Batman and Ethics

Batman and Ethics

Mark D. White

WILEY Blackwell

Registered Offices
John Wiley & Sons, Inc., 111 River Street, Hoboken, NJ 07030, USA
John Wiley & Sons Ltd, The Atrium, Southern Gate, Chichester, West Sussex, PO19 8SQ, UK

Editorial Office
9600 Garsington Road, Oxford, OX4 2DQ, UK

For details of our global editorial offices, customer services, and more information about Wiley products visit us at www.wiley.com.

Wiley also publishes its books in a variety of electronic formats and by print-on-demand. Some content that appears in standard print versions of this book may not be available in other formats.

Library of Congress Cataloging-in-Publication Data

Name: White, Mark D., 1971– author.
Title: Batman and ethics / Mark D. White.
Description: First edition. | Hoboken, NJ : Wiley-Blackwell, 2019. | Includes index. |
Identifiers: LCCN 2018052863 (print) | LCCN 2018052978 (ebook) |
   ISBN 9781119038047 (AdobePDF) | ISBN 9781119038030 (ePub) |
   ISBN 9781119038023 (paperback)
Subjects: LCSH: Batman (Fictitious character) | Comic books, strips, etc.–Moral and
   ethical aspects. | BISAC: PHILOSOPHY / Eastern.
Classification: LCC PN6728.B36 (ebook) | LCC PN6728.B36 W5 2019 (print) |
   DDC 741.5/973–dc23
LC record available at https://lccn.loc.gov/2018052863

Cover Design: Wiley
Cover Images: ©dovate/iStock.com, ©dwleindecker/iStock.com, ©panda3800/iStock.com, ©daboost/iStock.com

Set in 10.5/13pt Minion Pro by SPi Global, Pondicherry, India
Printed in Singapore by C.O.S. Printers Pte Ltd

10 9 8 7 6 5 4 3 2 1

Contents

Acknowledgments

I wish to thank the people at Wiley Blackwell that saw this project through from formulation to completion: Liam Cooper, Deirdre Ilkson, Rachel Greenberg, Manish Luthra, and especially Marissa Koors, who helped me see what I was trying to say with this book the entire time. I also thank Louise Spencely for her expert copyediting, and three anonymous reviewers for helpful comments and criticism.

I thank E. Paul Zehr (*Becoming Batman*) and Travis Langley (*Batman and Psychology*), my bearded brothers in the bat, for support and feedback at a crucial point in this project, and William Irwin, Rob Arp, and all the contributors to *Batman and Philosophy*, which is really where the current book (and all my popular writing on superheroes) began. I thank Jeff Peters, formerly of Commuter Comics, for helping me find my Batman love again after many years away, and Steve Nemeckay at Amazing Heroes for sustaining it ever since. And as always, I thank my friends that help preserve my spirit while writing: William Irwin, Lauren Hale, Anita Leirfall, Carol Borden, and Heidi Page.

Of course, I wouldn't be writing this book if not for the creative genius of Bob Kane and Bill Finger, nor all the writers, artists, editors, actors, directors, and producers that have put their indelible and invaluable stamp on Batman and his world. I owe each and every one of them more than I can ever put into words, so to them I dedicate this book, full of the best words I could come up with.

Introduction

You've decided to become a costumed crimefighter. Congratulations! You've got your outfit, having made the critical decisions regarding colors, mask or cowl, and cape or no cape. You've got your secret lair, your cool car (unless you can fly), and all the equipment you need to confront the criminal element and protect the innocent citizens of your fair city.

But wait … that's just the easy part. What are you going to do now? Are you going to look for muggers and burglars, or tackle corruption in government and business? Are there already supervillains to fight—or will they instead be inspired by you? How far are you willing to go in your crusade for justice? What degree of violence are you comfortable using? Will you break bones, put thugs in the hospital—or will you "cross the line" and end them once and for all?

The questions don't stop there. Who else will you enlist in your mission? Will you bring in a sidekick, maybe even a young boy or girl to watch your back and train to become a full-fledged hero someday? Will you cooperate with other masked crimefighters? What relationship will you cultivate with the local authorities? How far will you go to protect your secret identity? How will you balance your superhero life with your personal life, including your love life? Will you let your friends and family know what you're doing?

It turns out there's a lot more to being a costumed crimefighter than gearing up and jumping into the fray. As with many things in life, being able to do something is not the same thing as knowing what to do with it or the best way to do it. As a wise sage once said, "with great power must come great responsibility": deciding what to do with your power is the hard part,

Batman and Ethics, First Edition. Mark D. White.
© 2019 John Wiley & Sons Ltd. Published 2019 by John Wiley & Sons Ltd.

and the answer you choose separates the superheroes from the truly dangerous (if not villainous).

Being a superhero, then, opens a green hornet's nest of ethical conundrums—and if you're anything like me, you find those moral dilemmas just as interesting as the exciting, cataclysmic battles between good and evil. It turns out that stories about superheroes in comic books, TV shows, and movies are great ways to start discussions about ethics and morality. The difficult ethical spots that superheroes find themselves in may not always look like the ones you and I face, but they can be examined using the same basic schools of ethics that philosophers have developed over the last couple thousand years. Even better, they apply much more to our day-to-day moral issues than you might think.

That also happens to be why I wrote this book. But why did I choose Batman as my companion along the way? There are several reasons, but the simplest one is that he's incredibly cool! And I'm not alone in thinking that. Batman is one of the most popular and enduring superheroes all of time, appearing regularly in the comics since his introduction in 1939, becoming a TV star in the 1960s, and a movie star starting in the 1980s. He has appeared in many different forms, styles, and moods, yet there is an essential quality of "Batman-ness" that persists through all of them and continues to fascinate us.

One explanation commonly cited for Batman's enormous popularity is that he is "just" a regular person, a human being like you or me. He's not an alien visitor from another planet or an Amazon princess with powers granted from the gods, nor was he granted an all-powerful power ring, an enchanted hammer, or an ouchie from a radioactive spider. He's "just a guy"—well, a guy with a load of money and free time on his hands, but otherwise, a normal guy. Setting aside those small details, however, Batman stands as an example of what each of us could be if we wanted it badly enough and pushed ourselves hard enough. Ideally, we could hone our bodies to physical perfection, study criminology and forensic science until we've mastered it, and devote our entire lives to stamping out crime. In theory, each of us could be Batman—it's only our resolve (and our resources) that stand in the way.

Because he's human—despite the enormous wealth—we feel closer to his experiences, his adventures, and his moral struggles, than we do to those of his super friends. Furthermore, the moral struggles he faces as "merely a man" are more interesting because the choices he must make and the burdens he must bear are more familiar to us than those of Superman or

Wonder Woman, even as "normal" and down-to-earth as comics creators try to make these characters seem. Batman makes bad choices and he pays for them—and even worse, sometimes other people pay for them—and he regularly beats himself up over it. He constantly pushes himself to be better and do more, but there are limits to how much or how well he can do—limits he usually refuses to acknowledge, for reasons both pragmatic and principled.

In this book, we'll talk about a number of aspects of Batman's life and mission, his friends and colleagues, and his most dramatic and exciting adventures, and explore the ethics behind each of them. We'll see that Batman's moral code is not simple and does not fall neatly into any of the ethical schools we'll talk about—which is fine, because few of ours do either! Just like the rest of us, Batman's ethics are complicated and conflicting, different aspects of them being triggered by different circumstances, and Batman's moral choice in these situations may not be the same as you or I would make. Figuring out why … now *that's* the fun part!

Popular conceptions of moral philosophers have us knowing "the truth" about right and wrong and having "the answer" to any moral question. That is, frankly, ridiculous—neither part is accurate. What we moral philosophers do instead, especially when we teach, is highlight and explore different approaches to ethics, not to declare one of them "right" or the "best," but to emphasize different aspects of everyday moral thinking. (It would be very difficult to declare one approach to ethics "the best," anyway, because how you define "the best" depends on what ethical approach you take, and then you're assuming your answer, or what philosophers call "begging the question.") Sometimes people try to bring about the greatest amount of happiness; sometimes they try to follow rules and do the "right thing"; and sometimes they try to be the best people they can be. These three approaches correspond to the schools of moral philosophy known as utilitarianism, deontology, and virtue ethics, which we'll talk more about in the pages to come (especially the first two).

Often, those three approaches to ethics point in the same direction. For example, all three would say that, in general, lying is unethical and helping others is ethical, although they might provide different reasons with different bits of nuance. Most of the "big" moral issues are like this: killing, stealing, and poisoning the Gotham City water supply with Joker venom are all forbidden by all major schools of ethics. (Whew.)

However, in other cases the three schools do come into conflict—especially utilitarianism and deontology—especially when doing "good" and doing "right" point to different actions. You want to surprise your best friend on her birthday by taking her out to a show, but you promised another friend you'd watch his dog while he's away. Perhaps you have a chance to get a great job with health benefits to take care of your sick child, but you have to lie about your qualifications to get it. Or maybe you have a chance to stop your homicidal arch-nemesis from killing more innocent people, but only if you kill him, which you swore not to do.

The last case may not crop up in your life very often, but it is a recurring theme in Batman's stories and a constant question in every fan's mind: Why doesn't Batman kill the Joker? The Joker, easily the most deadly of Batman's colorful rogues' gallery, has killed countless citizens of Gotham City and elsewhere. He has also directly affected the Dark Knight himself: he killed Jason Todd, the second Robin; he shot and paralyzed Barbara Gordon, the original Batgirl and adopted daughter of his close friend, Jim Gordon; and he killed Sarah Essen, a Gotham City Police Department detective and commissioner (and wife of Jim Gordon). As we'll see later in this book, it's not only fans who wonder why Batman doesn't put a permanent end to the Joker's killing spree—many people in the DC Universe have confronted Batman about this, including Barbara Gordon and Jason Todd himself (after returning from the dead).

Here we see all three ethical approaches at play and in conflict. If Batman only wanted to do good, to save lives and protect innocent people, he likely would have killed the Joker a long time ago. But he also wants to do the right thing, and he feels strongly that killing is always wrong, even if it would save more deaths in the future. Finally, Batman does not want to be a killer; he does not want to become like the criminals he opposes and holds himself to a higher standard of character. The last two approaches speak to why he won't kill the Joker, reinforcing each other by emphasizing the lines Batman won't cross in his mission to protect the people of Gotham City, but that refusal to kill limits the success of that mission itself.

Does Batman make the right choice? We may assume *he* feels it's the right choice, but we may have our own opinion on the matter. The type of choice Batman finds himself in here is what philosophers call a *tragic dilemma*, a choice from which one cannot escape "with clean hands." Either Batman kills the Joker, sacrificing his moral principles and who he strives to be, or he accepts that the Joker will kill more innocent people, compromising Batman's core mission. He can't do both, but he must make a choice. Is there truly a "right" choice in such circumstances? What would *you* do, and why?

In the end, it comes down to *judgment*, which we use all the time to settle conflicts between important moral goals and principles. Most of us don't often encounter life-or-death conflicts like Batman does—unless you're a doctor or nurse, a police officer or firefighter, or in the military—but we can still appreciate the need for moral judgment to settle disputes between the good and the right, or even different types of one or the other. You want to donate money to a charity, but which one and how much? You accidentally make promises to different people and can't possibly keep them all, so which do you break? You have a chance to move to a better school district to give one child access to a better music program, while tearing your other child away from his friends—do you move?

None of these are clear-cut decisions that you can easily make with rules or formulae. These tools can help you clarify various aspects of an issue, but at the end these options are not easy to weigh against each other. It's not like comparing prices for an identical product, like a specific model of a new car or a washing machine—it's more like comparing different prices for different makes and models of cars of different ages with different features. You can analyze and compare and make lists until you're blue in the face, but at the end of the day you have to make a choice that feels right to you, and all you have at your disposal to make that choice is your judgment. Call it intuition, call it your gut, call it whatever you want—it's *you*, the real you, the person that has to make a choice that reflects and reinforces who you are.

Batman makes this choice every time he refuses to kill the Joker. He knows the arguments for and against doing it, and he sympathizes with those who want him to end the Clown of Crime once and for all. But there is no one right decision—only the one he feels is consistent with his values and the hero he wants to be.

With Batman, however, it's even more complicated than this, and this complication is the true motivation behind this book. It's not just that Batman has to make choices between the ethical ideas of doing good, doing right, and being a good person. Every superhero has to do this and, as I said, this is part of what makes superhero stories, whether in the comics, movies, or TV, fascinating as well as entertaining. With Batman more than most superheroes, the problem is that his conception of each of these moral principles is *inconsistent*. Sometimes his version of doing good is fighting crime and other times it's saving lives, two clearly good aims that are not the same thing and sometimes conflict. He refuses to kill because it's wrong, but is often extremely violent and sometimes engages in what can be called torture—again, two clear wrongs but only one of which he steadfastly avoids. In the end, how does he reconcile these inconsistent visions of the good and the right—or does he at all?

You could say that this is another aspect of Batman's inherent humanity: he is as inconsistently moral as any of us. But while having to balance the good against the right is a part of being a good person—doing it well can even be considered a sign of fine virtue—having conceptions of good and of the right that are inconsistent *within* themselves is not. It signals a lack of integrity in a formal sense, a sign that one's moral character is not as settled as it should be in order to be ethical in the world. In other words, Batman could be better, and so could we—and that's the real message of this book. It's wonderful to care about ethics and have many different thoughts about how to make the world better and more just while also being a good person, but if you can't reconcile those thoughts into a consistent code of ethics, your actions will reflect this sense of disorder. You may still be a good person and do ethical things, but not as much as you could or as reliably as you could.

In this book, we'll take a trip through the ethical landscape where Batman finds the various pieces that make up his moral code and consider the inconsistency in each one as well as how he balances them against each other. My intent is not to criticize him as a person or a hero—despite his imperfections he is a fine example of both. Instead, I use those imperfections to show how he can be better at both, and how we can all learn from his example to be better ourselves. (And talk about a lot of great comics in the process!)

Which Batman?

One question that naturally arises when you write about a massively popular multimedia character such as Batman is: which Batman are you referring to? There have been many versions of Batman over the years, not only in the comics but also on TV, including the campy, beloved live-action starring Adam West and Burt Ward and the more recent animated series, and in the movies, representing several distinct visions under different directors, screenwriters, and actors. Even if we focus only on the main Batman comics—excluding "imaginary" stories and those from alternate Earths—there have many different versions of him, from the original 1930s gun-wielding Batman and the goofy 1950s sci-fi version (Rainbow Batman!

Mermaid Batman!), through the Darknight Detective of the 1970s, the even Darker Knight of the 1980s, and beyond.

The brilliance of Batman, however, is that there are certain qualities of Batman-ness that carry through most all versions and make them identifiably the same character. The philosopher Ludwig Wittgenstein coined the term "family resemblance" to explain how various examples of a vague concept can be identified. For instance, he cited the difficulty with defining what a "game" is—every characteristic of a game you might suggest has a counterexample among something clearly called a game. But, Wittgenstein said, the various things we call games have enough in common, even if not among all games, to link them together, in the same way that blood relatives may share various similarities with other family members: the daughter may have the father's nose and the mother's eyes while the son has the father's mouth and the mother's hands. In the same way, the various iterations of Batman over the last 80 years share enough qualities with enough of the other versions that they are all recognizable as Batman.

If my purpose is to investigate the inconsistency in Batman's moral behavior, though, the best way to do that is to focus on one version of the character. It wouldn't be much to say, for instance, that Adam West's Batman from the 1960s TV show behaved differently than Ben Affleck's Batman in the film *Batman v Superman*, or that the goofy Batman of the 1950s comics behaved differently than the version in Frank Miller's 1980s classic *The Dark Knight Returns*, but it would be interesting to point out the same inconsistency in any one of these. Striking a balance between including too broad or narrow a range of material, in this book I will focus on a period in the comics of about 40 years, from the early 1970s through 2011, and will treat this version of Batman as a singular version of the character. Despite being written, drawn, and edited by hundreds of different people over these four decades, I feel Batman was portrayed as consistently during this period as ever—which makes the inconsistencies in his moral behavior that remain all the more apparent.

Why do I talk only about the version of Batman in the comics? It's not because the versions shown in the movies and television are any less valid or meaningful, to be sure. It's because I believe the comics are where his behavior and thought processes are best illustrated and explained—often they're stated explicitly, in copious dialogue, thought balloons, and exposition, which don't occur as often (or at all) in other media. This is not to say that the mainstream comics version of Batman is more legitimate or represents the "real" Batman—each version of Batman is the real Batman to somebody. It's simply that the ethical aspects of Batman I find most interesting are found in the comics from this period, beginning with the modernization of the character in the early 1970s by writer Denny O'Neil and artist Neal Adams, continuing on through the 1980s in the work of creators such as Doug Moench, Mike Barr, Jim Aparo, and of course Frank Miller, into the 1990s with Alan Grant, Norm Breyfogle, and Chuck Dixon, and the 2000s with Ed Brubaker, Greg Rucka, Scott McDaniel, and Grant Morrison.

(Why stop at 2011? I cut off my look at the comics there because this was the year that DC Comics rebooted their entire universe in the "New 52" initiative, which they only partially reversed in the 2016 with "DC Rebirth." The character of Batman was among the least affected by this change, and fantastic stories were told afterwards by Scott Snyder, Greg Capullo, Peter Tomasi, Tom King, and others, but the change was still significant enough to mark a break in continuity that provides a neat and tidy bow on the period I cover.)

I left many names out, of course, and they're all listed in the references. In most of this book, though, as you'll notice, I will rarely make reference to any particular creators' version of Batman. Instead, I treat Batman as one coherent character, as I believe he was for these four decades (and for the most part continues to be). He naturally changed over the years, of course, as we all do; and even during this period he was not entirely consistent in his actions, motivations, or justifications, again just like the rest of us. I talk about him as if he were a real person, which is a useful fiction, but this is not to ignore the fact that who we call the Batman is the creation over many years of hundreds of talented creators, and it is to them that this book is dedicated. I believe that his characterization matured in the early 1970s and stayed fairly constant through the ensuing decades—enough that we can talk about one "Batman" while still exploring the inconsistencies of his ethical behavior and motivations, and use this to consider our own.

PART I

What Batman Tries to Do—and How He Might Do It Better

The story has been told many times, each as chilling as the last. After seeing a Zorro movie at the movie theater, Thomas and Martha Wayne and their young son Bruce walk down an alley, only to face a mugger who demands money and jewelry. Thomas resists, and the mugger shoots him and then his wife, leaving their son in shock as the killer runs into the night. As Bruce kneels sobbing over his parents' bodies, he swears an oath to prevent this tragedy from happening to anybody else—and, in many ways, Batman was born that night.

Of course, Bruce was still a young boy then, and the cape and cowl, not to mention the cave and car, were years away. The Waynes' loyal butler Alfred Pennyworth (with the help of Thomas' friend and colleague Dr. Leslie Thompkins) raised Bruce to be the man his parents would have wanted him to be, while in solitude he began the intensive training that would prepare him for the role and the life he chose for himself that fateful night—in other words, "the mission." It is this mission to which Batman dedicates his life, sacrificing his every waking moment, much of his fortune, and any prospect of an independent life with joy or love. It is this mission and Batman's superhuman resolve to pursue it that inspire admiration among his fellow heroes in the DC Universe and his millions of fans in the real world—while at the same time they question his sanity for pursuing it with such single-minded devotion. And it is this mission, along with the steps he refuses to take in pursuit of it, that together define who Batman is in ethical terms.

In this part of the book, we'll explore the nature of that mission. We'll discuss various aspects of it, both positive and negative, and what each one implies about the priorities Batman puts on different sides of his overall

Batman and Ethics, First Edition. Mark D. White.

goal. We'll also see how Batman's mission can be described in terms of moral philosophy, specifically the school of ethics known as *utilitarianism*, which is focused on increasing and maximizing the amount of good in the world. We'll explore how Batman's mission falls short of the utilitarian ideal in important ways and try to explain why—and find out more about utilitarianism in the process. We'll even see that certain aspects of his mission are self-defeating, which shows how complicated ethical questions can be, even in the context of a very simple and straightforward goal. Most important, we'll discuss how Batman struggles with ethical dilemmas that, other than the cave, car, and cape, resemble ones we face every day, and as much as we can be inspired by his successes, we can learn from his failures. Batman isn't perfect, and neither are we—but we can all be better. Let's see how.

1

Utilitarianism and the Mission

One reason Batman is such a popular superhero (and fictional character in general) is that he has incredible devotion to his life's goal, or his *mission*. At the risk of seeming insensitive, given the tragic reason for his adopting that goal, many of us might be envious of Bruce Wayne's single-minded focus and belief in the purpose of his life. (I know I am!) What's more, that mission is altruistic, oriented toward making other people's lives better, and motivated by his own loss at a young age. We can of course argue that he goes too far in pursuing his mission, in that he sacrifices his own personal happiness and any chance at romantic love. Some would say that he doesn't go far enough, in that there are certain steps, such as killing his enemies, that he will not take even to further his mission. Yet others say that, if he really wants to help people, dressing up as a giant bat and beating up bad guys isn't the best way to go about it. Even though we may be critical of the mission itself or how he executes it—and we'll talk about that in later chapters—many of us admire Batman's devotion to it in general.

But what exactly *is* his mission? As with most things in the world of Batman—save for his famous, oft-quoted saying about criminals being a "cowardly and superstitious lot"—there is no definitive, canonical statement about his mission. However, there are several recurring elements of his mission which, although related and overlapping to some extent, reflect different aspects of it and shed light on its complexity as well as his devotion to it.

The most immediate one, which gets to the heart of what he does more than why he does it, is his never-ending war against crime in Gotham City and elsewhere: as the narration to one story reads, "it's what his life is about."[1]

Batman and Ethics, First Edition. Mark D. White.
© 2019 John Wiley & Sons Ltd. Published 2019 by John Wiley & Sons Ltd.

As Batman once said, "I made a promise. To honor my parents. Someday to rid Gotham City of the crime that took their lives."[2] Simply put, Batman is driven not only to fight crime but to *end* it, despite the futility of this goal, which he admits: as the narration to an overview of his early life and motivation reads, "he knows he's set himself an impossible goal. No man can ever eliminate crime. All he can do is try."[3] And this he does, in full awareness of this impossibility. "I've dedicated my life to eradicating crime," he thought to himself while combatting gangs in Gotham's Chinatown. "At best a hopeless cause. Sometimes all we can do is maintain the balance of power."[4]

Furthermore, Batman does not limit himself to major crimes or the antics of his colorfully costumed foes. On his way to catch Kite Man—yes, *Kite Man*—Batman heard a burglar alarm coming from a jewelry shop and considers driving by, but then thought, "a crime is a crime is a crime! It's isn't my job to judge them—just to stop them!"[5] Even these crimes must be confronted, even though he knows he can never deal with them all, even on a night of "casual crimes and momentary madnesses ... the same thousand sins of any normal night, anonymous evil I can never stop."[6] We'll come to the way Batman sets priorities later, but for now the point is that, in theory, he doesn't exclude any crime, no matter how small, from his mission—even if, in practice, he finds he must prioritize them somehow.

Although avenging the deaths of his parents played a clear and important role in driving his mission to eradicate crime—"turning a boy of bright hope into a man of dark vengeance," which we'll unpack later—Batman does not endure a constant battle against crime in Gotham City simply to make up for not saving his parents as a young boy.[7] Neither is fighting crime an end in itself; there is deeper purpose behind it, namely to help, protect, and save people, especially the residents of Gotham. Inspired by his father's devotion to medicine, Batman goes to extraordinary lengths to save innocent lives. As he dove off a cliff to catch a vial of deadly Ebola virus, the narration reads: "Millions of lives are at stake. Maybe all humanity. He doesn't hesitate for an instant."[8] He famously lets criminals escape if he needs to save a life. After doing just that, a person he saved asked, "But why did you bother? I thought you only cared about catching criminals!" to which Batman replied, "You're not alone in thinking that! I wish you were!"[9] And it is not only the lives of the innocent that he tries to save, but all lives, even those of the most heinous and evil. We see this in the numerous times he saves the Joker, even at the expense of the countless people the Crown Prince of Crime will surely kill later—a central moral dilemma in the Batman canon that we will talk about often in this book.

Utilitarianism: Bentham, Mill, and … Wayne?

These two simple goals—fighting crime and saving lives—cover most all of Batman's actions as the Dark Knight, but each is more complicated than it seems, in terms of how each must be implemented in itself as well as when they conflict with or contradict each other. We'll discuss those nuances soon enough, but in general they both reflect Batman's overall motivation to help people, which corresponds to a school of moral philosophy that grounds the first part of this book.

Whatever their method or motivation, most superheroes try to help people. When Superman diverts an asteroid hurtling toward the Earth, Wonder Woman prevents one of the Olympian gods from enslaving humanity, or the Flash stops a bank robbery before most people realized it had begun, they are protecting people from harm, including the loss of property, freedom, and life. They are also serving the cause of justice and preventing wrong from being done—very important considerations, especially when they conflict with helping people—but most of what superheroes do can be summed up as helping, protecting, and saving.

In other words, superheroes use their fantastic powers and abilities to make people better off, just as real-world heroes such as doctors, soldiers, and firefighters do with their skills, training, and courage. Implicitly, they regard people's well-being as something of moral importance, and they use their gifts to enhance that well-being (or prevent it from being lessened).

This way of choosing how to express heroism closely resembles the school of moral philosophy known as *utilitarianism*. Although the basic idea dates to antiquity, utilitarianism was introduced in its current form by Jeremy Bentham and John Stuart Mill, who were philosophers as well as social reformers who wanted to improve the lives of all people. Utilitarianism is a specific type of *consequentialism*, the general view that the outcome or result of an act is what matters as far as ethics is concerned. In other words, consequentialism judges actions by their consequences rather than the intention behind them or their correspondence with abstract rules or principles, considerations belonging to other ethical systems we'll talk about later.[10]

Utilitarianism is narrower than consequentialism because only one aspect of consequences is morally relevant: the total amount of *utility* they have. The word "utility" can mean benefit, happiness, or satisfaction, depending on which utilitarian you ask, but for our purposes, we can understand utility to mean whatever people regard as good to them.[11] Each person gets their own individual utility from choices they make (as well as things that happen to them), and the total utility of a group of people is computed simply by adding up the individual utilities of every person. Although this summing up may seem obvious, it can also be considered the most radical aspect of utilitarianism, in that it implies that the utility of *each and every person*, regardless of class, race, gender, or religion, counts equally in the total. This idea was heretical in the eighteenth and nineteenth centuries, when most societies were more formally stratified into classes, and would not be welcomed even today within some segments of even the most liberal democracies. It also represents an ideal of moral equality that gives utilitarianism much of its nobility, while at the same time generating problems when people with different capacities for utility, or "utility monsters," twist the sums in their favor by dominating the utilitarian calculus.[12] For example, if the Penguin derives twice as much utility from fresh halibut than anyone else, a goal of increasing total utility would imply that he should get more fish than other people would, even if they needed it more but enjoyed it less. This also points out the importance and difficulty of defining exactly what "utility" means, whether based on want or need, as well as the possibility of lessening the utility of some people to increase the utility of others if that will lead to a higher total—the controversial "ends justify the means" reasoning that we'll see later.

Getting back to the main point, utilitarians maintain that we should choose actions that give people *more* utility (or make them better off), and if we have several such options, we should choose the one that gives them the *most* utility. For example, if Bruce Wayne decides to give ten million dollars to his favorite country club, that is an ethical and generous act, but it would probably be better to give it to a homeless shelter club because it is likely to do more good for people who need it. (Indeed, many have wondered if it would be better for Bruce to give away his fortune rather than spending it on Batmobiles and batarangs … we'll get to that!) When an elderly and poor man asked Batman why he bothered to prevent him from being mugged rather than chasing "international criminals," the Caped Crusader told him, "Crime is crime … and to you, the loss of a dollar is more important than the loss of thousands to a banker!"[13] Batman's statement is based on *diminishing marginal utility*, a fancy term for the simple idea that, after a point, extra amounts of things bring a person less happiness, so an extra dollar means more to someone who has few of them than to someone who has many. Although giving is generally good regardless of the recipient, it can do more good by steering it to people who have less.

Not as Simple as It Seems

While utilitarianism sounds simple in theory, it is actually surprisingly difficult to implement well in practice, at least if you always aim for the one decision that will increase utility the most (or maximize it). One reason is that utility can be very difficult to measure. I loaded the deck a bit in the last paragraph when I gave Wayne the stark choice between giving money to a homeless shelter or a ritzy country club. But what if his choice were between two reputable charities? Wayne believes that each would do a lot of good with the money, but how is he supposed to compare the "lot of good" each would do? It would be hard enough to compare how much good it would do to donate money to one person or another: the money would certainly raise each person's utility, but how do you compare them to know which person would get more utility from it? Philosophers call this the problem of *interpersonal comparisons of utility*, and it has proven a thorny issue precisely because a person's feelings of happiness or utility are typically considered internal and therefore subjective, and there is no way for one person to express how happy they are in units that another person can also use. This isn't a fatal problem, though: Utilitarians can acknowledge it and still make their best estimate, because doing some good is better than nothing even if you're not sure you're doing the best you can.

Another problem with implementing utilitarianism, and indeed any type of consequentialism, is that most outcomes or results happen in the future and are therefore uncertain. Bruce can't be sure what the charity he donates to will do with the money or how much they will use it to help people versus padding their executives' bank accounts. As Batman, he can't know for certain which patrol route will lead to more criminals he can fight or people he can save. He doesn't know which heroes to invite onto teams like the Justice League or the Outsiders who will best aid him in his mission. And he definitely doesn't know how long it will take for the villains he puts away in Blackgate Prison or Arkham Asylum to escape and wreak more havoc. All he can do is make the best decision he can based on the information he has. Because he's Batman, he has as much information as anyone can have, and the experience to know how to craft it into a decision, but he must still make informed guesses before making a decision how to best further his mission in specific circumstances. All utilitarianism can ask is that we make the best decision we can, even if we can't hope to make a perfect decision, but this is still a very tough task—especially for someone who has sworn to do the impossible.[14]

The difficulties with putting utilitarianism into practice point to the importance of using *judgment* to fill the gaps in the information that is needed to do it perfectly. On the surface, utilitarianism may seem easily reduced to numbers, comparing the benefits and costs of various options, but we have seen that the numbers themselves are rarely obvious or clear. Even in the context of business investment, which is literally a numbers game in which people choose between opportunities with various rates of return and levels of risk, investors need to use judgment to decide which combinations of risk and return are most attractive. Also, the numbers themselves are based on estimates that someone arrived at using judgment, because they are all predictions about an uncertain future. But when the choices involved in a utilitarian decision are not so easily put into numbers—such as when they involve human lives—judgment is all the more important.

But the vague and indeterminate nature of these hard decisions also makes them more subject to being questioned or challenged. Superheroes often face hard moral choices in the comics, and other heroes, colleagues, and (of course) the readers all debate their decisions. Judgment is based in part on one's experiences and way of understanding ethics, beyond formulas and rules, and as a result each person's judgment is unique. Think of the nine justices on the United States Supreme Court, all brilliant and experienced legal minds, but each with a unique way of looking at the law and the hard cases they encounter. Even when they arrive at a unanimous 9–0 decision, each justice may justify her or his decision in a different way, as often expressed in their separate opinions and concurrences.

One of the issues we'll address throughout the first part of this book is whether Bruce Wayne is doing the most good he can as Batman, both in terms of being Batman at all and the way he conducts himself as Batman. Because there are so many factors involved in this determination, ultimately this is a judgment call. There is no simple ethical rule or formula that can definitely answer any of these questions, and as such there will inevitably be disagreement. For instance, Henri Ducard, a detective who helped train a young Bruce Wayne, disagreed with Batman's focus (even as Ducard starts to realize the two men are one and the same):

> While Batman busies himself with petty thieves and gaudy madmen, an abyss of rot yawns ever wider at his feet. He's a band-aid of a cancer patient. I am of course no moralist, but this Batman has a very poor understanding of the world.[15]

I guess we should be thankful he's not a moralist!

Many have questioned Batman's focus and methods, both within the context of his particular brand of utilitarianism and also how he integrates other moral perspectives to moderate and modify it. Although we can certainly question the decisions he makes and how he makes them, in particular situations as well as how he generally chooses to live his life, we must be generous enough to acknowledge that Bruce Wayne is trying to do good with the cards that life has dealt him, both the good and the bad. By examining his moral decisions, we can start to appreciate how difficult they are, and also how difficult our own moral decisions are—and by criticizing the way he makes them, we can begin to see how we can make better ones, especially through a better integration of the various aspects of our moral personalities or characters. We begin that task in the next chapter as we look at ways in which Batman limits his own utilitarianism by how he defines his mission.

Notes

1   *Batman: Shadow of the Bat* #0 (October 1994).
2   *Batman: Ghosts—A Legend of the Dark Knight Special* (1995). See also *Batman* #608 (December 2002), where his origin is retold: after his parents were killed, Bruce made "a vow to rid the city of the evil that had taken their lives."
3   *Batman: Shadow of the Bat* #0.
4   *Batman* #467 (Late August 1991).
5   *Batman* #315 (September 1979). Naturally, after I first wrote this, Kite Man was made relevant in the DC Rebirth era of Batman. (I could never have predicted this.)
6   *Batman* #525 (December 1995).
7   *Batman* #558 (September 1998).
8   *Batman: Shadow of the Bat* #54 (September 1996).
9   *Detective Comics* #486 (November 1979), "Murder by Thunderbolt."
10   The essential work in utilitarianism includes Bentham's *The Principles of Morals and Legislation* (1781), available at https://www.utilitarianism.com/jeremy-bentham/, and Mill's *Utilitarianism* (1863), available at https://www.utilitarianism.com/mill1.htm. As for consequentialism in general as well as its relationship to utilitarianism, see Walter Sinnott-Armstrong's 2015 entry in the *Stanford Encyclopedia of Philosophy* at https://plato.stanford.edu/entries/consequentialism/.
11   This is problematic if you think people don't know what's good for them. (I'm looking at you, Mr. Pennyworth.)

12   Utility monsters were introduced by Robert Nozick in his classic book *Anarchy, State, and Utopia* (New York: Basic Books, 1974), p. 41.

13   *Detective Comics* #457 (March 1976), "There Is No Hope in Crime Alley!"

14   We have only scratched the surface of utilitarianism here. For more on the complications and controversies with what is, to many, the most intuitively plausible and attractive school of ethics, see J.J.C. Smart and Bernard Williams, *Utilitarianism: For and Against* (Cambridge: Cambridge University Press, 1973), Amartya Sen and Bernard Williams (eds.), *Utilitarianism and Beyond* (Cambridge: Cambridge University Press, 1982), and Samuel Scheffler (ed.), *Consequentialism and Its Critics* (Oxford: Oxford University Press, 1988),

15   *Detective Comics* #600 (May 1989).

2

Limitations of the Mission

Even though Batman is at the simplest level a utilitarian, in that his mission is broadly oriented toward making people better off, it would be more accurate to call him a *limited utilitarian*. Although he uses his skills, abilities, and resources to increase total well-being, he does so in a way that is deliberately limited in a number of different ways. I'm not talking about moral influences from outside his utilitarianism that interfere with his ability to increase people's well-being, such as his refusal to kill murderous villains like the Joker even if it might save many more lives in the future. We'll ride that particular trolley in the second part of this book; in this chapter we're going to focus on ways in which Batman limits his pursuit of his utilitarian mission by narrowing its scope—and by going negative.

The Dark Utilitarian

The most important aspect of Batman's mission as it relates to utilitarianism is that it's mainly a negative conception: Batman doesn't often take actions to increase well-being, but rather those that prevent it from decreasing. As Bruce Wayne, he engages in a great deal of charitable activities, such as donating money and appearing at celebrity fundraisers, which have a positive effect on the total utility of people in Gotham City. As Batman, however, he primarily saves those same people from *losing* utility, by either preventing crime or saving lives. When Robin suggested that Batman wanted to "save the world," the older hero clarified, "My life is sworn to fighting crime … and protecting the people from its ravages, not 'saving the

Batman and Ethics, First Edition. Mark D. White.
© 2019 John Wiley & Sons Ltd. Published 2019 by John Wiley & Sons Ltd.

world."[1] In other words, if you live in Gotham City, Bruce Wayne may make your life better, but Batman will see that it doesn't get worse, by working "towards an end to unnecessary loss and suffering."[2]

To emphasize this distinction, we can present utilitarianism in a different way. Although, as we saw in the last chapter, the goal of utilitarianism is to maximize total utility, we could be more precise. Well-being, happiness, or utility is not simply a unitary "substance" that starts at zero and increases from there, a number that ethical actions then try to make as large as possible. Instead, a person's utility can be better thought of as the sum of many different influences, both positive and negative. Some things in our lives make us happier and some make us sadder, and our utility is the balance between the two—our "net" utility, or what's left of the positive effects after the negatives are subtracted. (This may, of course, be negative.)

Once we see utility this way, there are two ways to increase this net utility: raise the positive effects or lower the negative ones. Either of these—or both together—will increase the difference between good and bad and in turn increase total utility. As Jeremy Bentham wrote in his classic work on utilitarianism, *An Introduction to the Principles of Morals and Legislation*, "nature has placed mankind under the governance of two sovereign masters, *pain* and *pleasure*," and a person's interests are advanced by an action "when it tends to add to the sum total of his pleasures: or, what comes to the same thing, to diminish the sum total of his pains."[3] John Stuart Mill agrees, writing in his much more Gladwellian-titled *Utilitarianism* that "actions are right in proportion as they tend to promote happiness, wrong as they tend to produce the reverse of happiness."[4] If you think of your happiness as the sum total of your positive and negative experiences, then you will be happier if you have more positive things in your life, such as Batman comics, or fewer negative ones, such as Wolverine comics. (Just kidding: Wolverine comics are great for cushioning the ends of your longboxes so your Batman comics don't get damaged.)

Understood this way, Martha Wayne's little boy does good in both his civilian and masked identities, but in different ways. On the one hand, Bruce Wayne has a "direct" influence on utility as a philanthropist and public figure (as we'll discuss later), enhancing the positive experiences of the citizens of Gotham City by providing aid and jobs, or "adding to the sum total of pleasures." On the other hand, Batman has an "indirect" influence on utility by preventing people from being hurt by criminals, accidents, and natural disasters, or "diminishing the sum total of their pains." As he said to his parents' grave after the earthquake known as the Cataclysm killed

almost a million residents of Gotham City, "I vowed to protect the innocent. I promised that no one would suffer if I could do anything to stop it."[5]
Of course, Batman can do little to prevent earthquakes, or even most of the
crime that plagues Gotham, but that does not stop him from feeling remorse
that he cannot do more (as we'll see later).

Of course, Bruce is also Thomas Wayne's little boy, and both aspects of
the younger Wayne's utilitarianism show the influence of his father.
Although Thomas was a pillar of the Gotham community and an active
philanthropist, it is his role as a doctor that parallels Bruce's role as Batman
most strongly. Although it is increasingly common today for doctors to
practice "positive medicine" and try to improve the lives of their generally
healthy patients, traditionally doctors tended mostly to the sick and
injured, helping them get closer to their original level of health (or at least
a tolerable one).

Batman has often compared his mission to that of his father, citing his
medical work as the basis of Bruce's own dedication to protecting life: "Like
my father before me, I'm a surgeon ... and Gotham is my patient. I will
breathe life into her again."[6] While crouched atop one of his favorite Gotham
gargoyles on a stormy night, Batman wondered to himself, "It's odd ... that
on a night like this ... I remember my father. The phone would ring. There
was a medical emergency somewhere. He had to go. He was needed. There
was no choice. Is that why I'm here ...?"[7] As a young boy, Bruce told his
father, "I want to be just like you! You're a doctor—you help people!"
Thomas replied, "That's what life is all about, Bruce—helping people! Our
love—our compassion—are the only things that set us apart from the beasts
in the fields!"[8]

The word "compassionate" may not be one that immediately springs to
mind when thinking of the Dark Knight, but as we'll see throughout this
book, Batman's mission is driven as much by the compassion he learned
from his parents as by the tragedy of their deaths. When a young doctor
named Lynn Eagles helped a mysterious stranger—actually Bruce Wayne,
whom she called "Lazarus," with wounds suffered at the hands of the
Joker—she happened to tell him about the time she encountered Batman
when he saved her from an assault. After he "made short work" of the
attacker, she explained, she should have been afraid of him,

a crazy man in a Halloween costume. But he comforted me, Lazarus. He held
me, weeping in his arms till the police came. And I knew then, with all my
heart, that this wasn't a crazy-man. He was decent. Compassionate. In his

own odd way, I guess you could say he was a healer. Just like my father. Just like yours.[9]

As the narration to one story read, "the avenger within the Batman co-exists with the compassionate man" who is Bruce Wayne—each serving a unique role in their shared utilitarian mission.[10]

Another influence on young Bruce in the fashion of his father was Dr. Leslie Thompkins, a friend and colleague of Thomas who helped raise Bruce and remains a close friend (and ally to Batman) to this day. She was also a fierce critic of his methods, as we'll see in the second part of this book, and often contrasted his chosen path in life with that of his father. Early in his career, Leslie asked Bruce, "you seriously mean to honor the memory of your father—a doctor, Bruce, a man committed to life and healing—by putting yourself in the path of bullets?" He answered, "I cannot tolerate the tyranny of crime in this city. There has to be a way to make things better. In any case, it is my birthright to die trying."[11] Much later, after Batman helped Leslie perform a caesarian section under a collapsed building, she told him that he should consider "a career change" and become a doctor. "You've got the gift. You'd be saving lives without perpetuating this cycle of violence—" but Bruce cut her off, telling her that he has a career, and anyway, "it wasn't my father who instilled me with the sanctity of life. It was you."[12]

Thomas inspired Bruce in other ways, such as when he patched up the gunshot wound of a criminal's nephew, refused to accept dirty money for it, and then told the criminal he would report the gunshot to the police, part of "another oath doctors work under too—to uphold the law," despite the criminal's threats if he did so.[13] This more legalistic aspect of Dr. Wayne's code of ethics reminds us how Batman's brand of utilitarianism also resembles the role of a police officer. Despite Batman's often contentious relationship with the Gotham City Police Department—with the exception of his close friend Jim Gordon—they share a similar role in protecting citizens from crime, lessening the negative impact of criminal behavior and therefore raising net well-being. Of course, Batman is much more ... cavalier, shall we say, in how he goes about fighting crime than a police officer is—at least an honest police officer, of whom there are not many in Gotham City—and we'll look into that aspect of his activities in the second part of this book. For now, let's look more deeply into his mission to eradicate crime in Gotham City and what it implies about his particular brand of limited utilitarianism.

Fighting Crime and Only Fighting Crime

It is well known that Batman is obsessed with crime, and considers the fight against crime to be the primary way by which he makes the lives of the citizens of Gotham City better. "When you're the Batman," the narration to one story reads, "you hate crime with a passion that drives you to fight it every waking moment of your life."[14] Of course, a big part of this can be traced to the pivotal event that launched his career: seeing his parents shot and killed by a thief on what came to be known as Crime Alley. Explaining his mission to Alfred while being patched up after a night out, Bruce told him, "I hope to prevent some other child from seeing his family slaughtered."[15] As one retelling of his origin reads,

> He had failed to prevent the brutal murder of his parents, and he knew the failure was final. Two words boiled from the blackness of his mind: never again. The killer would become a symbol of the faceless crime lurking in every shadow, striking without warning, snuffing lives precious only to those whose futures are shattered by the loss.[16]

Although this passage focuses on murderers ("snuffing lives"), later in the same story his ideals are stated more generally: "stop crime and prevent horror."[17] Batman is driven to combat not only murder, but all crime that plagues innocent people, whatever the degree of harm, and recognizing that even just the threat of harm represents a horror that the innocent do not deserve and criminals have no right to impose.

Before we explore Batman's attitude toward crime, let's take a minute to think about what crime is. The simple answer, of course, is that a crime is an act that is against the law, but this is far too simple. After all, the law says that if Robin accidentally smashes his motorcycle into your car, he may be liable for the damages, but there was no crime committed, just a private injury (or *tort*). If a baker signs a contract with Alfred to provide dessert at a charity event held at Wayne Manor but no one puts the date on it, the law says the contract is null and void, but this is no crime (although the absence of dessert can easily be considered criminal). The law also says that each state in the United States has two seats in the Senate, but it isn't a crime if one of them is empty. There are countless ways that behavior or circumstances can conflict with the law, but only a certain portion of them constitute crimes.

As it turns out, crimes are somewhat difficult to define, but we can agree on several basic properties in general, all of which are relevant to Batman's mission.[18] At the simplest level, they are usually intentional; accidents are typically not crimes (although they can result from criminal negligence, such as driving under the influence). That's why Robin didn't commit a crime when he drove his motorcycle into your car—unless he was underage when he did it! So crimes are normally intentional harms, such as when someone commits murder, theft, or assault. (Surely, only a criminal would punch another person, right? Oh, wait ...)

But why are intentional acts that create harm considered crimes, deserving of the attention of police and prosecutors, rather than a private matter between the victim and the perpetrator? Again, if Robin hits your car by accident, the police only get involved to file a report for the insurance companies to determine liability—but if the Penguin has one of his henchmen ram into your car on purpose, the police will arrest the driver and the prosecutor will try him in court. The same thing happened in both cases—one car hit another—and the same physical damages may have resulted, but the official response in each case is very different. What is it about the second being intentional that makes a crime worthy of official intervention?

Batman knows the answer, because he uses it himself: *fear*. If two drivers have an accident in your neighborhood, it's regrettable for the people involved, but it won't trouble anyone else very much (unless some unsafe road conditions or signs contributed to the accident). But if one person uses a car to hit someone else's—or worse, to run someone over—it's likely to cause the neighbors to fear for their own safety precisely *because* it was an intentional infliction of harm. A person meant to hurt someone else, and this is more frightening than just a random occurrence, even if the harm done is the same.

The philosopher Lawrence Becker calls this effect "social volatility," and this is one theory about what justifies the involvement of the state in crimes, rather than simply being a private matter between two parties.[19] And the comics agree: as the narration to one Batman story reads, specifically in terms of murder,

> the taking of a human life is the most heinous of all crimes. There can be no correction if a mistake has been made. There can be no restoration of the status quo. Murder is forever. The effects of a murder spread out like ripples on a pond, washing over other lives ... The victim's wife and son ... The police, desensitized by the parade of deaths that passes daily through their lives ... And the neighbors. They'll be a little less trusting, a little more fearful, each of them wondering: "Will it be me, or my family next?"[20]

This is the horror that we mentioned earlier in terms of Batman's mission: fight crime and the fear it creates, even for those not directly affected by it. The victim of a murder is the main person affected, of course, but this heinous act has ripple effects through the community, affecting the victim's family, friends, and neighbors—even someone living two blocks away who did not know the victim will likely be shaken if they learn that someone was killed near their house. Not everyone in Gotham City will be a victim of crime, but they all live in a crime-ridden city, and this takes its toll, mentally and emotionally. It is poetic justice that, to lessen the fear that criminals impose on Gotham, Batman makes them experience that fear for themselves.

We can be sure that Batman realizes the true nature and crime and the widespread harm it causes. But what exactly does he try to do with regard to crime? In general, Batman wants to serve Gotham City, "to protect its people from the human wolves that prey upon it."[21] But he can do this in many ways—and the lengths he is or is not willing to go to in service of his goal will be the subject of the second part of this book. For now, we just want to focus on what he sets out to do to criminals in order to protect the citizens from Gotham—and we can go to the source and see what Batman himself has to say on this.

Most of the time, Batman describes his job much as a police officer would. As he told a young Dick Grayson early in his training, "The people we're after have broken the law. It's our job to find them, stop them, and arrest them. Do your job well, and you make that arrest stick. Do your job badly ... and you might not get a second chance."[22] As he explained to a Gotham City police detective who asked him how he handles seeing so much death, "I think of capturing the perpetrator. That reminds me what I'm here for."[23] As these two passages suggest, Batman's role is similar to an arresting officer, whether a beat cop or a detective: to solve crimes and bring in the suspects.

This is fairly limiting, however. In an enlightening exchange with Alfred, Bruce read a news report about the Joker's latest commitment to Arkham Asylum, from which he will inevitably escape, and said, "I can catch them, Alfred ... but that's it. I can't keep them locked up." Alfred responds.

> Nor can you prosecute them nor defend them nor help them seek out the root of their criminal drives. Yours is a singular task you've set for yourself, Master Bruce. It starts at this tunnel [of the Batcave] ... and it ends at the front of the police station ... where you drop off the trash.[24]

Whatever authority the police department deigns to grant him at any certain time, neither Bruce Wayne nor Batman has the authority or expertise to prosecute, defend, or judge the guilt of the criminals he catches. (In fact, even to call them "criminals" is presumptive, unless he catches them in the act.) Nonetheless, this fact weighs on him; as his journals tell us, what Batman hates the most about his mission is "the lack of emphasis on reparation or rehabilitation. The revolving doors of the penal system."[25] Batman can't do any more than catch criminals and trust the justice system to prosecute and punish them, but this doesn't mean he doesn't wish he could do more. Because there is always more to do, he cannot possibly do it all—and after the deaths of his parents and others close to him, this is perhaps his greatest regret (as we will see later when we discuss the futility of his impossible mission).

What about Vengeance and Justice?

However, Batman does not always think of himself as merely catching criminals and handing them over to the authorities, at least not when he talks about his mission.[26] As often as he mentions protecting innocent people from suffering as he and his parents did on that fateful night, he also cites a more abstract goal that sidesteps a compassionate mission for one based on a more personal and vengeful motivation.

The examples are numerous. As Batman traveled to North Korea in search of one of the men who trained him, he thought to himself, "as a youth I swore eternal vengeance on all criminals."[27] When Alfred asked him early on if he expects to "avenge his parents' murder," Bruce answered, "A little, maybe. Or maybe I can even the balance between the world's evil and the world's good just a bit."[28] After the earthquake that came to be known as the Cataclysm struck Gotham, Batman found himself faced with thousands of deaths but no criminal mastermind to go after, and thought, "there's no vengeance to reap from the cracked and sundered earth, no villain to hold responsible for this horror ... The dead are simply gone, with no one to blame."[29] Finally, when Batman boldly resigned from the Justice League of America due to their refusal to intervene in a revolution in Markovia, and set out to form a more pro-active team called the Outsiders, he told his fellow heroes,

> I've heard the cries of the dying ... and the mourning ... the victims of crime and injustice ... I swore I'd do everything in my power to avenge those deaths ... to protect innocent lives ... and if I fail to keep that promise ... my entire life is a lie![30]

All these passages and many more I could have quoted (don't tempt me!) invoke the idea of addressing wrongs rather than lessening harm or suffering, a motivation that could potentially compromise his generally utilitarian mission.

Although personal vengeance is typically understood to be an ethically unattractive emotion, it has a nobler and more general analogue in *retributivism*, the idea that wrongdoers must be punished for their crimes as a matter of justice rather than as a way to increase well-being or utility by preventing future crime (known as *deterrence*). These two justifications for punishment are usually presented as contrasting philosophies of criminal justice. Retributivism addresses past wrongs by holding criminals responsible for their wrongful actions, and deterrence increases utility going forward by lessening or preventing crimes in the future. To some extent, they work together: sentencing a convicted felon to prison for ten years punishes that person's crime and also sends a signal to potential criminals that the same may happen to them.[31] Many theories of punishment even combine the two, such as the "hybrid" theory of legal philosopher H.L.A. Hart, which recommends motivating criminal penalties with deterrence but relying on retributivist principles to ensure that only the guilty are punished and that their penalties "fit the crime."[32] But they can also diverge, such as when a frail and elderly criminal is sentenced to life in prison despite representing no serious threat in society and providing little value in terms of safety or prevention; when a violent criminal cuts a deal with the prosecutor for a light sentence in exchange for testimony to help nail the criminal's boss; or when convicts are punished too harshly compared to their crimes in order to "send a message."

There are strong arguments on the side of both deterrence and retributivism, but my point here is that Batman's language of vengeance is often at odds with his preventive mission to lessen suffering. This may lead to actions that, once again, compromise his more general utilitarian mission, such as when he spends an inordinate amount of time chasing one criminal to whom he has personal ties while ignoring other criminals who threaten harm to a larger number of people.

A focus on righting wrongs is also in conflict with Batman's limited role as an unofficial agent of the law. Vengeance is intimately connected to punishment, a concept Batman invokes quite often despite his restricted task of apprehending wrongdoers. On a quiet night, perched high above Gotham, Batman thought to himself, "with luck, I'll prevent or punish one or two of the night's small crimes."[33] A colleague once described Batman's mission as "trying to shield the innocent" but also "striving to punish the guilty."[34]

Despite the rhetoric, though, he is aware that punishment is not his job. At the end of a long adventure, after he caught the serial murderer known as the "Holiday Killer," Batman thought to himself, "I made a promise to my parents to protect this city from the evil that took their lives. If I am to succeed, I must be willing to deal out—the punishment." As Batman was about to strangle the man, Jim Gordon stopped him, saying he won't let him "do something that we'll both regret." Batman told Gordon, "then do what needs to be done," and Gordon did: he placed the murderer under arrest to face his crimes in a court of law.[35] It is natural for Batman to want to mete out punishment and vengeance himself, and he comes close to doing so on occasion—he is only human, after all—but he usually stops short of crossing that line, realizing in the end that punishment is not his to hand out.[36]

Similarly, Batman often states his mission in the language of *justice*, a term with many meanings but, in this specific case, representing retributivist justice as described above, evening the scales between good and evil. When Bruce introduced a young Dick Grayson to the Batcave and his second life, Alfred said what he does himself is irrational enough, but bringing a young boy into it is plainly wrong, to which Bruce responded, "We're seeking justice, Alfred. How can that ever be a mistake?"[37] Speaking over his parents' graves after the Cataclysm struck Gotham, he described his role as "an instrument of justice. Justice for you, justice for all."[38] As the narration to one tale reads, "Batman knows full well the meaning of his life—a never-ending quest for justice. A never-ending war against evil."[39] (We'll return to the meaning of Batman's life at the end of the first part of this book.)

However, justice—even retributivist justice—is distinct from naked revenge or vengeance. As Batman told a murderer named Grotesk who was seeking revenge but speaking of fighting evil, "you don't seek justice. You seek vengeance. They're not the same."[40] It's also a lesson he teaches his partners: when Batman scolded his second Robin, Jason Todd, for trying to kill Two-Face, Jason explained that he had discovered Two-Face may have been involved in the death of his father. Batman advised him, "Learning how to temper revenge with justice, well ... that's hard even for an adult," as he all too well knows, but it must be done.[41] Compared to justice, vengeance is often more personal, a drive to make things right for yourself and your loved ones, regardless of any general sense of justice involved. Justice, particularly retributivist justice, is properly conducted in a court by dispassionate people acting as prosecutors, judges, and juries, divorced from the strong emotions that drive the victims of crime or their family and friends. To some extent, Batman exemplifies this vengeful impulse, his mission to eradicate crime being driven by the violent deaths of his parents at the hands of a criminal—and this makes it all the more commendable that he usually holds back and recognizes his limited role in the criminal justice system (even if he needs a reminder from Jim Gordon once in a while).[42]

Even though furthering justice (impersonally and dispassionately) is an admirable goal, it has little to do with Batman's traditional role, similar to that of a police officer, as protecting the innocent and catching criminals. After all, courts, not officers of the law, dispense justice. As he told Alfred after becoming aware of the actions of the murderous political vigilante Anarky,

> His cause may be just but his methods certainly aren't … The fact is, no man can be allowed to set himself up as judge, jury, and executioner. So, while I may sympathize with this Anarky's ends, I'm duty-bound to use every power at my disposal to prevent him from carrying them out![43]

When Batman discovered that the Reaper, a murderous vigilante dressed as his grim namesake, was actually the Holocaust survivor Doctor Gruener, Batman accused him (like Grotesk) of pursuing personal vengeance, to which Gruener replied, "Who are you to judge me? You—who have not witnessed the horror of those days?" Batman answered, "True, I have no right to judge! Neither have you!"[44]

In the end, not only does Batman acknowledge that he has no right to judge and punish wrongdoers, but he also prevents others from doing the same, as shown most starkly by his reaction to Jean-Paul Valley, who took over for Batman after Bane broke his back.[45] Due to his training at the hands of the Order of Saint Dumas to be their vengeful agent Azrael, Valley began his tenure as the Dark Knight by taking the "dark" more seriously than Bruce Wayne ever did. Tim Drake, who was Robin at the time, was scared by Valley's behavior from the start, and explained to him that, to Batman—as utilitarian as his general mission may be—the ends don't always justify the means, at which Valley scoffs.[46] (We'll discuss Batman's uncomfortable relationship with ends-justify-the-means reasoning much more in the next part of the book.)

After Wayne recovered from his injury he confronted Valley, and the narration makes clear the distinction between the two (starting with the latter's scalloped armor):

> Jean-Paul Valley's Batman is a thing of metal and fire, all razor edges and bulletproof terror, a guise for punishment and retribution. For this Batman the

end justifies the means, and already two men have died because of him. Bruce Wayne's Batman stands for justice. He has sworn that no more life will be taken—and staked his own life on the result.[47]

We'll have much more to say about Valley's Batman and his contrasts with the classic formula later; for now, it's enough to recognize that he represents what Wayne could have become if he had embraced his vengeful impulses in action as well as word, and forgotten his larger mission to save and protect (which Valley ultimately comes to appreciate, but too late).

For all his talk about vengeance and justice—even proclaiming it the "meaning of his life" without which his "entire life is a lie"—in his actions Batman does not seem that motivated by revenge. As Sasha Bordeaux—Bruce Wayne's bodyguard, Batman's crimefighting partner, and "both" men's eventual love interest—reminisced while working alongside him, "it's not for revenge. It's not about righting the wrong done to him as a child … It's about protecting people."[48] In one of his weirdest but most meaningful tales, Batman and Robin are recruited by the mysterious Phantom Stranger to go to an alternate dimension in which Thomas and Martha Wayne have yet to be killed, giving Batman a chance to save another young Bruce the same hell he faced himself—and the same fate of becoming the Batman. Robin plays utilitarian here, wondering if, by saving the Waynes, they are denying this world one of its greatest heroes, implying that the deaths of the Waynes might be an acceptable cost, a harsh but understandable version of the ends justifying the means. In the end, however, Batman does save the Waynes, and young Bruce is inspired by the sight of the masked man to undergo a familiar training ritual, someday to "make a decision … choose a direction for his life … And when he does, it will not be a decision born of grief, or guilt, or vengeance … but of awe … and mystery … and gratitude."[49] Unlike this younger Batman-in-training, our Dark Knight cannot deny his deep-rooted hunger for vengeance and justice, but rather than indulging these, he uses his pain and anger to fuel his mission to do what he can to prevent crime and protect the innocent.

At the same time, however, even though it's not about vengeance for Batman, it's not always about protecting people either. Reminiscent of his reaction to Anarky, when faced with the possibility of two of his most murderous foes, Joker and Black Mask, killing each other, Batman thought, "Despite the many rumors to the contrary, any need I have for vengeance is mitigated by my sense of duty. And one can't ever set duty aside, even for an outcome that would clearly serve the greater good."[50] This is yet another exception to his generally utilitarian mission, one based on duty that some-times takes precedence over the safety and lives of innocents, and which represents the greatest challenge to Batman's stated mission. We'll return to this in the second part of this book, but for now it serves as a reminder that ethics are complex, especially for a hero who has devoted his life to doing the most good he can and also doing it in the right way.

Sticking to Gotham City

A simpler way in which Batman limits his utilitarianism is the narrow geographical focus of his activities. I don't like to repeat myself, so just flip back a few pages and see how many times he mentions Gotham City in his grand pronouncements. Batman doesn't set out to stop crime *everywhere*, or protect *all* innocent people of the world from the scourge of wrongdo-ers. He wants to help Gotham, save Gotham, and "cure" Gotham (as shown in the quote earlier, in the spirit of his father, about Gotham being Batman's "patient").

Speaking of the elder Wayne, while Bruce was investigating a slander-ous allegation against Thomas, he told Alfred that "my father felt a social obligation to the people of Gotham," to which Alfred added, "The apple doesn't fall far from the tree."[51] As the son of a prominent Gotham City family—dating back to his great-great-grandfather, the judge Solomon E. Wayne—Bruce feels a close bond with the city.[52] As the narration to one adventure reads:

> In the sincerest sense of the word, the Darknight Detective loves this city—feeling the pounding pulse of it as if it were his own! They are irrev-ocably entwined, the city and the man, each fulfilling a desperate need in the other—each sensing the other's secret sorrows and private pains ...[53]

According to Batman's journal after a battle against Two-Face, "This is my city. When she bleeds, I bleed. Even when I sleep ... I can hear Gotham screaming."[54] And again, he thought to himself, after all he and Gotham had endured during the Cataclysm and the viral outbreak known as the Contagion, "I kept fighting. I never stopped fighting. All for her. I'm every-thing because of her. I'm nothing without her. I care. How can I not? All those times, all those battles ... she's still screaming."[55] (Always screaming, it seems.)

Whether or not he's in the cowl and cape, most everything Bruce Wayne does is in service to his beloved Gotham City. After the Cataclysm struck, Gotham plunged into what became known as No Man's Land, eventually disavowed by the federal government and its bridges destroyed to cut it off from the rest of the nation. Before this happened, though, Bruce went to Washington to petition Congress to save Gotham rather than isolate it. For an entire issue, Bruce recounted his history and love for his city, praising the perseverance, determination, and generosity of its people despite its reputation as, in the words of one senator, "some kind of asylum. A nightmare carnival ride. An endless source of horror stories for the tabloids. A haven for the worst of the worst."[56] When another senator accused him of asking for federal money to line his own pockets, Bruce answered, "I've been accused of a lot of things in my life. Being one of the idle rich. A spoiled heir. A do-nothing playboy," and recalling when his back was broken by Bane, he continued, "But I've suffered setbacks in my time. I've failed and paid for mistakes and missteps. There were times I wanted to quit, to run far away. But I couldn't do that to Gotham." As he left the chambers, a reporter asked him, "With your wealth, you could live anywhere. Why do you care about Gotham so much?" and Bruce answered, "A very simply reason, actually. It's a promise I made a very long time ago."

As he said to the senator, Batman has endured great personal agony and sacrifice for Gotham. When Bane was sending all of Batman's foes at him to weaken him for their final battle, the Firefly used his flame guns to scorch our hero. As Batman fought on, he thought about how tired and injured he was, then caught himself: "Stop complaining. Keep moving. Your problems don't matter. You don't matter. Only Gotham matters."[57] Another time, as half the city lay without power, Batman thought to himself, "Tired ... I want to go to bed ... I don't really have a choice ... Gotham City. She chose me ... someone has to look after her ..."[58] In an earlier tale, after preventing Ra's al Ghul from wiping out Gotham by poisoning its water supply with a chemical that caused deadly reactions to sunlight, Batman apparently killed him, after which Ra's' daughter Talia, Batman's occasional lover and betrothed, left him. As they exited the scene, Robin said, "You may have lost her, yeah ... but you saved Gotham. That's something," to which Batman replied, "No, chum ... that's everything."[59] He is even willing to alienate the entire Gotham City Police Department to save the city, such as during the War Games incident, when one of his associates turned the cities' organized crime families against each other and Batman was forced to co-opt the police to quell the violence. When Alfred asked him afterwards how he planned to carry on "when the police force has orders to shoot you on sight," Bruce responded, "Just like we did in the beginning, old friend—very carefully … The city's changed. But there are still millions of people … I will protect … with my life."[60]

That promise and oath would sustain him through the No Man's Land period; as he told Alfred after Gotham was quarantined, "Gotham is my city. My responsibility. I took an oath to protect it. Bruce Wayne couldn't save it, so Batman must."[61] For a period of time between the Contagion, a crisis involving the breakout of a deadly pathogen (which returned after it was believed to be eradicated), to the Cataclysm and its "Aftershock," and through No Man's Land—from 1996 to 1999 in our world—Gotham City itself was under constant threat, not from petty crime, murder, or supervillains, but from large-scale destruction, putting Batman's mission to save lives to the test. Among other things, this series of catastrophes inspired soul-searching on the part of our Dark Knight, including the impassioned apologies at his parents' grave we saw earlier. "There's little I can do against disease and natural disasters," he said. "I hope you don't think I've failed in my promise."[62] As he told Nightwing—the adult Dick Grayson—while surveying the earthquake damage, "Crime isn't Gotham's biggest problem right now. Survival is. That takes something more long range than our nightly vigilance."[63]

During the second round of the contagion, we find Bruce and Tim frustrated in the cave, with Bruce telling Alfred that "I failed them. I swore to protect the innocent of Gotham and I failed them. They died painful deaths because I couldn't save them. I'll never forget those bodies. More than I could count." Alfred tried to assure the two that many more would have died if not for their help. "You'd do well to remember this the next time you're in Gotham—every face you see, should it be an innocent or the basest villain … each and every one of them owes you their lives."[64] But Batman is not one to focus on the good he did and the suffering he prevented, but only what he failed to do—and given the futility of his mission, he is guaranteed to fail to some degree, and therefore guaranteed to suffer.

However reasonable the motivation, we have to admit that Batman's choice to focus his nightly activities on Gotham City is morally arbitrary: there is no ethical relevant reason to restrict himself this way, especially within the context of his generally utilitarian mission to protect and save people. Although he doesn't strictly limit his superhero activities to its borders, he does concentrate his efforts on Gotham—which, among other things, predictably interferes with his participation with superhero teams.

Not long after he quit the Justice League of America to form the Outsiders so his hands would be less tied when people needed help, Batman left that group, telling his teammates, after a subterranean mission, that "innocents were murdered [in Gotham] while I was off under the earth, instead of here, where I was needed. I thought this would be different, but it's just like the Justice League—so busy saving the world, we lose sight of individuals," especially those in his hometown.[65] Years later, after rejoining the JLA, when Superman asked him if he was coming to a team meeting, Batman answered, "I have business … Gotham comes first."[66] Batman has very sentimental and deep-rooted reasons to focus on Gotham City, as we saw, but this would not seem to justify ignoring the world outside its Gates.

In general, is Batman justified in limiting the scope of his utilitarianism in this way? We've seen before that he also limits himself to certain means to increasing utility, such as fighting crime and saving people, which lessens suffering rather than increasing happiness. This seems to be acceptable, representing a focus on the type of altruism he is best suited to provide. However, the restriction of his activities to Gotham seems more arbitrary, suggesting that lives within Gotham are more worthy of focus than lives outside it.

This, of course, is absurd. Although Batman certainly focuses most of his time and energy on Gotham, he does not neglect the world outside it (his record with teamwork notwithstanding). In an early adventure, Jim Gordon was abducted and Batman believed he was taken to his own hometown of Chicago. When Alfred questioned the wisdom of going to Chicago to find him, a city where no one knew Batman and with which he was unfamiliar, Batman merely said, "It's all Gotham. Let's go."[67] Whether this meant that every city is essentially Gotham, so Batman would have no problem navigating it, or that "it's all Gotham" in the sense that he goes where he is needed, it shows that Batman does not, by rule, limit himself to his own city. When Batman received word—from his "clipping services all over the world," thank you 1980—of two priests who were mysteriously murdered in rural Spain, he immediately made plans to go there, and when Alfred asked him, "Gotham City is unusually quiet this week—why don't you simply rest?" Batman replied, "I wish I could, Alfred! With all my heart … I only wish I could!"[68] But crime is crime, anywhere he—or his clipping services— find it.

In fact, Batman's global exploits are the stuff of legend (or at least comic books), including jaunts to Scotland, where he has family roots, and Barcelona, where he is shown to have a stash of costumes and equipment (so he doesn't have to worry about getting his utility belt through customs).[69] His travels over the years to poverty-stricken areas such as Ethiopia and Calcutta triggered his compassionate instincts and philanthropic side.[70] In what was perhaps his most cosmopolitan moment, after returning from "the dead" (actually displaced in time by the almighty Darkseid), Batman decided to make his brand global, forming "Batman Incorporated" and traveling around the world training surrogates to fight crime "with the idea of Batman."[71] As he told Superman, "Once, I patrolled the dark alleys of Gotham alone. Now, Batman will be everywhere that it's dark."[72] As he explained to Dick Grayson, who served as Batman while Bruce was otherwise disposed and continued to do so at home while Bruce traveled the world, "I need you ... Gotham needs you. The world needs *us*."[73] In this way, Bruce continues to keep a special eye on Gotham by dedicating his best disciple to its protection—with his son Damian at Dick's side as Robin—while he expands his mission to the rest of the world.

The Futility of the Bat

This cosmopolitanism aside, is Batman's traditional focus on Gotham City really that unreasonable? One argument in favor of it is that it moderates what is, by any measure, an impossible task: to eradicate crime and to prevent the pain and suffering resulting from it. As the narration to an overview of his early career reads: "Bent on a mission he knew was impossible to accomplish—the elimination of crime in Gotham—he attacked it with obsession and every new resource at his command."[74] The elimination of crime is an impossible goal even when restricted to Gotham City, so in a sense it wouldn't help anybody to extend his domain outside Gotham—he has more than enough work to do there! As we saw above, Batman does help wherever he is needed or called, but he prefers to focus on Gotham when he can. It may be an arbitrary restriction to focus on one city and mostly ignore others, but it is not an unreasonable one, given his all-too-human limitations. Rather than dwell on his obsession with Gotham, we should emphasize the fact that he devotes his life to helping others at all, whether those others live in Gotham or not. (And it's not like Metropolis and Central City don't have their own costumed heroes running around anyway!)

Although it may excuse his focus on Gotham, the futility of Batman's mission even within its borders remains a concern. As we said above, it is

an impossible task wherever he chooses to pursue it—and time and time
again we see it get to him. Sometimes it's the individual he can't save, such
as the woman who jumped off a roof in front of Batman and Jim Gordon.
Batman caught her with a batarang on a rope, only to watch her swing
through a window and die. When Gordon told him, "It's not your fault,
Batman. You did all you could do for the poor girl," all Batman could think
was, "but it wasn't enough. It never is quite enough, is it? I can never do
enough. To stop people dying. To bring back the dead."[75] Other times, it's
the revolving door of the criminal justice system and Batman's failure to
reform any of his foes; as Alfred put it to a young Jason Todd, early in his
tenure as the second Robin,

> so much villainy under the bridge, as it were … so many brilliant, vital minds
> wasted on crime … and all the master has ever done is put them behind bars
> … which never hold them for long … With the exception of Catwoman and
> precious few others, Master Jason—he has convinced none of them to see the
> world as he does. In a sense, then, his repeated successes in jailing them are
> in fact failures.[76]

Most often, however, it's Batman's inability to be everywhere at once, such
as when he rushed to a convenience store hold-up after defeating Killer
Croc, apprehending the thief but arriving too late to prevent the clerk from
being shot and killed. As the introductory narration to that issue reads:
"The Dark Knight is not insane. He knows he cannot prevent every single
tragedy, accident, or crime to befall Gotham City—but he also knows that
he can't stop trying to."[77]

It is Batman's knowledge of the futility of his mission—even "merely"
within Gotham—that makes it all the more tragic, inspiring, and noble.
We've seen, in his frequent lamentations about his limitations over the
graves of his parents, how deeply he feels about his task, despite its enor-
mity. As he wrote in his diary during his earliest years as Gotham's
protector,

> It is now many months since I set out upon my war against crime, and I am
> no nearer an end than when I began. I am not despondent. Only a fool or a
> madman would feel that such a war can ever be won, and I am neither of
> those.[78]

In that same entry, he is surprisingly realistic concerning reports of his progress: "My friend Lieutenant Gordon tells me Gotham's violent crime has

fallen by 8 percent since I began my campaign … 8 percent. No victory, perhaps—but no mere trifle when measured in terms of human suffering."[79] Later, when Clayface tortured Batman, *Clockwork Orange*-style, with a movie designed to trigger his worst memories—including the deaths of his parents, the more recent death of Jason Todd, and the shooting of Barbara Gordon—Batman thought to himself, "I've always known I could never win. Always known that for every life I saved, a thousand others were lost to me."[80]

Perhaps the best statement of Batman's self-awareness of the futility of his mission was given by Sasha Bordeaux, during the same reflections quoted above:

> Carrying the fight forward to the streets of Gotham, trying to shield the innocent … striving to punish the guilty. Every night now for over ten years. Doomed to failure, again and again. Because it is a true Fool's Errand. Because his quest is impossible. Even if the lunatics did not exist … even if men like the Joker and women like Poison Ivy were locked securely away forever … parents would still be murdered … children would still become orphaned. And before someone thinks that the foolish errand makes the one who pursues it a fool himself, let me clarify: He knows all this better than anyone. But he does it anyway. Heedless of the cost to himself … painfully aware of the cost to others.[81]

The cost that this devotion to his mission imposes on him and those close to him will be a point of emphasis throughout this book—especially when it comes to those closest to him, the young boys he trains to be his partners in an increasingly violent crusade against crime.

If the futility of Batman's mission to eradicate crime isn't bad enough, remember that he set himself the task of protecting and saving the innocent people of Gotham in general, not just from the scourge of wrongdoers but also from other dangers, whether manmade or natural. We've already seen that he struggles with large-scale disasters such as the Contagion outbreak and Cataclysm earthquake, as well as the No Man's Land that followed, because there are no enemies to capture and bring to justice: "there's little I can do against disease and natural disasters."[82] After all, young Bruce Wayne was inspired by a bat to adopt its guise to strike fear in the hearts of evildoers, which doesn't help to put small children at ease when he's rescuing them from burning buildings or collapsed subway tunnels. At times like this, Gotham needs a Superman, Wonder Woman, or Green Lantern, so even as much as a Batman can do, it will never be enough—especially for him. It is this kind of realization that emphasizes the futility of his mission even within Gotham City, and further justifies this focus. One can hardly imagine the remorse he would endure if he felt responsible for every innocent life, inside and outside of Gotham. Even the legendary endurance of the bat could not tolerate that for long.

These considerations also cause Batman to doubt his own value and purpose in life on occasion, a topic we'll explore near the end of this part of the book. In the meantime, we'll turn to the second core aspect of his mission—saving lives—and explore the nuances and complexities involved when putting this goal into action. Can he save everyone? If not, whom does he save first? And is his mission to save everybody self-defeating when he saves those who will only go on to kill others? Holy headaches!

Notes

1   *Detective Comics* #568 (November 1986).
2   *Batman: Gotham Knights* #4 (June 2000), "Letting Go."
3   Jeremy Bentham, *An Introduction to the Principles of Morals and Legislation* (1781), ch. I.I, I.V, available at https://www.utilitarianism.com/jeremy-bentham/.
4   John Stuart Mill, *Utilitarianism* (1863), ch. 2, available at https://www.utilitarianism.com/mill1.htm.
5   *Detective Comics* #724 (August 1998).
6   *Batman Allies Secret Files and Origins* 2005 (August 2005), "A Friend in Need."
7   *Batman: Legend of the Dark Knight Special* #1 (December 1993).
8   *The Untold Legend of the Batman* #3 (September 1980).
9   *Batman: Legends of the Dark Knight* #67 (January 1995).
10 *Batman* #403 (January 1987).
11 *Batman: Gotham Knights* #7 (September 2000), "Oblation."
12 *Detective Comics* #793 (June 2004), "The Surrogate Part Three: Deliverance."
13 *Batman* #595 (November 2001).
14 *Detective Comics* #583 (February 1988).
15 *Batman: Legends of the Dark Knight* #129 (May 2000).
16 *Batman* #0 (October 1994).
17 Ibid.
18 For a thorough treatment, see Douglas Husak, "Criminal Law Theory," in Martin P. Golding and William A. Edmundson (eds.), *The Blackwell Guide to the Philosophy of Law and Legal Theory* (Malden, MA: Blackwell, 2005), pp. 107–121.

19 Lawrence C. Becker, "Criminal Attempts and the Theory of the Law of Crimes," *Philosophy and Public Affairs* 3 (1974): 262–294, available at http://digitalcommons.hollins.edu/cgi/viewcontent.cgi?article=1011&context=philfac.

20 *Batman: Shadow of the Bat* #71 (February 1998).

21 *Secret Origins* #6 (September 1986). Granted, this issue retold the origin of the Golden Age Batman, but … umm … hey, look, squirrel!

22 *Batman* #438 (September 1989).

23 *Detective Comics* #627 (March 1991), "The Case of the Chemical Syndicate" (a modern retelling of the original Batman story from *Detective Comics* #27 in 1939).

24 *Batman Confidential* #25 (March 2009).

25 *Batman: Gotham Knights* #5 (July 2000), "Locked." See note 76 below for more on rehabilitation and restorative justice.

26 Even in the aspects of his work that resemble police, he goes much farther, as we'll see later.

27 *Batman* #431 (March 1989). (The comic actually reads "*of* all criminals," but I assume it meant to say "*on* all criminals.")

28 *Batman: Legends of the Dark Knight* #129 (May 2000).

29 *Batman* #558 (September 1998).

30 *Batman and the Outsiders*, vol. 1, #1 (August 1983).

31 For a survey of philosophies of punishment, see Thom Brooks, *Punishment* (London: Routledge, 2012), and for more detailed debate, see H.B. Acton (ed.), *The Philosophy of Punishment: A Collection of Papers* (New York: St. Martin's Press, 1969), A. John Simmons et al. (eds.), *Punishment: A Philosophy & Public Affairs Reader* (Princeton, NJ: Princeton University Press, 1995), and Mark D. White (ed.), *Retributivism: Essays on Theory and Policy* (Oxford: Oxford University Press, 2011).

32 See H.L.A. Hart, *Punishment and Responsibility: Essays in the Philosophy of Law* (Oxford: Oxford University Press, 1968), and Brooks, *Punishment*, ch. 5.

33 *Batman* #525 (December 1995).

34 *Batman: 10-Cent Adventure* (March 2002).

35 *Batman: The Long Halloween* #13 (December 1997).

36 We'll see a technical exception to this in the section on torture in the second part of this book.

37 *Batman* #437 (August 1989). We discuss Alfred's reservations about training Robins later in this part of the book.

38 *Detective Comics* #724 (August 1998).

39 *Batman: Shadow of the Bat* #72 (March 1998). The narration continues: "But this is no time for philosophy." To the contrary—it is *always* time for philosophy!

40 *Batman* #659 (January 2007).

41 *Batman* #411 (September 1987).

42   On the difference between retributivism and vengeance, see Robert Nozick, *Philosophical Explanations* (Cambridge, MA: Harvard University Press, 1981), pp. 366–368. On the role of emotions in criminal justice and punishment more generally, see Jeffrie G. Murphy, *Punishment and the Moral Emotions* (Oxford: Oxford University Press, 2012), and Martha C. Nussbaum, *Anger and Forgiveness: Resentment, Generosity, Justice* (Oxford: Oxford University Press, 2016).

43   *Detective Comics* #608 (November 1989).

44   *Batman* #237 (December 1971).

45   Bane broke the back of the Bat in *Batman* #497 (July 1993), and Valley assumed the role of Batman (at Wayne's request) in the next issue, *Batman* #498 (August 1993).

46   *Detective Comics* #665 (August 1993).

47   *Batman: Shadow of the Bat* #30 (August 1994).

48   *Detective Comics* #765 (February 2002). Sasha reiterates this later while recounting his origin: "A vow made to his parents, to their memory. Not solely to avenge. To protect" (*Batman: 10-Cent Adventure*, March 2002).

49   *Detective Comics* #500 (March 1981), "To Kill a Legend."

50   *Batman* #644 (Late October 2005).

51   *Batman: Legends of the Dark Knight* #204 (Late June 2006).

52   On Solomon E. Wayne, founder of modern Gotham and a member of the Underground Railroad that helped Southern slaves escape to the north, see *Batman: Legends of the Dark Knight* #27 and #45 (February 1992 and December 1995, respectively), and *Batman Secret Files and Origins* (October 1997), "The Men Behind Gotham." See also the 2011 miniseries *Batman: Gates of Gotham* for the role of Solomon's son Alan in the further development of Gotham, alongside the Cobblepots and Elliots.

53   *Batman* #308 (February 1979). Before you think you caught me, I'll have you know that "Darknight" was typically spelled in one word early in its usage, particularly when modifying "detective."

54   *Batman: Two-Face—Crime and Punishment* (1995). See also *Batman: Legends of the Dark Knight* #116 (April 1999), when Batman wondered, in the early days of No Man's Land, if Gotham created him or, if considering all of its current problems, "did he create it?"

55   *Batman: No Man's Land* #0 (December 1999).

56   All quotes in this paragraph are from *Batman* #561 (January 1999), part of a storyline that could only be titled "Mr. Wayne Goes to Washington."

57   *Detective Comics* #662 (June 1993).

58   *Batman: Legend of the Dark Knight Halloween Special* #1 (December 1993).

59   *Batman Annual* #8 (1982). We'll discuss the matter of Batman's apparent and intentional killing of Ra's in a later chapter, don't you worry—even though, in *Batman* #400 (October 1986), Ra's returned, as he always does.

60 *Batman* #634 (January 2005). We'll talk much more about this episode when we discuss Batman's relationship with the police in the second part of this book.

61 *Detective Comics* #730 (March 1999).

62 *Detective Comics* #724 (August 1998); see also *Batman* #558 (September 1998).

63 *Detective Comics* #724 (September 1998). This issue also features a wonderful speech in which Batman told Nightwing of his dreams for Gotham from the time his parents were shot, hoping for a "brighter and cleaner" Gotham after he was gone. "Now Gotham is gone. And I'm still here."

64 *Detective Comics* #702 (October 1996).

65 *Batman and the Outsiders*, vol. 1, #32 (April 1986).

66 *JLA* #5 (May 1997).

67 *Batman: Legends of the Dark Knight* #159 (November 2002).

68 *Batman* #320 (February 1980).

69 *Batman: Scottish Connection* (1998); *Batman in Barcelona: Dragon's Knight* #1 (July 2009).

70 *Batman* #427 (December 1988) and #534 (September 1996), respectively; more on both adventures to come.

71 *Batman: The Return* #1 (January 2011), in a story that, not coincidentally, is titled "Planet Gotham."

72 *Superman* #710 (June 2011).

73 *Batman: The Return* #1 (January 2011).

74 *Batman* #0 (October 1994); compare to the quote from *Batman: Shadow of the Bat* #0, published around the same time.

75 *Batman* #452 (Early August 1990).

76 *Batman* #400 (October 1986); see also the passage from *Batman: Gotham Knights* #5 (July 2000), "Locked," quoted above. Both episodes refer to *rehabilitation*, an alternative orientation of punishment to retributivism and deterrence that focuses on the improvement of offenders in the hopes that they can re-enter society as lawful members. Another related theory of punishment is *restorative justice*, which takes a broader view toward healing victims, offenders, and the community as a whole. On these two ideas, see Brooks, *Punishment*, chs. 3 and 4 (respectively).

77 *Batman: Gotham Knights* #3 (May 2000), "Bad Karma." Incidentally, this sentiment is shared by another Gotham hero, albeit a distinctively super-powered one: Alan Scott, the Golden Age Green Lantern. When Scott joined Batman on a modern adventure, the older man said, "I've forgotten what Gotham feels like … Night after night, hopelessness just tries to beat down anything good. It wasn't this bad in the '40s, or the '50s … but it was still bad. I can remember those days so clearly, you know? Like they were only yesterday … Coming home black and blue from nights of fighting Grundy or Sportsmaster—but feeling like I'd really accomplished something. Then I'd turn on the radio and

hear about every place I hadn't been. All this pain, just washing up on Gotham's shores." Batman agreed, saying, "I know that feeling. That moment of satisfaction that's always ripped away too soon" (*Detective Comics* #785, October 2003, "Made of Wood: Part Two of Three").

78   *Batman: Legends of the Dark Knight* #172 (December 2003).

79   Ibid. This passage is followed by a parenthetical: "friend—Gordon? Odd, I think of him that way." There's more about their relationship in the second part of this book.

80   *Detective Comics* #606 (October 1989).

81   *Batman: 10-Cent Adventure* (March 2002).

82   *Detective Comics* #724 (August 1998).

3

Trade-Offs within the Mission

So far, we've described Batman's mission as a limited form of utilitarianism, in which he focuses on lessening pain and suffering, chiefly by fighting crime in Gotham City—a goal that can never be achieved or "finished," and is therefore futile in a sense, but which nonetheless provides purpose and meaning to his life. We've addressed the problems with this, especially the arbitrary restriction to one city and its immediate environs, while also acknowledging that given the futility of the mission in general, these self-imposed limitations may be justified in that they focus his Herculean efforts rather than spreading himself *even* thinner.

Now we set aside our discussion of his mission itself and turn our attention to how he makes choices *within* it. As we've seen, even while limiting his activities to Gotham, Batman is still merely one man—even when he lets the other kids play with his toys—and he cannot be everywhere at once. Superman is often faced with global choices such as preventing a nuclear weapon from hitting Europe or stopping a tsunami raging toward Indonesia, but Batman faces more "mundane" but also more immediately human choices, such as the incident with Killer Croc and the convenience store robbery that we discussed in the last chapter. Although he wasn't aware of the robbery until after he subdued Croc, there are many other cases in which he must make a choice between pursuing a criminal and saving an innocent person. This choice may have been easy for him—guess which option he chose—but he regularly faces more difficult choices, such as between saving one innocent person or another when he can't save both, or saving a villain and thereby possibly endangering more innocent lives down the road.

Batman and Ethics, First Edition. Mark D. White.
© 2019 John Wiley & Sons Ltd. Published 2019 by John Wiley & Sons Ltd.

Holy Decisions, Batman!

I don't think, at this point in our discussion, that we need to stress that Batman wants to save *everyone*. In his frantic search to find survivors of the Cataclysm, he made such dramatic proclamations as, "Where life has survived, it must be saved!"[1] Even though he appreciates the futility of his mission and knows rationally that he can't save everyone, that doesn't mean he won't try to save every person he can. When a little girl cried that she couldn't find her mother in the earthquake wreckage, Batman told Robin, "There're a million stories like it in Gotham right now." When Robin asked, "Does that mean we don't help?" Batman answered, "If I ever get that calloused I'll retire."[2] Much later, after he failed to stop a man from detonating explosives under a building, Batman thought, "No ... it was all for ... all for nothing. I only pray ... pray that I can save ... even one life."[3] Even while saving one person, he tries to help others: after he dove off a roof to catch a falling girl, Batman and the girl crashed through the window of an elderly woman's apartment. When he saw the woman's oxygen tank, he told her "You probably have mesothelioma. It's asbestos poisoning from this building's pipes. Get a lawyer."[4]

Naturally Batman will try to save every person he can—even from asbestos poisoning—but he is only one man and he cannot save them all. Given the nature of Gotham City, though, there will always be more people to save, help, or protect than he can attend to. As Sasha Bordeaux wrote,

> There's always something. He tries to stay on top of it. Computers in the cave monitor the emergency and the local news ... feeding him a constant stream of information through the radio in his cowl. ... He can never be fast enough. He doesn't discriminate. He just tries to save lives.[5]

This is one of the few reasons Batman ever acknowledges that it might be useful to take on a crimefighting partner, such as when he thought during a citywide gang war, "for the first time in a long time, I realize I need something I've never needed before. Help."[6] Most of the time, however, he flies solo, with nary a Robin at his side, even though this means he can save fewer people than if he played better with others.

This also means that Batman has to make choices about whom to save and whom not to save. Given his determination and the personal importance of his mission, he riles against this; as Sasha said above, he doesn't discriminate, but tries his best to save all. When he can't, though, he has to use some criterion to decide who receives his help first or which crime to tackle. Sometimes there's no way to make a choice. In one of his globetrotting episodes—"It is death that has brought the Batman to London"—a man was shot from two directions by two gunmen, and Batman admitted that "I can't nab both gunmen! Got to settle for the one I can see!"[7] In a case back at home, the Dynamic Duo were chasing Two-Face, but they arrived just in time to see, in Batman's words, "two getaway cars—same make, model, and color! The Batmobile can catch one of them—but which one?" Robin chose one, only to discover, after it crashed, "just some punk driver—and no Two-Face. I picked the wrong one." Batman told his partner, "It's not your fault, Robin—the best we could have done was flip a coin."[8] In even choices like this, in which there is literally no reason to choose one option rather than the other, even an experienced detective can do no more than follow his gut—or flip a coin. But at least it's promising that Batman acknowledges when he cannot catch two criminals heading in opposite directions—that's progress! This also explains his relief when, as the Joker and Black Mask tried to escape from him down an alley, he realized, "This time the alley is blocked on either end by the arriving police. This time I don't have to choose between capturing one and letting the other get away. Neither of them has enough room to maneuver. Neither of them can escape my reach. Not the worst way to spend an evening."[9]

Cases like this are what philosophers call *tragic dilemmas*, choices from which one cannot escape "with clean hands." Tragic dilemmas show up often in literature, television, and movies, such as when a parent can only save one of their two children and must make the impossible choice of which one lives and which one does not.[10] These are also the stock-in-trade of superhero comics and movies, in which our heroes are put in the unenviable position of having to choose whether to rescue someone close to them, such as a love interest, sidekick, or family member, or save many innocent strangers from a natural or manmade disaster. Of course, supervillains are very fond of putting the heroes in this position because it offers them a chance to torture the heroes emotionally, especially if they can't find a way to save everybody. The heroes rarely blame the villains who put them in that position, but rather blame themselves for failing to do the impossible— and that's part of what makes them noble, heroic, and tragic.

What makes a hero a *super*hero, though, is finding a way out of the tragic dilemma. This is easier, of course, for superpowered heroes like Superman, Wonder Woman, or the Flash, who can usually find a way to race around the world or perform some other amazing feat to save all the people. It's much harder for someone like Batman, who has only his wits, training, and wonderful toys, to do the same—but it makes it all the more impressive when he does!

Given what we know about Batman, we wouldn't expect him to accept tragic dilemmas lying down. We've already seen how he tortures himself for failing to save *anybody*, whether it was possible or not. As he said in one tale, when confronted with an impossible decision between two choices, "There's always another choice if you think hard enough."[11] Even if there isn't—and let's be realistic, sometimes there isn't—it can be good to pretend this is. When the Spectre, a supernatural member of the Justice Society of America who also moonlights as God's Spirit of Vengeance, instructed the Justice League not to intervene in a military operation to obliterate a city in order to prevent "the end of existence," arguing that "the losses will be acceptable. A few thousand at most," and concluded that "I can see no dilemma here," Batman responded, simply, "No loss is acceptable. Take it from me."[12] Even though the Spectre made a very sound and reasonable argument why the loss of a few thousand lives was preferable to the loss of ... well, *all* life ... Batman refused to accept this choice, and in the end the Justice League was able to save everybody. (And they didn't even tell the Spectre, "told ya so," likely because he would smite them down with righteous fury and wrath.)

But not all tragic dilemmas are as stark as choosing which of your children has to die—any choice between two unacceptable options can be considered a tragic dilemma, even if there is a way to identify one option as worse. This decision usually involves the use of *judgment* to determine where someone like Batman can do the most good. The problem with this is that knowing what "the most" means is often more complicated than it seems, and doesn't always provide a clear answer—especially when he resists such a comparison at all. When Alfred told Bruce about a homeless woman who was murdered, he had the costume ready to go, at which Bruce mused, "You know me too well, old friend ... almost too well!" Alfred replied, "Well enough to realize you could let no murderer go unpunished, Master Bruce—no matter how inconsequential his victim!" (That's cold, Alfred, very cold.) As Batman left to investigate, he said, "When I start making value judgments—deciding who's important enough to avenge—it'll be time to hang up my mask forever!"[13] Recall Batman's thought, quoted earlier, when he was chasing Kite Man but witnessed a burglary in progress: "A crime is a crime is a crime! It isn't my job to judge them—just to stop them!"[14]

As noble as these sentiments sound, they also come across as naïve. After all, if Kite Man were that dangerous—a big *if*, but bear with me—then Batman could surely do more good by bringing him down then by investigating a robbery. In fact, another time he came across a burglary, he thought to himself, "Still a crime—but I'd rather protect lives than money," suggesting that he does appreciate the difference between more and less significant crimes.[15] This is confirmed by a reflection one night:

> Wrong, damn it. Got to learn more self-control. Only amateurs stop for every little thing. I stopped two punks who skipped toilet-training from slicing each other up over a leather jacket. They both turned on me. Now I'm late for something I've spent two weeks setting up. A crack ring.[16]

Of course Batman wants to stop every crime and save every life, but he also knows he can't, so he acknowledges, in his brain if not his heart, that he has to make choices and pass up some crimes to tackle others that seem more important or harmful to innocent civilians.

The Partiality of the Bat

The simplest distinction between two crimes or criminals that Batman could make would be a simple "more lives" versus "fewer lives" scenario: all else the same, he should work to save more lives if he can, which is why he beats himself up for making the wrong choices or acting on impulse. Once, while chasing a psychopathic murderer, he saw a stabbing in progress in an alley and thought, "A monster loose in Gotham—every moment my hunt is delayed, lives may be in danger. Yet when I see cold-blooded murder, I can't ignore it!"[17] For the most part, however, he does make the wise decision to devote his time and effort to where it will do the most good, even when it's difficult. For example, when he really wanted to investigate a fascinating 100-year-old murder—talk about a cold case!—he nonetheless realized that "there are newer, more urgent crimes to be dealt with," and then devoted himself to them.[18] Sometimes he goes too far and fails to acknowledge that his life also matters. Once, as he prepared to leap off a roof after two falling people, he admitted to himself, "I deduce that if I go off that ledge, it's very likely that three people are going to die instead of two. But I have to turn off that part of my brain."[19]

In another, more personal case, Oracle called Batman, who was working with Nightwing to help people out of the wreckage of the Cataclysm, to tell him her father, Jim Gordon, was missing. Nightwing told Oracle they were on their way, but Batman told him to go alone, saying, "I can't spare the time away from here. There're too many lives at stake here to trade for one. Even James Gordon."[20] As he told his partner, even though Gordon is one of Batman's oldest and closest friends, as seen in many tales over decades of comics, Batman knew that his responsibility was to save as many lives as he could, even if it meant not saving the one that meant more to him than almost anyone else.

Would Batman have left to save Gordon if Nightwing (or someone else) hadn't been there to go instead? There's no way to know; Batman, after all, is only human, and it's natural for us humans to devote more attention to those we're close to. This is a topic of particular interest to moral philosophers because playing favorites, or showing *partiality* to some people over others, seems to go against the spirit of a moral system like utilitarianism that makes a point of treating everyone the same. One of our most famous modern utilitarians, Peter Singer, is well known for arguing that partiality leads affluent people in the first world to neglect the more dire plight of those in the third world.[21] There are many altruistic and philanthropic people in industrialized countries, but they give most of their money to people and organizations in their own countries rather than the more destitute people in other parts of the world. Much like Bruce Wayne giving money to a country club rather than a homeless shelter, any helping is good, but Singer argues very reasonably that charity should be directed to those who need it most—inspiring the modern *effective altruism* movement, which emphasizes the importance of doing the most good with one's philanthropic giving.[22]

Singer makes a very important point about shared humanity and looking beyond our own borders when trying to do good, which is relevant to Batman's focus on Gotham City as well as his choice of whom to save at any particular time. We could argue that Batman does the most good he can within Gotham City because he knows the city like the back of his glove and he has trained to combat the specific kind of crime that plagues it. Because of this, he may be able to do just as much good elsewhere, but it's reasonable to think that he couldn't do any *more*. (Remember, as told in the last chapter, that even Alfred questioned whether Batman should go to Chicago because he didn't know it well enough.)

Another reason even a utilitarian would support some degree of partiality is because helping those closer to you has positive effects of your own well-being. When Batman prevents a couple from being mugged or a cop from being killed by the Joker, this benefits not only the potential victims of these crimes but also furthers Batman's personal mission and his own well-being and satisfaction. Of course, this isn't the main reason Batman works so hard, but even if his personal satisfaction isn't what drives him, it is important to a utilitarian because his utility is included in the total as well. If we assume that Batman can do just as much good in Chicago, Caracas, or Cairo as he can in Gotham, but derives more personal satisfaction from working in his hometown, then it is better from a utilitarian point of view that he continue to do so.

When partiality rears its head in the tales of the Dark Knight, however, it's usually more personal and narrow, applying to one particular choice of whom to save rather than how he pursues his mission in general (an issue we'll come back in the next chapter). In one adventure, Batman searched in vain for the sister of a woman he had recently become involved with as Bruce Wayne. When Alfred informed him about another missing woman, Batman claimed he had no time to look into her disappearance, especially because he wasn't making any progress on the first case. When Alfred mentioned his personal connection, Batman snapped, accused Alfred of questioning his impartial judgment, and asked him, "What do you propose—flipping a coin?"[23] Given that Batman could pursue either case and both were equally worthy, there is nothing wrong with choosing the case that means more to him, assuming that the personal connection would not make him *less* effective at solving the case.

In another story, Batman investigated the murder of an amusement park owner who had befriended him as a child. After he caught the murderer, Alfred asked Bruce if he was pleased with the outcome, but he was surprised by the response: "No. In fact, I feel … ashamed." Bruce elaborated, "This city is full of killers, Alfred … but I went after Hart's. I let my emotions take control. Thought of myself—what I wanted—instead of others. That's dangerous."[24] But it is precisely this personal connection that allows him to make a meaningful distinction in otherwise interchangeable decisions. Batman could have investigated either murder, just as he could have pursued either missing woman in the earlier case, and either choice would have had an equal chance of doing the same amount of good (all else the same). By choosing cases that meant something to him, however, Batman did a little more good by helping someone else that also matters: himself.

It is rare for Batman to actually ignore his responsibilities because of a personal attachment. As we saw earlier, he sent Nightwing to help find Jim Gordon when he went missing because he felt he was needed to help people caught in the earthquake. On the surface this is a simple case of choosing to help many people instead of one, but it's still notable because the one in that case, Gordon, meant so much to him. Batman is hardly perfect on this count, however. In one striking instance, when a mysterious woman named Nocturna tried to take custody of his newly adopted ward (and second Robin) Jason Todd, Bruce decided to devote all of his resources to keeping him, including not only his wealth and the efforts of all of the Wayne Foundation's lawyers, but also his own time. When Alfred interrupted a meeting between Bruce and his lawyers to tell him about that glowing yellow light in the night sky, Bruce answered, "Alfred, I've never before failed to respond to that signal … but nor have I ever before been confronted by something more important," which meant it was more important to him than helping with whatever criminal situation Gordon was contacting him about.[25] However, later in Jason's short career as Robin, as he grew more rash and violent and Batman had to take him out of action, Jason ran away—at the same time that the Joker returned and got his hands on a nuclear missile. "Choices," Batman thought, continuing:

> Do I stay in Gotham to live up to my responsibilities as the boy's guardian? Or do I go after that madman and his nuclear weapon? It is painfully obvious which path I must choose. The question is: How will I ever be able to live with this decision?[26]

Even though he makes the right choice to save more people rather than fewer, Batman also feels the regret from letting the latter down, even though he had no reasonable alternative. Once again, this feeling is the hallmark of a hero who can never do enough, and although we may admire this, it is an impossible standard he holds himself to, and which drives some of his more, shall we say, obsessive behavior.[27]

If there's one thing that Batman allows to sway his judgment, it's not a particular person, but crime itself. This makes sense, given that it is his life's work to eradicate crime; we would hardly expect him to be dispassionate about it. At times he refuses to distinguish between more or less serious crimes and criminals; remember that he says things such as "a crime is a crime is a crime." (That never gets old.) When Batman and his favorite Gotham City police detective Harvey Bullock found Arnold Wesker, a.k.a. the Ventriloquist, dead, Harvey said, "This guy was bad. I mean not a Joker or Freeze level bad, but—" until Batman cut him off, saying, "All evil is bad. I don't have a sliding scale."[28] Bullock is just as quick to dismiss some criminals as beneath Batman's notice, especially when it comes to saving them. When Batman saved a stoned kid who jumped off a roof, Bullock said, "You could've skipped the heroics, though. No sense risking yourself on account of dopers! Sooner or later they all end up in the morgue." Of course, Batman disagreed: "I don't like drugs any more than you, Detective Bullock. But killing off the users isn't the way to stop them!"[29]

But some criminals do get to Batman more than others do. Exhibit A is the Joker, of course, whom we'll talk about a lot in this book. It isn't only the Clown Prince of Crime, though—all of Batman's archfoes trigger his rage from time to time. Take the Penguin, for instance, a cunningly intelligent and sadistic man who is driven by the same comical appearance that leads many to take him lightly. When Renee Montoya, another one of Gotham's finest, asked Batman why he focuses so much on the Penguin's thugs, asking him, "Is this really worth your time? Or ours?," Batman answered, "They're criminals. They were beating on someone. That's what it's about." But Montoya pressed on, arguing, "This is a not a major crime. This is about your feud with the Penguin … and those are two of the Penguin's bookies. Any other bookie in Gotham you would've left alone."[30] Another time, when it appeared the Penguin was dead, Batman thought to himself, "Can't say I'll miss his particular brand of mayhem. Better a dead Penguin—one less evil to haunt the night—than a crippled security guard, or a blinded bank clerk."[31] Here, Batman definitely distinguishes between greater and lesser crimes, but in a way that imputes a greater and lesser value to some lives than others, a position that flies in the face of his professed devotion to the value of all life, as we'll see later.[32]

There is one criminal Batman allows to get to him in a distinctly different way: Selina Kyle, the master thief known as the Catwoman, with whom he has an on-again, off-again romance through decades of comics despite her criminal activities (and perhaps a little bit because of them). During the Contagion outbreak, he told her, "I should do something about you. But whatever ever crimes you've committed, whatever crimes you may commit in the future—seem pretty insignificant beside the horror in the streets," making his neglect of her "minor" criminality explicit; this trade-off itself is not unreasonable, but does contradict his other language about "a crime is a crime."[33] Even the Gotham City police realize this: When Catwoman was suspected of murder, and a police officer suggested to the commissioner at the time, Michael Akins, that Batman might bring her in, Akins asked if he was kidding.[34] This blatant partiality may not be the heroic ideal we're accustomed to seeing from our masked marvels, but it does show the human side of Batman—especially considered against the background of the superhuman sacrifices to his own happiness he more often makes in the pursuit of his mission.

Save Rather Than Chase ... No Matter Who Needs Saving

One of Batman's most predictable choices regarding saving lives means letting criminals escape when there are innocent lives at stake. In fact, he is quite adamant about this not being a choice at all. When he stopped to help injured international ski champion Molly Post rather than chase homicidal environmental terrorist Ra's al Ghul, he thought, "Blast!—A rotten choice ... Chase Ra's ... or get Molly to medical help. No ... not really any choice at all!"[35] Later, while chasing the Sensei (of Ra's al Ghul's League of Assassins), Batman saw one of his henchmen run the other way with a hostage, and once again thought, "Rotten choice I have—let the Sensei escape or risk an innocent life! But it isn't really a choice!"[36] And while fighting Night-Slayer in a warehouse, a crate began to fall on a night watchman lying unconscious on the floor, and Batman thought, "Got to choose between saving the watchman and stopping the thief! Which means ... there's no choice at all."[37] (If it were a choice, though, I'm betting it would be a rotten one.)

Of course, Batman is fully aware of the trade-off he is making in these cases: when he was forced to save a group of kids from drowning when their boat was hit by flaming debris from a nearby explosion, rather than pursue his more dangerous quarry, he thought, "Couldn't let these kids drown! But I wish they'd been somewhere else! In rescuing them, I had to let my would-be killers go!"[38] Nonetheless, this is perhaps his firmest guiding principle, and one he regularly teaches his young partners. Early in Tim Drake's training, Batman told him, "The idea is to always minimize danger for any civilians in the area, as well as for yourself" before he does anything else, including chase criminals.[39] He taught the same lesson to Jason Todd: as Batman left to investigate a break-in at a local college and told Jason to get medical attention for a wounded civilian, the new Robin complained that he was stuck with the "unimportant stuff." Batman corrected him, saying:

> Remember when I said our purpose was to protect people from crime? What makes you think it's any less vital than pursuing criminals? Ensuring that the victims of crime are taken care of always comes first. Keep in mind—what's really important.[40]

Even Jean-Paul Valley, who took over as Batman after Bane broke Wayne's back, learned this lesson, though he resisted it at first. As he fought the villain Abattoir atop a school bus that was teetering over a cliff, Abattoir escaped and Jean-Paul wanted to pursue him, but understood that "there was no choice—I had to stay and save the kids. Definitely the way Bruce Wayne would have done it."[41]

But there's a problem with this principle being so well established. After all, Batman knows he has no choice when it comes to saving an innocent person or chasing a criminal, and all the Robins know it, and we know it. Guess who else knows it? *All of his enemies.* And they don't hesitate to use this information to help them escape the Dark Knight. Perhaps Clayface said it best as he dropped a napalm canister into a pool full of swimmers: "There's no way on earth you are going to be able to stop me—unless you're prepared to let those swimmers down there get burned to a crisp!"[42] As Clayface planned, Batman dove in to save them, and the malleable miscreant got away. Bane, the villain who would break the back of the bat, watched him carefully before facing him, and it didn't take him long to realize that Batman "will choose the saving of lives over the apprehension of killers ... He always does."[43] Bane used this information later when he faced Batman during the No Man's Land period in Gotham, bragging that he could walk away any time he wanted "because given the ethical choice—you will always make the correct decision and right now, you have only two choices—to continue this battle—and gamble on the outcome ... or defuse the dynamite bomb I planted in the sewer" beneath a soup kitchen. Of course, Batman leaves, and Bane gloats.[44] Even Batman's friends use his reliability on this point to their advantage. As Batman seemed ready to die in an epic battle with Black Mask at the end of a citywide gang war, Oracle took the drastic step of activating the self-destruct sequence in her watchtower headquarters. "Do you hear that, Batman? Do you see that this place is coming down around us?" she asked him. "I don't have any way out, unless you save me, Batman. Save me."[45] To Barbara, this wasn't a gamble because she knew this was the man who taught the principle of "save people first" to a young Batgirl years earlier.

But it took a certain felonious feline to point out the obvious to the Dark Knight. In a team-up early in both of their careers, Batman and Catwoman were chasing a cat-themed killer who targeted young women. As they faced him on a rooftop with one of his potential victims, the killer pushed the woman off the roof to get away, and Batman was forced to decide which way to go: "Left to save the woman—or right to stop the killer? Left." Of course, there was "no choice at all," and he saved the woman, who dangled by her fingertips off the ledge.[46] Later, Catwoman told Batman that the killer "was more than you could handle alone." Batman argued that "I chose to save this woman," but Catwoman already knew him too well: "There was no choice—it was what you always do. It's a strength, but he turned it into a weakness—used it to escape. You need help bringing him down. You need a partner."[47] This provides yet another reason Batman needs someone at his side to help him avoid choices such as save-or-chase, as well as more serious tragic dilemmas such as the choice of whom to save when one man, even a Batman, cannot save them all.

Even though Batman usually focuses on saving the innocent citizens of Gotham City from the criminals who would prey on them, he is careful to save criminals as well, even the worst of the worst (assuming that, like Harvey Bullock, we are willing to make such distinctions). On his first night in the costume, Batman fought burglars on a fire escape and clumsily knocked one over the railing. He was quick to catch him, thinking, "no—I'm no killer," and was careful to hold onto him even as the rest of the burglars attacked him, establishing several aspects of his mission from day one (or night one).[48] He also saves criminals from each other, such as when he saved the Riddler, hopped up on the venom that gives Bane his size and power, after Bane's goons shot him.[49] What's more, he even saves criminals from killing themselves. When a murderer Batman was chasing drove his car into a wall, Batman pulled him from the flames, with the narration telling of two men: "One says 'no' to life. Says the other—at all costs—'yes.'"[50] In another case, a henchman for the Penguin named Do-Boy (as in "do this, do that") jumped out a window rather than being caught by Batman, yelling, "Hey, Batman?" You ever hear the expression 'do or die'?" Batman caught him with a batarang and a rope, saying, "Hey, Do-Boy … never say die."[51]

Despite Batman's reputation, criminals are often surprised when he tries to save or help them. Speaking of henchmen, after Ivor, one of Poison Ivy's thugs, tried to kill him, Batman still looked after his well-being after defeating Ivy, prompting Ivor to ask, "You care … even after I tried … kill you …?"[52] Another story, narrated by a street punk named Barry Hemor, described how Batman confronted an angry mob Barry joined who were torching abandoned buildings to send a message to the authorities. After trying to convince their leader, Jeremiah Jones, to stop, Batman came across one such fire and dragged Jones into it to show him the harm he was doing. As the building began to fall, Batman and Jones barely escaped in time. Barry was ashamed that he had been a part of this, and said, "My shame was intensified when I saw Batman direct the others ... so that he could administer life-saving efforts ... to the man who was to blame for all that had occurred."[53] It's natural that criminals wouldn't expect the Batman to care for or save their lives; after all, the entire idea of dressing up as a bat is to strike fear into their hearts and scare them away from a life of crime. They don't see the compassionate side of the Dark Knight that ultimately cares about life, regardless of how it has been spent. When Catman, whom Batman was trying to save from making a fatal mistake, asked why he cares, Batman answered, "I thought you knew me better than that. I thought you saw me more clearly. I care what happens to everybody."[54]

As we've seen, Catwoman knows Batman better than most—at least more than most people on her side of the law do—including his refusal to let even those he fights die. When Bruce Wayne resumed his costumed identity after subduing his violent replacement Jean-Paul Valley, he rushed to save some criminals in a disabled helicopter about to topple off a tall building. As Catwoman returned a batarang to him, he told her he's going to save the criminals, and when she reminded him who they are, he merely says, "Doesn't matter. I can't let them die." The narration in the next panel makes it clear: "If the tingle she felt the first time she'd seen him left her in any doubt, it fades now. The man in the metal costume [Valley] would never risk her life for scum—she knows the real Batman is back."[55]

But even Catwoman can still be surprised by Batman's compassion for those he has sworn to fight. In one case, the two of them found some former henchmen of the Joker about to shoot mobster and murderer Tony "the Turk" Rulyanchik in the knee. (Clowns ... go figure.) Batman said, "Let's go," but Catwoman objected, "You kidding? Tony the Turk deserves to be walking with a limp ..." Batman cut her off, saying, "That's not the way I work." In the ensuing fight—to which words can't do justice, because comics are a visual medium, after all—Batman took a number of gunshots meant for Rulyanchik, the Kevlar lining in his costume shielding him but the agony nonetheless all too clear on his face.

Afterwards, as they lick their words, the two creatures of the night talk:

Catwoman: Y'know, you didn't have to let him shoot you that much ...
Batman: If I'd dodged, he would've hit Rulyanchik ...
Catwoman: I just don't understand you sometimes ... You stand there and
           take point blank shots for one of the big scuzzballs in Gotham ...
           I mean, I could understand if he was a decent human being, or a
           friend ... I'd jump in front of a bullet for a friend ...

Batman:	It's complicated.
Catwoman:	I thought you were the big protector of the innocent—what's complicated about that?
Batman:	Everything. Life complicates everything.[56]

What Catwoman doesn't know—but we lucky readers do—is that earlier Batman had been in Crime Alley reminiscing about the death of his parents; he first saw the clowns and Rulyanchik when their car almost hit two kids playing nearby. After the melee, Batman thought about "my codes, the rules I live by—these ideals came from my father ... from Thomas Wayne ... That's why I couldn't let even a killer like Tony Rulyanchik get shot. Because he wouldn't have either. He believed in the sanctity of all life."[57] As we noted earlier, young Bruce witnessed his father save criminals' lives many times, often at risk to his own life (especially when he would later inform the authorities), and this lesson stayed with Bruce as he went on to face villains more murderous and vile than his father could ever have imagined—and save their lives when he could, nonetheless.

Although Batman tries to save the lives of criminals as well as innocents, he does face significant internal conflict over this. Of course, he laments any deaths: during a rash of murders of mob bosses, Batman kept watch over the next target, with the narration reading, "How many have been killed so far? Four mob bosses in as many weeks. Batman should be pleased ... but somehow he can't bring himself to believe these executions are for the public good."[58] In the culmination of an adventure with Catwoman against the Scarecrow and Hugo Strange, Batman saved Scarecrow from a raging fire inadvertently started by Catwoman, who told Batman, "I should have known you wouldn't let this creep die." But it wasn't enough for Batman to save one foe when another one was also in danger; afterwards he had only regret, saying, "But ... water was ... too dark ... to find ... Hugo Strange."[59]

These cases reflect Batman's compassionate concern for life regardless of merit or desert, but at times he does indulge his rage at the criminal element, even if it doesn't change his actions. When a vigilante dressed as Batman dropped a mob assassin called the Snuffer off a roof, the real Batman swung by and caught him. When the very confused Snuffer said, "Thanks ... but what did you drop me for if you was gonna save me?" Batman snapped back, "Shut-up. I didn't drop you, but I almost wish I had. Saving your life is the most disgusting thing I've done in a long time."[60] When Batman saved a man who brutalizes women from a female vigilante named Pagan, the man thanked him, to which Batman again responded, "You have no reason to thank me ... I'm handing you over to the police.

And one more thing—don't ever thank me again!"[61] And sometimes, he has sentimental reasons to save a killer's life even if he has just as many sentimental reasons not to. When Batman saved the mercenary David Cain from fellow mercenary Deadshot—even though the former had a death wish—Cain asked Batman, "I killed someone you cared for. Tried to ruin your life. Put you in prison ... Why are you so troubled if someone wants to put me out of my misery?"[62] Batman answered that he was doing it for Cain's daughter Cassandra, who had recently taken the mantle of Batgirl under the tutelage of the original, Barbara Gordon.

Batman's negative feelings about criminals are even more apparent when he has to choose which people to save, either innocent civilians or those who would harm them—and if he can't save everybody, he does always give preference to the innocents. For example, after Batman defeated insurgents holding a pregnant couple hostage at a chemical plant, a doctor tried to tend to a wounded insurgent, but Batman told him, "That man can wait, Doctor," and directed him toward the couple. When the doctor objected, saying "he has some rights, you know," Batman replied, "That woman has more."[63] Similarly, during No Man's Land, Batman was furious that Leslie Thompkins planned to use the blood he brought her to save the vicious psychopathic killer Zsasz: "This is what I went through hell for? To save that monster? You will not use the blood I just brought you on him!" Leslie stood her ground, telling the man whom she helped raise,

> Yes, I will. And if you don't like it, you'll have to physically stop me! Let me make this clear: if he doesn't get that blood within the next couple of hours, he will die. Don't tell me this federal No Man's Land is making a killer out of you![64]

With all due respect to the good doctor, Batman doesn't want to kill Zsasz as much as he wants the blood to save innocent lives instead. If he could save everybody he would, but as we know, this isn't always possible. The choice is a tragic one when he has to decide which innocent person to save, but it isn't so difficult when the choice is between saving the innocent and saving the guilty (assuming he can safely make that judgment).

Save Everybody ... Even Those Who Would Kill?

Another aspect of the example above is that Zsasz is not your average criminal, but is actually a murderous psychopath who carves a notch into his flesh every time he kills. It is one thing to save the life of a petty thief, an anonymous henchman, or even a supervillain such as the Riddler who doesn't enjoy killing, but it is another to save the life of those who regularly take the lives of others with relish and are almost guaranteed to do so again.

This is a dilemma for which Batman has a keen appreciation. One time, he found the murderous villain, Black Spider, sneaking up on a much more murderous villain, Black Mask, planning to shoot him. As Batman stood ready to throw his batarang at Black Spider's hand, he questioned his own judgment: "Throw before or after he fires his gun? It's the difference between one or both going down … Now? Or three seconds from now?"[65] Batman chose the former, saving Black Mask's life, but also letting him escape while he apprehended Black Spider. As he reflected later,

> Never again will I permit anyone's murder—even when the preserved life masks a soul already dead. The disturbing thing is that I even paused … to choose … when there was no choice to consider. Even if Black Mask lives to kill tomorrow—or ten years from tomorrow—I can only hope I'll feel the same. If I don't—it'll be time to quit.[66]

While he kicked himself for even considering letting Black Spider kill Black Mask, he also recognized the consequences of letting him live and escape— that he may kill again—and he resolved not to let this affect his choice if a similar situation should arise again in the future.

At home in the Manor afterwards, Bruce stood under the portrait of his parents—presumably because their grave was too far away—and continued to reflect on saving Black Mask:

> After seeing you fall to a killer's gun, I must stop every other murder I can— no matter who the intended victim. But in this case, I prevented the murder of a man who himself might commit murder at any moment. And so tonight—maybe for many nights to come—I must try to stop him. I must try to stop Black Mask.[67]

These two monologues complement each other nicely, the first focusing on his responsibility not to allow killing, even when the person he saves might go on to kill innocent people, and the second emphasizing his responsibility to prevent those further killings. In a way, this compounds his already futile mission: not only must he save as many lives as he can, but he also has to prevent some of those he saves from taking more lives themselves.

Batman takes this position because he knows where his responsibility begins and where it ends. Once, he saved the life of Orca, a researcher named Dr. Grace Balin who transformed herself into a whale–human hybrid using experimental gene therapy and then tried to kill Camille Baden-Smythe, the woman who eliminated her job. Afterwards, Baden-Smythe told Batman, "That beast is a felon and an attempted murderer! ... The blood of all her victims will be on your hands!" and the Dark Knight responded, "We are each responsible for our actions. I cannot allow ... I will not allow ... her to die."[68] As with the Black Mask, Batman realizes that his job is to save lives, regardless of what those he saves will do with them later, which is their choice and their responsibility. If they choose to go on to hurt and kill people, it is his responsibility to stop them. As the narration read while Batman saved both women, "for the truly heroic, it is not acceptable for anyone to die," even Baden-Smythe, who was "aware of the irony that she herself will die ... as the direct result of the mortal wounds she inflicted on Orca. How fitting."[69] (That's the narrator talking, not Batman, although it's not hard to imagine him sharing that sentiment in a darker moment such as this.)

Just as Catwoman knew Batman wouldn't let the Scarecrow die in the story told earlier, the rest of his foes generally know about his refusal to let even other criminals die, and they use this to their advantage (as they do with innocent bystanders and hostages). When the Joker put a remote-controlled explosive pacemaker in Bruce Wayne's childhood friend Tommy Elliot—the Aristotle-quoting villain Hush who knows Batman's dual identity—Tommy asked Bruce to remove it. When Bruce stalled, Tommy said, "Bruce, as much as you hate me, you couldn't let me die if you could prevent it. It's your biggest virtue—and your greatest weakness."[70] Later, Hush had a very serious talk with Batman about his Joker problem, which we'll discuss more in the second part of the book, but even here we see that he understands this essential conflict in Batman's mission: that he's compelled to save the lives of those who would take them. And Hush is not the only one who knows this—for instance, take the Scarecrow again. (Please!) When he tried to break Joker out of jail to kill him, Batman stopped him, saying, "That cell stays locked, Scarecrow, and the Joker stays alive to receive his just punishment—as long as a single breath remains in my body!" Scarecrow replied, "Only you would risk your life to save a mortal enemy ... making it all the easier for the rest of us!"[71]

Speaking of the Clown Prince of Crime, appropriately enough we find him at the center of many of Batman's greatest moral dilemmas, especially those dealing with life and death. The Joker is perhaps Batman's most homicidal foe, and the one most deserving of his final reward if Batman were so inclined. Yet, Batman finds himself in the position of saving him more often than any of his lesser sparring partners.

In one telling of their first meeting, after a series of targeted individual killings that Batman fails to prevent, the Joker dumped poison into the Gotham City water supply. Batman blew up the viaduct, stopping the poison from getting into the system, then began to fight the Joker man-to-man. When one of the Joker's wild swings missed and he started to fall into the water, Batman caught him while thinking, "It would be so easy to let him fall into it. So many are already dead because of this man … I can't. Damn it. I can't."[72] (He did, however, beat the crap out him: "This'll have to do." Remember this when we get to Batman's penchant for violence and brutality in the second part of the book.) Later, Batman told Captain Jim Gordon that he felt somewhat responsible for the Joker, because he may have played a part in his creation (pushing him into a vat of chemicals that transformed the Red Hood into the Joker). Gordon told him what he later comes to realize for himself: "Did you put the hood on his head and the gun in his hand? No, you didn't."[73] Again, Batman isn't responsible for the choices criminals make. He is responsible only for protecting other people from those choices and stopping those truly responsible for them—and saving every life he can, no matter how unworthy.

In a much later adventure, during one of their many battles, Batman knocked the Joker off a rooftop, then caught him. Batman asked him, "Give me a reason why I shouldn't drop you," to which the Joker responded, "C'mon, Bats—we both know you won't do that. It's against the rules."[74] Batman may bluff at times, such as when he responded, "You're right, I don't do that. But maybe I should start," but like most of his foes, the Joker knows that Batman will never let him die if he can prevent it (much less kill him himself, as we'll see later). Like the Joker said, "it's against the rules," specifically Batman's personal code against allowing death when he can stop it. Even when Nightwing believed that the Joker had killed Tim Drake and beat him to death, Batman revived him. When the Huntress, the member of Batman's circle most inclined to kill, said, "We should have let him die," Batman replied, "We don't do that. Not even for him."[75] As we've seen, however, the sheer scale and scope of the Joker's murderous activities, and the reasonable belief that he will never stop, leads many to question Batman's determination to save every life he can in the face of his more general mission to save lives—a mission that is compromised by refusing to put an end to one of the greatest threats to innocent lives in Gotham City.

Batman, of course, is as aware of this trade-off as we are. When Etrigan the Demon—no relation to the Demon's Head, Ra's al Ghul—wanted to burn the Joker in supernatural flame, Batman thought to himself, "I can't stand fast and watch a man killed ... not even a man like the Joker." After Batman went into the flame to save the Joker, he reflected: "Etrigan saw my choice—risking life itself to save the Joker as an act of goodness. And yet I was also ensuring the continued existence of evil."[76] Although he stands fast and resolute in his devotion to protecting specific lives, even killers such as the Joker and the Black Mask, he is aware that doing this interferes with protecting more lives in a broader sense.

In the second part of this book, we'll talk about Batman's refusal to kill and the unique issues this raises, but refusing to let criminals die has the same effect on his overall mission. One could even argue that the latter should be less of an issue for Batman because it doesn't involve his taking a positive action, but merely looking the other way, or waiting just a second to react (as he considered doing when the Black Spider was set to kill Black Mask). As Oracle—herself a victim of the Joker's madness—said when Batman prepared to save the clown from Ra's al Ghul, "Like I said before, to hell with the Joker. They deserve each other. Maybe they'll kill each other." When Batman told her, "I can't let this go, Barbara," she asks, "Why can't you? You'll risk your life saving that homicidal maniac? You saved the Joker's life before. Justice could have been served, but you had to be noble."[77] Later, as he watched the Joker and Black Mask try to kill each other, Batman thought, "I'm honestly tempted to let them. But, as much as that would solve so many problems, I can't."[78] This is merely the first of many instances we'll see in this book in which Batman puts his own moral code and personal virtue above the mission he has sworn to pursue and the "so many problems" he could solve by setting his principles aside, just one example of the inconsistency in Batman's moral code that we may recognize in ourselves but must nonetheless work to improve.

The Problem of the Robins

Batman's core mission, as we've said, is to save and protect life, inspired by the tragic deaths of his parents when he was a young boy. But a second tragedy, which affected him almost as much as the first, belies this mission to some extent, because it struck someone Batman had a special responsibility to protect: Jason Todd, the second Robin, who was brutally murdered at the hands of the Joker. Although this was obviously the worst thing to happen to one of Batman's confederates—even if Jason did "get better," as we'll see later—the various young men that have worn the red and yellow plumage of Robin have suffered injuries that would fell the most hardened boxer, have seen death and violence more often associated with war zones, and generally engage in an extremely risky lifestyle, all for the sake of a mission and the man who holds it.

This brings up serious questions about what costs Batman is willing to impose on other people—in particular, those who help him, and especially those who are children—in pursuit of his mission to eliminate crime and save lives in Gotham City. Gordon nailed it when he asked Batman, early in Dick Grayson's career as Robin, "What's with the boy?" He zeroed in on the primary ethical conundrum this raises when he continued, "You've vowed to protect the innocent and yet you have an adolescent tagging along. I thought maybe you had him as an assistant on one particular case … But it's been months now. He's still here. I don't get it."[79]

As Gordon pointed out, Batman's mission is to protect and save the innocent, especially the potential victims of crime in Gotham City. He goes to significant lengths to make sure that no innocents come to harm, and even risks his own life to save evildoers so they can face justice and possibly reform. Yet, as Gordon told him on another occasion, "You're training some kid to follow in your footsteps! Putting him in the path of bullets and madmen!"[80] Batman repeatedly puts the safety and lives of children in danger, *even though* he realizes the risks, *even though* he questions this practice each time one gets hurt (or worse), and *even though* he knows he shouldn't.

There are a number of ways he rationalizes this, and he has plenty of help from the Robins themselves, who are often eager participants—but what teen or preteen wouldn't be excited to join Batman on adventures? Even Alfred, often the harshest critic of Batman's apprenticeship program, usually ends up getting on board and sometimes arguing in favor of Robins for Batman's own sake. As we trace through the history of the Robins, we'll see that the main reason Batman continues to use them is for his own good, even more than the good of the mission, which makes this contradiction of the terms of his mission itself possibly his most egregious moral failing.

There have been a number of Robins, so we may as well start with the original. Paralleling Bruce Wayne's own story more closely than any of his successors, young Dick Grayson witnessed his parents die during a Flying Graysons acrobatic performance at Haly's Circus—an event Bruce Wayne was also present to witness, after which he offered to take Dick in as his ward. After realizing the boy didn't want vengeance as much as he wanted to make sure no other child has to suffer the same fate, Bruce revealed his double identity and offered to train Dick to be his partner, the first Robin.

Although most of Dick's adventures took place in a more whimsical and less violent period in Batman's career, nonetheless there were times at which his life was in significant danger, including two incidents when he was near death, one at the beginning of his career as Robin and another near the end. The first involved Two-Face, who would develop a reputation of being an even more dedicated foe of Robins than the Joker is. After Gordon told Batman that Two-Face kidnapped a judge—and expressed his concerns about there being a Robin at all—Batman decided to bench Dick for his own safety. The new Robin defied orders and followed his mentor to Two-Face, who caught him and beat him within an inch of his life with a baseball bat. After defeating Two-Face and leaving him for the police, Batman scooped up Robin in his arms and asked Alfred to drive them to Leslie Thompkins' clinic, in the first of many such scenes to come.[81]

Two-Face told Gordon during interrogation that he killed Robin; when Gordon asked Batman about this, the Dark Knight assured him that the boy was alive, but had retired as his partner. As Dick recovered, Batman told him, "This was all a terrible error in judgment. Gordon was right. You're just a boy. What the hell was I thinking?" and he "fired" him.[82] Dick soon ran away from home and went undercover to infiltrate Two-Face's gang, ultimately helping Batman bring him down. When they returned to the Batcave and Alfred, Batman told Dick he would take him back as Robin, apparently realizing the value of having a partner despite the risks. But he gave Dick conditions that he gave every Robin going forward: be a good soldier, follow commands, and don't question them, even if Batman's own life is in danger. Dick agreed, and after Batman left, he told Alfred, "Somebody's gotta help him ... might as well be me."[83]

On another occasion, after Alfred expressed concern about the risks he was taking, Dick told him, "I know the danger, and I really try to be careful. But I also know I'm doing good, that I'm helping people. I think in a way I'm helping Bruce too." When Alfred asks how, Dick explained that he helps Batman be Bruce Wayne: "Mom and Dad always taught me to enjoy myself. I think maybe I'm helping Bruce to sometimes enjoy himself, too."[84] This desire to help Batman personally as well as professionally is a theme we will see again, especially in the third Robin, Tim Drake, who got the job after arguing to Batman that he needed a Robin, no matter who is behind the mask.

More important, we see Batman setting aside any reasonable reservations he had about leading a child into danger, even after that child was nearly killed, simply because he contributed to the success of the mission. Alfred, usually the voice of reason in a cave full of bats, giant coins, and a life-size Tyrannosaurus rex, recorded his own doubts in a journal, writing that "I have made it clear to [Master Bruce] that I believe the recruitment of Master Richard into his exploits to be potentially dangerous," but that advice was ignored. Nonetheless, having a young partner around "has made a difference in him. I do believe I saw him smile" and even laugh. "But smiles and laughter do not assuage my guilt. For I fear that I am once more watching a child barter his youth away in the service of 'justice' … a thankless cause to be sure."[85] Then, Alfred was more concerned about Dick devoting his childhood to the same mission that cost Bruce his, but later he would also reflect on the mortal danger these children would be in.

The second incident occurred near the end of Dick Grayson's time as Robin, when he was shot by the Joker and fell over the side of a building. A passing newscopter witnessed everything, and soon the newspapers and TV reporters were asking if Robin was dead (one reporter raising the issue of "virtual child abuse"). In an echo of the previous tale, when Gordon asked Batman if Robin was dead, Batman answered, "Literally? No. To all intents and purposes? Yes." And once again, Bruce talked to Dick while he healed, and told him he was planning to let the world believe Robin is dead, explaining that he almost died for real, and if he had, "the Joker would not have been responsible. I would." When Dick asked if he hadn't been a help, Bruce assures him, "you have, son—but we've been lucky. In what I do, there is no place for a child." To be fair, Dick was hardly a child at this point, being nineteen, so Bruce corrected himself: "You are a man now—man enough to accept my decision." We see that Dick is already thinking ahead to becoming Nightwing, and Batman goes solo … for a while.[86]

One might assume from these two important bookends to the career of the first Robin that there would never have been a second. However, on his next annual pilgrimage to Crime Alley on the anniversary of his parents' death, Batman found a young orphan stealing the tires off the Batmobile and, admiring the kid's gumption, he decided to take him home and make him the second Robin.[87] Jason's father was a minor crime figure who was killed by Two-Face, a secret Batman unsuccessfully kept from the young boy, which prompted Alfred to tell Batman, "You're protecting the boy … and yet you plan to make him your new partner, after you swore you would not endanger another child."[88]

This statement led to Batman's official justification for making Jason his second Robin: "Alfred, this 'child' is already a streetwise adventurer—who left to his own devices would undoubtedly go down the same criminal road that took his father to an early death."[89] When Nightwing confronted Batman about his new replacement—whom he had to read about in the newspaper—Batman once again argued that

> if left on his own, the boy would be dead by now. Hard times have given him no great abundance of self-esteem. Training him to be Robin has channeled those self-destructive energies toward a more positive goal. In my own way, I think I may have saved Jason's life.[90]

When Jason was shot by the Mad Hatter and Batman rushed him to Leslie's clinic, she scolded him, telling him that "Jason wouldn't have been out there, if not for you. Didn't that close call with Dick teach you anything?" Batman reiterated what he told Alfred and Nightwing: "Do you think I do this for me? I did it for him—for the boy I saved from a life of crime—for the boy who saved himself," elaborating later that "I wanted to give Jason an outlet for his rage ... wanted him to expunge his anger, and get on with his life ... and instead, I may have killed him. I always thought this was my probable end ... but not for him."[91] Batman showed the same hint of regret on another occasion when Jason was (only) nearly shot, the narration reading, "The call is very close ... and its narrow margin between life and death proves to be the measure of one man's conflicting conscience." This happened in the midst of a challenge to Bruce's adoption of Jason, which made Batman mutter to himself, "Maybe they're right to take you away—you almost got shot—the danger ..."[92]

Batman did end up giving Jason an outlet for his rage, but it was not as tightly controlled as his mentor would have liked. As we'll discuss more in the second part of this book, Jason gradually became more reckless and violent; when Batman suspected him of pushing a criminal off a fire escape to his death, he asked Barbara Gordon to come out of retirement as Batgirl and spend some time with the new Robin to get her impressions of him. Afterwards, she warned him that Jason is losing control, saying that "he's carrying emotional baggage ... plus, he's hauling a gigantic chip on his shoulder and daring anyone and everyone to knock it off."[93] She also warned Batman, who was once again in pursuit of the Joker, that his foes didn't need to strike at him directly, but could also target those close to him. Batman dismissed this, saying he knows his foes better than that, but that's exactly what the Joker later did to Barbara Gordon when he shot her, and soon after to Jason Todd when he beat him senseless with a crowbar and left him to die in an explosion. At Jason's funeral, Barbara whispered to Bruce from her wheelchair, "I told you."[94]

After Jason's death, Batman went through a period of deep remorse and self-recrimination. As he searched for the body in the rubble of the explosion, he reflected:

> Why didn't I see that you were too young for this kind of work? How could I have been so stupid? It's just that I felt so adrift when I lost Dick Grayson as a partner. The Batman needed a Robin. But that was a different, less dangerous time. I guess the truth is that I was lonely ... didn't want to go it alone. So what do I do? I bring a young innocent into this mad game ... I must be insane.[95]

He remembered his oft-stated reasoning for taking Jason in and training him to be Robin, just as he had with Dick, "but this kid had a rebellious streak in him. I told myself he'd work it out of his system in time. Yes, I blinded myself to so much." And then his thoughts turned to his own motivations: "Jason and I were going to be a great team. That was all that mattered."[96] He came to realize that adopting a new partner, as much as he claimed it was for Jason, was chiefly done for himself—I mean, for his mission. (Of course.)

Once again, Batman vowed never to take on a partner, never to train another Robin, never to place another child in harm's way for the sake of himself or his mission. When Nightwing offered his help on a case, Batman told him, "I don't need any partners. Not ever again," and Alfred explained to the former Robin, "He's afraid. Afraid that what happened to Jason could happen again."[97] Batman took a more reckless and violent turn himself, which was obvious not only to Alfred and Nightwing, but also to a new player in our drama: a young boy named Timothy Drake, who deduced the true identities of Batman, the original Robin (now Nightwing), and the recently deceased Robin.

More than anyone else, Tim argued that it was important for Batman himself to have a Robin, whether Dick Grayson (Tim's first choice) or eventually Tim himself. As he told Dick upon their first meeting, Batman needed a Robin "to remember what he used to be. Before his parents died."[98] After Dick brought Tim to the Batcave and introduced him to Alfred, he changed to Nightwing to help Batman, but Tim stressed that he doesn't need

Nightwing, he needs Robin—and Alfred suggested to Tim that maybe that's why Dick brought him to the cave.[99] Alfred agreed with Tim, telling Dick that "the lad may have a point. Master Bruce has not been the same—since he lost Robin ... a second time." Tim agreed: "It's true, Dick. He needs a partner again. Someone to care about ... someone who cares about him."[100] Later, Tim told Alfred, "I saw how Batman changed without there being a Robin to care about."[101] Note that this entire discussion is in terms of what *Batman* needs, not to advance his mission but for his own personal good. This is a caring sentiment to be sure, but one that ignores the other side of the equation, namely the means they endorse for Batman's sake: putting yet another child's life in danger.

In this case, Batman realized the dangers of a new Robin more than his confederates did. After Tim put on a Robin costume to save Batman and Nightwing, Batman ripped off the boy's mask and said, "I don't know who you are—but you're not Robin! There is no more Robin!" When Nightwing and Alfred argued on behalf of Tim and his detective skills, Batman asked them, "What are you trying to do? One boy died wearing that costume. I'm not taking that risk a third time." Tim explained the benefits to Batman: "You need someone to make you slow down just a bit and wonder what could happen. I mean, how many times have you been hurt these past months?" But Batman went to the heart of the issue when he asked, "So, for my sake, I should put some child in danger?" After arguing more, Batman told Tim, "What I do is dangerous," to which Tim responded, "I know. And that's exactly why you need me."[102] In the end, Batman hesitantly agreed to think about it, leading to the third time he dismissed his better judgment and chose to put a child's life in danger to further his mission and benefit himself—at the encouragement of not only Tim himself, but adults such as Dick and Alfred who should have known better.

Unfortunately, we see Batman's waffling over this issue through Tim's tenure as Robin as he vacillates between protecting the boy from danger and putting him in the middle of it. At first Batman refused to let Tim out in the field, telling him "I'm not making any mistakes this time," and thinking to himself, "What do I need another partner for? This can be ended now before the boy is hurt ... like ... like Jason."[103] When the Joker returned, Batman sent Tim out of town, saying to Alfred, "The Joker's return punctuates how foolish it is for me to have a partner. I won't allow another boy to die because of me."[104] It is over a year and a half in our world before Tim's first night out as Robin, which Batman enjoyed, thinking, "This is a night I never thought I'd see again—a night I thought I'd never allow myself to see. But he's doing well, and I'm feeling good about it … almost as if some part of me had been missing—and now it's back."[105] By now, though, this reads as mere rationalization, as if Batman were trying to make himself feel better about doing something he knows is wrong—the epitome of moral insincerity and self-deception, both serious issues with Batman's moral character (on top of the more practical issues with putting a child's life in danger).

Batman continued to make Tim stay back when he thought it too dangerous. When gangs seemed to be targeting Robin, Batman went out alone and was beaten badly. Tim lashed out at him:

> I used to worry that you'd be too concerned for my safety to be effective out there. That you were actually better off on your own … You're reckless without me. As long as you're looking out for me, you're thinking of yourself. You need me there to keep your feet on the ground and watch your back.[106]

With this statement, Tim advocated putting himself in danger for the sole purpose of making Batman more careful, a noble sacrifice for a young boy to make but not an offer or argument a mature, responsible adult should ever accept—especially one sworn to save and protect lives.

To his credit, Batman usually doesn't buy this reasoning, instead thinking of the danger a young sidekick could pose as a distraction. One time he grounded his new partner, Batman thought to himself, "if there's even a chance of undue danger to Robin, I can't risk taking it. And more selfishly, it's easier not having to worry about Tim."[107] When Alfred asked why Batman was going out solo so often, he replied, "sometimes Robin only creates more turbulence, Alfred—another factor to juggle." When Alfred argued that Tim is "the most capable of your three partners," Batman agreed, but countered that "it's different out there now. Automatic weapons are routine, and the danger is—" Alfred cut him off, pointing out that "no one is more dangerous, sir, than your earliest foes—Two-Face, the Joker …" but Batman said, "And look what the Joker did to Tim's predecessor." Batman admitted that he was still thinking of Jason when he shielded Tim from danger, "but whether the problem is Tim or me, Robin can still be a distraction."[108] Although he doesn't accept Tim's reasoning about being a helpful distraction, Batman's logic just accentuates the problem with accepting him as a partner by weakening the case for Robin being a positive contributor to the mission. If he is, in fact, a distraction, this compromises any argument for putting him in danger.

Even after he agreed to take Tim on, Batman never forgot what happened to Jason, which contributed to his schizophrenic attitude toward letting Tim out as Robin, despite his expertise, enthusiasm, and levelheadedness. Alfred tried to explain to Tim that "he has to have a clear mind. He has to know you're safe." When Tim argued that he didn't want to be protected, Alfred reminded him that "it's not only you he's protecting. You know there's only one thing he fears." After Tim risked his own life to save Batman's, only to be scolded again, Batman told him, "My life is not important. I'd rather … I'd rather …" Tim finished his sentence: "You'd rather give your life than risk mine. When are you going to realize … I'm not Jason Todd."[109] But Batman did treat him like his predecessor, even though the two couldn't be more different. Another time Tim did something Batman felt was too risky, Batman tore into the boy: "You were cocky! He could have killed you. I might not have been there to save you." Tim struggled to reply, and Batman continued, "You took a chance. You got lucky." When Tim looked despondent, Batman realized he went too far and apologized. When Tim told him it was okay, Batman reiterated, "No. I'm really sorry. I just worry that you'll start thinking of this as a game"—like Jason often did.[110]

Even after Tim proved himself time and time again in the field, the ghost of Jason Todd continued to hover over him. As he told Catwoman during the first episode with Hush, "The entire time I've been Robin—every lesson—every move that Batman has taught me—is intended to keep what happened to Jason from happening to me."[111] Again, Batman's cautious impulse, informed by the brutal murder of the last Robin, would be more admirable if it had actually prevented him from taking on a successor rather than repeating his mistake and then equivocating about it endlessly. In a recent adventure—15 years in our world since Tim became Robin—Batman encountered a new foe and told Tim to stay behind, despite all his experience, because of the uncertainty of a new threat.[112] But around the same time, after Tim told Batman to chill out, Batman thought to himself, "I've gone through times doubting the need for a—sidekick. Now I see. The brightness of him. I need to see that light more."[113] Despite all the dangers, Batman still focused on the benefit to himself of having a Robin, another example of a muddled moral perspective on an undeniable ethical dilemma.[114]

Aside from the problems with child endangerment itself and how it contradicts his stated mission to protect the innocent—a mission that, it bears repeating, leads him to risk his life to save others, even the criminals he fights—it is the inconsistency in his thinking regarding Robins that is most relevant to the overall theme of this book. When it comes down to it, despite all the dangers to the young boys he trains and takes out to face homicidal maniacs, he still finds the practice useful to himself and the mission. Remember what he told Alfred about holding Tim back: "if there's even a chance of undue danger to Robin, I can't risk taking it." This sounds very careful and prudent until you ask, what level of danger is "undue"? At the risk of reading too much into his language, in moral and legal terms, "due" indicates a certain level of expectations (or "duty"), such as doing one's "due diligence" or taking "due precaution," both defined in terms of one's position and the obligations thereof. In term of Robins, this suggests that there is a certain level of danger that *is* due, expected, or at the very least permitted. This may be reasonable—even a child playing softball or soccer has to accept some nontrivial amount of risk—but the problem comes in when we ask what level of danger is due and what is considered undue. Another time Batman left Tim at home, he thought to himself, "unless there's a good reason … the only life I'll endanger will be my own!"[115] Taken together, we could conclude that it is Batman's idea of what makes a "good reason" that also determines whether a Robin faces "undue danger" or not—in other words, danger is undue only if it is more than needed to further the mission in the broadest sense, including any benefit or cost to Batman himself as the chief "pursuant" of that mission.

For better or for worse, this fits with Batman's generally utilitarian orientation toward his mission to fight crime and save the people of Gotham: everything he does is a means to that end. His continued endangerment of children serving as his partners represents one of several moral principles that Batman casually ignores out of devotion to his mission, and therefore serves as a cautionary tale about the excesses of utilitarianism untethered to any other moral considerations.[116] Unlike most of the other rules he breaks, like those against violence, torture, or lawlessness—all discussed in the second part of this book—keeping child sidekicks does very little to further the mission, as seen by the number of times Batman chooses to leave Robin behind when heading out on a case. Even when he does have a Robin, Batman acts on his own a tremendous amount of the time, such as when Dick Grayson was away at college or Tim Drake was at boarding school. Having a Robin seems much less essential to the success of the mission than to the well-being of the man pursuing it. When Bruce tried to tell Dick he trained Jason Todd to be a new Robin because "the Batman needs a Robin. Fighting crime in Gotham City is not a one-man job. I couldn't do the job alone," Dick called bull—and if anyone has the right to say this, it would be him.[117] In this sense, Robins act as support staff, much in the same way that Alfred and Oracle do. (Both mean much more to him personally, of course; this is speaking to the mission only.) But there is a critical difference: both Alfred and Oracle are adults, and they are not put in mortal danger nearly as often as are the Robins, all for the sake of the mission Batman accepted for himself and which focuses on the protection of innocents.

Let's give the most steadfast critic of the Robin program the final word. Recall that when Dick Grayson was just beginning as Batman's sidekick, Jim Gordon told the Dark Knight, "You've vowed to protect the innocent and yet you have an adolescent tagging along ... I don't get it."[118] Years later, after Dick was nearly killed and Batman declared that Robin was retired, Jim Gordon told him, "I can't say I disagree with your decision to go solo—the dangers of working with a youth, even as able a youth as Robin, outweigh all advantages."[119] Even though he puts the decision in the terms of utilitarian logic, Gordon makes clear that the dangers are so high that no imaginable advantages can overwhelm them. This resembles *rule utilitarianism*, which supports following rules, not based on principle, but on utilitarian conclusions that can be generalized over a broad range of cases. For example, rule utilitarians often say that people shouldn't lie, not because it's wrong in and of itself, but because lying almost always leads to harm in excess of any benefits. Gordon isn't ruling out any benefits to Batman and his mission from having a Robin, but is merely saying that however significant those benefits may be, over time they are unlikely to exceed the costs from putting a child in mortal danger. In cases like this, principle and calculation lead to similar conclusions—and make it even more striking that Batman refuses to follow either as he continues training and using Robins in his fight against crime.

Hopefully this chapter has provided a fairly thorough picture of how complex and fraught it can be to make decisions within a broadly utilitarian framework. Although utilitarianism seems like a simple and intuitive ethical framework on the surface, the ins and outs of putting it into practice are much more complicated and demand the use of judgment to fill in the gaps. This judgment can work in many different ways, and each person will have his or her own approach to it. But each person's pattern of judgments should be fairly consistent, and we have seen above that Batman's judgment in the various situations he finds himself in does not meet this standard. Although his general devotion to saving lives is unquestionable, many of the choices he makes in terms of whom to save, which crimes to investigate, which criminals to pursue, and whom he takes on as partners in his efforts, are difficult to reconcile with his mission and his claims about it. We do not have to question Batman's heroism and dedication to criticize specific decisions he makes in his day-to-day activities, or to draw lessons from them that we can apply to our lives (as humdrum as they may seem in comparison).

In the next chapter, however, we will step back from the Dark Knight's individual decisions and take a bat's-eye view of his heroism and dedication by examining his value and contribution to the well-being of Gotham City, its millions of innocent citizens—and himself. Is being Batman the best way to do good in the world, either according to general utilitarianism or his specific mission within it? And is it the best thing *for him* to do?

Notes

1   *Batman: Shadow of the Bat* #76 (July 1998).
2   *Detective Comics* #722 (June 1998). I mean, really, Robin?
3   *Detective Comics* #832 (July 2007).
4   *Batman Confidential* #49 (December 2010).
5   *Batman: 10-Cent Adventure* (March 2002).
6   *Batman: Legends of the Dark Knight* #182 (October 2004). We'll see later that Catwoman tells him the same thing after a forced loss.
7   *Detective Comics* #481 (January 1979), "Ticket to Tragedy."
8   *Batman* #397 (July 1986).
9   *Batman* #644 (Late October 2005).
10 The paradigmatic case is *Sophie's Choice*, either the 1979 novel by William Styron or the 1982 film directed by Alan J. Pakula and starring Meryl Streep. For more on tragic dilemmas, see Rosalind Hursthouse's *On Virtue Ethics* (Oxford: Oxford University Press, 2001), ch. 3, and Lisa Tessman's two books, *Moral Failure: On the Impossible Demands of Morality* (Oxford: Oxford University Press, 2014) and *When Doing the Right Thing Is Impossible* (Oxford: Oxford University Press, 2017).
11 *Batman* #575 (March 2000).
12 *JLA Secret Files and Origins* #1 (September 1997), "Star-Seed."
13 *Batman* #307 (January 1979).
14 *Batman* #315 (September 1979).
15 *Batman* #548 (November 1997).
16 *Batman: Legends of the Dark Knight* #83 (June 1996).
17 *Detective Comics* #589 (August 1988), "The Burning Pit."
18 *Batman: Legends of the Dark Knight* #54 (November 1993).
19 *Batman Confidential* #49 (December 2010).

20 *Detective Comics* #721 (May 1998).

21 Peter Singer, "Famine, Affluence, and Morality," *Philosophy and Public Affairs* 1 (1972): 229-243, available at https://www.utilitarian.net/singer/by/1972----.htm.

22 See William MacAskill, *Doing Good Better: How Effective Altruism Can Help You Make a Difference* (New York: Avery, 2015), and Peter Singer, *The Most Good You Can Do: How Effective Altruism Is Changing Ideas about Living Ethically* (New Haven, CT: Yale University Press, 2016).

23 *Batman: Legends of the Dark Knight* #209 (October 2006).

24 *The Batman Chronicles* #8 (Spring 1997), "Secrets of the Batcave: Dinosaur Island." This story reveals the origin of the famous Tyrannosaurus rex in the Batcave: Batman brought it home from the amusement park, Dinosaur Island, as a memento to remind him of the good he does (and not just the good he fails to do).

25 *Detective Comics* #542 (September 1984), "Between Two Nights." To be clear, this was the original Jason Todd, who made Dick Grayson look like a bad seed, not the brash and insolent version introduced after *Crisis on Infinite Earths* that no one in their right mind would want to take away from Bruce.

26 *Batman* #426 (December 1988).

27 As Sasha Bourdeaux wrote, "he can never be fast enough" (*Batman: 10-Cent Adventure*, March 2002), but even when he manages to save everybody, that isn't enough: After he saved a family from drowning in their car, he apologized for taking so long (*Detective Comics* #757, June 2001, "Air Time").

28 *Batman* #652 (June 2006).

29 *Batman* #475 (March 1992).

30 *Batman* #585 (January 2001).

31 *Detective Comics* #610 (January 1990).

32 Criminals suspect Batman of this attitude as well. For example, mob boss Carmine Falcone accused Batman of not trying hard enough to catch the Holiday Killer because he or she only killed mobsters. After his nephew was killed on Halloween, Falcone told Batman, "It could have stopped there. But it didn't. And we both know why. You and the cops just let it continue because he was killing our people. *Mia famiglia!* And you stand here and act like your hands are clean" (*Batman: The Long Halloween* #12, November 1997).

33 *Azrael* #16 (April 1996).

34 *Gotham Central* #26 (February 2005).

35 *Batman* #244 (September 1972), "The Demon Lives Again!"

36 *Detective Comics* #489 (April 1980), "Where Strike the Assassins."

37 *Detective Comics* #529 (August 1983), "The Thief of Night!"

38 *Detective Comics* #486 (November 1979), "Murder by Thunderbolt."

39 *Batman* #443 (January 1990).

40 *Detective Comics* #568 (November 1986).

41 *Batman* #505 (March 1994).

42 *Detective Comics* #496 (November 1980), "Murder on the Mystery Ship."

43 *Batman* #491 (April 1993).

44 *Detective Comics* #736 (September 1999).

45 *Batman* #633 (December 2004).

46 *Batman: Legends of the Dark Knight* #46 (June 1993).

47 *Batman: Legends of the Dark Knight* #47 (July 1993). Ironically, when Catwoman was shot during a robbery led by Harley Quinn at an opera house— during an opera Bruce Wayne and Selina Kyle were enjoying at the time, thank you very much—Batman saved her and let Harley escape. As he held her in his arms, Catwoman whispers to him, "if you ever choose to … rescue … me again … over catching the bad guy … I swear, I'll scratch your eyes out" (*Batman* #613, May 2003).

48 *Batman* #405 (March 1987).

49 *Batman* #490 (March 1993).

50 *Detective Comics* #783 (August 2003), "More Perfect Than Perfect."

51 *Batman: Gotham Knights* #27 (May 2002), "Never Say Die." (Or maybe that was Ozzy!)

52 *Batman* #344 (February 1982). Batman answers, "You aren't the only man who ever fell under Ivy's spell, Ivor."

53 *Batman* #347 (May 1982), "The Shadow of the Batman."

54 *Secret Six*, vol. 3, #2 (December 2008).

55 *Batman: Shadow of the Bat* #30 (August 1994).

56 *Batman* #604 (August 2002). Another time Batman's foes were killing each other while trying to kill him, Catwoman said, "In case you're wondering, I think you're crazy to put your life on the line to save these freaks … Let them pick each other off and you can bring in the last man standing." When he replied, "That's not how I work," she said, "Oh, I know. I know all too well" (*Detective Comics* #780, May 2003, "Dead Reckoning Part Four").

57 *Batman* #604 (August 2002).

58 *Batman* #436 (August 1989).

59 *Batman: Legends of the Dark Knight* #141 (May 2001).

60 *Batman* #402 (December 1986). (Yes, the comic reads "shut-up" with the hyphen. Stay back, overzealous copyeditor!)

61 *Batman* #479 (Early June 2002).

62 *Batman* #607 (November 2002).

63 *Batman: Son of the Demon* (September 1987).

64 *The Batman Chronicles* #18 (September 1999).

65 *Batman* #519 (June 1995).

66 Ibid.

67 *Batman* #520 (July 1995).

68 *Batman* #581 (September 2000).

69 Ibid.

70 *Batman: Gotham Knights* #74 (April 2006). Later, Batman suggested to Hush that he actually didn't have the pacemaker removed: "How did you recover so fast? Why didn't you have any post-op effects?" When Hush accused him of bluffing, Batman simply asked, "Am I?" Hush told him, "You don't do this! It's not who you are!" Later, we find out he wasn't bluffing: The Joker triggered a heart-attack, but Hush recovered the remote-control just in time, and had the pacemaker removed thereafter (as revealed in *Detective Comics* #849, December 2008).

71 *Batman* #373 (July 1984). In a rare gaffe, Ra's al Ghul overplayed his hand with respect to Batman and the Joker: As Batman prepared to lower a dying Joker into the rejuvenating Lazarus Pit so he could tell Batman where Ra's was and what he was planning, Alfred said, "It is the Demon's way to taunt you like this … He offers you a dilemma. To save the world you must save the life of your gravest enemy." But Batman would have saved him anyway; discovering Ra's' evil plan was just icing on the cake (*Batman: Legends of the Dark Knight* #145, September 2001).

72 *Batman: The Man Who Laughs* (2005).

73 Ibid. When Gordon told him, "you saved the entire city from that deranged madman. Give yourself a pat on the back, I say," Batman simply responded, "I'll take it under advisement." (Gordon: "You do that.")

74 *Batman: Gotham Knights* #74 (April 2006). We'll see later that Batman some-times breaks his own rules, though, especially when he apparently failed to save Joker after the Clown Prince of Crime killed Jason Todd.

75 *Joker: Last Laugh* #6 (January 2002).

76 *Batman* #546 (September 1997).

77 *Batman: Legends of the Dark Knight* #143 (July 2001).

78 *Batman* #644 (Late October 2005).

79 *Robin: Year One* #2 (November 2000). James DiGiovanna confronted similar issues in his chapter "Is It Right to Make a Robin?" in Mark D. White and Robert Arp (eds.), *Batman and Philosophy: The Dark Knight of the Soul* (Hoboken, NJ: Wiley Blackwell, 2008), pp. 17–27.

80 *Batman: Turning Points* #2 (January 2001).

81 *Robin: Year One* #2 (November 2000).

82 *Robin: Year One* #3 (December 2000).

83 *Robin: Year One* #4 (January 2001).

84 *Batman* #438 (September 1989).

85 *Robin: Year One* #3 (December 2000).

86 *Batman* #408 (June 1987); in *Batman* #416 (February 1988), Dick said he was 19 when Batman fired him. Stepping outside the comics for a second, this sequence of events is told differently from time to time. Originally, he resigned as Robin in *New Teen Titans*, vol. 1, #39 (February 1984), telling his fellow Teen Titans that "Robin will always be the back half of 'Batman and—.' But

Robin belongs with Batman, fighting at his side. Trouble is—I don't," and then appeared as Nightwing for the first time in *Tales of the New Teen Titans* #44 (July 1984). After the Joker episode recounted above, Dick returned 18 months later as Nightwing, telling Batman he had joined the New Teen Titans as Robin, then changed his name to Nightwing (*Batman* #416). In yet another telling, Batman fired Dick for spending too much time with the Titans: "This is a war, Dick. Robin is my second ... my lieutenant. Anything less than total devotion to this cause is simply wasting my time" (*Nightwing*, vol. 2, #101, March 2005). (Who knows what's supposed to have happened since the New 52 began!)

87   *Batman* #408 (June 1987). Again, this is the revised story following the *Crisis on Infinite Earths* "reboot," which has been canon since 1987 (and even into the New 52); before that, Jason was a circus acrobat whose parents were killed. (Hmm ... at least he had red hair ... until they changed it to look *just like* ... well, you know.)

88   *Batman* #410 (August 1987).

89   Ibid. This is more relevant to Batman's son Damian, who was trained by his mother Talia with the League of Assassins to be an expert killer, and whom Batman made Robin to temper these murderous impulses. Nonetheless, Damian was killed by an agent of Ra's al Ghul after the New 52 began, only to be brought back to the land of the living by his father ... never mind.

90   *Batman* #416 (February 1988).

91   *Detective Comics* #574 (May 1987). In one case, Batman actually gave the same reason for his first Robin; as he tells Gordon, "I'm helping him not get killed. I'm not training him as much as guiding him, Jim ... You can't imagine what he's been through ... the pain and anger inside this boy. There had to be an outlet somewhere ... or he would have self-destructed, probably taking others with him. I'm just trying to stop a cycle we've both seen too many times" (*Batman: Turning Points* #2, January 2001.)

92   *Detective Comics* #542 (September 1984). (It is doubtful this adoption storyline survived the *Crisis on Infinite Earths*, but it's still in my funny books, dammit.)

93   *Batman: Gotham Knights* #43 (September 2003), "Batgirl & Robin."

94   *Batman: Gotham Knights* #44 (October 2003), "Body of Evidence." Incidentally, these last two stories and the next featured an agent from Child Protective Services who investigates the series of boys who have passed through Bruce Wayne's care, especially the one who died. (This isn't the first time CPS looked into Wayne Manor; they also looked into Jason's stay in *Batman* #375, September 1984.) After asking questions of Dick, Tim, Alfred, and lastly Bruce (and making some particularly tasteless insinuations regarding his relationship with the boys), the agent left satisfied, but advised Bruce "to think long and hard before you take it upon yourself to bring another child into this

home" (*Batman: Gotham Knights* #45, November 2003, "Knights Passed"). If only the agent knew what went on underground!

95 *Batman* #428 (December 1988).

96 Ibid. This echoes what Batman told Nightwing when his former Robin pressed him for the real reason he took in Jason: "I admit it. I was lonely. I missed you" (*Batman* #416, February 1988).

97 *Batman* #439 (September 1989).

98 *New Titans* #60 (November 1989).

99 *Batman* #441 (November 1989).

100 *New Titans* #61 (December 1989).

101 *Batman* #442 (December 1989).

102 Ibid.

103 *Batman* #443 (January 1990).

104 *Batman* #450 (Early July 1990).

105 *Batman* #465 (Late July 1991).

106 *Batman* #468 (Early September 1991).

107 *Batman* #521 (August 1995).

108 *Batman* #526 (January 1996).

109 *Batman* #469 (Late September 1991).

110 *Detective Comics* #646 (July 1992).

111 *Batman* #618 (October 2003).

112 *Detective Comics* #821 (September 2006).

113 *Batman* #652 (June 2006).

114 This is not even to mention Alfred's suspicion about Batman's taking on Stephanie Brown as Tim's replacement: "Promise me one thing. This isn't some scheme to lure Tim back, is it?" (*Robin*, vol. 4, #126, July 2004). Batman simply ignored him, as he did Barbara Gordon when she raised the same concern (*Detective Comics* #796, September 2004, "... And Red All Over"). If Alfred and Barbara were right, this is the most heinous justification Batman ever employed for taking in a Robin, all the more tragic given Stephanie's apparent death not long after he dismissed her as Robin soon thereafter (*Batman* #633, December 2004).

115 *Batman: Bride of the Demon* (December 1990).

116 Of course, there is one means that Batman does not consider justified by the end: killing, a personal rule that takes precedence over the mission, regardless of how many lives are threatened, ruined, or lost as a result. This is one moral principle that he will not violate, although as we will see in the second part of this book, it may have more to do with the preservation of his moral self-image than his presumed dedication to the sanctity of life.

117 *Batman* #416 (February 1988). (This is when he pressed Bruce to admit that he missed his original Robin.)

118 *Robin: Year One* #2 (November 2000).

119 *Batman* #408 (June 1987).

4

The Value and Meaning of the Bat

Batman is often criticized—more by people in the real world than in the comics—for selfishly using most of his fortune to fund his activities as a costumed crimefighter, supporting him and his partners with gadgets, computers, vehicles, and grand hide-outs. As Hush said when he fell down the stairs into the Batcave in a fight with Batman, "Bruce, you bastard! This is magnificent! … I wonder what Thomas and Martha would think of the self-indulgent way you're squandering their fortune. All this to salve a spoiled brat's broken heart."[1] (Hush sure knows how to hurt a guy.)

This final chapter of our discussion of Batman's mission abstracts from his individual actions and asks various questions about whether Batman serves the purpose that Bruce Wayne intends for him. Should Wayne be using his incredible resources—not just his wealth, but also his intellect, influence, and determination—in different ways than dressing up as a bat and prowling the night? Has being Batman made a difference in Gotham— and does he believe he has? And finally, does being Batman make Batman happy, and does it give his life meaning—despite the futility of the mission itself?

Is Being Batman the Best He Can Do?

The argument usually goes like this: If Bruce Wayne truly wants to help the people of Gotham City, there are better ways for him to do it than put on a costume and punch bad guys. All of the money he spends on the equipment in the Batcave (and his other stashes throughout the world), his various

Batman and Ethics, First Edition. Mark D. White.
© 2019 John Wiley & Sons Ltd. Published 2019 by John Wiley & Sons Ltd.

Bat-vehicles, and all of his wonderful toys—in addition to his time, attention, and intellect—could do more good for others if used in more direct, positive charitable efforts. By devoting so much of his wealth and time to being Batman, then, he is actually compromising the mission he swore to pursue, hiding from the world under a cape and cowl rather than engaging with it openly and freely.

Batman himself has criticized others for the same thing. Once, he met a hermit named Haven living in the woods, who explained that he was a man who "despaired of civilization … and who has tried in his way to find peace … So I left the world behind me … journeyed out into these woods … and built a new world with my bare hands." Batman challenged him, asking, "Isn't that a cop-out? Running away and hiding from the world rather than trying to change it?"[2] Some would say Batman has done the same thing, running around in a disguise, helping the people of Gotham avoid undue pain from crime but not doing enough to lift them up in a more positive way.

This is fair question to ask of anyone who claims to try to help the world: Are you doing it as much as you can or in the best way you can? As we saw earlier, the effective altruism movement focuses on this, asking us to not merely do (some) good but do the most good we can do, specifically for the people who need it the most. We have already seen, however, that Bruce Wayne decidedly does *not* do this: As he tells Robin, "My life is sworn to fighting crime … and protecting the people from its ravages, not 'saving the world.'"[3] As we know, his mission is deliberately narrower than general utilitarianism: to save lives, primarily by fighting crime, and mainly in Gotham City. If we accept this restricted and negative mission as a valid goal, then the choice to be a masked vigilante doesn't seem so strange—well, in the context of superhero comics, at least—especially given his skepticism regarding the effectiveness of those usually tasked with this goal. (We'll have more to say about Batman's relationship to the police in the second part of the book.)

Even if we doubt the contribution of his nighttime self to his mission, or question his mission itself as too limited, we should acknowledge that Bruce Wayne does much more than just cast a wicked shadow under a Gotham City streetlight. Although he obviously does devote considerable resources to fighting crime, he also dedicates much of his money—and some of his time, when he is awake at all during the daylight hours—to helping Gotham City and its citizens in other ways.

He didn't start out this way, to be sure. As he trained to fight crime, before that intrepid bat flew through his window, young Bruce Wayne planned to devote all of his time and wealth to his mission against crime. While in Paris, he met Lucius Fox for the first time, who proposed they partner up to help Gotham and the world: "My expertise is in finance—and with your family fortune, we could really do something extraordinary," to which Bruce responded, "No, that money—like me—has already been committed elsewhere." As he reflected later, "Lucius wouldn't have understood. No one could. I made a promise. To honor my parents. Someday to rid Gotham of the crime that took their lives."[4]

Later, however, he had a change of heart. After one of his gravesite confessionals, Bruce returned home to the manor and Alfred, and told his trusted butler, "I want to use more of my parents' money, Alfred, to build a better foundation." Alfred assumed he meant Batman, and said as much, but Bruce corrected him: "No, Alfred, my father's charitable foundation— for the victims of crime ... and for the victims of the poverty that spawns crime ... its work redoubled and rededicated ... in my parents' memory."[5] The Wayne Foundation would go on to become the primary means through which Bruce engages in philanthropy. Years later, when the Wayne Foundation was taken over and the Wayne fortune appropriated to pay off its debts, Batman reflected on his newfound poverty and revealed the extent of his largess:

> Never thought about my money very much—it was always there. And now that it's gone, I can't quite decide how I feel. Most of it's always gone toward charitable ends ... and as for the rest of it, aside from the upkeep of the manor, it has ironically been the Batman—rather than "playboy" Bruce Wayne—who spends the most ...[6]

It comes as no surprise that the Batman "operation" absorbs a lot of Wayne resources—and the Wayne lifestyle very little—but this statement suggests that the expense of crimefighting pales in comparison to his charitable efforts.

As stark a distinction as Batman often draws between the lives in and out of the mask, his philanthropy and his nightlife are two sides of the same coin, whether that coin represents his more focused mission to fight crime or his more general one to save the residents of Gotham City. As his comment to Alfred above suggests, he is well aware that poverty "spawns crime." As he boarded socialite Camille Baden-Smythe's yacht—leading to the episode with Orca recounted in the last chapter—she told him she was surprised to see him there, to which he replied, "You've never hosted a benefit for the Gotham Orphanage before, Camille." They debated the merits of helping the less fortunate, with Bruce at one point paraphrasing Charles Dickens from *A Christmas Carol*: "our work is mankind." When Baden-Smythe accused him of wanting to support "drug addicts, winos, bag ladies and the mentally ill," Wayne answered, "I'm not a proponent of supporting the dysfunctional ... but that money could build and support a youth center in the inner city. It could save a lot of kids from a life of crime," showing that he acknowledges the role that deprivation plays in the development of the criminal (even though he believes that it doesn't absolve criminals of responsibility for their actions). When she hit back with "I don't see you turning Wayne Manor into a halfway house!" Bruce simply said, "I do my bit in other ways."[7]

As suggested by this exchange, Bruce Wayne is particularly concerned with housing and the plight of children in Gotham City, areas in which he focuses much of his philanthropic energy. After a night of unsuccessfully tracking a criminal, Batman told Alfred,

> I've checked every flophouse and fleabag this guy's visited—and the only crime in each is that people have to live in them! God, it's enough to turn my stomach—and make me double my efforts to help rebuild those areas with Wayne Foundation funds![8]

Another time, Bruce Wayne sympathized with a homeless veteran complaining about high-priced real-estate development in Gotham, and told a nearby police officer, "The city would have earned itself less money, but a lot more good will, if they'd sold the land for low-rent housing."[9] Among the wide variety of the Wayne Foundation's charitable efforts following the Cataclysm earthquake and its aftershocks was the provision of shelter and food to the displaced, while they also coordinated with FEMA and other federal aid agencies to help people rebuild their homes or relocate.[10]

Given his own history, it's natural that Batman would have a soft spot in his heart for the well-being of children. In one case, he searched for the family of a young girl in foster care whom Leslie Thompkins was treating in her clinic; when he found her home, he discovered half a dozen more children sleeping on the floor, in a clear case of foster abuse. "Makes my stomach turn," he thought to himself. "Kids. Abandoned. Neglected. Abused. Orphaned ... treated like this. The Wayne Foundation will try to get these kids moved to a decent home. But ... it doesn't seem like it's enough."[11] And he doesn't only help through his family's foundation—he also gets personally involved. One night during patrol, Batman and Robin happened across a couple of college kids breaking into grocery store. "I know those boys," Batman said. "Bruce Wayne sponsors their schooling through the [I Have a Dream] program. I'd like to do a little checking on them." And check in on them he does—as Bruce Wayne, which may have been only a little less scary than if he had arrived as Batman—and offered them research jobs on the weekends with the Wayne Foundation.[12]

In line with his belief that poverty breeds crime, Bruce Wayne is also extremely vested in the Gotham City economy. During a mayoral election in which both candidates focused on the failing police department and the threat of vigilantism—no idea who they were worried about there—Batman worried that neither will "address the real issues—urban decay, a shrinking tax base, and industrial stagnation ... And all of us in Gotham are the poorer because of it."[13] As we saw earlier, he dedicated not only the Wayne Foundation but also Wayne Enterprises to helping the city rebuild after the Cataclysm, going so far as to tell his chief accountant, "Until this city is back on its feet, job performance will be judged by criteria other than profits ... By the swift improvement of everyday life in Gotham ..."[14] He also pleaded with his fellow business leaders to keep their headquarters and operations in Gotham after the quake (and before the city was quarantined in the No Man's Land), arguing that "Gotham is my city. Its people are my people. They're your people, too! They're already reeling from the quake. If your companies leave, you'll be dealing them a blow they might never recover from!" When another businessman objects that Wayne doesn't understand business, Wayne responded, "And you don't seem to realize a city is a living, breathing entity! Cut off its oxygen—the means by which its people earn a living—and you'll effectively starve the city to death!"[15]

Wayne isn't successful in that attempt, but continued to steer his enterprises toward philanthropy as well as business enterprises that help the Gotham economy as well as employees and stockholders. We see this when he returned to Wayne Enterprises after being framed for murder and jumped back in with both feet, steering corporate charity, donating new bulletproof vests to the Blüdhaven Police Department (where Dick Grayson happens to work), and giving a high school student working in the mailroom a scholarship to college.[16] In a more recent story, Batman discovered that Athena, the head of the criminal cartel known as the Network, was actually Celia Kazantkakis, CEO of Wayne Enterprises. When Oracle discovered that the Network was planning to steal two billion dollars from Wayne's company during an engineered blackout, he thought, "If Athena manages to walk away with the two billion, not only will Wayne Enterprises collapse ... thousands of people will lose their jobs, and the Gotham economy will suffer a staggering downturn."[17]

There are many instances, as we've seen, in which Bruce Wayne is the true hero of Gotham City (or at least tries to be). After all, it was Bruce Wayne, not Batman, who tried to convince other business leaders to stay in Gotham after the Cataclysm, and who testified in front of Congress to argue for Gotham's future and try to prevent No Man's Land—both unsuccessfully, as it turns out, but he surely stood a better chance in a suit and tie than a cape and cowl.[18] As Batman (in his cape and cowl) told Nightwing at that time, "Maybe Bruce Wayne can do more to help Gotham than Batman can. Wayne's money, properties. I can't believe I'm saying this, but his place in the community. They might mean more right now than any good a vigilante can do."[19] Even in better times, there are things Bruce Wayne can do that Batman cannot. When Wayne was framed for murder, Batman visited Leslie Thompkins at her clinic, telling her, "If you need my help—" which Leslie cut off, saying,

> I really don't. No help that Batman can provide, at least. I'm short-staffed, short on supplies, and short on equipment ... Batman can do nothing about those things. On the other hand, Bruce Wayne, well ... he was a very rich man. In more ways than he recognized, I think.[20]

Of course, this doesn't mean that Batman doesn't have a role to play—as we'll see very soon—but simply that Bruce Wayne is important to Gotham City as well, a role that, despite Leslie's insinuations, he hardly neglects.

And it isn't just Gotham City that benefits from Bruce Wayne's philanthropy. As he does with his crimefighting skills, Bruce Wayne also extends his charitable efforts around the globe. After a case on an Native American Indian reservation that reflected centuries of injustice, Batman called into the Wayne Foundation and asked (in his Bruce Wayne voice) for "a dozen suggestions as to how we can help the Native Americans."[21] When he traveled to Calcutta, he compared it to Gotham, a city down on its luck but with strength and spirit, and sorely in need of help. After Batman and the assassin Shiva beat some thugs, Batman took a ring off one of them and gave it to a merchant to feed a boy who helped him. When Shiva said, "Calcutta is home to eleven million people, most of them hungry. You can't feed them all," Batman replied, "I don't know them all, Shiva, but sometimes ... it takes just one to make a difference."[22] This recognition of the futility of helping everybody mirrors the futility of his mission to eliminate crime, and in both cases, even Bruce Wayne can only do what he can, and every bit helps, even if only a bit. We see this again when he traveled to Ethiopia with Jason Todd, was saddened by the conditions, and resolved that "When I return to Gotham, I'll send out another check to help the effort and try to forget what I've seen here. I'm no different from anyone else." Wayne follows this with an open admission of futility: "There's only so much even Bruce Wayne—or Batman—can do."[23]

We should not forget the global initiative of Batman Incorporated, which Batman initiated after his "return from the dead." Not only was this an expansion of his crimefighting activity and reach, to make sure "Batman will be everywhere it's dark," but also an extension of Wayne's philanthropy. As he told Lucius Fox, "I'm authorizing a massive cash injection, Lucius. We're investing in bleeding edge technology and working prototypes to support Batman's war on crime."[24] Although Wayne obviously spent a good deal of his own fortune on his crimefighting activities, this was possibly the first time he used his corporate and foundation resources explicitly to do the same. When a journalist asked Bruce Wayne if this put him, his employees, and shareholders in danger—physical as well as financial, we can assume—Wayne was forthright, saying "it's the responsibility of people in my position to more actively support the fight for a better, safer world."[25] In this effort, Bruce Wayne's sense of civic responsibility to Gotham City and the world dovetails with his work as Batman, while not neglecting his other philanthropic duties.

Even though Batman's mission may be limited to fighting crime and saving people from its effects, Bruce Wayne works toward a broader utilitarian purpose of helping all—even if, to some extent, his activities as Batman compromise the amount of good he can do in that context. Batman may not be out to save the world, but Bruce Wayne is trying to do just that. We can criticize him for the specific approach to helping people that he adopted as Batman, saying he should take a broader approach to charity and giving like he does as Bruce Wayne—and perhaps spend more or all of his money and time in the latter way. But it's not fair to accuse him of neglecting more positive ways of increasing utility; it's just not his only focus.

This argument also shows that utilitarianism, in its simplest and more direct form, is a uniquely perfectionist system of ethics. Utilitarians are expected to act only in those ways that are likely to maximize total well-being. Increasing it by a certain amount, no matter how large, is not enough if it could be increased by even more. But this is unreasonable, and not even effective altruists such Peter Singer advocate absolute self-sacrifice and the quest for perfection. They merely recommend that we give more than we already do and put effort into making sure our giving is directed to where it can do the most good. Not only does this relax the pressure to "maximize total utility," but it allows individual utilitarians some leeway in crafting how they will act to improve the world. Each of us has certain talents, abilities, and motivations that steer our altruistic efforts in one direction or another: some toward animal rights, others toward environmentalism, and yet others to help refugees of war. None of these are guaranteed to be *the best* way that person could help the world in general, but as long as each person helps in a way they can that also engages them, their effort is undeniably good.

Perhaps Bruce Wayne could do even more good if he devoted some of his crimefighting resources to more directly charitable activities. But we should also acknowledge that he already does a tremendous amount of good, both in his philanthropy as Bruce Wayne and his fight against crime as Batman, and this leaves him little obligation to change his behavior to do *even more* good.

But Is Batman Good for Gotham?

We've been avoiding one crucial question in our discussion about the good that Batman does as a crimefighter and as Bruce Wayne, billionaire philan-thropist: in general, how much good does Batman do? (We could ask the same about Wayne's charitable giving, but that would be less fun.) Regarding Batman's career choice, there are some—this time, more in his world than in ours—who doubt his value to Gotham City. As we'll see, Batman questions this as much as anyone, often wondering if being Batman is worth his effort and dedication, especially given the personal sacrifices he makes himself for the mission (including his own happiness).

Let's start with the most focused criticism: that rather than lessening the scourge of crime in Gotham City, Batman actually worsens it through attracting and perhaps even creating many of the more colorful villains he fights. We see this sense of responsibility in Batman's "confession" to Gordon after his first run-in with the Joker, that he "created" him during his encounter with the Red Hood and bears some responsibility for his later actions.[26] Anarky had the same opinion as he watched Batman in action:

> The evil of Gotham City is all Batman's fault! He's set himself up as a vigilante elite—a costumed hero who issues a challenge to all: "Gotham is my city—take it if you can!" And the maniacs have accepted! ... They only exist as an answer to his challenge! Batman creates his own villains. He is the city's true enemy![27]

This is echoed by Gotham City police detective Sarah Essen when she yelled at Batman when her husband Jim Gordon was in danger:

> While you're flitting around in a Halloween costume, he's doing his job as police commissioner. And he's better than you—because he does it the right way! You take down the weird ones, the freaks who wouldn't even be here if not for you! You attract them—while he deals with the "normal" crime—the simple atrocities committed with guns and knives and baseball bats—all the dirty work that's beneath you![28]

Essen interestingly connects Batman's battles against his costumed foes to the police's burden of handling the street crime. Certainly, you might think common thieves, muggers, and even organized crime figures are deterred from operating in Gotham by Batman's relentless efforts to thwart them. But to the extent he's often preoccupied by clowns, penguins, and poisoned ivy, ordinary criminals may enjoy even more freedom to operate, contributing to Gotham's reputation as a crime-ridden cesspool.

The latter point can be easily dismissed, especially considering the Gotham City Police Department's responsibility to tackle ordinary crime. Granted, the GCPD is in a strange position, operating in a city with costumed vigilantes and outlandish themed villains, as the 2002–2006 series *Gotham Central* showed well. But this doesn't dismiss their traditional role as enforcers of the law and protectors of the citizens of Gotham from garden-variety crime. Gotham was a criminal haven long before Batman arrived, and even if he were somehow to blame for the rise in "super" villains since his arrival, he can't be blamed for ordinary crime or for the police department's difficulties in dealing with it (many of them due to the GCPD's historical corruption).

The theory that Batman "created" the Scarecrow, Killer Croc, and the rest is more interesting, especially given the widely held understanding that the Batman and the Joker are "necessary opposites," neither capable of existing without the other.[29] This is what detective Henri Ducard was thinking as he assessed the Dark Knight:

> ... he functions as a lightning rod for a certain breed of psychotic. They specialize in absurdly grandiose schemes, and whatever the ostensible rationale—greed, revenge, the seizure of power ... their true agenda is always the same: to cast Batman in the role of nemesis ... He always triumphs. If he failed, they'd be bereft. The *pas de deux* would have no point ... Thus "good" conquers "evil." True evil seldom announces itself so loudly.[30]

In Ducard's opinion, the costumed villains' evil is a less serious variety, more focused on toying with Batman and seeking the attention of a disapproving "parent," rather than pursuing evil for its own sake (or even for more mundane material ends). This theory links Batman to the emergence of his costumed foes, but also minimizes their impact on the citizens of Gotham City, which as we know all too well is significant and often tragic.

If anyone is going to blame Batman for the costumed villains that plague Gotham, it would be Commissioner Jim Gordon. He suggested this when visiting Arkham Asylum with Batman, saying, "So many are here. Nearly double from when you first appeared. Not that there is a direct correlation, but … do you give it any thought?" Batman said no while thinking to himself, "I know what Gordon is implying. That my … presence … somehow attracts these men and women to my city," and went on to recognize that although the police do the best they can with limited resources, "Gotham City needs Batman to protect her" from the more serious threats.[31] (Note that he didn't refute Gordon's implication, though.) But we must remember Gordon's response to Batman after defeating the Joker for the first time: "Did you put the hood on his head and the gun in his hand? No, you didn't."[32] Later, Jim assured his friend again: when Batman claimed that "I made the monsters," Gordon told him, "No, you didn't. You want to go down the road of cause and effect, we'll just end up at some caveman hitting another on the head for the hell of it. This is a sick world sometimes. That isn't your fault."[33] Batman set out to protect the citizens of Gotham from the scourge of crime before there were costumed villains vying for his attention. He cannot be held responsible if, as Ducard and Anarky believe, some criminals chose to challenge him—to fight the toughest kid on the playground and make their bones, so to speak.

Nonetheless, from a generally utilitarian standpoint, responsibility is not the main concern—consequences are. If Batman has a net negative effect on Gotham by attracting more murderous and destructive crime to its streets, this has to be counted as a loss in the ledger. Against this we have to consider his constant battle against ordinary crime and all the lives he has saved and the suffering he has prevented. There is no way to quantify or even estimate this, of course. How much do the costumed villains detract from his routine patrols, and to what degree do they embolden the street criminals? Is the GCPD less or more burdened because of Batman? These are impossible questions to answer—especially given the scant evidence available from the comics "record." It also serves, more broadly, as a critique of utilitarian judgment on the basis of insufficient information: although it may be impossible to judge the overall value of Batman to Gotham City, it is much easier to say that he generally serves the cause of right and justice, doing much good in individual actions day to day. And even if he is somehow responsible, causally if not morally, for "supercrime" in Gotham, that bell can't be unrung, and the best he can do is fight it, proving Batman's value going forward if not in retrospect. As Gordon told him when he was considering his responsibility for the "monsters" in Gotham, "the genie is out of the bottle and it turns out he's only granting his wishes you don't want. So even if you buy into that load of hogwash … that you created Gotham's nightmares … they're still out there."[34]

A broader critique of Batman's value to Gotham City has to do with his contribution to the cycle of violence, a critique that comes from someone very close to Batman's heart. If Alfred Pennyworth easily slid into the role of father figure to Bruce Wayne after the death of his parents, then Leslie Thompkins certainly adopted the cause of foster mother. While Alfred snidely disapproves of Bruce's chosen vocation but enables it at the same time, Leslie is more firm in her objection to the Batman's behavior based on her dedication to pacifism. We'll discuss Batman's penchant for violence in the second part of this book; for now I want to focus on Leslie's thoughts about the value of Batman given how he relies on violence and contributes to the cycle of violence in Gotham City.

When we first meet Leslie, Batman had saved her from several muggers near her home in Crime Alley who wanted the money she was collecting for neighborhood children. When he asked her why she continues to live there, she told him,

> I once saw a hideous thing—a child who parents were murdered in front of his eyes! I've never forgotten the lad! I've devoted my life to doing what I can to prevent such tragedy! Forgive me … but I live for the time when you and your kind will be unnecessary![35]

Leslie's sentiment here casts her in profound opposition to Batman, both of them reacting to the same horrific tragedy in polar-opposite ways that defined them for their lives—and set them at odds as well.

We learn much more about Leslie over the years, and with each retelling of her backstory she became more involved in Bruce's upbringing, not just comforting him that fateful night but also helping Alfred raise him into a man.[36] Most important, her pacifism became one of her defining character traits, alongside her life as a doctor tending to the poor, both in Gotham City and developing countries. In one of Batman's early tales, Leslie and Bruce were witness to a group of "Bat-men," local vigilantes inspired by Batman who took the law into their own violent hands against local crime. In her ignorance of Bruce's double life, she told him how glad she was that he didn't turn out like the "bat-men," and that "I was wrong to be angry with them. They're just a symptom ... a symptom of the violence glorified by the Batman."[37] Her ignorance didn't last long, as she discovered Batman's true identity while treating him for gunshot wounds suffered at the hands of one of the bat-men who wanted to kill a drug dealer he was questioning. Leslie was angry at first, but at the end of the tale, she told him she was sorry she failed him, that if only she had raised him better, he wouldn't feel the need to risk his life to fight crime.[38]

Leslie would go on to emphasize Batman's contribution to the cycle of violence in Gotham City many times. After the episode in which they delivered a baby by caesarian section only to lose the mother soon afterwards, Batman told Leslie he was leaving to find Mr. Freeze, who knew who was ultimately responsible for the turf battle that led to the young mother's plight. "Are you joking?" she asked. "After all this you're going to battle some 'super villain'?" Even after Batman explained the connection between the woman and Freeze, she wasn't satisfied, continuing:

> My god, Bruce, don't you see? You beat these madmen senseless, hand them over to the authorities, only to have them walking the streets again, now only angrier and more violent than before. And you respond in kind. When does it end?[39]

Leslie reached the end of her rope when she found herself in the middle of the "War Games," a manmade catastrophe in which Gotham exploded in violence between the city's rival gangs, the police, and Batman and his colleagues. After Catwoman brought a gunshot victim to the hospital, she and Leslie heard a news report of violence at Tim Drake's high school and Leslie raged that Bruce was putting people she cared about at risk for "his damn mission." When Catwoman said the war wasn't his fault, Leslie argued,

> And you think he and his people aren't culpable in this? His tactics are almost as bad as those gangbangers, sometimes trying to lower the crime rate by terrifying people. It's—it's ludicrous. It just becomes part of the cycle of violence that gave birth to the Batman in the first place.[40]

Again, she blamed herself for what she saw as her own part in continuing the cycle: "How could I have failed that child so badly, that he would think violence ever accomplishes anything positive? I'm ashamed of myself, Selina ..."[41]

Nonetheless, as much as she hates the way Batman does his job, she still loves the man beneath the mask and appreciates what he does for Gotham. During the episode with Zsasz during No Man's Land—when Batman was angry she was planning to use the blood he brought her to save Zsasz's life—she told him angrily, "I am grateful every day for what you do for this city, but I do not approve of the way you do it!" But later, after they reconciled and he was despondent, she told him, "You keep working toward peace in this city, and I'll keep working toward peace in your heart."[42] After the caesarian and the mother's death (but before leaving to find Mr. Freeze), Batman himself lost it, saying "People are dead, Leslie." Here she played a similar role to Alfred's, reminding him, "And more would be if not for you. Including me. Bruce, Gotham would be dead if not for you. But you are not responsible for everyone in this city."[43] After that episode was over, she told him again, "It's no secret that I don't always approve of what you ... do. But your devotion to the sanctity of life is so beautiful ... I see your father in you."[44]

In an earlier scene with Leslie, Batman was again despondent about his mission and its futility, remembering his early days and telling her, "In those days, I really thought I could make a difference ..." Leslie asked, "You don't know?" and he answered, "Sometimes, no ... Maybe you're right, Leslie ... maybe there's no more need for me ..." Leslie told him, "Bruce, wait—I don't deny that I pray for the day when no one will die from crime or injustice ... when you and your kind are unnecessary ... but until then, there is a need for you—and I'm glad you're here to fill it."[45] Despite her opposition to violence, she realizes that Gotham is a violent city, and even if she refuses to raise a hand in opposition to it, she's glad that he does, even if it breaks her heart to watch (and stitch him up, often alongside Alfred, whenever he needs it).

As these episodes with Leslie show, no one has greater doubts about Batman's value to Gotham than the man himself. Once, after Gordon told him that he should be satisfied that he did his job, Batman answered, cynically, "No doubt ... I suppose I've justified my existence for one more night."[46] Not long into his work as the city's Dark Knight, he said to Alfred, "It's been over a year since I put on this mask, and yet all I've done is react, respond, retaliate. How can I expect to make a difference in this city when all I do is mop up the bloodstains ...?"[47] It doesn't help, either, that the police—ostensibly his partners in the fight against crime—are often against him, telling him he's more bother than he's worth, with even the public occasionally joining in. After being framed for murder by Ra's al Ghul, Batman became a fugitive from justice; as he overheard people debating whether Batman is a hero, he thought, "All the years I've spent watching over them—guarding the streets while they slept—and they turn on me in a minute—like I was Attila the Hun! Sometimes it can make you wonder if it's all worth it!"[48]

In part, the malaise Batman suffers from is related to the futility of his mission, the fact that he will never eradicate crime in Gotham City, never save every life from being ended prematurely at the end of a gun, and never protect everyone from loss and suffering. He knows this full well, of course, but every life he fails to save means more than a hundred he does, and this prevents him from appreciating the full value of what he does and who he is. When Bruce Wayne returns after Dick Grayson's first spell as Batman (following Jean-Paul Valley's time in the costume), Dick accused his mentor of never questioning or examining himself, but Bruce set him straight: "You don't know how I question myself and everything I've become. The right of it. The wrong of it. Not allowing myself any reward for the good. Damning myself for every mistake."[49] As we've seen, Alfred often has to reassure Bruce that for every crime he fails to stop, he succeeds at stopping many more, and it's when he's doubting his purpose and value that he needs to remember this more than ever.

Although he agonizes over every crime he can't prevent, the major events and catastrophes incite the deepest ruminations of the bat. The first was probably when Bane broke Batman's back and Bruce appointed Valley, the brainwashed religious warrior Azrael, to be his successor, only to see the new Batman cross lines the original never dreamed of. After Bruce defeated Valley and reclaimed his mantle, Tim Drake found him in the cave, and Bruce opened up: "All of this has been due to my poor judgment. I left the city in unstable hands. Jean-Paul was a disastrous choice." When Tim said there wasn't time, Bruce continued:

> No excuse! There's no margin for error here. I should have been prepared for any contingency! I should have had a successor in the wings. Until I found out about Jean-Paul's ... indiscretions I was prepared to live the rest of my life as Bruce Wayne and nothing more. Now I'm back and it's as if nothing has happened. I have to rethink it all, make some changes. I'm going to reappraise a lot of things about Bruce Wayne ... and Batman.[50]

And reappraise things he did. As the narration read, referring to both his appointment of Valley as his successor and his physical return from having his back broken:

> It is these two factors—mistake and recovery—that have spawned his current doubts and questions. Still haunted by the horror that gave him birth, he is reborn with a new but unfocused perspective. Shattered before he was

formed, Bruce Wayne became nothing but a stitched-together mask ... but what if the Batman, too, is nothing but a mask? Who is he, really? What has he created? And is it worth being?[51]

After a night of reflection, he stopped a mugging, and then saw the light. The narration continues:

> His doubts are settled: Even in the darkness of obsession, even at the risk of his sanity, this creature of the night is worth the shaping. This angel in the devil's dark guise is worth being. Someone must haunt the shadows, scare the demons, slay the horror ... save the victims. He knows it now, knows it again—just as he knew it when his eight-year-old soul was forever shattered. The eternal night of Gotham needs the Batman.[52]

There is much room for interpretation here, but as I read it, Bruce is questioning himself after facing trials and ordeals like none he'd ever faced before, and feeling that he'd failed at all of them. (Feel free to add Jason Todd's death and Barbara Gordon's shooting to the mix as well if you wish.) But it was a routine mugging—an example of ordinary street crime that nonetheless might have changed an innocent person's life forever—that reminded Batman of his purpose, the meaning of his life, the mission that propels him through the occasional doubt. He swore to fight crime and protect the innocent, and Batman is the best way he knows to fulfill that oath and pursue the mission it set him on.

The adequacy of that "way" is never more challenged than during large-scale disasters such as the Contagion and its return, the Cataclysm and its aftershocks, and the No Man's Land period of Gotham City's exile from the rest of the world. We've already seen Batman's frustration—often expressed at his parents' gravesite—at his inability to fight when there is no enemy, and to manage death on such a large scale when the deaths of only two human beings were enough to shatter him. Three hours after the Cataclysm struck, Batman surveyed the devastation it caused to his city. As the narration read:

> Fighting crime—finding clues, solving riddles, uncovering motives—stopping thieves and killers and madmen—these are all things he knows. But his city in ruins ... even in his worst nightmares, he never imagined this. With the power down, the stars above seem to shine unnaturally bright ... as if the immensity of the cosmos is mocking him. He feels small and feeble. A tidal wave of helplessness and despair threatens to engulf him. What can he do? What can one man do for an entire city?[53]

All of this is enough to drive the bat from the city he loves. After unsuccessfully asking his fellow business leaders to stay in Gotham after the earthquake, and pleading with Washington to save Gotham City from being cut off from the rest of the country, Batman fled to Monaco and played at being Bruce Wayne for a while. After a week, he picked a fight with some local thugs and let them beat him to a pulp. Talia, daughter of Ra's al Ghul and one of the women closest to Batman, found him in his hotel and tended to his wounds while shaming him: "All that magnificent ability … used to punish yourself. You are a disgrace—to yourself, to your teachers—and to your parents." When she offered to accept him nonetheless as her betrothed, he declined, telling her that "I am for another."[54] After that realization, he returned to Gotham, snuck into the No Man's Land, activated his secret batcaves hidden throughout the city, and hatched his plan to save his true love. As with the mugging above, it is usually one person crying out for his help—or a beautiful woman offering to love him—that snaps Batman out of his reflection and reminds him that he just has to save one person at a time, over and over again, even in the absence of crime *per se*, he can still save lives, even if he can't save them all.[55]

Is Batman … Happy?

If Batman were a more "holistic" utilitarian, concerned not only with saving the innocent citizens of Gotham City from the harmful effects of crime but also with happiness and well-being in general, he would be forced to consider the well-being of those very close to him. This includes his friends such as Jim Gordon, "co-workers" such as his fellow superheroes, love interests such as Catwoman, and his "family," including the Robins, Leslie, and Alfred. Of course, he clearly takes the well-being of all these people into account, and is tortured when any of them is in danger, especially due to his own crimefighting efforts, but this is usually not the focus of his mission (especially, as we discussed, when it comes to the safety of the Robins).

But I'm not talking about them. I mean Batman or Bruce Wayne himself, whose well-being counts just as much in a general utilitarian calculation as anyone else's (which we discussed in the context of making choices in tragic dilemmas). In terms of common-sense ethics, thinking of one's own interests is often regarded as selfish, but most schools of moral philosophy stress the need to look out for yourself—provided you don't look out for *only* yourself! It is indeed selfish to always put your own interests above everybody else's, and this is why you don't hear much about promoting your own happiness in discussions of ethics. You can usually count on people to look after themselves, but it usually takes a little prodding—either from their own consciences or role models such as parents, teachers, and religious leaders—to remind them to take other's interests into account too.

It's the nature of the hero, however, to ignore his or her own interests and sacrifice everything to help others. Firefighters run into burning buildings, doctors and journalists go into disaster areas, and soldiers face mortar fire, all to improve the lives of people they've never even met. As they do these things, they're not thinking of themselves, whether by habit or by force of will; that's the only way they can focus on helping others when their own lives are at risk. Remember when Batman leapt off the building to save two people, knowing he was risking his life as well, "but I have to turn off that part of my brain"—if he didn't, he likely would have hesitated, and he wouldn't have been able to save anybody.[56]

Throughout this book so far, I've recounted many instances of Batman risking his life to save others, including both innocent civilians and wicked criminals. But this is not the only thing he gives up for his mission: he also sacrifices his own happiness, which in some ways is just as important as his life.

At this point we have to note that there are many types of happiness that philosophers talk about.[57] One is the deep satisfaction that comes from having purpose and meaning in your life: the ancient Greeks called this *eudaimonia*, which we today typically translate as "flourishing." As frustrated as Batman often becomes with the futility of his mission, he also realizes that it is that mission that gives his life value and meaning. In the real world, this is the kind of happiness that we most often fail to achieve, as shown by the countless books, articles, and websites devoted to helping people find meaning in their lives, whether in work, play, or love. Even though it may not seem like it, Batman has that kind of happiness locked down, and that is no small thing.

We'll come back to the meaning of Batman's life in the next section. For now, I want to focus on another type of happiness, one that is more familiar: the joy or pleasure felt in the moment rather than over the span of a life. This is the kind of happiness that makes you smile with glee, even if only for a short time, and may come easier for many of us than the deeper kind that only comes with finding one's purpose in it. But most of the time, this type of happiness is not for the Dark Knight. Despite his wealth, position, and movie-star looks—how many superheroes can say they look like George Clooney *and* Ben Affleck?—Batman's life was launched in tragedy, and every waking minute of it has been spent fulfilling a promise to prevent that tragedy for others (not to mention the endless nights spent reliving that single evening). He could easily give it all up and devote his life to flights of hedonism few of us could imagine, but that isn't the life he chose (and the few times he has tried to indulge it, such as the beginning of No Man's Land, it bored him). He made a choice, early on, to sacrifice the temporary, day-to-day happiness many of us take for granted in favor of a hard life filled with purpose and meaning, achieving the deeper satisfaction many of us crave in vain, but at the cost of the simpler pleasures. "It means that some of my heart's desires may go unfulfilled," he thinks. "But many more are satisfied ... It *is* a good choice."[58]

It is clear from the comics that Batman disregards the need for this simpler kind of happiness. In a dream induced by Ra's al Ghul's potion in which Bruce spoke with his parents, Thomas told him, "We wanted what every parent wants for their child, Bruce. We wanted you to live a long, healthy, and happy life. So far, well ... you seem healthy enough, I suppose," to which Bruce replied, in his defense, "The cost is one I've always been willing to pay ... For your memory, and the memory of my loss."[59] Whether or not Bruce is happy is a topic that also comes up often with his "adopted" mother, Dr. Leslie Thompkins. In the story in which she first learned of his double life, after she apologized for not doing a better job raising him, he told her: "I don't know if I'm happy ... but I'm content," suggesting that he's satisfied with his life of purpose and meaning, but not happy in the moment, a subtle yet important distinction.[60]

Soon thereafter, in his second year of fighting crime in Gotham, Bruce showed Leslie the Thomas Wayne Memorial Clinic that he set up for her in Crime Alley, and told her, "I only hope it makes you happy, Leslie." When she asked him, "What about you, Bruce? Are you happy?" he answered, simply, "It doesn't matter."[61] In a follow-up story, Bruce Wayne asked Rachel Caspian, who joined a convent after learning her father was a murderer, "Are you happy?" to which she answered, "Perhaps we can never have exactly what we want, Bruce. I've learned to live with that. I'm content. That's more than many people have." At the end of the story, Rachel asked Batman, "Tell me ... do you know Bruce Wayne?" Even though Batman said that he didn't know Wayne well, she asked him, "Is he happy?" Batman answered, "He's content, Miss Caspian. That's more than many people have."[62] Not only did he echo her previous words to Bruce Wayne, he also reaffirmed that he is content with the life he has chosen, even if he is not happy in the here and now.

This isn't to say that Batman never enjoys any true happiness. A year and a half after first donning the cape and cowl, Bruce meditated in the cave and reflects.

> I've avoided a basic fact about my secret life. For mother ... for father ... for all the good reasons, all the right choices ... a part of me still scampers over rooftops in the dark for the sheer pleasure of it. I'm mortified to admit just how much I love being Batman.[63]

It wasn't until he was captured, repeatedly electrocuted and beaten, and nearly died in agony—agony that carries his mind back to the night his parents were shot—that he thought of his tormentor as "relentlessly mocking a time only days past when, heaven help me—I'd actually begun to consider my career as Batman fun." As he struggled to fight back, he thought, "If pain is all that is left behind—then it must be pain that—sustains me."[64] But Batman is human, after all, and sometimes even he pines for the carefree life of simple pleasures that he works so hard to make sure others can enjoy. In one moment of particular (albeit chemically induced) frustration, he cries out, "I've always responded to those in need, without an instant's hesitation—but what about my needs? What about me?"[65] These are merely occasional lapses in what is usually a steadfast, silent devotion to sacrifice and ... contentment.

There is one source of happiness that has been denied Batman—or perhaps that Batman has denied himself—and that is romantic love. Bruce Wayne has had a number of pivotal love interests in his life, including Julie Madison (from his earliest stories), Vicki Vale, Silver St. Cloud, Talia al Ghul, Vesper Fairchild, Sasha Bordeaux, and of course Selina Kyle, aka Catwoman. Whether they knew his secret life or not—and most did, whether he told them or they figured it out—they all represented the possibility of true happiness for a tortured soul, but also one more person to protect (and to fail to protect).

Most important to him, though, was that love represented a distraction from the mission that he felt he could not afford. Batman learned this lesson mere days into his crimefighting career, when he repeatedly had to cancel plans with a socialite named Viveca Beausoleil. After they finally enjoyed an evening together, he returned home to hear that criminals he left tied up for the police before leaving for his date managed to escape and got into a firefight with the police, resulting in the deaths of two criminals, one police officer, and a nine-year-old girl watching from her window above. After solemn reflection, he calls Ms. Beausoleil, telling her "I hate like hell to do this, but I don't have any choice … Yes, you're right, baby … there is someone else" … his true love, Gotham.[66]

You'll remember that Bruce said something very similar to Talia when she found him beaten in Monaco as No Man's Land began. Chosen by her father Ra's al Ghul to be his successor, and regarded by her as "my beloved," Batman was drawn to Talia from their first meeting.[67] Nonetheless, when they were married by her father, Batman told her, "if I were anyone else, I'd cherish you for the rest of my life! But I can't consider our marriage real! I have a mission—and you'd keep me from doing what I must!"[68] He reaffirmed this soon thereafter when she helped him heal from a laser wound: She offered herself to him again, but he demurred, telling her that "you tempt me … but there's too much to do. And frankly, I don't want another relationship now. The last few have been too … painful. And I can't permit more pain to cloud my judgment. Not now."[69] Later, when tempted to revisit the topic of their marriage, he told her "there's never been any room in my life for a woman … that is what I told myself, after every liaison I've ever known shattered."[70] Talia would forever be in his life—the last episode described here, in which he failed to resist her, resulted in their son Damian—but they would be rarely be as close again as she become more like her father and battled Batman for control of their son.

Of all the women in his life, none has meant more to Batman than his feline counterpart, Catwoman. Similar to Talia, Nocturna, and Poison Ivy, Selina Kyle has a darker side that for some reason appeals to the Dark Knight, but that also dooms their love. As Nocturna put it, "you love me because I'm dark and dangerous … yet if I do something dark and dangerous—you can't love me."[71] But as we know, Batman has managed to reconcile his feelings for Catwoman with her occasional criminal activities, in what has been his longest-running (albeit intermittent) relationship, and by all accounts his one true love. Alfred sees the way she lights him up and lightens his heart, and he encouraged Bruce and Selina's early relationship before either knew about the other's double life.[72] Even after they were mutually aware, Alfred appreciated what she did for him in whatever their "relationship" was. During Batman's initial encounter with Hush, after he brought Catwoman to the cave for the first time so Alfred could patch him up, Alfred told her, "you began this evening asking what you could do to help. You are doing it, Miss Kyle. And please continue to do so."[73]

Speaking of Hush, when he later wanted to strike at Batman where it would hurt the most, he went after Selina, and as they fought he told her that, compared to the other women, Bruce has "always had a softer spot for you. The dance with the forbidden partner, I suppose. Were he to take that one step over his own moral line and truly embrace everything you are, he would crumble."[74] After he subdued her, Hush used his surgical skills to remove her heart and delivered her to the local hospital for Batman to find. Batman asked several Justice Society members, Dr. Mid-Nite (an actual medical doctor) and Mr. Terrific (a scientific and technological genius), to examine her, and after he left to find Hush, Mid-Nite tells Terrific, "if you ever doubted Batman had a human side, this is proof. I don't think there's ever been another woman who has gotten so close to him. Whether he allowed her to or not."[75] After Batman defeated Hush and Selina began to recover, Batman confessed his love for her, but the relationship continues its on-and-off path. Perhaps Hush was right when he said Batman finds it difficult to ever fully embrace Catwoman because, as with the other "dark and dangerous" women he's attracted to, they remain forever out of reach of a man dedicated to a mission that condemns them.[76]

Despite his reluctance to embrace romantic love or any other sources of worldly pleasure, Batman nonetheless does occasionally enjoy glimpses of joy, which are all the better when combined with the deeper satisfaction that comes from a life with purpose. While swinging around Gotham City at 6:12 a.m., he thought to himself,

> There's a moment—right before my grapple cable goes taut … when it's just me and the ground hovering somewhere far below … a moment of freefall … a moment of total calm. I will never tell anyone how much I enjoy that moment. Or how good it feels on some mornings to see the sun rising over my city … after a full night's work. In the light of a new day, it almost feels like Gotham is lifting itself out of the mire … Feels like all my work, all my sacrifice, is worthwhile. Seeing the sun gleaming off those skyscrapers—gives me something I need to go on each night. Helps me carry on my mission.[77]

Batman doesn't need success or happiness to persist in his mission; the mission is enough.[78] But once again, he is human, and taking some little bit of joy and happiness in what we do is sometimes necessary to help carry us through when our goals, purpose, or source of meaning—our missions, if you will—weigh on us and the futility raises its ugly head and mocks us. It is to Batman's credit that he presses on, day after day, year after year, fighting crime and protecting the citizens of Gotham. It may not be good for him, but it is good for Gotham, and it is very admirable of Bruce Wayne, man and Batman.

What Being Batman Means ... to Batman

Even if he's not often happy in the sense of immediate pleasure and joy, we have acknowledged that Batman may be happier in the deeper sense of satisfaction and meaningfulness that many of us covet these days. This is an intriguing thought, especially considering that his mission, by his own admission, is an impossible and futile one that Batman will never stop pursuing. After the episode at the convenience store described earlier, when Batman failed to thwart a deadly robbery because he was busy subduing Killer Croc, he was beating himself up (as expected). When Alfred reminded him that he did some good, the Dark Knight yelled back, "It's not enough!" Although it probably landed on deaf ears, Alfred asked, "Will it ever be enough, Master Bruce?"[79] Similarly, when Leslie Thompkins asked him on another occasion, "You have such a good heart, Bruce. When are you going to give all this up?" Batman predictably answered, "When I'm finished."[80] Of course, he'll never be finished, and he knows that all too well.

But ... does he really *want* to be finished? At one level, he does, of course: He would like nothing more than for crime to be a distant memory for the residents of Gotham City, for no person to suffer again as he and his parents did that night so long ago. As the Dynamic Duo listened to a blowhard argue against costumed heroes, Robin said, "It's enough to make a guy wanna hang up his cape and stay home!" to which Batman responded, "You should look forward to that." When Robin raised the issue of Batman's dedication to his mission, the older hero said, "The day I can 'hang up my cape and stay home' is the day I'm working toward."[81] On another level, though, Batman's mission has become his *raison d'être*, his reason for being. As we saw earlier, "Batman knows full well the meaning of his life—a never-ending quest for justice. A never-ending war against evil."[82] This means that eliminating crime is not simply an end to be achieved (ideally) or pursued (more realistically), but the thing that gives his life purpose.

The concept of the meaning of one's life crosses two distinct areas of philosophy, one of which is the central focus of this book, and the other which takes us a bit outside it. The meaning of one's life is a topic of ethics insofar as it contributes to *eudaimonia*, the version of happiness mentioned earlier which is roughly translated as fulfillment or flourishing (or what modern psychologists tend to call "life satisfaction" to distinguish it from temporary, fleeting pleasures). We don't have to be utilitarians to acknowledge that happiness is of significant moral value to a good life, even if other considerations are more important in certain situations. Normal day-to-day happiness eludes the Batman, but as we've seen, he "happily" gives it up for the deeper satisfaction of pursuing a mission that is meaningful to him and gives his life purpose.

We see signs of this in several interesting episodes in which Batman has an opportunity to give up his mission, seeing the scourge of crime ended in Gotham City, but also threatening to rob him of his life's purpose and meaning. In one, an immortal killer named Matatoa, who takes on the characteristics and goals of those he kills, made Batman an offer it seemed he couldn't refuse: If Batman lets Matatoa kill him, as Matatoa explains, "I could protect your city for all eternity."[83] In the end, Batman refused, and Nightwing called him on it: "I mean, that is what you want, isn't it? To know that Gotham will be protected forever?"[84] Batman told his former protégé that Matatoa's magic was corrupted and perverted, stolen from a Maori medicine man who would have used it for healing, not killing. But the real reason for his refusal may have been more selfish: it isn't only protecting Gotham that matters to Batman, but also that *he* be the one to do it.

Batman faced a similar dilemma in an earlier tale in which Ra's al Ghul made him an offer to realize Ra's' goal of making Batman his partner in ruling the world, heir to his wealth, and husband of his daughter Talia. After freeing most of Batman's more extravagant foes from prison and Arkham Asylum, Ra's gave Batman the following proposition:

> Join me in reshaping the world, Detective, and I will help you recapture your foes … or, should you prefer, even eliminate them forever … Once they are eliminated, your obligation to Gotham would cease—freeing you to join me in the rest of the world. In the past, your sense of duty has preventing you from embracing me. Now I sweeten the temptation, by offering to release you from that duty.[85]

The choice is easier for Batman in this case: whereas Matatoa truly may have been transformed into a new savior for Gotham if the Dark Knight had accepted his offer, Ra's al Ghul "may be the worst villain of them all," as Batman told him. "I'd simply be trading a pack of demons for the devil himself."[86]

But more important, once again we see that Batman's duty, his mission, is not simply *a* goal but *his* goal, and one that he feels a special responsibility, derived from the promise he made his parents, to fulfill himself. Doctor Simon Hurt, a psychologically devious foe who claimed to be Thomas Wayne come back to life, explained to Batman that, as part of his plan, he "stemmed the tide of crime in Gotham City, undermining your reason to be" and thereby forcing his retirement.[87] Doctor Hurt knew that Batman's mission is essentially personal in nature—an aspect of his overall ethical code that, as we shall see throughout this book, drives him harder at the same time that it compromises the amount of good he can do by his own definition (such as preventing him from killing even his most murderous foes).[88]

Although it lies somewhat outside the scope of this book, the area of philosophy that focuses more directly on the meaning of life is *existentialism*. Existentialism is a loosely defined field of philosophy which explores the experience of living as a human being with purpose and meaning in a world with neither—a state of affairs that existentialists such as Søren Kierkegaard and Albert Camus quite accurately describe as *absurd*.[89] The perspective of the existentialist can seem dismal, stressing that we are born, we live, and we die, all for no preordained reason and with no given purpose. Batman is no stranger to this particular brand of malaise; as the narration to one tale read, "Sometimes life is a series of lonely nights, spent peering into darkness," suggesting existentialist philosopher Friedrich Nietzsche's famous saying that "if you gaze long into an abyss, the abyss also gazes into you."[90]

The bright side to this "empty" view of existence, however, is that we are free—*radically free*, as the existentialists put it—to determine our own path and purpose for ourselves. As Cristina Llanero, an old friend with whom Bruce Wayne reconnects in Barcelona, advised him after he played the playboy act a bit too convincingly: "Write the story of your future. Chart a destiny for yourself, Bruce Wayne. Live a life of meaning."[91] In fact, existentialists maintain that self-determination is our responsibility, under which we must live an *authentic* life steered by our own ideas of who we want to be, shunning the influence and pressure of others, whether individuals or society. Our circumstances, such as our genetic heritage and socioeconomic position, determine what we start out with in life, but it is up to us to determine what we make out of it and who we are going to be.[92]

Batman certainly knows the meaning of his life: fighting crime and protecting the citizens of Gotham City. He didn't start this way, though.

According to a bit of clever narration from the point of view of the inspirational bat who flew through the window of Wayne Manor that fateful night, Bruce Wayne "was bleeding to death, hopeless, with a bell in his hand. A lost knight without a standard. A soldier with a wounded heart. A warrior without a totem. A life without meaning."[93] Soon he would know his life's purpose, but did he decide this for himself, or did he accept his mission as his "destiny"?

There are conflicting accounts of this. Much later, when the Joker apparently killed Batman, Bruce Wayne went into hiding and contemplated the possibility of pursuing a new life without the cape and cowl. After he faced the Joker once again, however, he thought to himself (rather confrontationally), "I didn't ask for this. I— Listen to me! As if what I want even matters. This is what I do. This is who I am. This is what fate made of me. And I hate it."[94] This reflection suggests that Batman merely accepted his "fate" rather than determining his mission for himself. We heard a similar thing when he brought Jason Todd to Leslie Thompkins' clinic after being shot. When she accused him of putting the young boy in danger, he told her, "I didn't choose Jason for my work. He was chosen by it … as I was chosen … to do the work I was born to do …"[95] Finally, in (yet another) speech delivered over his parents' grave after a frustrating night of failure to eradicate crime completely from Gotham, he said:

> The beginning of your long sleep was the start of my awakening. Your deaths cast my young mind into darkness … shadowed my soul … until the loss assumed almost supernatural power. And the power … the power of your deaths … created my new life.[96]

In these quotations, we see the recurring theme of his path in life being set by circumstances rather than determined by his own will, which is far from the existentialist ideal of embracing of one's freedom and setting one's own path and purpose in life.

There remains hope for the Dark Knight, however. Later in the same cemetery soliloquy quoted above, he leaned toward self-determination, giving his own life meaning while he does the same for his parent's deaths: "I hope to use my new life to give your deaths some greater purpose, some higher meaning … by preventing other senseless deaths … dark, empty holes in the fabric of life … losses without meaning."[97] This is even clearer later while investigating the mysterious deaths of people close to the superhero community, when Batman thought to himself,

People think it's an obsession. A compulsion. As if there were an irresistible impulse to act. It's never been like that. I chose this life. I know what I'm doing. And on any given day, I could stop doing it. Today, however, isn't that day. And tomorrow won't be either.[98]

Yet another time, reflecting on the end of a case, Bruce thought to himself, "I thought that I didn't have a choice about being the Batman. That Gotham City chose me to protect her. That is wrong. Ever since the night my parents were taken from me, I made the choice."[99]

When Leslie Thompkins first learned Bruce's secret, she apologized for not raising him better, but he assured her, "what I am, I am of my own choice."[100] By making that choice, Batman decided for himself who he was to be and what he was to do, making the mission part of who he was—and this explains why he is so hesitant to give that up, even if it would mean satisfying the mission itself once and for all. This can also help us understand why he chose such a futile mission to begin with and continues to pursue it: if it's impossible to achieve his goal, it will always be a part of who he is, and therefore his life will always have its purpose as he determined it the night he swore an oath to his parents.[101]

And as so often is the case, Alfred is the voice of reason in Batman's pointy ear: sometimes a voice of ancient Greek wisdom, other times one of Eastern moderation, and yet other times one of existential insight, especially concerning the importance of self-determination. As the narration to one tale reads, "Alfred Pennyworth knows you must invest life with your own meaning. You decide which ideals you're going to serve, and then you never waver from that task."[102] In the wild and vivid dream caused by a potion that Ra's al Ghul promised would enable Batman to talk to the dead, his parents accused him of throwing his life away and becoming so wrapped up in the mission that he forgot the grief that inspired it.[103] When he awoke, he told Alfred of the dream but dismissed it as a figment of Ra's' alchemy. Alfred nonetheless asked him, if the vision had been real and his parents had asked him to give up his mission, whether he would have. When Bruce said yes, Alfred accused him of being disingenuous:

If your mother and father had begged you on bended knee to give up what you are, what you do … you would have refused them. You cast your life to a purpose, regardless of the catalyst, Bruce. Simply put, you are the Batman because it is who you are meant to be.[104]

Here, Alfred affirms that Bruce chose this life for himself, even if it was inspired by events he could not control. He made out of his life what he wanted to and what he felt he had to, and no one, not even the ghosts of his parents, could talk him out of it—unlike if he had simply accepted his mission from someone else. As one of Batman's Eastern masters told him (albeit in yet other hallucination), "You have pursued the destiny you yourself have set," and it remains his choice to follow through with it or not.[105] I don't think there's much doubt that he will continue as long as he can (and perhaps even longer), or as he told Leslie Thompkins, he'll be finished "when I'm finished."

Are *we* finished? We're only getting started! Before we move on to talk about several things Batman will or will not do in service of his broadly utilitarian mission, though, we'll have a brief intermezzo to sum up where he stands in terms of that mission, taking into account what we've seen to this point.

Notes

1 *Detective Comics* #850 (January 2009).
2 *Detective Comics* #514 (May 1982), "Haven!"
3 *Detective Comics* #568 (November 1986).
4 *Batman: Ghosts—A Legend of the Dark Knight Special* (1995).
5 *Batman: Legends of the Dark Knight* #140 (April 2001).
6 *Batman Annual* #10 (1986).
7 *Batman* #579 (July 2000).
8 *Batman* #306 (December 1978), "The Mystery Murderer of 'Mrs. Batman'!"
9 *Detective Comics* #609 (December 1989).
10 *Batman* #556 (July 1998).
11 *Detective Comics* #791 (April 2004), "The Surrogate Part One: Lost and Found."
12 *Batman* #465 (Late July 1991).
13 *Batman* #345 (March 1982). Ironically, this was also around the time he resigned from his role at the Wayne Foundation to focus exclusively on being Batman—a largely symbolic move, given that the Wayne Foundation continued in its charitable mission, but suggestive nonetheless.
14 *Batman* #556 (July 1998).
15 *Batman: Shadow of the Bat* #78 (September 1998). After the meeting, Bruce ran a play from the 1936 Frank Capra film *Mr. Deeds Goes to Town*, agreeing to finance thousands of small business loans to help Gotham's citizens get back on their feet. Soon thereafter, in *Batman* #560–562 (December 1998–February

1999), he would go to Washington to argue for Gotham's fate in a story titled "Mr. Wayne Goes to Washington," after the 1939 Capra film, *Mr. Smith Goes to Washington*. (This Capra fan approves!)

16 *Batman: Gotham Knights* #32 (October 2002), "24/7."

17 *Batman: Family* #8 (February 2003).

18 *Batman* #560–562 (December 1998–February 1999).

19 *Detective Comics* #725 (September 1998).

20 *Detective Comics* #768 (May 2002), "Purity: Part 1 of 3." (A nod to Capra's *It's a Wonderful Life*, anybody?)

21 *Batman* #464 (Early July 1991).

22 *Batman* #534 (September 1996).

23 *Batman* #427 (December 1988).

24 *Batman: The Return* #1 (January 2011).

25 *Batman Incorporated* #6 (June 2011).

26 *Batman: The Man Who Laughs* (2005).

27 *Batman: Shadow of the Bat* #16 (Early September 1993).

28 *Batman* #487 (December 1992).

29 This is pervasive, especially in more recent Batman stories featuring the Joker, including *Batman* #614 (June 2003), in which Batman beats the Joker while thinking that Dick Grayson "explained to me once that the Joker and I are forever linked in constant battle. That in some sick way, the Joker exists because of me. How I represent the order that is necessary to live in Gotham City and the Joker is the chaos that disrupts that order."

30 *Detective Comics* #600 (May 1989).

31 *Batman: The Long Halloween* #3 (February 1997).

32 Ibid. When Gordon tells him, "you saved the entire city from that deranged madman. Give yourself a pat on the back, I say," Batman simply responds, "I'll take it under advisement." (Gordon: "You do that.")

33 *Detective Comics* #780 (May 2003), "Dead Reckoning Part Four."

34 *Batman: Turning Points* #3 (January 2001). After his pep talk, Batman asked Jim, "promise me you won't say 'hogwash' anymore."

35 *Detective Comics* #457 (March 1976), "There Is No Hope in Crime Alley!"

36 If you'll allow me to step out of the story for a second: As recently as 1980, the comics showed Alfred coming to work for Bruce only after he became Batman and brought Dick Grayson to live with him and serve beside him as Robin. (See, for instance, Alfred's "origin" in *The Untold Legend of the Batman* #2, August 1980.) It is only fairly recently—after the *Crisis on Infinite Earths* in the mid-1980s and Batman's soft reboot in "Batman: Year One" (*Batman* #404–407, February–May 1986)—that it became canon that Alfred started working for the Waynes before Thomas and Martha were shot, and raised Bruce thereafter. (Leslie's history followed a similar path as she became more involved with his upbringing over the years.)

37 *Batman: Legends of the Dark Knight* #22 (September 1991).

38 *Batman: Legends of the Dark Knight* #23 (October 1991). Incidentally, at the end of this issue, a young boy thrilled to news reports of the Batman, and told his father he hopes they'll see him when their circus gets to Gotham.

39 *Detective Comics* #793 (June 2004), "The Surrogate Part Three: Deliverance."

40 *Catwoman*, vol. 3, #34 (October 2004).

41 Ibid. I would love to go into Leslie's actions at the end of this storyline—which fans thought was a horrible betrayal of her character—as well as Batman's reaction to them, the truth behind them, and the aftermath, but I would need another book to do it justice. Suffice it to say the story was convoluted and ill-conceived, and I will discuss it no more. (I said *no more!*)

42 *The Batman Chronicles* #18 (September 1999).

43 *Detective Comics* #793 (June 2004), "The Surrogate Part Three: Deliverance."

44 Ibid. (before telling him he should consider becoming a doctor, as recounted above).

45 *Detective Comics* #574 (May 1987).

46 *Detective Comics* #598 (March 1989).

47 *Batman Confidential* #1 (February 2007).

48 *Detective Comics* #447 (May 1975), "Enter: The Creeper."

49 *Robin*, vol. 4, #13 (January 1995).

50 *Robin*, vol. 4, #9 (August 1994).

51 *Batman* #0 (October 1994).

52 Ibid. But the Batman it needed would be Dick Grayson for a while, as the student replaced the teacher for the first time (*Batman* #512, November 1994); it was upon his return that Bruce and Dick had the exchange related above.

53 *Batman: Shadow of the Bat* #74 (May 1998).

54 *Batman: No Man's Land* #0 (December 1999).

55 Sometimes, of course, he doesn't have to. In one brilliant story, Batman leapt from incident to incident, discovering every time that there was no crime in progress (or, when there was, that he interfered with a police sting operation). At the end of the night, the only crime he had prevented was a case of littering; the litterer apologized and thanked Batman for watching over the city. Upon his return to the cave, Batman told his trusty butler, "Worst night of my life, Alfred. Absolutely, without a doubt, the most miserable night of my life" (*Detective Comics* #567, October 1986, "The Night of Thanks, But No Thanks!").

56 *Batman Confidential* #49 (December 2010).

57 For a concise summary of the philosophy and psychology of happiness, see Daniel Haybron, *Happiness: A Very Short Introduction* (Oxford: Oxford University Press, 2013), and for more depth on the topic, see his book *The Pursuit of Unhappiness: The Elusive Psychology of Well-Being* (Oxford: Oxford University Press, 2008).

58 *Batman: Legend of the Dark Knight Halloween Special* #1 (December 1993).
59 *Batman: Death and the Maidens* #6 (March 2004).
60 *Batman: Legends of the Dark Knight* #23 (October 1991).
61 *Detective Comics* #578 (September 1987).
62 *Batman: Full Circle* (1991).
63 *Batman: Legends of the Dark Knight* #24 (November 1991).
64 *Batman: Legends of the Dark Knight* #26 (January 1992).
65 *The Untold Legend of the Batman* #3 (September 1980).
66 *The Batman Chronicles* #19 (Winter 2000), "Got a Date with an Angel." It was then he realized that with great power comes great ... oh sorry, that's another guy.
67 *Detective Comics* #411 (May 1971), "Into the Den of the Death-Dealers!"
68 *DC Special Series* #15 (June 1978), "I Now Pronounce You Batman and Wife!"
69 *Batman* #333 (March 1981), "The China Syndrome!"
70 *Batman: Son of the Demon* (September 1987).
71 *Batman* #390 (December 1985). At the end of this story, Catwoman, now reformed, was injured, and Batman realized that although he still cared about her, his feelings had faded, and he wondered if it was because she was no longer "dark and dangerous." When she recovered, he told her he loved her, but she replied, "You loved me when I was dangerous, Batman ... and you think you love me now ... only because you know it's wrong to love someone still as dangerous as Nocturna" (*Detective Comics* #557, December 1985, "Still Beating"). (*General Hospital* has nothing on this stuff!)
72 *Batman: Dark Victory* #2 (January 2000).
73 *Wizard the Comics Magazine* #0 (September 2003), "Interlude: The Cave."
74 *Detective Comics* #848 (November 2008).
75 *Detective Comics* #849 (December 2008).
76 Nevertheless, in the current "DC Rebirth" continuity, "Bat" did take the extraordinary step of proposing to "Cat," who accepted, but the wedding did not take place—Selina selflessly left him because she feared that making him happy would compromise his effectiveness as Batman, giving him momentary happiness and denying him the deeper satisfaction he gets from his mission (and also robbing Gotham of its greatest savior). (See *Batman*, vol. 3, #50, September 2018, by writer Tom King and dozens of artists.)
77 *Detective Comics* #784 (September 2003), "Made of Wood: Part One of Three."
78 And, in reference to the recent events recounted in note 76, some believe that happiness may interfere with the mission.
79 *Batman: Gotham Knights* #3 (May 2000), "Bad Karma."
80 *Batman: Legends of the Dark Knight* #202 (Late May 2006).
81 *Detective Comics* #568 (November 1986).
82 *Batman: Shadow of the Bat* #72 (March 1998).
83 *Batman: Gotham Knights* #16 (June 2001), "Matatoa Part 1 of 2."
84 *Batman: Gotham Knights* #17 (July 2001), "Matatoa Part 2 of 2."

85 *Batman* #400 (October 1986),

86 Ibid.

87 *Batman* #681 (December 2008).

88 Batman does at times recognize his own mortality, but also acknowledges the need for the concept or identity of Batman to live on to carry on the mission. When people were trapped in a collapsed subway tunnel near the Batcave, Batman proposed letting them escape through the cave and Wayne Manor, which would mean exposing his secret. When Robin (Tim Drake) questioned this, Batman said, "The loss of Bruce Wayne's secret won't 'kill' anything, Robin. The Batman will go on—with or without the manor, with or without the cave … and even with or without me … The Batman will never die …," going on to suggest that he hopes Tim will carry on for him after his passing (*Batman* #555, June 1998).

89 See particular Albert Camus' 1942 essay *The Myth of Sisyphus* (available in many editions and collections), which famously describes Sisyphus from Greek mythology, condemned by the gods to push a boulder up a hill each day, only to watch it roll back down—much like Batman putting his villains in jail only to see them escape again.

90 *Batman: Shadow of the Bat* #72 (March 1998); Friedrich Nietzsche, *Beyond Good and Evil*, aphorism 146. Keep this in mind later when we discuss why Batman refuses to kill.

91 *Batman in Barcelona: Dragon's Knight* (July 2009).

92 For an introduction to existentialism, see Walter Kaufmann (ed.), *Existentialism from Dostoevsky to Sartre*, rev. and exp. edn. (New York: Penguin, 1975) and William Barrett, *Irrational Man: A Study in Existential Philosophy* (New York: Anchor Books, 1958). For a more contemporary treatment, see Sarah Bakewell, *At the Existentialist Café: Freedom, Being, and Apricot Cocktails* (New York: Other Press, 2016).

93 *Batman: The Return* #1 (January 2011).

94 *Batman: Legends of the Dark Knight* #68 (February 1995).

95 *Detective Comics* #574 (May 1987).

96 *Batman: Legends of the Dark Knight* #140 (April 2001).

97 Ibid.

98 *Identity Crisis* #4 (November 2004).

99 *Batman: Legend of the Dark Knight Halloween Special* #1 (December 1993) (in response to the earlier quote from this issue).

100 *Batman: Legends of the Dark Knight* #23 (October 1991).

101 There is, of course, always the possibility of adopting a new mission, but determining one's purpose in life once is hard enough, so we can forgive Batman not wanting to do it twice!

102 *Batman: Shadow of the Bat* #72 (March 1998). For more on Alfred and existentialism, see Christopher M. Drohan's chapter "Alfred, the Dark Knight of

Faith: Batman and Kierkegaard," in Mark D. White and Robert Arp (eds.), *Batman and Philosophy: The Dark Knight of the Soul* (Hoboken, NJ: Wiley Blackwell, 2008), pp. 183–197.

103 *Batman: Death and the Maidens* #6 (March 2004).
104 *Batman: Death and the Maidens* #7 (April 2004).
105 *Batman: Legends of the Dark Knight Annual* #1 (1991).

Intermezzo

In the first part of this book, we discussed a number of aspects of Batman's mission: what he tries to do, what he doesn't try to do, and how he makes hard choices within his chosen goal, as well as the value of his mission to Gotham and to himself. Generally speaking, Batman tries to do good, working to make the world a better place for those who live in it, but he does so in a very specific and limited way. Rather than work to improve the positive things in people's lives, he strives to lessen the negative ones by protecting them from the harmful effects of crime. Driven by his personal tragedy in Crime Alley, he wants to make sure no one else has to suffer the same unimaginable loss, at least not if he can help it. He devotes every waking minute (and there aren't many sleeping ones), every ounce of his energy, and every bit of his resolve, to this purpose. Because utility can be understood as the difference between the positive and negative things in life, Batman does just as much good for people by lessening their bad as he would by increasing their good. (And we mustn't forget that much, if not most, of the Wayne fortune does go to helping people, helping with the good while Batman protects them from the bad.)

However, to a hardcore advocate of utilitarianism—which we know is a very demanding and perfectionist ethical system—Batman might be falling short of how much good he could do if he made different choices about how he conducts his life. Most generally, although he does an incredible amount of good both as Batman and Bruce Wayne, there is always the possibility that he could do even more good using the entirety of his fortune—and his talents and time as a Very Smart Person—to help people in a more positive way. The incredible amount of philanthropy Wayne does engage in

Batman and Ethics, First Edition. Mark D. White.
© 2019 John Wiley & Sons Ltd. Published 2019 by John Wiley & Sons Ltd.

would certainly satisfy most advocates for increasing charity from the wealthy, but if he could do more, a utilitarian would say he should do more—and if more altruism from Bruce Wayne would do more good than the heroism of the Dark Knight, then the utilitarian would judge that an ethically necessary step.

More narrowly, the true utilitarian would also say that, if Bruce Wayne insists on devoting much of his time and energy to being Batman, he should at least be Batman where it would do the most good. Gotham City is certainly portrayed as a cesspool of crime—with or without the costumed villains that Batman may or may not attract—and Batman certainly spends most of his time in the back alleys of Gotham rather than watching over the jewels and paintings of his wealthy neighbors outside the city limits. He has made it clear that he prefers to watch out for the "little people," those who cannot afford fancy locks or private security and therefore need his help more (especially when the Gotham City police are overwhelmed themselves). Nonetheless, there may be other cities, towns, or rural areas in the United States where Batman can do more good, even if just to spread his imposing presence—and this goes just as well for the rest of world. He seemed to acknowledge this fact with the Batman Incorporated initiative, but that didn't last long before Batman was once again focused on Gotham.[1] He certainly has sentimental reasons for protecting the citizens of Gotham City mostly to the exclusion of the world on the other side of its bridges. But that sentiment, as important as it is to him, doesn't go very far in excusing a gross misallocation of his resources if he could do significantly more good elsewhere.

Finally, some of the choices he makes in specific situations don't reflect what an ideal utilitarian would do, all things considered. Remember that one of the most important and noble aspects of utilitarianism is that it treats each person's well-being equally in the calculation of total utility. In general, then, saving more people rather than fewer people is better, but when he must choose between saving one person or another, there is often no clear way to decide.

But it gets more complicated. Just because each person's utility is counted equally in the total does not imply that any one person's utility is actually equal to any other person's utility. One person may enjoy life more than another, and technically the first person's life would contribute more to total utility and would therefore be more "important" in terms of increasing the total (and therefore more important to protect). Luckily for the anxious ethicist, this is impossible to know for sure. We can't compare one person's level of utility with another's, like we can with height or weight. Happiness, well-being, or utility are inherently vague and subjective ideas, and can't be expressed or measured precisely enough to make meaningful comparisons between persons. So we are safe in acting as if each person has equal happiness and in that sense contributes the same amount to total utility.

But that's not all. While we can assume for the sake of argument that each person enjoys roughly the same utility as the next, not every person contributes the same amount of utility to society through their actions. Some people add more to society than others—think of the doctors who cure diseases, the teachers who educate and inspire us, and all the real-world heroes who save lives, just to name a few. As repugnant as it may sound, they add more utility to the total than many other people, regardless of whether they're "better" people in the sense of moral worth or virtue. (Even Bruce Wayne's fellow billionaire Lex Luthor provides thousands of LexCorp employees with jobs.) This is the basis for hypothetical "lifeboat dilemmas," in which a small group of people can't all survive and they must decide somehow which of them should be sacrificed to save the rest—dilemmas which usually come down to decisions regarding worth, despite our automatic and normally unspoken assumption that each human life is equally valuable.[2]

Batman shares this belief in the unquestionable and absolute sanctity of all life, passed down from his father the surgeon, who would never turn down an opportunity to save someone no matter how little they contributed to society—or, in the case of criminals, how much they took from it. And this is a noble position, motivating Batman to expend the same effort to save a homeless person as he would a socialite. It is a position that puts the essential dignity of each and every person above their "practical" value to society. But as such, it is not a utilitarian position, and it does not serve the cause of total well-being and utility. Certainly, we can infer from the many times Batman puts his own life at risk to save others that he does not regard his life to be of any more value than anyone else's—which is understandable given his own doubts about the value of what he does.

Nowhere is this as obvious as when Batman saves the life of a vicious murderer, including many of his arch-foes, such as the Joker and the Black Mask, as well as more common thugs and mob bosses. As much as he believes that every human life has value, that even the most heinous criminal is redeemable, he also realizes that some people will kill if they have a chance, which, given the apparent revolving door in the Gotham City criminal justice system, is inevitable. If he knows this—and we know he does, based on the passages quoted earlier—then he knows that saving the life of a killer will most likely result in more deaths down the road that he may not be able to prevent. We've seen that, when given the choice in the moment to save an innocent person or a criminal, he will choose the former. But his reasoning doesn't seem to extend through time, which would justify saving one or more innocent lives down the road by letting a likely murderer die now (or, as we'll see in the next part of the book, by killing the murderer).

Perhaps it is exactly the length of time involved that leads Batman to act differently in these cases. We saw, after he saved Black Mask's life, that he realized that he must take responsibility for stopping him from killing again, even though he can't be sure he can prevent further murders. But he also believes people, even Black Mask and the Joker, are redeemable. If this belief is strong enough, then every murderer he saves is a candidate for redemption with no loss of life down the road. Again, this is a noble and beautiful sentiment, and one that may be surprising coming from a man who regularly encounters the vilest scum imaginable. And given the nature of this scum, his faith seems misplaced—with horribly tragic consequences in terms of the innocent people he puts in the way of danger. Maintaining this belief in the good in all people may help keep him going in his otherwise futile mission, but he must ask himself: Is it worth the cost?

We will have occasion to discuss this issue in bolder terms when we talk about Batman's one firm rule, no killing, which has the same implications regarding the intentional sacrifice of innocent life. It also involves a more direct and personal role of the part of the Dark Knight, and invokes a type of ethics, *deontology*, that emphasizes principles and rules rather than outcomes and consequences. It is this moral approach that treats each life as equally deserving of value and consideration despite differing effects on total utility, and helps us understand this deviation from his otherwise utilitarian mission of saving as many lives as he can.

Even though he is a fictional superhero, Batman operates in a fairly realistic world in which choices are not easy and even the best decisions often have tragic consequences. This makes Batman a lot like you and me, even if we don't wear capes or fight criminals. We all make our way through life with our own moral codes, and chances are that our moral codes are not as clear-cut as those that philosophers like me teach and write about (but, to be honest, rarely live up to). If you consider yourself a utilitarian, trying to do the most good in the world that you can, then you know that making decisions with uncertain impacts on the people around you, both near and far, is an incredible task and burden. Even if you're devoted to making the world a better place in terms of happiness, well-being, or utility, you're never going to do it perfectly, nor could you ever know if you did. It's enough to do the best you can—and remember that your happiness matters too.

This is the benefit of examining Batman's own brand of utilitarianism and finding it decidedly imperfect in so many ways: We see that it mirrors our own imperfect moral codes and behavior. This is yet another way in which he is one of the most realistic superheroes in comics, TV, movies, and animation. But we shouldn't rest comfortably in this moral imperfection. In this respect, Batman isn't a role model to be emulated. Having an inconsistent moral code is not a good thing, and signals a failure to successfully integrate your moral beliefs and actions. If you're going to be a utilitarian, you do have an obligation to put some effort into trying to do the right thing, and if you decide to limit those efforts in some way, as Batman does, you need to defend that. You also can't regularly or repeatedly take actions that you know don't increase utility, without justification, and still claim to be a utilitarian.

Batman doesn't claim to be a utilitarian, of course, but he does claim to have a mission to save lives, and his continued devotion to saving the lives of killers—and putting young boys, like his Robins, into danger—is not consistent with that claim. The need for moral consistency that Batman lacks is the central message of this book. Batman doesn't have it all right, just like us, but that doesn't mean he can't do better—he can.

And so can we.

Notes

1   Admittedly, the minor detail of the entire DC Universe being rebooted in 2011 may have had a little to do with that.

2   For a Batman tale very similar to a lifeboat dilemma, see *Batman* #477–478 (May 1992), in which Batman was trapped with two other people in an airtight vault and they were forced to decide which person they would sacrifice to save the other two. (We'll discuss this story more in Chapter 7.)

PART II

What Batman Is Willing to Do—and What He Isn't

We spent the first part of the book talking about what Batman tries to do in general: fight crime and save innocent people from the tragedy and suffering it causes. We talked about way he limits this mission, such as focusing on Gotham City, as well as choices he makes regarding which criminals to fight and which people to save, choices that are often difficult and sometimes controversial, especially when it leads him to save criminals who will likely go on to hurt more innocent people.

The similarity of this last point to Batman's famous rule against killing even his most homicidal foes leads us into the second part of this book. Here, we focus on specific morally questionable actions Batman will or will not engage in as part of his mission. Some of them, such as violence, torture, and lawbreaking in general, support the mission but do so by violating an important moral rule or principle. His refusal to kill, on the other hand, follows an obvious moral principle but, like saving the lives of murderers, compromises the mission by putting more innocent lives in danger.

As we will see, Batman may have reasonable explanations for each of his questionable actions, but taken together they are often morally inconsistent. For example, he refuses to kill even the most vicious murderers, but he is perfectly willing to use extreme violence and to torture people for information—often people that haven't even been implicated in a crime, as long as they might have information Batman needs to catch someone who has. Although these actions may further his mission to fight crime and save people, it is nonetheless behavior that is widely regarded as immoral, *especially* when practiced on people who haven't done anything wrong (not that it would necessarily be justified or excused if they had). In other words,

Batman and Ethics, First Edition. Mark D. White.
© 2019 John Wiley & Sons Ltd. Published 2019 by John Wiley & Sons Ltd.

Batman is using these people simply as means to his own ends, a common criticism of utilitarianism that points instead to *deontology*, the ethical school that grounds the second half of this book.

Furthermore, the fact that he will violate many moral principles but *not* the one against killing, which some would argue is less heinous than torture, again reveals Batman's moral code to be a bit confused—even more so than his utilitarianism itself. The waters of Gotham Harbor get even murkier as we explore the specific actions of the bat …

5

Deontology and the Rules

Although Batman's overall mission is grounded in utilitarianism, many actions he takes in pursuit of it are questionable from the view of commonsense morality. After all, we normally consider violence, torture, and lawbreaking to be wrong in a basic sense, regardless of the good intentions behind them or positive consequences resulting from them. This is not to say such behavior can never be justified, but the bar is often significantly higher than simply pointing to the good outcomes, which would exemplify the "ends justify the means" reasoning that is one of the main criticisms of utilitarianism.

In this short chapter, we'll introduce an alternative to utilitarianism known as *deontology*, which focuses on issues of right and wrong, based on moral principle, rather than good and bad (or better and worse), based on outcomes. We'll also explore the contrasts between these two schools of ethics, which form a large part of the conflict in Batman's moral code—and our own. We'll see that deontology offers a firm grounding for our intuitive feelings of the wrongness of some actions, which will lay the foundation for our discussion of these various actions of the Dark Knight that some may find particularly disturbing—as well as the one rule he (almost) never breaks, despite the potentially enormous number of lives he could save if he did.

The Deontological Knight

In general, deontology judges the morality of an action based on the nature of the act itself rather than by its consequences in a particular situation.[1] For example, a deontologist would be likely to say that telling a lie is wrong in

Batman and Ethics, First Edition. Mark D. White.
© 2019 John Wiley & Sons Ltd. Published 2019 by John Wiley & Sons Ltd.

general, regardless of the circumstances in a specific case, whereas a utilitarian would say that telling a lie in a particular situation would be wrong only if it led to negative consequences in that case. This doesn't give utilitarians enough credit, though. They would be likely to agree that lying is wrong in general, not because it violates a moral principle, but because it *usually* leads to negative consequences, even if on rare occasions a lie may be beneficial. In other words, utilitarianism can lead to rules of thumb against behavior that leads to negative outcomes more often than not, but still leaves the possibility open that such behavior might be justified in particular situations.

This dependence of utilitarianism on individual circumstances lends it a certain sense of contingency. After all, actions like lying are not judged by utilitarians to be *always wrong*, but just *usually bad*, and even the utilitarian that takes this to heart will still be tempted—if not obligated—to consider whether a lie in a particular case might lead to higher utility. Take Batman's attitude toward lying, for instance: generally he is an honest person, but he has no problem keeping his identity as Bruce Wayne a secret and lying to protect it. Even if he acknowledges the utilitarian costs of lying in general, he justifies that significant and ongoing lie as protecting his loved ones and the mission itself. (We'll talk more about this in the conclusion to the book.)

Deontology, however, tends to be more firm, declaring certain actions right or wrong depending on something intrinsic to the act itself, which doesn't vary with individual circumstances. Lying is wrong, full stop, even if a lie in a specific instance would do a lot of good. This isn't to say that lying can never be justified, but it would normally only be justified by recourse to another moral principle that might be violated. If Batman had made a promise to Alfred that he would never reveal his true identity, for example, then keeping that promise might serve as a justification for lying that is based on principle rather than consequences.

But exactly what is it about an action that makes it right or wrong if not its consequences? There are many different varieties of deontology, but most of them hold actions up to some moral principle, right, or duty, to judge it as right or wrong. One possible principle, from the work of the most famous deontologist, Immanuel Kant, is the respect owed to each and every person, based on a belief in their essential dignity or worth. Lying would violate this due respect regardless of the circumstances around the lie or the intent behind it, which implies a duty not to lie. According to one version of Kant's famous categorical imperative (his formulation of "the moral law"), a person must always "act in such a way that you treat humanity, whether in your own person or in the person of another, always at the same time as an end and never simply as a means."[2] When you lie to someone, according to Kant, you use them merely as a means to your own end, regardless of how noble that end may be. Everyone deserves to be treated as an "end-in-themselves," which demands that they not be deceived or coerced (the two general ways people can be used merely as means).

Deontological principles or rules can be based on many other factors as well. W.D. Ross, another prominent deontologist, believed that right and wrong were intuitive, in the sense that "everyone knows" lying is wrong, and this alone is enough to ground a duty not to lie.[3] Individuals' deontological principles can also be based on deeply held sentiments. For instance, Batman's belief in the sanctity of life grounds his refusal to kill or let someone die if he can prevent it, and his deep hatred of guns makes him uncomfortable with using them (although he has on occasion when he thought it necessary).[4] He also teaches his rule against guns to his Robins (while nonetheless training them in their use). During a tough fight with the Beast, Tim Drake saw a gun nearby and thought, "Maybe this is the time to think about survival. Maybe this is one of those times the rules don't count. No. The rules always count."[5] Tim held this rule inviolable, even when it might have increased his chances of winning the fight sooner. This isn't to say that deontologists are unreasonably rigid—one principle can be overridden by another more important principle—but their judgments are much less likely to change than those of utilitarians according to the circumstances of a specific moral dilemma.

Some of you are undoubtedly thinking: "Why, these moral principles are just made up! They're arbitrary and *ad hoc*, so why should anybody adhere to them?" That's a great point. But *every* moral system has to start with at least one assumption or axiom that is taken for granted and from which the rest of the system is derived. With deontology it's some set of moral principles, rights, or duties. With utilitarianism, it's the importance of utility or the "good" that results from actions, which is no less arbitrary as a starting point than principles are for deontology. The intrinsic ethical value of consequences may seem natural, but this doesn't make it any less arbitrary; others may think respect for persons or the sanctity of life is just as natural. Just because something seems "natural" doesn't make it right or wrong—this is what philosophers call the *naturalistic fallacy*. If you want to believe that what makes things right is whether they're natural, then fine, but others may not accept that "natural" has ethical value. To argue simply that something's right *because* it's natural is to *beg the question* or assume your conclusions ("the natural is best because it's natural").[6]

The Brave and the Bold: Utilitarianism vs. Deontology

Deontology is an important school of ethics in and of itself, but for our purposes it is enough to judge the actions Batman will or will not take in pursuit of his mission. In general, we could say that Batman's deontological side—chiefly the part of him that refuses to kill or let someone die, even if they threaten to take more lives in the future—tempers his otherwise single-minded utilitarian drive to stop crime and save lives. This is most apparent when we contrast Batman with other self-professed heroes who *are* willing to kill to stop criminals once and for all, including run-of-the-mill vigilantes or even potential allies such as Jean-Paul Valley and the Huntress who are willing to cross the line that their mentor isn't.

Why does utilitarianism need to be restrained anyway? What could be wrong with an ethical system that guides you to do the most good you can do? Sometimes acting for the sake of the greater good involves doing things that are morally questionable from a deontological point of view. We've already seen this in our discussion of Batman saving criminals and murderers: Batman feels it would be wrong to let them die, even though it would prevent much needless pain and death in the future. A simple utilitarian analysis might say to let them die and the world will be a better place (in terms of higher total utility), but Batman feels it would be wrong to let a person die if he can save them. In this case, his principle of the sanctity of life prevents him from letting a person die—or, as we'll see in the next chapter, killing them himself—even though doing so might promote overall utility and good.

To explore the worst-case scenario associated with utilitarianism, consider a person or group that pursues their vision of the greater good with no deontological "filters" whatsoever. Lucky for us, we have just such a person in the world of Batman: Ra's al Ghul, the Demon's Head. Like the man he simply calls "Detective," Ra's has a mission: to save the earth from the plague that is humanity. As he told his daughter Talia after his latest dip in the life-restoring Lazarus Pit, "I must begin putting into effect my plan ... my plans to restore harmony to our sad planet! ... I have a vision ... of an earth as clean and pure as a snow-swept mountain ... or the desert outside."[7] Ra's said the same thing to Batman before he described his plan to use the sun's rays, filtered through a special lens into a destructive beam, to obliterate all human life on earth with "a liquid which, when ingested, would react to the beam, destroying all living tissue."[8] Other times, he seems to have more humane goals—"An end to hunger. An end to disease.

An end to crime"—all leading to his vision of "a pristine world," which may or may not include any ... you know ... people.[9] Yet other times, Ra's seems content to rule the world, "a better world, sailing a calmer course, a perfect destiny ... who better to chart the future?" When Batman accused him of doing so "by trammeling the spirits of everyone alive—the good right along with the bad," Ra's responded, "Perhaps ... and perhaps such is the price of harmony."[10]

It is the utilitarian language of a "price to be paid" for a better world that is repugnant to a deontologist, who normally makes no concessions to a moral wrong based on its positive consequences. Even if deontologists were willing to bend on this point—and we'll see later in what circumstances they might—there is still a concern if that "price" is too high or is "paid" by someone other than the one making the choice. As Ra's tried to convince his other daughter, Nyssa, to join him, she argued that the price was too high: "The cities you have razed, the villages you have let be devoured by the desert. The thousands lost to time, remembered only by us. It is too much." Ra's replied, "The work pains me as much as it pains you, Nyssa. I feel the pain of every death I cause," but, he argued, "it is for a greater good. Everything I have done, I do for the greater good."[11] Naturally, he did not have to pay this price himself (aside from the "pain" he "feels").

In general, though, the point isn't that the price is too high compared to the benefits, which would be a normal utilitarian calculation, and one that Ra's would presumably think works out in his favor. It is that the success of his goal depends on doing things that are wrong in a deontological sense: chiefly, the sacrifice of innocent lives. When Batman caught Vox, a terrorist who threatened to blow up Wayne Tower, Vox said, "I thought you of all people would understand. Have you never been so moved, so struck by an injustice that you'd do anything to correct it?" Batman replied, "No injustice—is worth the slaughter of innocents."[12] When Ra's offered to kill all of Batman's enemies to "release him from his duty," freeing him to join Ra's in ruling the world, Batman refused (of course), saying he would never consent to mass murder, "even of fiends like the Joker."[13] In fact, Batman does not believe that human life can be "priced" at all. After Bruce prevented socialite Camille Baden-Smythe's security forces from firing into the crowd on the yacht in an effort to recover a diamond worth six million dollars, she berated him for interfering. When he explained that "I just saved you from a number of wrongful death lawsuits, Camille," she argued that "my lawyers could have settled them for a lot less than six million!" He asked her, "Is the value of a human life negotiable?" to which she answered,

"There isn't anything under the sun that's not negotiable."[14] To Batman, like Immanuel Kant, human life is not to be priced, especially to weigh it against mere things, even six-million-dollar diamonds or, in Ra's case, bringing about a "pristine earth."[15]

Unlike Ra's, there are things Batman will not do in service of his mission, wrongful acts that are not justified by the good consequences that may result from them. Ra's may be a twisted caricature of a utilitarian—for one, it is unclear exactly whose utility he seeks to maximize, given that he plans to wipe out *all the people*—but he does exemplify the main critique of utilitarianism, that the "ends justify the means." Ra's is willing to eliminate the human race to achieve his dream of a "pristine Earth," and however pained he may be by this loss, it is not his loss to bear. Batman often invokes this point about ends and means in the case of vigilantes. For example, when he and Jason Todd debated about whether the new Robin should go out on a dangerous mission to find a murderous vigilante named Tommy Carma, Jason argued that "danger is what my job's supposed to be about!" Batman responded, "Not danger, Jason. Justice. Let's not confuse the ends with the means. Tommy Carma's confusion about the ends and the means is what makes him a very dangerous man."[16] Unlike vigilantes who practice this philosophy on a small scale, or Ra's who takes it global, Batman believes that no life is worth sacrificing for a case, no matter how worthy (even, as we've seen, the protection of other lives, a wrinkle we'll explore in the coming pages).

On this point, Ra's al Ghul's own "ends justify the means" thinking invokes one of the strongest arguments against utilitarianism: that it could justify the deliberate sacrifice of a few innocent lives to save many others. As the typical nightmare scenario goes, a benevolent dictatorship faces a popular uprising that threatens to turn violent and could result in the deaths of many protestors (as well as police and security forces). The government considers picking a random person out of the crowd and publicly executing him to instill fear in the crowd and stop the protest. The argument is that the sacrifice of one innocent life will prevent the deaths of many more—or more generally, the survival of the many justifies the sacrifice of the few.[17] We see a milder version of this when Batman was fighting a mind-controlled mob and was "trying not to injure any of them permanently. But maintaining the status quo wasn't a workable strategy. I'd have to break something." He breaks the little finger of a nearby man, which makes the rest back away.[18] This doesn't rise to the level of sacrificing one life to save many, of course, but it shares the spirit of intentionally doing a little harm to prevent much more.

To a utilitarian, this is simple logic—more lives saved versus fewer—applied to a tragic dilemma with no "good" solution. To a deontologist, however, it represents a wrongful action to matter how beneficial the consequences. As Batman said in a similar situation, "I've never taken it upon myself to decide who lives and who dies. I never threw another corpse on the pile, thinking, 'This will show them all! This will bring everyone to their senses!' That's a sick idea from an evil mind."[19] Utilitarians normally distance themselves from the implications of this thought experiment in various ways, arguing that it's unrealistic or overly simplistic. It avoids issues of responsibility on the part of the government for whatever inspired the citizens to revolt, or it neglects the fact that, in the long run, random executions will likely worsen total utility by causing the people's trust in the government to deteriorate even further. But these arguments are all contingent on other circumstances in the hypothetical situation and do not get to the core issue: does utilitarianism allow for wrongful acts in the service of total utility? And if it does, is this a problem?

Despite the angelic glow I may have given the Dark Knight in the preceding contrast with the man literally called the Demon's Head, Batman does not have an unambiguous answer to this question. He is steadfast in following one rule—against killing or failing to save a life—but he is very comfortable breaking other ones, such as engaging in violence and torture, lying, and breaking the law. Actually, Batman neatly summarized the extent of his deontological limitations when he told the Huntress (hopefully to the tune of a Meat Loaf song), "I'll do whatever it takes short of killing to preserve what I do."[20] There isn't much the Batman won't do in the fight against crime, including many acts that would ordinarily be considered criminal and immoral in themselves. As we go through these acts (including Batman's sole no-no), we'll discuss the implications of each one for his mission as well as his moral integrity. And we just may find that the most troubling aspect of his deontology is the one rule he won't break—and why.

Notes

1   For more on deontology, see Larry Alexander and Michael S. Moore's entry in the *Stanford Encyclopedia of Philosophy*, at https://plato.stanford.edu/entries/ethics-deontological/.
2   Immanuel Kant, *Grounding for the Metaphysics of Morals*, trans. James W. Ellington (Indianapolis, IN: Hackett Publishing Company, 1785/1993), p. 429.

As he explains in *Grounding*, Kant derives the dignity of persons from their *autonomy*, the capacity of every rational being to make decisions in accordance with the moral law despite inclinations to the contrary. For more, see Roger J. Sullivan, *An Introduction to Kant's Ethics* (Cambridge: Cambridge University Press, 1994).

3 W.D. Ross, *The Right and the Good* (Oxford: Oxford University Press, 1930). The title reflects the popular characterization of the contrast between deontology ("the right") and utilitarianism ("the good").

4 For example, Batman used a rifle to stop an assassin in *Detective Comics* #710 (June 1997); later he told Robin and Alfred that Henri Ducard trained him in long-range sniping (!). (And of course, he killed Darkseid with a gun in *Final Crisis* #6, January 2009, but he told the evil god from Apokolips that it was a "once-in-a-lifetime exception.") For a great debate between Batman and Catwoman over the issues of guns, see *Batman/Catwoman: Trail of the Gun* #1–2 (October–November 2004).

5 *Robin*, vol. 4, #14 (February 1995). We see Batman training Jason Todd in the use of guns in *Batman* #410 (August 1987).

6 This doesn't even scratch the surface of how we decide that something's "natural," which can too easily mask biases, such as believing that female empowerment or homosexuality aren't natural, when both can be regarded as much more natural than, say, air travel, cell phones, or—*gasp*—Batman.

7 *Batman* #244 (September 1972), "The Demon Lives Again!"

8 *Batman Annual* #8 (1982).

9 *Batman: Death and the Maidens* #1 (October 2003).

10 *Batman* #400 (October 1986).

11 *Batman: Death and the Maidens* #2 (November 2003). As opposed to Bryan Adams, who would say "everything I have done, I do it for the greater good."

12 *Detective Comics* #830 (Late May 2007).

13 *Batman* #400 (October 1986).

14 *Batman* #579 (July 2000).

15 Kant famously used dignity to differentiate between person and things: "whatever has a price can be replaced by something else as its equivalent … whatever is above all price, and therefore admits of no equivalent, has a dignity" (*Grounding*, p. 434).

16 *Batman* #402 (December 1986).

17 Readers of Alan Moore and Dave Gibbons' 1986–1987 series *Watchmen* (or the 2009 film, directed by Zack Snyder) will see Ozymandias' plan as another example of this.

18 *Hawkgirl* #63 (June 2007).

19 *Batman* #644 (Late October 2005).

20 *Batman: Gotham Knights* #40 (2003), "Knight Moves Part Three: Checkmate."

6

Killing

In case I didn't mention it earlier, Batman does not kill. As the narration to one retelling of his origin read, his mission is to "stop crime and prevent horror," but with the proviso that "because the lives lost were so precious, he decided all life was so. He would therefore use force when necessary, but he would never kill …"[1] This is not to say he doesn't want to. Several months after he began his mission, he recorded in his journal:

> I have one hard and fast rule: I will not kill—though often every fiber yearns to dispense that ultimate sanction. It was murder that brought me to this pass—the murder of two innocents—and I will not go down that road. When the sanctity of human life no longer has meaning, that way does lie insanity.[2]

Another time, while Batman dragged an injured Joker to safety, his most viciously homicidal foe asked him if he was finally going to kill him. Batman answered no, "because if I did, I'd be violating the belief that has sustained me all these years. I believe in the absolute sacredness of human life. I may not really believe in anything else."[3]

Everyone in Batman's world and ours knows about his refusal to kill. His subordinates all know it, because all Robins, Batgirls, and other assorted costumed confederates are trained not to kill. As Tim Drake was helping to train Jean-Paul Valley, long before the former assassin would assume the mantle of the bat, Jean-Paul wished for his sword, at which point Tim told him, "there's one thing you've gotta know … Batman never kills. Life is sacred to him. In his book, life even beats out justice," a priority which we

Batman and Ethics, First Edition. Mark D. White.
© 2019 John Wiley & Sons Ltd. Published 2019 by John Wiley & Sons Ltd.

saw in our discussion of saving lives even at the cost of letting criminals escape.[4] Tim had to say the same thing to Bruce's son Damian soon after their first meeting, when the young Wayne showed up in the Batcave carrying the head of a criminal who was holding the mayor hostage: "You can't do that! We don't kill!"[5] And even Batman's enemies know it (and often use it against him). When Bane first met Batman after observing and studying his behavior, he said, "You do not kill. That is strange. A creature cloaked in nightmare. A figure of terror in a city of terror. And yet you will not break the sixth commandment."[6]

All of these quotations combine to form a definite statement of his position on killing. The rule itself is simple, but the ramifications of it for his moral character are anything but. In this chapter we will explore how he enforces this rule on his crimefighting partners, the various reasons behind it—which go far beyond the sanctity of life—and most important, what it means for his mission. Did I mention we'll enjoy a trolley ride in the process? So much fun ahead.

Thou Shalt Not Kill

Just as revealing as Batman's reflections and statements about his refusal to kill are the lengths to which he goes to ensure that no one that works with him uses lethal measures either. For example, one of the clearest signs that Jason Todd was losing control was when Batman suspected him of tossing a criminal off a fire escape (which Jason denied), eventually leading Batman to "ground" his new Robin.[7] Much later, Jason openly defied Batman's code, telling his former mentor, "You never cross that line. But I will. Death will come to those who deserve death. And death may come to those who stand in my way of doing what's right."[8] After Batman asked the Huntress if she was responsible for the recent death of an important mob figure—and she told him to "go to hell"—he promised, "If I find out there's blood on your hands … I'll take you down myself."[9] In one of his more surreal moments, Batman even stopped the Demon Etrigan from killing two criminals, saying "These two may be evil, but they'll get the justice decreed by law—not die at some mad demon's whim!"[10]

Of course, he tries to prevent his young protégés from ever developing a taste for killing. When Arthur Brown, the Cluemaster, takes the young hero Spoiler hostage and threatens to kill her, Batman tells Brown that Spoiler is actually his daughter Stephanie, which surprises him enough for Spoiler to subdue him. When Spoiler explained that her father destroyed her life and she wants to kill him, Batman told her, "He hurt you. But if you kill him it won't be Arthur Brown who destroyed your life. It will be you," and she stopped.[11] Later we see that Spoiler learned this lesson well: during the city-wide gang war, Black Mask captured and tortured her. When she escaped and pulled his own gun on him, Black Mask goaded her, even pointing out the reasons she *should* kill him: "You beat me. You got me. Now all you've got left to do is pull the trigger and you save all those lives. And everyone I might kill after tonight. All you have to do to decide to become judge, jury, and executioner." But Spoiler told him, "I could do it. I could! Maybe even I should. But that would mean ignoring everything Batman has taught me. And I've already done too much to betray his trust" (including setting off the gang war itself).[12]

Batman also takes steps to reform past killers. When Batman started training Jean-Paul Valley, he was well aware of his past as an assassin. When Robin asked, "So we're taking him under wing to counteract his brainwash programming?" Batman replied, "Something like that. Call it an attempt to … guide and mold him … more naturally," to which Robin added, "And to cut a potential killer off at the pass."[13] Similarly, when the mysterious Cassandra Cain appeared during the No Man's Land period and ingratiated herself first to Barbara Gordon and then to Batman, he defended her to a skeptical Nightwing:

> She has no name. Her father is the assassin Cain. He raised her to be a perfect killer, the ultimate fighter. She rebelled. Fled with him. She came here. Oracle found her. She's been learning for the last five months. The young woman is as well-trained and committed as any of you. She will never take a life. She will never surrender a fight.

When Nightwing asked how he could be so certain, Batman replied, "Her father was one of the men who trained me," and when Robin questioned this, Batman continued, "Knowing how to kill doesn't mean you must kill. That's why she left him. That's why she's here, now."[14] Batman's faith in Cassandra—who would soon become Batgirl under Barbara Gordon's tutelage—is reminiscent of his own training with Shiva after Bane broke his back, during which he refused to kill even though she trained him to do just that.[15]

Batman's position on the sanctity of life and his resulting refusal to kill puts him at clear odds with anybody who would kill in the name of fighting crime or battling evil. Sometimes they are random thugs who consider themselves vigilantes. One such young man was the Electrocutioner, who while getting beaten up by the Batman told him, "we're two of a kind, you and I! We're both dedicated to ridding the world of the human parasites—that prey on—" but Batman cut him off, asking him, "Me? On your side? On the side of a sadistic, bloodthirsty self-appointed executioner? Are you out of your mind? They'll be making snowmen in hell before I'm ever on your side, mister!"[16] Such "noble" killers typically justify their actions based on their "final" results, but this logic doesn't work well with Batman, who has certainly considered this argument time and time again himself. When a group of self-styled vigilantes told Batman, "You got no gripe with us? We're on the same side!" Batman told them, "Never count me on the side of murderers." Nonetheless, they defended themselves: "You call it murder—we call it justice! Rough—but more effective than your brand."[17] Others justify their actions by focusing on the victims of violent crime: the religious leader and vigilante known as the Deacon argued with Batman about the revolving door of the criminal justice system that "doesn't work for the poor and unfortunate innocent!"[18] Batman has no disagreement with these people's concerns, which he shares, but only with the way they execute them. (No pun intended.)

It isn't just the occasional citizen who decides to use violent means to stem the scourge of crime, though—sometimes it's fellow heroes that Batman considers protégés, successors, or colleagues. We've already seen that he disapproves of the Huntress's propensity to kill, motivated by her experience as a young child seeing her parents, members of a prominent organized crime family in Gotham, gunned down by a rival mob.[19] When Batman came across the Huntress bludgeoning a criminal, he told her, "I won't let you cripple this man. No matter what he's done." When Huntress told him, "Actually, I was going to kill him," he said, "Not in my town." Unlike most of Batman's partners, Huntress didn't accept this mandate, telling him, "This has opened my eyes, Batman. I don't think I want to be part of your happy little family. Not if the rules mean letting murdering trash like this walk the streets."[20] Later, Batman invited the Huntress to join the Justice League of America to help combat her violent impulse, but then ejected her when he witnessed her about to kill the villain Prometheus: "I don't need killers in the League. Consider your JLA membership revoked."[21]

Jean-Paul Valley, whom Batman chose as his successor after his back was broken by Bane, also considered killing to be an acceptable tool in fighting crime. After he left the villain Abattoir to die, the narration read, "Tonight, a line has been crossed. Tonight, for the first time, a man has died because of him … He doesn't feel good, and he doesn't feel bad. Jean-Paul Valley feels righteous."[22] While Bruce Wayne was away recuperating, it fell to Jim Gordon to confront Valley, who didn't fool him for a second. "The Batman I know—not that I know him very well!—would never bring dishonor to the cause he serves. Batman would never commit murder!" Valley defended himself:

> So one man died. Against that death, weigh this: Abattoir had already slaugh-tered at least twenty-five people. His insanity was incurable. He seems to escape from jail at will. How many more do you think he'd have killed? I didn't murder him … I left him to die so the decent folk of Gotham need never fear him again!

When Jim argued that it wasn't Valley's decision to make, but was up to the legal system, Valley told him that Batman had always worked outside the law, and "your rules do not apply to me!" When Jim asked Valley if he would kill again, the new Batman answered, "I'm telling you I'll carry out my mission—my crusade—using whatever means I deem fit!"[23] Eventually, as we've seen, Bruce Wayne returned from recuperation (and some time train-ing with Lady Shiva) to take Valley down, but continued training him to resist his assassin's training and value life as much as the true Batman does.[24]

It is not only Batman's protégés that cross the line into killing, but his peers in the superhero community as well. The most startling case may be the Amazing Amazon herself, Wonder Woman, and her execution of Maxwell Lord, a megalomaniac with psychic abilities. Lord managed to take control of Superman's mind and made him believe that his greatest foes, such as Lex Luthor, Brainiac, and Doomsday, killed several of his loved ones, including his wife Lois Lane. Superman flew into a rage against those he thought were the murderers, but in actuality he attacked a very surprised Batman, whom he nearly killed. Wonder Woman intervened just in time to save the Dark Knight's life, and then confronted Lord and Superman. Lord forced Superman to attack Wonder Woman, but then stopped him, just to prove he could. Lord told Wonder Woman, while bound by the lasso of truth, "The next time he'll kill Batman … or Lois … or you. You think I've lied to you but I haven't. I can't. He's mine. I'll never let him go." Wonder Woman ordered Lord to tell her how she could stop him, and when he said, "Kill me," she did, with a dead-eye stare.[25]

Soon thereafter, Wonder Woman visited Batman to explain—and justify—what she did. "I made my decision," she told him. "I stand by it as the proper one." She made an important distinction between her remorse over the tragic dilemma she found herself in and her conviction that the choice she made was right: "I was pained by what had happened. I regretted that there had been a need for Max Lord's death. But I was not sorry for what I had done, I shed no tears for my actions." Regardless of how she arrived at the decision, once she determined it was the right thing to do, she resolved to do it: "It was a question of doing what needs to be done. A question of doing it without hesitation. I know you understand that, more than most." She appealed directly to Batman's own morality, integrity, and confidence when she said, "Like you, I do not often find myself justifying my actions. I do not often find myself needing to, after all." Nonetheless, she argued in conclusion that "I have told you that I am not ashamed of what I have done. I did what was required to save not only Kal, but countless others."[26]

Despite Wonder Woman's candid and heartfelt plea, Bruce nonetheless uttered just two short words: "Get out." Even considering the undeniably high stakes and the impossible position Lord put Wonder Woman in, Bruce could not see a way to excuse what she did. Later, when she argued again that "there was no choice," he replied that "there's always a choice for people like us," implying that people with their powers, abilities, and resources should be able to find a way out of a tragic dilemma without compromising the principles that make them heroes.[27] Is this realistic, though? We'll talk more about this near the end of this chapter, but given the trade-offs inherent in any choices, especially tragic dilemmas, Batman's position comes off as noble yet naïve.

To the Bat-Trolley!

Although Batman's refusal to kill comes from a good place—a belief in the sanctity of life handed down by his father Thomas Wayne and reinforced by Leslie Thompkins—it does pose problems for the pursuit of his mission. This is perhaps the greatest conflict between the two main components of Batman's moral code, utilitarianism and deontology, which are often at odds in many decisions we face in our day-to-day lives. Furthermore, we may even need to bring in a third school of ethics to find the best explanation for why he sticks to this rule above all others.

The problems with the mission posed by his refusal to kill are similar to those introduced by his compulsion to save every life, no matter how underserving we may feel they are. For example, the fact that his rule against killing is so well known among the criminal set has a distinct downside in that it makes his threats of "talk or I'll kill you" less credible. In the beginning, before word of his methods had time to spread through the underworld, such threats could still work. In his first year in the cowl, Batman tied a thug to a flagpole high up a building. When the guy pleaded, "You can't do this! You can't leave me here! What if the pole snaps?" Batman answered, "Don't worry. The ground will break your fall!" When the criminal argued that his boss will kill him, Batman asked "You think I won't?" The guy accused him: "You're bluffing—trying to trick me! You wouldn't kill me in cold blood!" After Batman started to leave, the criminal gave in to his fear and offered to talk, showing that before his refusal to kill was well-known, Batman's bluffs could still work.[28]

But this gambit would more often fail as time went on. After the Cataclysm, Batman met with Penguin to warn him not to loot during the chaos and even asked him to help with the damages. When Batman implied that his men will be in danger otherwise, Penguin scoffed. "Psh! You've never killed anybody in your life, Batman!" When Batman told him, "That was then, Penguin. This is now. The old rules are dead and buried," Penguin knew better, saying, "You're bluffing!"—and he was right, of course.[29] When Batman dangled Abbot, one Ra's al Ghul's thugs, off the roof to get information, and asked, "Do I need to explain the rules to you?" Abbot confidently replied, "Oh, I know the rules, Detective. And I know you. You forget, I serve the Demon's Head. You have no secrets from Ra's al Ghul. You won't kill me. And an empty threat is no threat at all. You'll get nothing out of me."[30] Of course, Batman realizes this, and tries to convince criminals otherwise. One time, Batman threatened to throw a Gotham City alderman out of a window if he didn't talk, but the alderman said Batman was bluffing and that, in any case, "killing me won't get you what you want." Batman conceded that but added, "It will convince the next person I question that I'm not bluffing."[31] That time it worked, but eventually a person has to carry out a threat in order for it to remain credible, and Batman is not willing to make good on it, as most of his criminals know all too well.

What's more, because of his well-known rule against killing, Batman finds he is less imposing than others who are so willing. After the legendary assassin Deadshot intimidated a witness into refusing to testify at a criminal's trial, Batman found he couldn't convince him otherwise; instead, the witness told him, "as much as you scare me … he scares me worse." Batman later said to Alfred, "I put on this suit because I knew one of my greatest weapons would be exploiting the cowardice of criminals. But it looks like fear of Deadshot trumps fear of Batman." Alfred commiserated: "Not surprising, sir. Fear of the Batman is based on speculation—rumors of things you'd never actually do. It's no secret what Deadshot is capable of."[32]

This last example brings Batman's inability to bluff about killing together with his underlying refusal to kill, which costs untold numbers of innocent lives taken by his most murderous foes, the worst being genocidal terrorists like Ra's al Ghul, psychopaths like Zsasz, or the criminally insane like the Joker. As we saw in the discussion of saving lives of pathological killers, this central moral dilemma comes down to either killing one serial murderer to save their many future victims, or allowing them to live while acknowledging they will almost certainly kill again (if Batman doesn't stop them in time whenever they manage to escape from prison or Arkham).

Lucky for us, this perennial dilemma of Batman's closely resembles a classic thought experiment in philosophy called the *trolley problem*. (Surprisingly, the original formulation of the trolley problem was lacking any reference to Batman whatsoever. Philosophers are weird.) In the typical story, a trolley car carrying five passengers is out of control and hurtling toward a broken section of track. If the trolley reaches that point, the trolley will crash and the five passengers will be killed. A bystander happens to be standing next to a railway switch that can divert the trolley onto another track, saving the lives of the five passengers. But there's a hitch: there's a person doing maintenance on the other track who would not hear the trolley coming and would be killed if it is diverted there.[33] The trolley problem brilliantly and intuitively brings to light many aspects of moral philosophy, including the conflict between utilitarianism (saving the greatest number of lives) and deontology (not directly acting to kill), as well as the subsidiary idea of killing being a greater moral wrong than passively allowing to die (which supports the deontological choice of not pulling the switch). And that's just scratching the surface—like Ace the Bat-Hound, we'll scratch much deeper soon enough.

As I told the story of the trolley, you would be excused for thinking that I was recounting another exciting Batman adventure! OK, maybe it's a little less thrilling, and lacking in the hyperdramatic comic book dialogue or overwrought narration we've come to expect, but the hallmarks of Batman's familiar dilemma are here: in his worst-case scenarios, he can save numerous innocent people only if he acts to kill someone else. Let's see how some specific examples of this conflict played out in Batman's stories and how they change the parameters of the classic trolley problem story.

The stakes. In the typical trolley problem, the number of people on the trolley is small, typically five. Of course, this number can be increased to make the "cost" of inaction even higher and possibly tempt those who would not pull the switch to save "only" five people to reconsider their position. Typically, you would think people who were on the fence about acting in the standard situation would be more likely to pull the switch if the number of people they would be saving increased.

The stakes in Batman's typical cases differ from the standard trolley problem in two important ways. First, the number of lives he is potentially saving is much greater than five, given the extent of his worst foes' murderous intent and capacity. There are no reliable numbers given, but it is a safe bet that the Joker, Zsasz, and Ra's al Ghul have each killed hundreds if not thousands of people throughout their "careers." Among these three, however, the sheer scale and scope of the Joker's activities is emphasized the most, presumably because of his position of prominence among Batman's twisted rogues' gallery. Not only has Joker killed a comparable number of people to Zsasz and Ra's, but these actions have affected Batman very personally, killing or injuring individuals extremely close to him. The Joker shot Barbara Gordon, the original Batgirl, in the spine, paralyzing her from the waist down (but with no impact on her spirit or heroic impulse, as she continued to serve the superhero community as Oracle, an information and communications wizard).[34] He also killed Gotham City police Lieutenant Sarah Essen in cold blood, in front of her husband Jim Gordon (who also witnessed Barbara's tragedy), after throwing a live baby to her so she would drop her weapon.[35]

But neither of those heinous crimes hit Batman as hard as the murder of Jason Todd, the second Robin, whom the Joker bludgeoned with a crowbar and then left in a building he rigged to explode.[36] Of course, this being comics, the death didn't "stick," and about 15 years later (in real time), Jason Todd reappeared, as an angry young man, no longer concerned with following Batman's strict moral code.[37] Confronting Batman first as a new incarnation of the Red Hood—the name under which Batman first met the Joker—Jason soon revealed his true identity to Batman and told him, "If you had killed Joker, years ago ... beyond what happened to me ... you know what hell you would have saved the world. But no. His murder is a long list of sane acts you refuse to commit."[38] During a later confrontation, Jason again emphasized the scale of the damage done by the Joker: "Ignoring what he's done in the past. Blindly, stupidly, disregarding the entire graveyards he's filled, the thousands who have suffered ... the friends he's crippled ... I thought ... I thought killing me—that I'd be the last person you'd ever let him hurt."[39]

Jason's words highlight not only the fact that the Joker has taken countless anonymous lives that Batman swore to protect, but that he also ended the life of Batman's chosen protégé, one of the handful of people in the world closer to him than anybody else. It would be similar to the bystander in the trolley problem having lost a close friend or relative to a similar trolley incident in the past, and then finding out another person close to them was on the current runaway trolley. In that case, it isn't "just" a random stranger at risk—not that random strangers don't matter, of course—but someone very close to the bystander, a consideration which, as we saw earlier, naturally elicits some heightened concern due to reasonable sentiments of partiality. As Jason said, he thought his would be the death that finally drove the Batman to cross that line, that the personal nature of that particular loss would be enough to make him kill the Joker. But not even the murder of a Robin was enough to force Batman to finally end the Joker's life—and as Jason implies, if not that, then what?

Others besides Jason have stressed the scope of the Joker's harm as well. When Batman argued to the Spectre, the agent of God's vengeance, that Joker didn't deserve to die for his sins, but instead should be returned to Arkham Asylum, the Spectre told him, "To escape again?! To kill again?! How many innocent lives must be taken before we end a guilty one?! Your methods are an exercise in futility!"[40] Closer to our mortal realm, Hush—himself the victim of the Joker's remote-controlled pacemaker, as seen in the last chapter—confronted Batman with the litany of the Joker's other crimes and asked Batman how many more he's willing to accept.

> How many people would be alive today if you had just stopped the Joker the first time? Permanently. A hundred? More? You ever say sorry to Barbara Gordon? No matter what you tell yourself, no matter how many lives you think you've saved, you've caused far more deaths. You've orphaned far more boys. Widowed far more women. Ruined far more families.[41]

Certainly, Batman is well aware of the harm that the Joker has caused. In fact, it was after the Joker apparently killed Tommy Elliot (before Batman knew he was actually Hush) that Batman flew into a rage against the Joker, recounting for an entire issue his many crimes against Gotham City and those close to him, including Jason and Barbara, while he seemed more determined than ever to finally put an end to his killing spree. When

Catwoman, who had been shot earlier by the Joker's on-and-off girlfriend Harley Quinn, tried to stop Batman from killing the Joker, he struck her in her wound to stop her, thinking, "I tell myself she will understand someday ... Selina ... Don't you see that our relationship only allows for the possibility that one night ... it will be you I find killed by the Joker? I cannot ... I will not ... allow that nightmare to become a reality."[42] After all the personal loss he had suffered at the hands of the Joker, Batman seemed to have decided that the possibility of more death, especially of another person very close to him, was too much to bear. The cost of allowing the Joker to live may have finally become too high.

In the end, Jim Gordon stopped Batman from killing the Joker with the same message Batman used to stop the Spoiler from killing her father. When Batman asked him, "How many more lives are we going to let him ruin?" Jim answered, "I don't care. I won't let him ruin yours."[43] But the concept of the cost of one's principles becoming too high to maintain them has some foundation in ethics, even in deontological thinking that normally enforces principles without any consideration of consequences. In particular, *threshold deontology* allows for such a change of heart: It maintains that deontological principles are to be followed unless the costs of doing so increase to an intolerable level (or threshold), after which the decision-maker is allowed, even expected, to switch to utilitarian thinking and do whatever is necessary to minimize costs or damage. So even those who would not pull the switch to save five passengers may do so to save ten, or fifty, or a thousand.

Threshold deontology was originally suggested in a discussion of torture and "ticking bomb" scenarios in which a suspected terrorist is believed to know the location of a bomb that could potentially kill thousands, even millions, of people, and torture is assumed to be effective in getting that information.[44] The question then becomes: even for those who oppose torture on principled grounds, how many potential deaths would they be willing to accept to maintain that stance? We'll talk more about torture in the next chapter, but the basic idea is the same with respect to killing a murderer like the Joker: how many deaths are enough to make Batman "pull that trigger" himself? There may be no such number for him, but there is precedent in ethics for having one even in the face of a strongly held principle.

The uncertainty. The question of how many more people the Joker will kill if Batman allows him to live is one the Dark Knight must face every time he confronts the Clown Prince of Crime and has a chance to kill him.

This also represents another complication to the classic trolley dilemma story. There, it is assumed that if the trolley is left on its current track, its five passengers *will* die. In the case of the Joker, however, his future victims are merely potential ones. It is highly likely, given his past behavior, that he will kill again if allowed to live, but this cannot be known with absolute certainty. He could see the light and become a reformed man. This is the hope, for example, when the Spectre let the Joker experience "a sense of right and wrong," after which he became catatonic: "he tasted his own guilt and it has proven too much for him."[45] (It didn't take.) Recall that the possibility of reforming his foes is one of Batman's greatest dreams, and the meliorability of human nature, the belief that our moral characters can always improve, is part of his more general belief in the sanctity of life that grounds his refusal to kill.

We can safely assume that the Joker will always be the Joker, and that if he is free and able, he will kill again. However, he may not be free or able. He is sent to Arkham Asylum regularly—for treatment rather than imprisonment, *wink wink*—and while he stays there it is much more difficult for him to kill. (We'll talk more about the apparently inept corrections system in Gotham City soon.) Even when he's free, though, he could be prevented from killing. For example, the Joker could die from other causes before he has a chance to kill again, or he could be rendered unable to kill by an illness or an accident. In general, something *could* happen to the Joker that would prevent him from killing any more people, even if Batman lets him live, which would make his own murder a moral wrong with no benefit to possibly justify it.

When Batman considers the magnitude of the Joker's future crimes, then, he has to consider that they are merely possibilities, even very high probabilities, but not certainties. He knows all too well what the Joker has done in the past, and may use this knowledge to form an accurate prediction of what the Joker is likely to do in the future, but he cannot *know* what the Joker will do. And this may be a critical point in rationalizing Batman's refusal to kill the Joker: it is one thing to kill someone in the process of committing murder (if there is no other way to stop them), but it is another thing altogether to kill someone whom you merely suspect will commit murder in the future.

In the context of the trolley problem, this would be like diverting the trolley to the other track because you think the five passengers *might* die otherwise, trading one certain death for the possible deaths of five. This is basically the ticking-bomb scenario in the debates over torture, in which authorities *believe* there is a bomb somewhere that may kill a number of people, but they don't know with certainty. However, the scale of the damage may offset the lack of certainty and thereby exceed the threshold for sticking to deontological principle. While the chance of a bomb that could kill ten people would not justify torture in many people's minds, an equal chance of one that could kill a million might. By the same token, a 5 percent chance of killing a thousand people may not be enough to justify torture, but a 75 percent chance of killing the same number might. Even if we stop short of computing the "expected loss of life" by discounting the number of deaths by the likelihood of those deaths, the scale and likelihood will still be substitutes to some extent, either likely to trigger an extreme action if it gets too large.

Also, killing people to prevent their future crimes is an extreme example of *pre-punishment*, the idea of holding people accountable for crimes they may commit in the future. Normally, as we saw in Chapter 2, society imposes punishment for a crime a person is found guilty of for one of two reasons: to address the crime itself (retributivism) or to prevent future ones (deterrence). One argument in support of retributivism is that it respects the dignity and humanity of criminals by holding them responsible for their actions, rather than using them and their punishment as a means to serve society's ends (however worthy they may be). In this spirit, retributivism demands that only the guilty be punished and also punished proportionately for their crimes, neither too harshly nor too leniently.

As you may have figured out by now, retributivism is roughly deontological in nature, focusing on the right more than the good. The other goal, deterrence, which focuses instead on preventing or lessening future crime, is basically utilitarian in that it seeks to improve overall well-being rather than promoting justice as an ideal. Similar to the utilitarian nightmare scenario of a government executing innocent civilians to stem a violent uprising, critics of deterrence argue that such a criminal justice system may be less concerned about the guilt of specific criminals, because punishment would serve the same societal purpose regardless of their guilt or innocence. Also, a system promoting deterrence is more likely to enact disproportionately severe sentences to offenders to "send a message" to potential criminals.

Exacting punishment *before* crimes are committed, however, is a nightmare scenario of a deterrence-based system gone wild, in which overzealous authorities attempt to predict who is more likely to commit crimes and then surveil, arrest, and punish them before they can act.[46] But in practice, even a criminal justice system predicated solely on deterrence, which makes use of the threat of punishment as an incentive to deter crimes, requires that an actual crime was committed for which a person was convicted, before punishment can be imposed.

What about the Joker, then? He should certainly be held accountable for his crimes according to whatever concepts of responsibility and insanity apply to him (on which more soon). But for Batman to exact the ultimate penalty, to end his life, as a punishment for crimes he has yet to commit is an offense against most principles of criminal punishment as well as the Joker's own dignity and humanity. These ideas demand that Batman (and the actual criminal justice system) address acts the Joker has actually performed, not those he has yet to perform but may be expected to—which leads us back to the fact that no one knows for certain what he will do if he remains free to act. The standard trolley problem doesn't account for this, but Batman, and the criminal justice system in general, must.

The element of responsibility. Another aspect of Batman's particular trolley problem that makes it unique has to do with the responsibility of the various actors in the situation. One of the central questions raised by the standard trolley problem is whether the bystander's *ability* to pull the switch and divert the trolley car implies *responsibility* for the outcome. If the bystander pulls the switch to save the five passengers on the trolley, is she responsible for the death of the single person on the other track? And if she doesn't pull the switch, is she responsible for the deaths of the five passengers?

This is where the distinction between killing and letting die comes into play. For many people, reluctance to pull the switch is based on the belief that you'd be responsible for the single death you'd cause if you pulled the switch, but you wouldn't be responsible for the deaths of the five passengers if you simply did nothing. After all, you had nothing to do with the situation the passengers were in, and if you hadn't happened to be near the switch when the trolley car approached, you'd have nothing to do with the situation at all. Does the fact that you happened to be present and were able to pull the switch make you responsible for the lives of the various people involved? And if you did pull the switch, you'd be actively causing the death of the person on the other track, regardless of how strong a justification you might have—and for some people that is enough for them to make them say they would not do it.

This distinction is also invoked whenever a "duty to rescue" or "Good Samaritan law" is proposed. The typical example in philosophy is walking by a shallow pond when you see a small child drowning, described most famously by Peter Singer.[47] To save her, all you would have to do to is bend over and give her a hand to help her out of the pool—you wouldn't even get your shoes wet! The question is: Do you have a moral obligation to save the child? To be precise, this is not the same as asking whether it would be a good, nice, or minimally decent thing to do—of course it would. But are you *required* in some sense to do so?

Utilitarians would say "duh, of course," and Peter Singer is famous for using this example to lead into his plea for greater charity on the part of the wealthy. Some people, however, would say no, especially those deontologists who argue that the only strictly binding duties we have toward each other are duties of noninterference, such as "don't kill" or "don't steal." Even Immanuel Kant, who emphasized positive duties of aid and generosity as well as negative duties such as not killing, did not go as far as to say any specific action out of positive duty was required, but only that we should act on these duties when we can, in consideration of our many other duties, including our duties to ourselves.[48] Such deontologists would agree that we should help the kids out of the pool, understanding the word "should" in a casual sense, but would stop short of making it a strict obligation, allowing for the role of judgment in determining choices in specific circumstances. Common sense would dictate that one would save the child in the case described, but if we increase the cost or risk involved—such as putting the child in a deeper pool, in the middle of a lake, or in a burning building—it is not as easy to say that saving her is a strict obligation.

If philosophers can't even agree that a person should bend over to help a small child drowning in a shallow pool, it's hard to imagine they would agree on an obligation to pull a switch to save five passengers on a trolley car, especially when doing so involves killing an innocent person. That would be like saying you were obligated to knock one kid into the pool to save five kids from drowning in it—or, in another popular version of the trolley problem, having to push a large man off a bridge onto the track to stop the trolley from reaching the broken section of track.[49]

This brings us back to the idea of being held responsible for the death of the one person if you act to save the five, but not responsible for the deaths of the five if you do nothing. Basically, a person is usually not considered responsible for choosing *not* to inject themselves into a casual chain of events, but if they do, they're responsible for the consequences of doing so. This moral position could explain the greater resistance to "pull the trigger" in variations of the trolley problem that demand more direct involvement, such as pushing the large man off the bridge. This has the same effect as pulling the switch in the classic problem, but some people willing to pull the switch recoil at the thought of pushing the man, possibly because it emphasizes their active role in the situation, or because the man becomes the direct means to save the passengers rather than an unintended casualty (or "collateral damage") of pulling the switch.[50]

The question that is often ignored in this scenario is: who is responsible for the morally fraught situation in the first place? In the case of the small child drowning in the pool, it may be the child's fault—although she would not be held responsible for it, being a child and all—or perhaps the negligence of her caretaker, who was so engrossed in her book about Batman's ethics that she failed to notice. In the classic trolley problem, we have to assume that some person or party was responsible for the failure of the trolley's brakes as well as the faulty track that would lead to the deadly crash. Although the bystander at the switch has the ability to make a critical decision regarding the fates of the people involved, the ultimate responsibility, regardless of the outcome, would seem to lie with those in charge of maintenance of the track and trolley. Unfortunately, this doesn't make the bystander's decision any easier, but it does serve to shift the focus of blame and responsibility to the more appropriate parties.

Batman has a keen appreciation for this aspect of the trolley problem. In a story during the mystical "Underworld Unleashed" event that comes as close to the trolley dilemma as Batman will ever get, an Arkham Asylum patient named Kryppen made a deal with the devil for Batman's soul. Kryppen told Batman that he poisoned 200 of his fellow patients, staff, and doctors in Arkham, and offered to give them the antidote if Batman killed one of them—"refuse, and every last man here will die!" This is analogous to the version of the trolley problem with the large man on the bridge, because Batman has to directly kill one person as a means to save the rest.[51] Batman told him, firmly, "I don't kill, Kryppen. Not for you. Not for a devil. Not ever." When Kryppen asked, "Not even to save two hundred lives?" Batman replied, "No. Every man has to take responsibility for his own actions. You can't push these deaths off onto my conscience."[52] Here, Batman acknowledges that it isn't his responsibility to make this decision—especially the way Kryppen plans—because it was Kryppen who set up the scenario following the devil's instructions. (Philosophy has a long history of putting evil demons in their thought experiments, but I've never seen one associated with the trolley problem ... until now![53]) Situations like these are common in adventure stories from comics, TV, and film, in which the villain tells the hero he or she must kill one person to save others, but very rarely does the hero assert that he or she doesn't have to play along because it was the villain, not the hero, who chose to put the victims in danger. Batman realized this, however, and when Kryppen told him, "Kill one—or they all die," he knew this is Kryppen's choice, not his. (We'll see later how he solved this particular trolley problem his own way.)

But Batman isn't always so sure about this. As we saw earlier, he often struggles with questions about his responsibility for the costumed villains he may have attracted or inspired, especially the Joker, given his own role in "creating" him the night the Red Hood fell into a vat of chemicals. As Jim Gordon reassured him once, "Did you put the hood on his head and the gun in his hand? No, you didn't."[54] Just as Batman sometimes feels responsible for the creation of his foes, he often feels responsible for their actions, including the crimes they commit because he refuses to kill them. As he beat the Joker after he apparently killed Tommy Elliot, Batman pondered his responsibility regarding the Joker, thinking to himself, "I cannot ... I will not ... accept any responsibility ... for the Joker. Except that I should have killed him long ago."[55] This sentiment of Batman's—which, as we will see, is very common and often expressed—refers as much to his past crimes as his future ones, including the likelihood in Batman's mind that someday the Joker will kill Catwoman. In his rage, Batman wants both to kill the Joker for his past murders—"there is nothing I can do that would cause him the agony that he has brought upon others," expressing a clear retributivist sentiment—and also to prevent him from killing again—"it is what should have been done a long time ago," representing more of a deterrent one, albeit in hindsight.[56] It is part of Batman's mission to protect Gotham from the scourge of crime that makes him feel responsible for the deaths he cannot prevent because of the immense task he set himself—and ultimately a futile one, which sets him up for an incredible amount of guilt and remorse at his own human limitations.[57]

So, if Batman is not responsible for the situations the Joker puts him in, is the Joker responsible for them? On the surface, the answer seems to be a simple "yes," bordering on an "of course he is" with a dollop of "how could he not be, are you kidding me with this $%^&?" And if he were like most of Batman's other foes, such as the Penguin, Poison Ivy, or the Riddler, I would tend to agree. As we just said, the person who sets the trolley problem in motion, who creates the circumstances that lead to the bystander having to make that impossible choice, bears ultimate responsibility for the outcome. And the villain setting the master plan in motion isn't the only guilty party

here. The criminal justice and correctional systems in Gotham City—
including Arkham Asylum—deserve a hefty amount of blame for the
infamous "revolving door" that lets all of the inmates and patients break
free time and again. As gentle a soul as Alfred Pennyworth once noted,
"Sometimes I wonder if your vow never to kill was the right one, Master
Bruce. You catch them—the courts jail them—then they break free, and the
slaughter begins all over again!"[58] (Of course, Master Bruce acknowledged
the sentiment without endorsing the conclusion.) The Gotham City Police
Department certainly wouldn't have to work so hard, and Batman wouldn't
have to deal with all these trolley problems, if the city's prisons and mental
health facilities would just beef up their security a little bit!

Aside from the obvious flair, what is it that sets the Joker apart from the
rest of the pack? It's his mental state, usually described as insanity, which
has significant ramifications for his responsibility in both the moral and
legal senses of the term. When Batman reflected on his history with the
Joker after he seemed to kill Tommy Elliot, the Dark Knight seemed skeptical about the Joker's typical diagnosis, thinking to himself that after the
Joker shot Barbara Gordon, he was "deemed 'insane' by the courts" and
therefore never went to prison for the crime.[59] But Batman knows all too
well that, regardless of his actual mental state, the Joker will meet the courts'
traditional definition of sanity under the *M'Naghten rule*: that to be convicted of crime, a person must appreciate the difference between right and
wrong and understand how their actions were wrong.[60]

We can give the Dark Knight a pass for the sarcasm—as we have seen, he
wasn't quite himself at that time, considering killing the Joker more seriously than ever. Most other times, Batman is much more understanding
and even sympathetic to the Joker because of his mental state. After the
Joker killed Jason Todd and Batman prepared to face him at the United
Nations, he tossed the situation back in forth in his mind, and at one point
thought to himself, "the man's hopelessly insane. How can I hold him
responsible even for what happened to Jason?"[61] When the Spectre wanted
to exact holy vengeance on the Joker, Batman came to his defense, arguing
that "the Joker is sick. He belongs in an asylum and that's why I'm here—to
take him back to Arkham." When the Spectre asserted his divine authority,
Batman pointed out that the God he serves made the Joker the way he is:

> You're not part of my god and I don't recognize your authority! The Joker
> himself in a kind of unholy innocent—a sociopath! He has no real concept of
> good or evil! How can you sin unless you know you sin?! If the Joker lacks

that ability, if that is the way God created him, how do you dare punish him?! My stand is based on morality—what is yours?![62]

Similar to the legal sense, moral responsibility for a wrongful act also hinges on whether the person who performed it knew what they were doing was wrong and meant to do it anyway. Sometimes this comes down to a mistake of fact: for example, if the Penguin picks up somebody else's umbrella by mistake on his way out of the bank, that isn't a crime. (If he threatens to kill someone with it, that's a different story.) Other times, it's a failure to understand that an act was wrong, such as when a child takes something that doesn't belong to them, or hits another child before being told it's wrong. Batman is arguing that the Joker makes that mistake: although obviously intelligent, he lacks the basic conception of right and wrong that would give him the appreciation of his actions necessary to render him morally or legally responsible for them. As Batman said, a person can't act wrongly if they don't know it's wrong; in such cases, what they did may be harmful and tragic, but the person can't be held responsible for it.

This also implies such a person can't be punished for crimes they committed, because punishment, as we saw, assumes guilt, which in turns assumes responsibility. But at the same time, if a person is a danger to others—as the Joker most definitely is—he must be quarantined from the rest of society. This is why even criminal defendants found "not guilty for reason of insanity" may nonetheless be confined to a mental health facility, both to pursue treatment as well as separate them from others they may hurt again.

It follows that, as Batman told the Spectre, criminals who are judged insane should definitely not be killed as punishment for their crimes— something he often emphasizes in reference to another of his frequent foes, Two-Face. As he told government agent King Faraday, who told Batman to stay away from him while he chased Two-Face,

> You know that Two-Face was once district attorney Harvey Dent—before acid scarred half his face and drove him hopelessly insane! Well, I owe a debt to the man that was! I owe it to the memory of Harvey Dent to put Two-Face where he'll never harm anyone ever again.[63]

By this we can presume he did not mean prison, because after preventing Faraday from shooting Dent, Batman tells him, "Two-Face isn't simply a criminal—he's mentally ill! The man needs help—not killing!"[64] As Bruce told Alfred later, when Two-Face showed his unique face again, "Trauma made Harvey Dent the killer he is. But underneath, sometimes I still see the man I knew—a friend … a good man."[65] The difference with the Joker, of course, is that he is no friend at all to Batman, but he gets consideration based on his mental illness nonetheless, which is an exemplary display of Batman's principle and compassion (even if he loses sight of them from time to time).

Personal feelings. Even though Batman's own "Joker issue" differs from the classic trolley problem in these important ways, it still leaves the essential conflict the same: should he kill someone who has ended many lives and is almost certain to end many more if allowed to live? Batman isn't alone—many superheroes face similar problems when their worst foes are particularly homicidal or target those close to them—but the interaction of the Joker's murderous psychopathy with the deaths of Bruce Wayne's parents (and Jason Todd at the hands of the Joker himself) make this a particularly emotional dilemma for him, a consideration usually absent in trolley problems in which all the people involved are anonymous strangers.

Let us be clear: Batman *does* want to kill the Joker, very much so, and sometimes he even resolves to (although never follows through on it). At the United Nations, shortly after the Joker killed Jason Todd, he shot and killed a UN delegate, and Batman thought, "Another innocent sacrifice to the Joker's mania. Wherever he goes … death … Another hapless victim to haunt my sleep. Let there be an end to it! No more!"[66] Later, after the Joker's apparent murder of Tommy Elliot, Batman came as close as ever to killing the Joker (as we've seen already) and recalled many of his past crimes. He remembered when the Joker shot Lieutenant Essen, and thought, "the Joker's life should have ended then and there." He remembered when the Joker shot Barbara Gordon, paralyzing her from the neck down, and thought that "snapping the Joker's neck becomes that much easier." When Catwoman arrived and told Batman he would regret killing the Joker, he thought, "How could I regret what should have been done a long time ago?" Finally, when he considered the possibility of his beloved Selina becoming the Joker's next victim, Batman decided: "He dies tonight by my hand."[67]

As we know, Jim Gordon was the one who stopped Batman from betraying his one firm rule, which is appropriate considering he nearly killed the Joker himself after the murder of Sarah Essen, his wife. Immediately after her body fell to the ground, the Joker surrendered to the police. Gordon punched him and then pulled his weapon, saying, "He's gone too far.

He paralyzed my daughter, my little girl … He just murdered my bride, my Sarah … too much … too far …" Even though Batman said, "I won't stop you," and the Joker taunted Gordon ("You have a little boy, too, don't you?"), Gordon shot the Joker in the knee and told the surrounding police, "Arrest him. Charge is murder."[68] A similar scene played out when Gordon and Batman caught the Joker soon after he shot Barbara Gordon. "I could end it here and now … close the Joker out forever," Jim said. "The world would thank me for it. Just a squeeze of my trigger …" When he coughed, the Joker took the opportunity to attack him, and after Batman caught him he asked Jim, "You wanted the Joker. Decide what you want us to do with him." Even though the Joker taunted him again, saying "I'd kill me if I were me … C'mon, Commish. This is your chance to put me out of my misery," Jim told Batman, "The same as you want. But we'll book him anyway."[69]

Gordon isn't the only person Batman confides in about his desire for the Joker's death. After the episode recounted above, Batman admitted to Nightwing, "I almost killed the Joker … I honestly wanted to," to which the former Robin replied, with a hand on his mentor's shoulder, "whatever your impulse was, you didn't act on it."[70] When Batman discovered that the Joker has begun conjuring demons (including his old pal Etrigan), Alfred asked what he was going to do about it, to which he answered, "Keep up my nightly patrols—wait for some word or sign of whatever he's up to this time—hope I can stop it before anyone's hurt," not killing him, but admitting, "Hope he kills himself this time—hope he goes to hell for good and forever."[71]

Perhaps Batman's most heartfelt admission regarding wanting the Joker dead was to one of the few people alive who had reason to want it even more. When Jason Todd confronted him about never killing the Joker, Batman poured his heart out—yes, really—telling his former Robin:

> All I ever wanted to do is kill him. For years a day hasn't gone by where I haven't envisioned taking him … taking him and spending an entire month putting him through the most horrendous, mind-boggling forms of torture. All of it building to an end with him broken, butchered and maimed … pleading—screaming—in the worst kind of agony as he careens to a monstrous death. I want him dead—maybe more than I've ever wanted anything.[72]

Batman even told the Joker himself as much, as he dragged his injured foe across the snowy mountaintop. When the Joker asked him, "Will you do it? Kill me? Release the burden that torments both of us?" Batman answered,

"No. Oh, I want to—I've never wanted anything so much. But I won't."[73] But he still dreams about it, imagining telling the Joker, "Too many people have died because of you! Those poor souls haunt my nightmares! No more!" As Batman hacked his foe apart—again, in his dream—he thought to himself, "It feels great! Why did I wait so long? ... Too bad it's just ... a dream."[74] In the face of this much pent-up rage and an understandable human desire to get vengeance, the fact that Batman has not yet killed his greatest foe is a testament to his devotion to his pledge and duty (if not his mission) over indulging his desires.

This pent-up desire suggests another reason Batman abstains from killing, aside from his belief in the sanctity of life, even in extreme cases such as the Joker: he acknowledges his own human weakness. He recognizes that once he stops resisting, once he crosses that line just once, he may never come back from it. We saw this already when he told Hush, "I can go out into the darkness and still find my way back. You, the others, you got lost out there."[75] When the Joker reappeared after seeming to die in a helicopter explosion soon after he killed Jason Todd, Batman told Alfred, "I wanted to kill the Joker back in that helicopter. I still don't know why I didn't. I should have. Yet I couldn't. But what happens the next time Batman sees that grinning face? What if I don't ... can't control myself?" Alfred rested a hand on his shoulder and told him, "You always have, sir," but Batman knew that was no guarantee: "That doesn't mean I always will."[76] Batman is well known for his seemingly superhuman resolve, determination, and willpower, but even the strongest among us occasionally lapse—and it stands to reason that someone who values his mission and principles as much as Batman does would be even more concerned about betraying them, despite his nearly perfect record. This is well illustrated during a time Batman was under the influence of the Scarecrow's fear gas: when he thought he saw the Joker, he reminded himself, "The Batman doesn't kill! The Batman is better than that! I'm the best because I have to be! I can't take any short cuts! I can never fail!"[77] We know that Batman demands perfection from himself more than from anyone else, and his awareness of his own human imperfections makes him strive even harder for it.

The idea that killing would be a "short cut" comes up in one of the discussions between Batman and the revived Jason Todd about (not) killing the Joker. When Batman accused Jason of never understanding the problem with killing, Jason responded, "What? Your moral code just won't allow for that? It's too hard to 'cross that line'?" Batman's answer is surprising: "No. God almighty ... no. It'd be too damned easy." He went on to tell Jason how he's fantasized about the torture he would inflict on the Joker (as quoted above), followed by a line reminiscent of what he said to Hush around the same time: "But if I do that, if I allow myself to go down into that place ... I'll never come back." Jason had heard this before, though, and wasn't about to let Batman get away that easily. "Why do all the cub scouts in spandex always say that? 'If I cross that line, there's no coming back.' I'm not talking about killing Cobblepot and Scarecrow or Clayface. Not Riddler or Dent ... I'm talking about him. Just him. And doing it because ... because he took me away from you."[78]

Batman didn't elaborate, saying merely, "I can't. I'm sorry. I just can't," but we can easily imagine his reason: that once he starts by killing the Joker, he won't stop there. Having dismissed that constraint and allowing himself to kill when he deems it necessary, he's afraid he will "deem it necessary" in more and more cases. It's similar to addicts who cannot take one drink, smoke one cigarette, or place one bet, because they're afraid that they won't be able to stop at one.[79] As the theory of "bright lines" says, it's much easier to stick to zero versus one than one versus two—the former is none versus some, while the latter is some versus some *more*.[80] Because Batman's desire to end the lives of his enemies is so strong, his self-imposed duty to resist this desire has to remain even stronger, and he has to be vigilant against any temptation to slip ... even once.

The Real Reason Batman Refuses to Kill ... and the Problem with It

While threatening students and Gotham City police officer Renee Montoya in a college library, Zsasz accused Batman of being a hunter like him. When Batman asserted that he doesn't kill, Zsasz mocked him, saying:

> Ah yes, your "saving grace"—the one factor that allows the zombies to sanction your actions ... But you'd like to kill them, if only they'd let you get away with it ... because it would make your work so much easier, wouldn't it? And ever so much more satisfying.[81]

Batman told him he's wrong, of course, but to be fair to Zsasz, he really isn't. We've seen that killing his enemies—at least the most murderous of them—would promote Batman's mission by preventing significant loss of life, as well as making his threats more credible. For what it's worth, it would also (as Zsasz guesses) satisfy Batman's more vengeful desires, as well as whatever stake he puts in retributivist justice or making criminals pay for their crimes. So why is this, of all things, the one line he refuses to cross?

We've already discussed his belief in the sanctity of life, learned at the feet of his father, Doctor Thomas Wayne, who risked his career and his life helping anybody who needed it, whether innocent or criminal. This rationale is certainly noble in a way, but ultimately ends up being self-defeating. As we saw earlier in this chapter, Hush told him that many more lives were lost because he refuses to take even one: "No matter what you tell yourself, no matter how many lives you think you've saved, you've caused far more deaths. You've orphaned far more boys. Widowed far more women. Ruined far more families."[82] By refusing to kill even a person who is sure to kill again, Batman is putting the principle of not taking a life above that of saving lives—not an inconsistent position in itself, as we saw on our recent trolley trip, but inconsistent with his repeated emphasis on that particular aspect of his mission.

Other than the sanctity of life, the most common explanation that Batman gives for his refusal to kill is that he doesn't want to become like the murderers he is sworn to defeat. This reflects an ethical perspective very different from either utilitarianism or deontology, one grounded less in morally questionable actions and more in the person performing them: *virtue ethics*. Originally developed by ancient philosophers such as Aristotle and the Stoics, and revived in the mid-twentieth century by philosophers such as Elizabeth Anscombe and Alasdair MacIntyre, virtue ethics focuses on a person's moral character, which influences his or her actions. A person with good or ethical character traits or *virtues*, such as honesty, courage, or generosity, will generally do good or ethical things based on them, and a person with bad traits or *vices*, such as deceitfulness, cowardice, or avarice ... well, you know the rest.[83] Whereas utilitarianism and deontology focus on whether particular acts are moral or not, such as killing or lying, virtue ethics highlights the qualities of a person that leads to performing such acts.[84]

Generally speaking, superheroes are widely considered to be paragons of virtue, but in the terms that moral philosophers use, things are a little more complicated. Just because a person is ethical doesn't mean they're ethical in the sense of virtue ethics specifically—they could be excellent utilitarians or deontologists instead (or one of the many other equally valid but lesser known schools of ethics). Some heroes, such as Superman and Wonder Woman, may be best thought of as agents of virtue, taking actions chosen on the basis of their heroic character traits rather than the pursuit of any particular utilitarian goal or devotion to deontological principles.[85] Although I've described Batman as a limited utilitarian limited by principle (even if just one), there are nonetheless some aspects of his ethical behavior that are best explained with the language of virtue ethics.

To the extent that Batman's refusal to kill—despite the significant contribution it would make to his stated mission—is based on being the kind of person he wants to be, his motivation is consistent with virtue ethics. He wants to maintain a certain quality of character and not adopt the character traits of those he fights. When Batman explained to a young Jason Todd why they must never kill, he said, "I'm not a murderer, son. Murder is the line we must not cross," adding, "If we're no better than the lice who snuff out human life like it's worth nothing at all, then, well—then it's time I hung up my cowl."[86] After Bruce Wayne recovered from his broken back, he confronted Jean-Paul Valley, his vengeful and violent replacement, about the deaths of Abattoir and Graham Etchison. When Valley argued that he didn't kill Abattoir *per se*, Wayne answered, "You let him die—and a result, Graham Etchison died! You're out of control—just as bad as what you profess to fight!"[87]

It may be a bit insensitive, but Batman is adamant in emphasizing this argument to those he fights—even while they're actually fighting. When the Joker asked if Batman was going to kill him while trekking through the snowy mountains, the Dark Knight explained how important life is to him (as we saw above), and adds, "If I did as you ask, I'd be no better than my enemies—I'd be the insane avenger some people are certain I already am."[88] After Batman nearly killed the Joker after he apparently killed Tommy Elliot, he thought to himself, "I made a promise on the grave of my parents that I would rid this city of the evil that took their lives. Tonight ... I nearly became a part of that evil ..."[89] Speaking of Mr. Elliot, when Hush and Batman argued about the costs of not killing the Joker, Hush suggested, "Let me kill him and you'll have one less freak to worry about. Let me do what you can't. What you won't." Batman replied, "No. That would make me no different from you."[90] He even upped the stakes with Ra's al Ghul: when Ra's offered to kill all the villains that he released from prison and Arkham if Batman joined him, the Dark Knight called him the devil, and added that "if I consented to mass murder—even of fiends like the Joker—I'd be worse than the devil ... because I know better."[91]

Sometimes, Batman seems to take his metaphor of "becoming that which I fight" almost literally, and his concern becomes more about what killing will do to *him* than the act itself. "I can't let my anger get the better of me," he

thought during one search for the Joker. "I can't lose control. Then I'll be playing it his way. I'll be caught in the current of his madness." After he found the
Joker he beat him, while again thinking, "Control. Control! Don't cross the
line. Don't step into the current. Or you may never find your way back." It
turned out the man he beat was not the Joker, so Batman kept looking, berat-
ing himself for being sloppy, and telling himself, "this is where it ends. I stop
him. I take him in. And I do it my way, not his. Because as soon as I begin to
echo that lunatic, in even the subtlest ways … I'm finished. I might as well
have pulled the trigger on the gun that killed my parents."[92] A bit dramatic,
perhaps, but it shows the seriousness with which Batman takes the threat that
he'll slip into the Joker's methods and madness once and for all.

Alfred sometimes contributes to this concern as well. When Batman
enlisted his old mentor Henri Ducard in his hunt for Ra's al Ghul and the
Joker, Alfred told Batman he doesn't like that they enlisted Ducard's help,
upset with his penchant for killing and torture. Batman explained that
"Ducard is the best manhunter in the world today," but Alfred objected further, adding, "And an unprincipled killer. But I suppose 'the end justifies the
means' in this instance." A frustrated Batman told his old friend, "I don't
have time for your ethical niceties. Ra's al Ghul and the Joker must be found.
By any means," to which Alfred replied, "In many ways the Joker has already
won. He brings out a brutality in you I find disquieting."[93]

The same anxiety is on display when Bruce Wayne sought out the Lady
Shiva to retrain him after his back injury, and she was impatient with his
relentless refusal to make the final, killing blow: "For your skill to attain full
form, you must be willing to kill—efficiently and without hesitation." When
Bruce answered, "That is the nature of my ultimate test—my true oppo-
nent—and everything I'm pledged to stop," Shiva replied, "Then to stop it,
you must become it." Bruce remained firm: "No. By assuming the mask and
mantle of the bat, I chose to oppose darkness with darkness, and to fight fire
with fire … but only to a point. I will not become the enemy—and I will not
be burned."[94] When they saw each other later in Calcutta, Shiva congratu-
lated him on his return, and wondered, if he had instead been Valley,
whether she "would have helped him … or killed him." When Batman commented, "Ever bent on death, Shiva. Is there no point at which it spoils your
life?" Shiva invoked her version of the warrior code: "My life is that of the
warrior, and the warrior's way is always death." Batman said, "Is it? I've
killed no one … and I'm still standing," to which Shiva responded, "Only
because you are both less than a warrior … and more than a warrior. You
are … a mystery." When a boy who had helped Batman find Shiva was shot

trying to save him, Shiva told the Dark Knight, "Be proud of him—he chose the way of a warrior," but Batman corrected her: "No, Shiva. He almost died, but he killed no one ... he chose the way of a hero."[95]

We see this tradition of heroism being opposed to killing in Shiva's daughter, Cassandra Cain, whom Batman helped train to continue the legacy of Batgirl—and who herself sought out Shiva to train her, secretly hoping to be killed as penance for a murder she was forced to commit ten years earlier.[96] Shiva helped to train Tim Drake when he started out as Robin, and he also resisted her orders to kill, sounding much like his mentor as he explained that "I won't fight murderers by becoming one. I've taken a pledge to my mentor and myself that I won't kill. Even to save my life."[97] Refusing to kill is also harder, as Batman teaches his son Damian, who had been trained by the League of Assassins and had to be "retrained" in his father's nonlethal methods: "our way is stronger, and more disciplined, than the assassin's way. It requires more skill."[98]

Of course, Batman isn't the best person to talk to about what it feels like to kill, his pain coming from the other end of a gun. When a man suffering from the virus that struck Gotham during the Contagion pulled a gun on Jim Gordon, the police commissioner shot and killed him in self-defense. When Batman told Jim, "you did him a favor. You saved him from an agonizing death," Jim corrected him, saying, "You'd know how wrong that was if you'd ever killed a man. Nothing makes it easier."[99] And then there is Alfred Pennyworth, who may know a thing or two about killing from his days in the British military. When Bruce Wayne was set up for the murder of his girlfriend Vesper Fairchild—so convincingly that even those closest to him had doubts about his innocence—Alfred delivered a soliloquy to his master's collection of costumes in the Batcave, one worthy of his other background, on the stage:

> There are reasons not to kill. We've discussed these before. To say that murder is immoral is too vague. Killing, even once, even with reasons, strips you of your humanity. I do not mean this in an abstract way. Though we move about the world as individuals, the human race as a whole is spiritually—necessarily, scientifically—a single entity. You cannot afford to revoke that citizenship. You cannot work meaningfully for humanity from outside of it. I know you know this. I know you.[100]

Of course, Bruce Wayne did not kill Ms. Fairchild, but Alfred's comments are among the most profound in the Batman canon regarding the effects of killing on the killer, emphasizing that it is a betrayal of our common humanity and, in effect, it exiles you from the moral community.[101] This is also a fine explanation of Batman's fear of "crossing the line," compromising his own character and virtue as well as exacting irreparable harm on another.

Holding your moral character to a high standard may be a good thing in and of itself, but as with moral principles, it may come at too high a cost. In this case, Batman is treating his own self-image and moral character as more important than his mission to save lives. It's as if he said, "I will do anything to save lives except anything that makes me feel like less of a hero." Jason Todd suggested this when he told Batman, during their confrontation in front of the Joker, "I don't know what clouds your judgment worse. Your guilt or your antiquated sense of morality."[102] The bystander in the classic trolley problem who refuses to pull the switch because *she* doesn't want to be a killer is putting herself and her virtue above the lives of those involved. There are principled reasons not to pull the switch, of course, but refusing to do so because *you* don't want to be the one to do it is to condemn people to death because *you* don't want to act to prevent it. It is difficult for Batman to say, on the one hand, that he values all life and will do anything to protect it, and on the other to refuse to do the one thing that would do so most effectively because it would compromise his own self-image. As he thought to himself before he administered truth serum to Lady Shiva to find out if she was Jason Todd's mother, "Every fiber of my being is revolted by the thought of what I'm about to do. It won't stop me, though. That's the biggest trouble with this line of work—you can't always get the job done and remain a hero in your own eyes."[103] When it comes to killing, however, he does choose to remain a hero in his own eyes, at the expense of getting the job done. This may be the greatest inconsistency in Batman's moral character, and one that is very difficult to justify or explain away.

The suggestion that Batman's refusal to kill is more about his own moral self-image than the sanctity of life is supported also by the fact that he is much more forgiving with other people killing, despite his repeated exhortations to his fellow crimefighters. In a battle with the entire Bat-family, the Joker led Nightwing to believe that the Clown Prince of Crime had killed yet another Robin—this time, Tim Drake. Nightwing lost control, thrashing Joker while he continued to taunt the former Boy Wonder—"Aw ... jeez ... I hit Jason a lot harder than that. His name was Jason, right?"—and by the time Tim showed up to assure Dick he was alive, he discovered that Dick had killed the Joker. Making the ultimate heroic sacrifice, the Huntress gave the Joker mouth-to-mouth, and when he came to, she told Batman, "We should have let him die." Of course, he replied, "We don't do that. Not even for him," which mirrors Nightwing's own guilt at what he did: as Dick told Robin and the Spoiler, "I did it. I killed him … I lost all control. I let anger carry me. He was dead and I was … I was happy about it. He won." As he walked away and Robin wanted to go after him, Batman merely said, "Let him go, Robin. He has to face what he's done," hardly the condemnation we would expect given his repeated refusal to kill the Joker himself.[104]

Nightwing's guilt lasted longer when he stood still while the Tarantula, his partner in both heroing and romance, killed the villain Blockbuster.[105] After he returned to Gotham to help Batman with the citywide gang war, Dick was awkward around his former mentor, and thought to himself, "All I can think about is Blockbuster, my part in his murder … Batman must not know yet. If he did, how could he continue to send me out in his name?"[106] But afterwards, as he and Bruce sat together in Wayne Manor, Dick thought, "He knows. Don't know how he does. But I know he knows—I let Tarantula kill Blockbuster. I did nothing. Except get out of her way. But I still can't bring myself to say it out loud. And neither can he."[107] Once again, Batman did nothing—perhaps because Dick was his first Robin, or because he realized how different they are, or that Dick was punishing himself more than Bruce ever could. This may also explain the times James Gordon had the Joker in his sights and wanted to kill him for shooting his wife and adopted daughter, and Batman didn't stop him (although he may have if Jim had actually gone through with it), presumably out of respect for a man who does so much good and deserves to slip once in a while.

Batman may strive for perfection and beat himself when he falls short, but that doesn't mean he has to hold everyone else to the same standard. Nonetheless, these examples support the argument that Batman's refusal to kill is based more on making sure *he* isn't a killer than on being concerned about killers dying, and again emphasizes the inconsistency between pursuing his mission and foreclosing the one option that would most effectively help further it.

"There's Always a Choice for People Like Us" … But Is There Really?

Maybe we've been too quick to condemn Batman for what should be a noble stand on moral principle. After all, he is a superhero, and the hallmark of the superhero is to never take the easy way out, but to always find a better solution, one that doesn't involve doing wrong for the greater good.

Perhaps Batman avoids killing because he wants to find other options to deal with criminals that will serve the mission of saving lives while not requiring him to take one. For instance, the Spectre, who exacts holy vengeance on criminals for their crimes, mocked Batman for his refusal to kill, asking him, "And what would you have done? 'Rehabilitated' them?" Batman answered, "I would have stopped them. I would have isolated them. I would have put them in cages where they could harm only themselves. But never would I have killed them!"[108] It isn't that Batman opposes punishment, of course—he wants criminals to pay for what they've done—but he strives to find an option other than killing them, especially considering the finality of death. As he told Alfred, "If you're wrong, you don't get a second chance. That's a position of judgment I can never adopt" (unlike the Spectre, who has the authority of divine judgment on his side).[109]

Batman's belief that there is "always another choice" arises often in life-and-death situations when he is tempted to kill or must prevent others from doing so. In one fight with Zsasz, Batman dislocated his shoulder and considered that "even with one arm, I could snap his neck. And end this, forever. But I can't ... I won't ever ... become like him. There is always ... another way."[110] When his new Robin—Stephanie Brown, former Spoiler and future Batgirl—pulled Zsasz off Batman by yanking his nose up from behind, Batman scolded her: "You broke the rule, Stephanie. You resorted to deadly force." When she pleaded that Zsasz was still alive, Batman explained, "If his nose wasn't already broken, the cartilage would've splintered into his brain ... and you'd have killed him!" She tried to explain that she had to save Batman's life, but he stood firm: "Regardless, from your position there were a dozen ways to dispose of him safely. And you, whether consciously or not, went right for the kill." She argued that Zsasz almost killed them—and did kill hundreds of others—but Batman told her, "There are always other options than to kill. And if you can't learn to see those options first—then I can't have you as a partner."[111]

Of course, as they often do with his other rules, some in Batman's orbit challenge him on the idea that there are always other choices. After knocking out a terrorist named Hovar Brenc who had a ticking bomb strapped to his chest, Huntress threw him in a nearby van and drove it off a pier into the water, where it exploded without hurting anybody—other than Brenc, who died in the blast. After Huntress came to, Batman told her, "There were other options instead of killing Brenc. Maybe I could have disarmed Brenc's device." Huntress fought back, citing the risks of trying to save Brenc: "Maybe you could have been blown to itty bits along with lots of innocent bystanders. The world won't exactly miss that lunatic." When Batman said, predictably, that "That's not the way I work. I'm not a killer," Huntress muttered under her breath, "You sanctimonious ..." before saying out loud, "You're looking for fair play in Gotham? I got you all wrong, Batman. I thought we became what we are for the same reasons, because the streets took away everything we loved. I thought I knew what you were about."[112] Huntress resents the limits that Batman imposes on those he works with, believing they tie heroes' hands when they're dealing with criminals with no such self-imposed limits, and this imbalance leads to situations in which there may be no other option than to take a life to save others.

The same issue arose when, as described earlier, Wonder Woman killed Max Lord to save him from using a mind-controlled Superman to go on a killing spree.[113] We saw that Batman could not accept her actions, even after she justified them as the only way to prevent countless deaths. Later, during a heated debate between Wonder Woman, Batman, and Superman, the conversation turned to the Lord incident, and Diana once again found herself defending her actions, telling Superman, "That maniac murdered Ted Kord [the hero known as the Blue Beetle]. And he was going to use you to do the same to Bruce. There was no choice." Batman interjected, "There's always a choice for people like us," but Wonder Woman disagreed: "No, there isn't. Sometimes there is no other choice."[114]

Is there always another choice, as Batman claims, or is Wonder Woman right? As we saw in Chapter 3, it's easy to construct situations in which there is not, tragic dilemmas in which a person is forced to choose between two unacceptable options and therefore cannot escape "with clean hands." Even if another person is responsible for creating the situation—like the Arkham prisoner Kryppen who gave Batman a choice between killing one person or letting 200 die—and therefore bears ultimate responsibility, the person forced into making a choice still has to make it in the knowledge that it will have horrible consequences no matter what they decide. Even a deontologist who refuses to take an action such as killing or torture may be swayed if the price of maintaining that position becomes too high. One of the purposes of the trolley problem and its variants is to force people to consider just such a tragic dilemma—in particular, one that they had no role in creating, no responsibility to intervene in, but nonetheless one in which they must make a choice, either of which has a fatal impact on innocent lives.

Batman meant more than this, however, when he told Wonder Woman that "there's always a choice for people like us." Everyday heroes make sacrifices for the good of others, but superheroes do the impossible, denying the tragic aspect of the dilemma and instead finding a way to defeat it. Not satisfied with the options presented to them, they find a way to solve the problem without incurring either unacceptable outcome, including compromising their principles.[115]

Batman exemplifies this hope in two of the stories we described previously. In the case of Kryppen's ultimatum in Arkham Asylum, after Kryppen explained the stakes to Batman and taunted him sufficiently, he asked, "Still you hesitate? Evil is easy, Batman. It has already won the war against good. Your battle is already lost." Batman responded, "Then in a lost cause—I fight on!"[116] Batman attacked Kryppen and gave him the same poison that Kryppen gave the rest of the Arkham population, forcing him to hand over the antidote to save himself—and the 200 people he poisoned. Batman refused to accept the terms of the tragic dilemma as Kryppen defined them, and instead turned the situation against him, forcing his own solution and avoiding both dire consequences.

Also, in the climax of the battle between Batman and Jason Todd over killing the Joker, Jason slid a gun over to Batman, telling him cryptically that, even though he has always refused to kill his greatest foe, this time "you won't have a choice." When Batman affirmed yet again that he wouldn't do it, Jason said, "This is it. This is the time you decide." He grabbed the Joker, put a gun to his head, and gave Batman a very personal tragic dilemma: "If you won't kill this psychotic piece of filth ... I will. You want to stop me? You're going to have to kill me." When a visibly distraught Batman pleaded with his former Robin, "Stop this. Enough. You know I won't—," Jason explained, "All you've got is a head-shot. I'm going to blow his addled, deranged brains out—and if you want to stop it ... you're going to have to shoot me. Right in my face." They continue to go back and forth, and Jason counted to three ... but at the last instant, a batarang sliced across Jason's throat, forcing him to drop both the gun and the Joker as he covered his gaping neck wound. Appropriately, the Joker had the final word, gushing to Batman, "Oh, God!! I love it!! You managed to find a way to win ... and everybody still loses."[117]

Once again, Batman found a way to defeat the tragic dilemma because he is Batman. But unlike the earlier case, Batman still lost in a sense when he had to injure the living embodiment of his most profound guilt—just to save the person truly responsible for it. You could say that it's in the poetic nature of Batman, or the hero in general, that even when he manages to escape a tragic dilemma, he loses something in the process. He didn't have to betray his principle against killing, but he did have to hurt one of the people closest to him, and demonstrate to Jason once again that he will do anything to prevent life from being taken—even the Joker's life, and even from the boy he bludgeoned to death years ago.

Of course, these are but two examples of Batman overcoming the tragic dilemma. We could still argue that all the times he refused to kill the Joker (or the others), he accepted and chose the option that preserved his personal virtue at the expense of the murderers' future victims. His "other options" usually involve incarceration or institutionalization, which always fail to stop the criminals for long—and even though this isn't Batman's fault or responsibility, it does result in more deaths that he could prevent if he chose to. As a matter of right and justice, he shouldn't have to make up for the failures of the criminal justice and mental health systems of Gotham City, but as a matter of his utilitarian mission, he has to deal with the horrible hand dealt him and play it the best he can—and as long as he refuses to kill, or saves murderers from dying at another's hand, he's leaving cards on the table and more bodies in the morgue.

But He *Has* Killed ... and More Than Once ...

Even though Batman's refusal to kill is well known and repeatedly proclaimed by him and his subordinates, it has never been absolute. I'm not talking about cases in which criminals died by their own hand while fighting Batman, or fell off a building and he couldn't catch them.[118] I'm talking about cases in which Batman actively caused the death of someone or left them to die without making an effort to save them. Without claiming to be exhaustive, there are four significant cases in which Batman's actions definitely seem to betray his most solemn principle, the only one he claims to adhere to without exception.

The first has to do with—no big surprise here—the Joker. Although we've seen several cases in which Batman *almost* killed him, most notably after the Joker seemed to kill Tommy Elliot, Batman's vow not to kill seems most ironclad when it comes to the Clown Prince of Crime. What's more, Batman has probably saved the Joker's life more times than he has been tempted to take it.

However, there was one time when he seems to leave the Joker to die, saving himself with little thought for his longtime foe. After the incident at the United Nations following Jason Todd's murder, the Joker escaped on a helicopter, which Batman grabbed onto just as it was taking off. After a gunfight broke out on the helicopter—don't try this at home, kids—it began to careen into a nearby building. "Not quite the way I imagined the scenario ending," Batman thought. "I'll be lucky to escape with my life." Looking at the Joker, who had been shot in the chest during the firefight, the Dark Knight thought, "Farewell, old foe," and dove out of the copter into the water below, after which the helicopter crashed and exploded.[119] At no time do we see Batman try to stem the Joker's chest wound or even throw him out of the helicopter ahead of him, which would have given him at least a chance of surviving. The Joker did survive, of course, but no thanks to Batman, who, by all accounts, left him on that helicopter to die. (This also makes Batman's admission to Alfred later that "I wanted to kill the Joker back in that helicopter. I still don't know why I didn't. I should have. Yet I couldn't" seem more than a bit disingenuous.[120])

Another villain the Batman often expresses a desire to kill—and actually does, more than once—is Ra's al Ghul, the Demon's Head and father of Batman's sort-of-wife Talia. Several times in their initial meetings, Batman made threats to his life that sound like more than his ordinary bluffs to get information out of random street thugs. When Ra's offered help finding the killers of Kathy Kane (the original Batwoman), Batman said, "Keep it! I won't accept your help! Because someday soon I'll drop you down the deepest hole I can find—and when I do, I won't want any reason to show you mercy!"[121] One time he even made references to his rule against killing, but citing Ra's as the exception: "Though I've never intentionally killed ... I swear you will not leave here alive unless you surrender!"[122]

There are at least two times, however, that Batman did knowingly and intentionally kill him—although, like the proverbial bad penny (and our old friend the Joker), he always comes back, except in the case of Ra's he literally returns from the dead, thanks to the healing powers of the Lazarus Pit.[123] The first time was after Ra's poisoned the Gotham City water supply with a potion that triggered a fatal reaction to sunlight. Never ones to avoid the dramatic, Ra's and Batman agreed to a duel on the madman's satellite, before which they each drank the potion and then fought while trying to avoid an artificial sun ray. When the United States military attacked the satellite, Batman, Robin, and Talia escaped in one emergency craft while Ra's fled in another—which Batman booby-trapped to fly toward the sun rather than away from it, and also to open the hatch. As the Dynamic Duo watched the ashes of the Demon's Head float out of the spacecraft, Robin asked Batman, "Did you know what that sunlight would do to him?" Batman answered, "I knew, Robin, but I had to do it," but didn't say why. When Robin emphasized, "But Batman … you've killed him!" Batman merely asked, "Have I, Robin?"[124] Granted, Ra's is effectively immortal, but that assumes his body can be lowered into a Lazarus Pit, which he has done numerous times over his long life. But it is difficult to see how that could be done if his ashes were being drawn into the sun! So the answer to Batman's question would seem to be yes, but again, without explanation or justification.

Ra's did survive, of course. Soon thereafter, he visited the Batcave after releasing all of Batman's villains, offering to catch and kill them if Batman will agree to join him in his bid for world conquest. When Batman asked him how he was alive, Ra's explained that although he did die, the ashes that drifted from the spacecraft were not his, and he "was forced to undergo processes even more remarkable than mere immersion in the Lazarus Pit."[125] Later, after Batman had fought with nearly all of his key villains, he found Ra's in a deserted windmill, emerging from a Lazarus Pit for the first time without dying first, which gave him the strength of ten men. They did battle, with Ra's still trying to convince Batman to join him (and even to take a bath in the Pit himself) as the windmill began to collapse. Finally, Batman threw Ra's into the Pit, and according to the narration, "he will be forever haunted by the thrashing and shrieking of frenzied death beaten into a vessel of unnatural life."[126] Soon thereafter, the entire windmill collapsed, burying the pit. Even if he didn't intend to throw him into the Pit and he was unaware how it would affect him, as with the Joker on the helicopter, Batman seemed to make no attempt to save Ra's, but instead stood "pausing, letting it burn into his brain," before following the others out of the windmill. Even with someone as easily reanimated—if that's the best word—as Ra's al Ghul, Batman nonetheless shows stunning indifference to causing or allowing his death.

Perhaps the most callous and blatant example of Batman killing a criminal was the case of the Beast, or "KGBeast," a cybernetically enhanced assassin from the Soviet Union who was sent to America to kill important political, military, and scientific targets. Batman failed to prevent the Beast from taking out most of his targets (and over 100 people at a banquet), and in their final hand-to-hand fight in a sewer, Batman was spent, nearly dead on his feet, thinking "I feel a couple of ribs go. Only my training and reflexes save me from a fractured skull. My lungs are already beginning to burn" from the Beast's tear-gas gun. Nevertheless, he managed to trap the Beast in a room in the sewers, and when the Beast taunted him to continue their fight, Batman stood outside the door and calmly said:

> A few years ago I would have jumped at the chance to test myself against you. But time has taught me many valuable lessons. There's no reason for me to risk my life coming in there after you. It would neither accomplish anything nor prove anything worthwhile.[127]

As he barred the door, locking the Beast inside, Batman thought to himself, "Sometimes you have to ignore the rules. Sometimes circumstances are such that the rules pervert justice. I'm not in this business to protect the rules. I serve justice."[128]

Here, Batman *admits* that he has decided his own inviolable rule is no longer inviolable, and that the pursuit of justice—making sure the Beast, who has diplomatic immunity, is not extradited to the USSR where he'll escape punishment—justifies breaking his rule against killing him (or leaving him to die). Just in case there's any doubt, Batman told CIA agent Ralph Bundy, when he asked about the Beast, "You needn't worry about him anymore."[129] Bundy is visibly shaken—as we should be as well! Later, when Nightwing accused Batman of crossing the line in the rage after Jason Todd's death, "bludgeoning thugs instead of interrogating them," reminding him of the time he "nearly let one of them die, locked away in a subway tunnel," Batman said, "I informed the police." Nightwing replied, "Hours later. On second thought. It doesn't matter that he had already escaped—you considered letting him die."[130]

Just like in the satellite as they watched what they thought were Ra's al Ghul's ashes floating into the sun, Dick Grayson had it right with respect to the Beast: Even though it didn't take in either case, Batman did intend to kill (or leave for dead), and with no reasonable justification.[131] Did his refusal to give a good reason reflect the very failure of his moral virtue that he fears most? Or was it a silent acknowledgment that his mission sometimes necessitates killing his most heinous foes?

In this chapter, we discussed the one rule Batman (almost) never breaks, even though it would contribute immeasurably to the success of his proclaimed mission, which we noted was one of the most significant aspects of Batman's moral inconsistency. In the next two chapters, we will look at some widely held moral principles that he *will* break in pursuit of the mission. Even though this behavior shows more consistency within the mission itself, the similarity between these actions he will perform and the one he won't raises different issues with respect to consistency—once again, issues that may seem familiar to those of us without capes or cowls.

Notes

1   *Batman* #0 (October 1994).

2   *Batman: Legends of the Dark Knight* #172 (December 2003).

3   *Batman: Legends of the Dark Knight Annual* #1 (1991).

4   *Batman* #488 (January 1993).

5   *Batman* #657 (November 2006).

6   *Batman: Vengeance of Bane* #1 (January 1993).

7   *Batman* #424 (October 1988).

8   *Batman* #641 (August 2005). This was after Jason died and … got better. We'll get to that soon.

9   *Batman/Huntress: Cry for Blood* #1 (June 2000).

10   *Detective Comics* #603 (August 1989).

11   *Detective Comics* #649 (Early September 1992). And yes, since you asked: Stephanie Brown later become Robin for about as long as it took for you to read this endnote, and then Batgirl for about as long as it took for you to read this book.

12   *Robin*, vol. 4, #131 (December 2004).

13   *Batman* #488 (January 1993).

14   *Batman: Legends of the Dark Knight* #120 (August 1999).

15   Eventually (in *Batgirl*, vol. 1, #73, April 2006), Cassandra learns that Shiva is her mother. (Small world, huh?)

16   *Batman* #331 (January 1981).

17   *Batman: Legends of the Dark Knight* #173 (January 2004).

18   *Batman: The Cult* #1 (August 1988).

19   *The Huntress* #1 (April 1989), retold in *Huntress: Year One* #1 (July 2008). (The original Huntress was the daughter of the Golden Age Batman and Catwoman on Earth-2, before *Crisis on Infinite Earths*, and had none of the later version's murderous tendencies.)

20   *Detective Comics* #721 (May 1998).

21   *JLA* #39 (March 2000).

22   *Batman: Shadow of the Bat* #28 (June 1994).

23   Ibid.

24   To be fair, it isn't that Valley didn't value life, but he does make a distinction that Batman rarely does. After Gordon took a swing at him, asking him, "Does human life mean nothing to you, you cold, calculating—!" he stumbled off the rooftop. Valley caught him and said, "On the contrary, Commissioner—human life means everything to me. *Decent* human life" (ibid.).

25   *Wonder Woman*, vol. 2, #219 (September 2005). I discuss this episode further in my chapter "'What I Had to Do': The Ethics of Wonder Woman's Execution of Maxwell Lord," in *Wonder Woman and Philosophy: The Amazonian Mystique*, edited by Jacob M. Held (Malden, MA: Wiley Blackwell, 2017), pp. 104–114.

26 *Wonder Woman*, vol. 2, #220 (October 2005).

27 *Infinity Crisis* #1 (November 2005). And, like the hypothetical example from the last chapter of the government executing an innocent citizen to quell a violent uprising, there was negative fallout from Wonder Woman's actions, including imitators who felt justified in using violence, increased distrust of superheroes in general, and eventually a hearing at the International Court of Criminal Justice. See *Infinity Crisis* #1; *Wonder Woman*, vol. 2, #220 (October 2005); and *Manhunter*, vol. 3, #26 (February 2007).

28 *Batman: Shadow of the Bat Annual* #3 (1995).

29 *Batman: Shadow of the Bat* #74 (May 1998).

30 *Detective Comics* #746 (July 2000), "Evolution IV: Aftertaste."

31 *Batman: Legends of the Dark Knight* #160 (December 2002). One time he used Cassandra Cain, when she was new to Gotham, to bluff: when a guy Batman wanted information out of said "everybody knows the bat don't kill," Batman asked, "Then tell me this. The girl behind me. Has she killed any of your men?" When the guy said no, Batman continued, "Good. I trust her not to. I'll trust her not to kill you, either, when I leave the two of you alone. I'd be very upset with her if she did something like that" (*Batgirl*, vol. 1, #3, June 2000).

32 *Batman: Legends of the Dark Knight* #214 (March 2007).

33 The classic formulations are found in Philippa Foot, *Virtues and Vices* (Oxford: Oxford University Press, 2002), ch. 2, and Judith Jarvis Thompson, *Rights, Restitution, & Risk: Essays in Moral Theory* (Cambridge, MA: Harvard University Press, 1986), chs. 6 and 7. There has been a massive revival of interest in the trolley dilemma in recent years; two recent popular treatments are David Edmonds, *Would You Kill the Fat Man? The Trolley Problem and What Your Answer Tells Us about Right and Wrong* (Princeton, NJ: Princeton University Press, 2013), and Thomas Cathcart, *The Trolley Problem, or Would You Throw the Fat Guy Off the Bridge: A Philosophical Conundrum* (New York: Workman, 2013). For a more scholarly analysis (including commentary from Thomson and others), see F.M. Kamm, *The Trolley Problem Mysteries* (Oxford: Oxford University Press, 2016).

34 The tragic event occurred in *Batman: The Killing Joke* (1988), and Barbara first took up the identity of Oracle in *Suicide Squad* #23 (January 1989), becoming a major presence in all the Batman titles and especially *Birds of Prey*, in which she led a team of mostly female heroes in a rotating line-up that usually included Black Canary and the Huntress. (As of the beginning of the New 52, Barbara's paralysis had been cured and she returned to her original role of Batgirl.)

35 *Detective Comics* #741 (February 2000).

36 *Batman* #427 (December 1988).

37 The resurrection of Jason Todd was explained in *Batman Annual* #25 (May 2006), and involved Ra's al Ghul, his daughter Talia, and the continuity-shattering punch of Superboy-Prime. (Don't ask about the last one.)

38   *Batman* #641 (August 2005).

39   *Batman* #650 (April 2006).

40   *The Spectre* #51 (March 1997).

41   *Batman: Gotham Knights* #74 (April 2006). Note that this issue and *Batman* #650 both came out the same month—and just in time for a wet-behind-the-ears philosopher to start writing a chapter on Batman, Joker, and the trolley problem for a book he was lucky enough to have the chance to co-edit. (Thanks, Bill!)

42   *Batman* #614 (June 2003). Later, after the Black Mask seems to have killed Spoiler, Catwoman told Batman she should have killed him when she had the chance, given all the people close to her that he killed, in a clear analogue to Batman's issues with killing the Joker (*Detective Comics* #800, January 2005, "Alone at Night").

43   Ibid.

44   See Michael S. Moore, "Torture and the Balance of Evils," *Israel Law Review* 23 (1989): 280–344.

45   *The Spectre* #51 (March 1997). See also the "Going Sane" storyline in *Batman: Legends of the Dark Knight* #65–68 (November 1994–February 1995), in which Joker "goes sane" after he thinks he finally killed Batman, but he reverts to his old self even before he realizes Batman is still alive.

46   This threat was well spelled out in Philip K. Dick's 1956 short story "The Minority Report," included in a collection of the same name (New York: Citadel, 2016) and made into a film in 2002 and a TV series in 2015.

47   Peter Singer, "The Drowning Child," *The Internationalist*, April 5, 1997, available at https://newint.org/features/1997/04/05/drowning.

48   The question of how binding Kant's positive duties are is a major point of contention among Kant scholars that equals any rivalry behind fans of Batman and Superman. For example, see Mary J. Gregor, *Laws of Freedom: A Study of Kant's Method of Applying the Categorical Imperative in the "Metaphysik der Sitten"* (Oxford: Basil Blackwell, 1963), ch. 7; Thomas E. Hill, Jr., *Dignity and Practical Reason in Kant's Moral Theory* (Ithaca, NY: Cornell University Press, 1992), ch. 8; and Marcia Baron, *Kantian Ethics Almost Without Apology* (Ithaca, NY: Cornell University Press, 1995), ch. 3.

49   Hence the provocative titles to Edmonds' and Catcart's books (says the guy who titled a book chapter and newspaper op-ed "Should Batman Kill the Joker?").

50   In fact, Foot's original trolley problem was presented in an analysis of the "doctrine of double effect," a controversial ethical idea that distinguishes between intended and incidental effects of an action.

51   There is another variation of the trolley dilemma, the "surgeon problem," that this case resembles. In it, you are a surgeon with five patients, each of whom will die within hours without an organ transplant (unique to each). A healthy

patient comes into the office for a check-up, and you find he has all five healthy organs your other five patients need. Do you kill the healthy patient and give his organs to the five? This version definitely has a more visceral nature to it, but the essence is the same—and reactions to it are often widely different from the classic trolley problem, which raises interesting questions about the aspects of the problem that make them different (discussed by Thomson in her book cited earlier).

52 *Underworld Unleashed: Batman—Devil's Asylum* #1 (1995).

53 For example, in his *Meditations on First Philosophy* (1641), René Descartes suggested that an evil demon may be responsible for the world we experience (as part of his larger skeptical argument about what knowledge we can be sure of), which is discussed in Harry Frankfurt's book *Demons, Dreamers and Madmen: The Defense of Reason in Descartes's Meditations* (Princeton, NJ: Princeton University Press, 2007). As it happens, Frankfurt has his own evil demon that he invokes in a challenge to conventional ideas about moral responsibility and free will (see "Alternate Possibilities and Moral Responsibility," reprinted as the first chapter in his book *The Importance of What We Care About: Philosophical Essays*, Cambridge: Cambridge University Press, 1988).

54 Ibid. When Gordon tells him, "you saved the entire city from that deranged madman. Give yourself a pat on the back, I say," Batman simply responds, "I'll take it under advisement." (Gordon: "You do that.")

55 *Batman* #614 (June 2003).

56 Ibid.

57 Remember also that Batman acknowledges his responsibility to stop the criminals he lets live from hurting innocent people again, as we saw when he saved the Black Mask's life, knowing full well he saved the life of a man who will go on to kill again (*Batman* #520, July 1995).

58 *Batman: Shadow of the Bat* #62 (May 1997).

59 *Batman* #614 (June 2003).

60 For more, see various chapters in my edited volume, *The Insanity Defense: Multidisciplinary Views on Its History, Trends, and Controversies* (Santa Barbara, CA: Praeger, 2017).

61 *Batman* #429 (January 1989). Did I mention Iran named him their ambassador to the UN in the previous issue? Oh yes, they did.

62 *The Spectre* #51 (March 1997).

63 *Batman* #313 (July 1979).

64 Ibid.

65 *Batman: Shadow of the Bat* #62 (May 1997). Ironically, earlier in this issue, a therapist at Arkham told Harvey he lets his coin "choose" his actions "to absolve you of any responsibility for the atrocities you commit—for the evil deeds that your 'good' side cannot accept." Despite Harvey's delusions, we

know full well that he still bears responsibility for his actions, because he chose
to use the coin in that way.

66 *Batman* #429 (January 1989).

67 *Batman* #614 (June 2003).

68 *Detective Comics* #741 (February 2000).

69 *Batman* #451 (Late July 1990).

70 *Batman* #615 (July 2003). Much earlier, Batman also admitted to Nightwing
that he was afraid he'd kill Boss Zucco, the man who ordered Dick's parents
killed. When Zucco was released from prison, Batman and Nightwing watched
as rival criminals shot him as he walked through the prison gates. When
Nightwing asked Batman why he just stood there, he said, "I watched him and
I was shaking. I was ... afraid I'd strangle him for" what he had done to the
Graysons (*Batman* #438–439, September 1989).

71 *Batman* #544 (July 1997).

72 *Batman* #650 (April 2006). And this sometimes goes for minor criminals as
well. Early in Jason Todd's training, he and Batman were pursuing a vigilante
who was killing the same criminals the Dynamic Duo hunt, and after Batman
reiterated that they don't kill, Jason said, "I guess. But I'm still glad those guys
are dead," and Batman agreed: "Me, too, Jason—but I'm not proud of it"
(*Batman* #402, December 1986).

73 *Batman: Legends of the Dark Knight Annual* #1 (1991).

74 *Batman: The Cult* #1 (August 1988).

75 *Batman: Gotham Knights* #74 (April 2006).

76 *Batman* #450 (Early July 1990).

77 *Batman: Dark Detective* #2 (July 2005).

78 *Batman* #650 (April 2006).

79 At the same time, though, some prefer to keep temptation to remind them of
the danger of relapse. When the Deacon wanted Batman to kill him, Batman
refused, thinking, "It would be so easy ... But it would be too easy. The only
way to keep that keen edge is to run along it occasionally" (*Batman: The Cult*
#4, November 1988).

80 See George Ainslie, *Breakdown of Will* (Cambridge: Cambridge University
Press, 2001), pp. 94–100.

81 *Batman* #493 (May 1993).

82 *Batman: Gotham Knights* #74 (April 2006).

83 Technically, a virtue is what Aristotle called the "golden mean" between two
extremes. For example, courage is the mean between cowardice and
foolhardiness, and honesty is the mean between deceitfulness and forthright-
ness. Either of the extremes is considered a vice, although in the pairs given
here, the "lesser" extreme is more harmful to others, while the "higher"
extreme is more harmful to oneself. For our purposes, we can simply treat
virtues and vices as goods and bads (with apologies to all my virtue ethics

friends, assuming I have any left after this). For a more accurate and thorough application of virtue ethics to a superhero, see my book cited in note 85 below.

84   For more on virtue ethics, see Rosalind Hursthouse and Glen Pettigrove's entry in the *Stanford Encyclopedia of Philosophy*, at https://plato.stanford.edu/entries/ethics-virtue/.

85   In another book, *The Virtues of Captain America: Modern-Day Lessons on Character from a World War II Superhero* (Hoboken, NJ: Wiley Blackwell, 2014), I described the titular hero as exemplifying virtue ethics with a particular emphasis on principle (borrowed from deontology). (An early suggestion for the title of the book you're currently enjoying was *The Vices of Batman*, but I'm afraid that might have made even Batman question his vow not to kill!)

86   *Batman* #402 (December 1986).

87   *Batman* #510 (August 1994). I particularly like his choice of terms, given that I profess for a living.

88   *Batman: Legends of the Dark Knight Annual* #1 (1991).

89   *Batman* #614 (June 2003).

90   *Batman: Gotham Knights* #74 (April 2006).

91   *Batman* #400 (October 1986).

92   *Batman: Legends of the Dark Knight* #65 (November 1994).

93   *Batman: Legends of the Dark Knight* #144 (August 2001).

94   *Batman* #509 (July 1994).

95   *Batman* #534 (September 1996).

96   *Batgirl*, vol. 1, #23 (February 2002).

97   *Robin*, vol. 1, #4 (April 1991).

98   *Batman* #658 (December 2006).

99   *Detective Comics* #696 (April 1996).

100   *Batman: Gotham Knights* #26 (April 2002), "Innocent Until." As Alfred told Jason Todd years earlier, "the closest I've ever come to a criminal act … was an especially anemic performance as Petrucchio in *The Taming of the Shrew* when I was an actor in England" (*Batman: Legends of the Dark Knight* #100, November 1997, "A Great Day for Everyone").

101   This is reminiscent of Immanuel Kant's *kingdom of ends*, the highest stage of moral community when all persons respect and support each other out of respect for their shared dignity and autonomy; see *Grounding for the Metaphysics of Morals*, trans. James W. Ellington (Indianapolis, IN: Hackett Publishing Company, 1785/1993), pp. 433–437.

102   *Batman* #650 (April 2006).

103   *Batman* #427 (December 1988). She wasn't, by the way.

104   *Joker: Last Laugh* #6 (January 2002).

105   *Nightwing*, vol. 2, #93 (July 2004).

106   *Nightwing*, vol. 2, #98 (December 2004).

107 *Batman* #634 (January 2005).

108 *Batman* #541 (April 1997).

109 *Batman: Shadow of the Bat* #62 (May 1997).

110 *Detective Comics* #796 (September 2004), "... And Red All Over."

111 Ibid. Stephanie didn't last long as Robin—not because she crossed the line, but because she disobeyed a direct order (*Robin*, vol. 4, #128, September 2004).

112 *Detective Comics* #653 (November 1992).

113 *Wonder Woman*, vol. 2, #219 (September 2005).

114 *Infinite Crisis* #1 (December 2005).

115 The problem with the ending of the 2013 film *Man of Steel* was that the writers painted Superman into a corner where he couldn't find a way out of his tragic dilemma and was forced to kill Zod, betraying the promise that superheroes will solve problems on their own terms and thereby defeating the very concept of Superman. For more, see "My Thoughts on *Man of Steel*," *The Comics Professor*, June 16, 2013, at http://www.comicsprofessor.com/2013/06/my-thoughts-on-man-of-steel.html.

116 *Underworld Unleashed: Batman—Devil's Asylum* #1 (1995).

117 *Batman* #650 (April 2006).

118 I'm also not referring to his earliest days when he carried a gun and shot criminals—remember, I'm sticking to the modern portrayal of Batman beginning in the early 1970s. Nor am I discussing alternate versions of Batman where he was all trigger-happy. Any one of those may be your Batman, but he sure ain't mine.

119 *Batman* #429 (January 1989).

120 *Batman* #450 (Early July 1990).

121 *Detective Comics* #485 (September 1979), "The Vengeance Vow!"

122 *Batman* #244 (September 1972), "The Demon Lives Again!"

123 Good philosophers always qualify their claims, especially empirical ones that can be so easily disputed. I don't think there are more cases of Batman killing Ra's al Ghul, so I'm sure someone will tell me two hours after this book is published if there are!

124 *Batman Annual* #8 (1982).

125 *Batman* #400 (October 1986).

126 Ibid.

127 *Batman* #420 (June 1988).

128 Ibid.

129 Ibid.

130 *Batman* #439 (September 1989).

131 There's one more interesting story that doesn't quite rise to the level of killing, but is notable anyway because it is possible that Batman may have killed if circumstances hadn't intervened. During his second year as Batman, he

found his parents' killer, Joe Chill, and actually swore to his dead father that he'd kill him with the same gun Chill used to kill the Waynes (*Detective Comics* #577, August 1987). Later, Batman revealed his identity and his backstory to Chill and then pointed the gun at him, but before he had a chance to pull the trigger, the villainous Reaper shot Chill himself (*Detective Comics* #578, September 1987). Would Batman have killed Chill? We will never know.

7

Torture and Violence

As Batman often says, he'll do anything to further this mission other than kill—and as we'll see in this chapter and the next, he meant it. Although he draws the line at killing (or letting someone die), Batman willfully engages in practices such as torture, extreme violence, and a flagrant disregard for the law, each of which is widely considered a serious violation of moral rules or principles, but which he nonetheless disregards as essential to his mission, and apparently in ways that killing is not. The violation of moral principles for the sake of his utilitarian goals, no matter how we may judge it, is not inconsistent as such. However, the similarity between the many things he will do and the one thing he will not, without any reasonable explanation for the difference, does reflect significant inconsistencies in his overall moral code.

Part 1: Torture

In a recent story, Bruce Wayne's journal read, "normally—famously—the Dark Knight Detective does not—will not—torture, maim—nor kill."[1] As we know well from the last chapter, he certainly doesn't kill (with a handful of exceptions), and as we will see later in this chapter, although he is violent, it is rare that he "maims" his foes.

But it is difficult to say that Batman "does not torture." As he told a member of the Ghost Dragons after he took out the rest of the gang, "I don't kill. But I am not averse to inflicting pain … unless I get some answers."[2] When Batman interrogated Ra's al Ghul's man Abbot, Abbot told him, "You won't

Batman and Ethics, First Edition. Mark D. White.

torture me. You're out of options." Batman held up an injector and said, "Not quite." Abbot yelled, "No! No, you can't ..." but Batman said, "Just did. I don't like using chemicals. This one is particularly nasty. Makes sodium pentothal look like mother's milk."[3] Under most definitions, the infliction or threat of pain, if serious enough, with the intention of getting someone to talk, does constitute torture—and as we shall see, he practices it often, brutally, and, perhaps most disturbing, very casually.

We might expect this to be the most ethically disturbing and widely discussed aspect of Batman's crimefighting methods. Actually, though, it raises very few eyebrows, and it is often cheered and celebrated as Batman "doing what he has to do" to people who "must have deserved it." (I must warn you, I do break out of story quite a bit in this section—it's very difficult not to, given the widespread portrayals of torture in our popular culture.) It isn't only Batman, of course; we see "heroes" in popular fiction inflict torture all the time, especially "rogue" cops or government agents on TV shows and in movies, whom audiences cheer because they "get the job done," and because the people they torture are "obviously" bad guys (usually suspected terrorists) with information about plans to kill thousands of people.[4] This section will explore the problems with this, using real-world arguments regarding torture to comment on its portrayal in Batman stories (and other fiction).

Does Batman Practice Torture?

Batman is often very lackadaisical about his use of torture. For example, when he and Jim Gordon were investigating heavily armed gangs, Batman told him to "give me an hour" to get information from them. After subduing the crew of a tank and trapping most of them inside with a gas pellet, Batman hung the last one upside-down and said, "Now it's time to answer a few questions." When he returned to Gordon, the older man commented, "Fifty-nine minutes. You said you'd have answers," to which Batman replied, "I should never have made that promise. I got those answers in half an hour," and we can only assume how he did it.[5] In another case, Batman dangled a guy off a bridge over the river to get information; when he said he didn't remember much, Batman said, "Then I guess you're no good to me," after which the guy spilled everything (and then some).[6] What makes this second example notable is not just how much the guy talked about every little detail he knew, which is played for humor, but that it happened in an issue dedicated to Batman being in a fantastic mood after clearing Bruce

Wayne's name from a murder charge and getting on with his life: reconnecting with his "family," rewarding his employees at Wayne Enterprises, and playing chess with Two-Face in Arkham Asylum.

Before we go any further, we should be careful to distinguish "mere" violence from torture. As I'm using the terms—nothing extraordinary here, but specific to the subject matter—violence describes the mostly hand-to-hand combat that Batman engages in when fighting his foes, which Leslie Thompkins regularly argues perpetuates the cycle of violence and tragedy in Gotham City. When Batman beats up a bunch of henchman to get to their boss, or punches out a mugger before he can prey on an elderly couple, Batman is countering violence with violence and sometimes even pre-empting it. His use of violence has moral questions attached to it, no doubt, and we'll look at those in the next section, but I don't consider this to be equivalent to torture.

Torture is a notoriously difficult concept to define, involving more abstract ideas of harm, rights, and intention. One particularly useful and widely known statement is in the 1984 United Nations Convention against Torture and Other Cruel, Inhuman or Degrading Treatment or Punishment, which defines torture as "any act by which severe pain or suffering, whether physical or mental, is intentionally inflicted on a person for such purposes as obtaining from him, or a third person, information or a confession" as well as for punishment or intimidation.[7] Similar to this, I use the term here to describe the extreme violence Batman uses or threatens in order to get information out of people. For example, he often hangs someone upside down out a window or off a tall building or bridge, implying if not openly saying ("I hope you can fly") that he'll drop them unless they talk, which uses mental suffering to compel cooperation against the person's will.[8]

In one notable tale, Batman wanted a white-collar criminal named Leland Lindsay to testify against a mob boss, but Lindsay said, "It'll take more than a bat suit and a spooky voice to make me talk." Batman dropped him off the roof, with Lindsay shouting "I'll talk! I'll talk!" as he fell. Batman caught him at the last minute, saying, "Must've miscalculated. I wanted what little hair you have left to scrape the pavement. I'll give it a little more play next time." Lindsay promised to talk but asked for protection, which Batman promised, adding, "And if you get any ideas about changing your mind, remember … there are a lot of tall buildings in Gotham."[9] Even though most people know that Batman doesn't kill, compromising his ability to bluff (as we saw in the last chapter), the possibility that he might make an exception in *their* case is sometimes enough to get them to reveal what he wants to know. Although usually he'll simply beat someone until they talk—as he says to a bar full of thugs, "the beatings stop when you start talking"—he can be more creative, as when he told a Russian mobster, "trust me, I have many ways to make you talk to me."[10]

The common thread here is the way Batman uses fear of extreme pain, injury, or death to get people to talk. It isn't just that he hits them, or hangs them outside a window, but that there is always the implicit threat of more pain to come (if not death): "We can do this the easy way ... or I can hurt you."[11] He doesn't need to actually inflict pain; Batman can be very delicate as he dangles someone over a busy street a hundred feet below. All that he needs is for the person to experience enough fear that they will say whatever he wants to hear to avoid the dreaded consequence—and this fear itself constitutes torture.

In fact, all torture can be considered psychological in nature, and this is part of what distinguishes it from Batman's "ordinary" violence. It isn't the experience of pain but the fear and anticipation of it—or more of it—that transforms mere violence into torture. In one case, Batman beat a room full of mercenaries senseless and then wanted their leader to talk. "See, I did some recon before we stationed here," their leader said. "Got the whole brief of Gotham—the overambitious P.D., the criminal element, the Batman ... Batman won't kill me. We have no intel on Batman ever killing anyone." Batman replied, "What you mean is that you have no evidence. I'm not sure why you'd think I'd leave any. But you're right, I won't kill you. I'll just incapacitate your men." And then he proceeded to name each of his men and the specific injuries of each that he could exploit, such as "Deren, Robert. Age twenty-three. Gave a kidney to his diabetic sister two years ago. Probably needs the other one." He went around the room, standing on one guy's knee injured in football, grabbing another by the shoulder where he took shrapnel in the war and, as he grimaced, said, "still takes painkillers for it." He came to the last one and said, "Perfect medical record. *So far.*"[12] The leader dropped his head and told Batman what he wanted to know, not because he feared what Batman would do to him—Batman never touched him—but what he would do to his men (other than beating them senseless). In effect, this is no different than criminals holding a hostage until the police or superhero gives them what they want, other than the fact that this was Batman doing it.

Other times Batman's torture is purely psychological, such as the time he concocted an entire lifeboat scenario in which he and two other people were "trapped" in an airtight room and had to decide who would sacrifice themselves to save the other two—all to get one of the other people in the room to confess to a crime. As Batman explained when it was over,

> All a sham. An elaborate one, I'll admit, but it had to be convincing. You had to believe it. There was only one way you'd ever admit your guilt. You had to believe concealment no longer mattered … *You had to believe you were going to die.*[13]

Batman didn't lay a finger on the man who confessed, but made him face his own impending mortality all the same, in a particularly twisted kind of torture. He used a similar technique when he locked a criminal named Nico in a morgue locker—while wearing a straitjacket, no less—and left him there, returning periodically to pull out the drawer and ask for information about the Penguin. One time, when Nico said he wanted to make a deal, Batman responded, "I don't make deals," and left again. Finally, even though Nico argued that the Penguin would have him killed, Batman stared him down until he cracked—although there is no doubt that it was his extended stay in the morgue, facing his own mortality in a different way, that did the trick.[14] Other times, of course, Batman is much more direct, such as when he held a mobster's head against an unlit burner on a gas stove next to one with a high flame, threatening to light the one under his head if he didn't talk.[15] This is a particularly visceral form of torture that eschews violence for the frightening prospect of a fiery death to motivate the victim to talk.

Sometimes Batman starts with run-of-the-mill violence but escalates it in way that heightens the anticipation of future pain, which can be as simple as repeated pummeling or dunks in water (over 30 times, in one case, before the victim talked).[16] A story of Batman's early years gives us one example. When trying to get information on a vigilante from a gunrunner named Micky, Batman slammed his car trunk lid down on his hand, breaking it. "Think carefully, Micky" he said. "From here on— wrong answers bring you pain," and when Micky didn't give him what he wanted, Batman said, "Wrong answer, Micky!" and slammed the door down on his hand again.[17] When he didn't get enough information from Micky, he tortured other people, finally visiting one man at a pork processing plant and telling him about what he did to the last few guys before hanging him over a giant meat grinder, switching it on, and then slowly lowering the man toward the swirling blades until he talked.[18] In another case, Batman thrust his fingers into the chest of the man he's interrogating and asked him,

> Are you familiar with Dim Mak? It's an ancient form of martial arts where you strike vital points of an opponent's body causing paralysis, intense and prolonged pain or death. The pain you're experiencing is one of a hundred levels I can hit that are increasingly more painful as we go. So, I ask you again ...[19]

Batman got the information he wanted without having to go to level two—simply the threat of escalating degrees of pain instilled enough fear to get the response he wanted.

But ... isn't Batman the "good guy," and aren't the people he beats and tortures for information the "bad guys"? It's very easy to think that, and doing so helps people that are repulsed by torture in the real world enjoy it in fiction, in which case we can rest easy that it's being used on the "right" people and for the "right" reasons. For example, a retired police detective named Gary Sloan who responded to the call the night Thomas and Martha Wayne were murdered asked Batman about a later case in which a suspect didn't respond to police interrogation, but after seeing Batman he confessed to everything. When Sloan asked Batman how he got him to change his mind so quickly, the Dark Knight said, "Held him upside down in front of an oncoming train," to which Sloan responded, "Oh ... good call."[20] The people Batman interrogates, however, are not always the people he's looking for, but often merely people who might have information he needs to find the real culprits. They may be shady characters, but not the suspected criminals he has sworn to fight—and if they are suspected of a crime, Batman should be capturing and handing them over to the police, not torturing them in a perverse sort of punishment. If they're not suspected of a crime, then his torturous behavior is even more unjustified—in that case, they're not even the "bad guys," and they're not deserving of any "punishment" at all.

We see this conflict when Batman suspended Alex Kosov over the tracks in front of an upcoming train to get information about the Black Mask. As he told her, "You're here for punishment ... You're responsible for the 'Alamo High massacre.' You aligned with the Black Mask ... and helped turn my city against me. You deserve much worse." When Kosov told him, "You ... you don't kill," he replied, "The dead don't talk. You know what I want, Alex." When she told him the Black Mask would kill her if she talked, he simply said good-bye, and only returned to rescue her at the last moment after she gave him the information he wanted.[21] It's one thing for a prosecutor to cut a deal with a lesser criminal to get information to catch a more important one, but that is an offer, not a threat at the end of a fist or a rope. Most of the people Batman tortures, however, have not been convicted of a crime, and most have not even been charged or accused—the only thing that qualifies them for his treatment is that they have information he wants, and he'll use whatever means available to get this information.

In an astonishing twist, it is the murderous crime lord Black Mask who most eloquently states the problem with Batman's behavior. Broadcasting from a mobile reporter's camera during the citywide gang war, Black Mask proclaimed himself "the new, undisputed, absolute crime lord of Gotham City." He then turned on the Dark Knight:

> For years, all of Gotham has been terrorized by that sick, psychopathic Halloween reject, with his ridiculous bat tights and cape ... In the name of his own self-proclaimed "war on crime" this lunatic has beaten, tortured and crippled countless individuals ... I mean—excuse me? So it's not a crime when a masked vigilante brutally assaults a "suspected" burglar or drug addict? Let's not kid ourselves, people. The Batman's no different from Scarface, or the Joker, or even yours truly. The man is a menace. A dangerous criminal.[22]

Black Mask's allegations encompass all of Batman's illegal activities, focusing on his use of violence and torture as well as the fact that his victims are suspects (at best), not convicted criminals (who deserve state punishment rather than private vengeance or torture). This contrasts nicely with an earlier story in which a KGB agent working with Batman and the GCPD wanted to torture a suspect for information, saying, "If our time is on such a short fuse—why not force him to talk? His individual pain is nothing in the face of the consequences." Batman told her, however, "I'm afraid we don't do it that way in this country"—at least not officially, and definitely not with the endorsement of the Gotham City Police Department (at least as run by Jim Gordon).[23]

The Ethics of Torture

What makes torture so problematic ethically? After all, the KGB agent's rationale seems reasonable: in the big picture, the pain and agony of one person, especially if that person is withholding valuable information, is "nothing" compared to the well-being of all the people who would benefit if the authorities had that information. In terms of the simple utilitarianism that the KGB agent is expressing, this argument makes some sense. Even if they had the wrong person, it seems a small cost to impose pain or fear on one person for the chance of saving the lives of many others—the benefits would seem to exceed the cost, as high as that cost is for the person tortured.

The argument that torture is wrong is usually rooted, as we might expect, in deontology rather than utilitarianism—and we'll get to those arguments soon—but, to be sure, there are also utilitarian reasons to oppose torture. The most direct argument is that torture simply doesn't work. If the purpose of torture is to elicit truthful and accurate information, putting a person under severe psychological distress isn't likely to serve that purpose. If the victims talk at all, they will say anything to make the torture stop, whether it's what the victims think their tormentors want to hear or just something, *anything*, to make the harsh treatment stop for even a minute. Usually, providing accurate information requires some degree of clear, rational thinking, and the kind of mindset torture puts one under is anything but.[24] A less direct argument is similar to the one against sacrificing the innocent civilian to quell the violent mob: even if it works in the short run, chances are torture will only make things worse in the long run as news of the practice spreads, political resistance builds, and the act becomes less effective as potential victims prepare for it. Endorsing torture as an official tactic may encourage the development of a government that is increasingly willing to do anything to achieve its ends; much like Batman's refusal to kill because he doesn't want to head down that path, governments should also be wary of crossing ethical lines from which they may never be able to return. (So should a certain caped crusader, come to think of it.)

Of course, Batman's torture is almost always shown to be effective. In the worst case scenario, the people he threatens or beats up to get information don't know anything, but usually they lead him to his target (or to someone else who knows more, such as with poor Micky). Perhaps Batman is just really good at what he does—he certainly gets enough practice—or maybe our view is selective, and we only see the success and not the failures. But even when he has to beat up a dozen guys to find the one who knows what he needs to know, what gets ignored here is that he beat up a dozen guys—who may not have done anything to deserve their beatings—to get information from one, inflicting an enormous amount of undeserved pain for very little return (not to mention the implications of violating their rights, which we'll discuss next). What makes this even worse is that most of the cases he investigates are not mass murderers such as the Joker and Ra's al Ghul. For instance, when searching for Dawn Golden, a childhood friend of his, Batman beat up the Penguin—hardly the most physically imposing of Batman's archvillains—going so far as to break both of his arms to find out where Golden was. This elicited a strong reaction of shock and disgust from Alfred, watching remotely, his mouth wide open, and asking, "Sir ... what are you doing?"[25] Thefts, kidnapping, and single murders are serious crimes in their own right, of course, but hardly the "ticking bomb" scenario often used to justify the extreme measure of torture and its attendant harms.

But the ineffectual nature of torture isn't the reason most of its opponents feel it's unethical. Their reasoning is usually based on principle, maintaining that it's simply wrong from a deontological point of view grounded in the basic dignity and respect that every person deserves, regardless of their character or behavior, which prohibits any treatment that diminishes their humanity. As law professor Charles Fried and philosopher Gregory Fried write, "Torture grossly offends the bedrock premise that every human being is a locus of inestimable value," which Immanuel Kant called dignity.[26] In Kant's moral philosophy, persons should never be treated in ways that deny them their value as persons—particularly those that compromise their very faculties of reason, as torture does. Persons must always be treated as ends in themselves, which allows them the possibility of consenting to their treatment, a possibility that is denied them in more common instances of deceit or coercion—and torture can be considered an extreme form of the latter. In addition to imposing physical or psychological torment, torture denies its victims the ability to refuse consent, in much the same way that drugging someone in order to sexually assault them does—or even giving them a truth serum, as Batman also does (and occasionally expresses qualms about, as he did with Abbot).

This is another reason deontologists (especially those of a Kantian persuasion) oppose torture: it's a perfect example of using one person simply as a means to an end. In a literal sense, torture "uses up" a person, compromising and potentially destroying their mind and spirit in order to further another end, however worthy it is. Philosopher Bob Brecher puts it even more dramatically when he writes that "torture breaks people," elaborating that "the tortured person's capacity to act is broken" and, without the capacity to act, "the tortured subject is no longer a person."[27] In this sense, then, torture can be considered a worse offense against a person than killing them, because torture breaks them but leaves them alive to suffer their broken state. Although ending a life is irreversible in a more obvious way, torture diminishes its victims, robbing them of their rational faculties and inflicting mental trauma, not unlike the PTSD resulting from combat or rape, injuries that can last a lifetime. Paradoxical as it might sound, killing someone can be considered to pay them more respect than torturing them, because it does not force them to lead a compromised life afterward, similar to arguments in favor of the "death with dignity" movement that promotes the right to end one's own life before lapsing into dementia or a vegetative state.[28]

Looking at it this way, we can see why Batman's refusal to take a life conflicts so problematically with his willingness to damage a person through the psychological injury of torture. Granted, not all of his interrogation techniques rise to this level—punching someone in the face repeatedly may not be as traumatizing as threatening to drop them off a building or light a stove burner under their face—but they all indicate a lack of respect for the dignity of persons, even "scumbags," that would seem to contradict his father's teachings regarding the sanctity of life. Batman will not take a life but he is willing to destroy them—and to make matters worse, he usually does this merely to get information to catch another criminal, leaving the person he tortured to suffer, whereas the criminals he's most tempted to kill, but doesn't, are vicious serial murderers themselves. To be blunt, killing the Joker would further the mission much more than torturing one of the Joker's henchman to find out where he is (only to stop short of killing his boss).

Furthermore, to the extent that Batman's refusal to kill is based on preserving his moral character, ensuring he can still believe himself a hero and different from those he fights, his embrace of torture leads us to wonder what exactly that heroic self-image means. Certainly he would recoil if he saw the Joker, the Penguin, or Zsasz torturing someone, even a fellow criminal. Not only does Batman regularly threaten to injure, drop, and drown people to get information, he positively relishes it, contradicting all his high-minded statements about violence being a necessary evil, only to be used when absolutely necessary (about which we'll talk more in the next section).

While he refuses to kill villains such as the Joker despite his desire to, he revels in torturing even the most insignificant of criminals (assuming they're criminals at all).[29] When trying to get information out of two thugs, he tied them to the Batmobile and dragged them behind him; when they refused to talk, he said, "Fine by me … I've got a full tank of gas."[30] When he needed information from a travel agent who arranged trips for people seeking black market organs, Batman hung the man's car (with the man inside) from a junkyard magnet. After he told Batman everything he knew—but not everything Batman wanted to know—the man asked, "You're gonna let me down now, right?" Batman just grinned and told him, "They'll let you down in the morning. Play the radio."[31] Of course, Batman also does this with his more significant foes. When he wanted information out of Mr. Freeze—hardly the most murderous of his rogues' gallery—Batman turned up the heat in the room they were in and then revealed he had the helmet Freeze uses to keep his body temperature low. When Freeze pleaded with him, "Give me that, I'll die without it," Batman grinned and said, "Yes. But it'll take a little while"—just long enough for him to talk.[32] If Batman is concerned with his heroic self-image so much that he refuses to kill, one has to wonder how it survives the torture he inflicts on people—and the joy he takes in it.

Part 2: Violence

Even if Batman did not rely on torture to get information, his widespread and often brutal use of violence would remain a concern. While torture is, for most of us, a theoretical possibility or a thought experiment, violence is an everyday occurrence for many people around the world. For those of us fortunate enough to live in areas where we rarely experience violence, its prevalence outside our comfort zone is made more than apparent from even a cursory glance at the news. As an offense against the bodily integrity of another person, violence is almost universally considered immoral, absent a justification or excuse such as self-defense or the defense of others. For this reason, most societies restrict its use to the police or military (with oversight and accountability), and the burden on private citizens to justify their own use of violence is much higher.

Batman walks a curious middle ground here, being a private citizen who has an ever-changing relationship with the Gotham City Police Department. As we'll see in the next chapter, sometimes they sanction his activities, other times they merely tolerate and resent him, and often they actively oppose his presence. Even in the best of times, however, Batman's use of violence goes far beyond what would normally be tolerated from a police officer, more closely resembling what we might expect from a soldier in a war zone. Despite his frequent rhetoric about his "war on crime," however, the circumstances Batman finds himself in—or puts himself in—are not those that usually justify military techniques. For the most part, Batman employs military-level violence in civilian situations, and does so unofficially, making his methods problematic at best.

Although Batman almost never acknowledges his use of torture as such, he is very well aware that his methods are violent, and often seems rather conflicted about them. As we'll see in the rest of the chapter, his attitude about violence, especially as he teaches it to his crimefighting partners, doesn't always correspond to his actions. His most frequent sparring partner on this topic is Leslie Thompkins, the woman who helped raise him, and a dedicated pacifist; in Chapter 4 we talked about her feelings about Batman, what he does, and how he does it, particularly in terms of his contribution to the "cycle of violence" in Gotham City. We'll draw on some of those conversations again, but here we'll focus more on what Batman's violence says about him and his moral code, representing yet another thing he's willing to do to further his mission (while not crossing the line into killing). Although it's not as extreme as torture, violence embodies a similar diminution of the humanity of others even when used for good reasons, and its embrace—as much as Batman denies it—indicates the same character flaws as well.

What Batman Says About Violence

Batman often makes grand statements about using violence only when necessary, as a means to an end but nothing more. The statement of his ideals that we quoted earlier says that life is precious, and "he would therefore use force when necessary," before the obligatory "but he would never kill."[33] As Batman and Alfred watched a TV broadcast showing Anarky torturing a corporate polluter, Alfred called him a "kindred spirit," to which Batman strenuously objected: "His cause may be just—but his methods certainly aren't." When Alfred questioned this, Batman conceded, "I know, I know—my own methods aren't always legal, either. But there is a difference, Alfred … I only use violence when it's absolutely necessary, not as a form of punishment …"[34] In fact, humanity's penchant for violence disgusts Batman, who on another occasion asked his old friend, "What is it about us, Alfred? What makes us such easy prey for violence and depravity?" Alfred demurred, claiming to be a butler, not a psychologist, but did offer that "I'm sure you understand the repulsions—and attractions—of violence far better than I ever will. You are, after all, something of a specialist on the subject!"

Again, Batman objected, arguing, "I serve justice, Alfred. I meet violence with whatever it takes to overcome it. I take no pleasure in it!"[35]

Batman often strikes this note when training his Robins, some of whom are distinctly more prone to violence than others. Dick Grayson was never violent by nature, taking a swashbuckling joy in heroics that his mentor could only hope to emulate. This was apparent from the moment they met on the night Dick's parents were killed in the middle of their circus act. When Batman stopped a knifeman hoping to finish off the last Flying Grayson and beats the man senseless, young Dick asked, "He's out cold, mister. Do you have to keep hitting him?" Batman stopped, admitting, "No. I don't."[36] When Dick started training to be Batman's partner, learning to use logic and the new-fangled computing machines, Batman emphasized that "we can't just rely on physical force anymore. That's to be used only when absolutely necessary. We're not brutalizers. We've got to think with our heads, not with our fists."[37]

Batman taught the same lesson to his next Robin, Jason Todd:

> This job isn't all flash and color. If you want that, join the Justice League instead. No, what we do is more about thought and logic. We solve crimes. The punching and hitting and swinging-about is only a small part of it. That's the part people see ... the part of our existence people perceive as glamorous. But that isn't the important part.[38]

Even though Batman taught his new Robin "that 'violence' is merely a tool, to be used 'judiciously and without joy,'" Jason had trouble controlling his inherent violent impulses, gradually becoming more brutal with the criminals they fought.[39] When Jason accidentally hit GCPD detective Harvey Bullock with a batarang, Batman told him, "You've got to learn more control, patience ... Never act until you're certain the act is necessary."[40] Batman often berated Jason for this, such as the time he told the young boy after he defeated a thug, "You shattered his collarbone! There were at least ten different ways you could have ended that—none of them had to involve that kind of damage."[41] When Batman caught Jason beating on a pimp and told him, "I think he's had enough, Robin. What were you trying to do, kill him?" Jason asked, "Would it've been that big of a loss if I had?"[42] After Batman had reason to suspect that Jason pushed a man to his death and that he was acting so recklessly that he was endangering his own life, Batman pulled Jason off duty, which led to the events that culminated in his untimely death at the hands of the Joker—an event that haunted Batman every day for years (until Jason's miraculous return).

Tim Drake was more like Dick in that he rarely had issues with anger or violence, but even he had his moments, particularly after the Obeah Man killed his mother and put his father in a wheelchair.[43] The day of his mother's funeral, Tim stood in the cave and raged in front of the display case containing Jason's costume. "I know why they do it now. Why they put on the suits, and the masks, and go out into the night. They're angry. Full of rage. They want to hit back. They want to fill the hole that's burning inside them!" When Bruce found him there, he told him there's more to it than that, "but don't fight against the anger. It's natural. Accept it. Live with it. One day it'll be your friend."[44] Happily, Tim did not embrace this anger, and continued more in the tradition of the first Robin than the second (or the mentor they shared).

Tim's very temporary replacement as Robin, Stephanie Brown, was more prone to overreacting, as we saw in the last chapter regarding the incident with Zsasz, whom she almost killed trying to save Batman, and also her role in starting the citywide gang war that ended in her near-death.[45] As we've also seen, Batman often has to counsel others of his "family" on control and violence, such as Jean-Paul Valley (a duty that fell more to Tim Drake than Bruce Wayne himself) and Helena Bertinelli, also known as the Huntress. During the No Man's Land period, Helena discovered that she would be more intimidating if she cast the shadow of the bat, so she adopted a costume like Batman's. Once he became aware of this, Batman allowed her to continue, until a rash decision on her part resulted in the deaths of six people. Sharing the responsibility for this with her, he nonetheless told her, "You lack discipline. You lack control. You're too emotional," took her "Batgirl" costume away, and gave it to Cassandra Cain, a trained assassin whose restraint he admired and wanted to nurture.[46]

Batman's frequent language about using violence "only when necessary" reflects his utilitarian justification of it. Although he recognizes that violence is wrong *per se*, he nonetheless regards it as necessary to the pursuit of his mission, fighting criminals to protect the victims of crime. This is consistent with his general statement that he will do anything in service of his mission (except kill), and it's the same logic that justifies the limited use of violence on the part of the police and the military: violent threats often have to be met with violence in order to save innocent people from its effects. When a doctor treating Batman in the emergency room—a rare sight, to be sure—criticized him for presuming to do the job of the police and filling up his hospital with injured thugs, Batman responded, "Believe me, Doctor— violence is far from my idea of a good time. But sometimes there's no other way to prevent even worse violence!"[47] Even though violence is a moral wrong in general, when responding to the violence of others who are not bothered by its immorality, it must often be considered by even those who oppose it, yet another instance of a tragic dilemma from which one cannot escape with "clean hands."[48]

We see the more enlightened side of Batman's impressions of violence later in the story featuring the emergency room doctor. Definitely invoking the punishment he told Alfred was no part of his violence, Batman told Milton Sladek, a producer of "designer violence" videos, "I could beat you senseless—break every bone—pay you back in kind for the evil you've dealt out to others—." When Sladek begged him not to, Batman assured him, "Don't worry, slime. That's your game, not mine." At the end of the story, Batman reflected, thinking to himself:

> Violence ... sometimes it seems there's nothing else in the world. Man beats wife beats kid beats dog bites man ... a closed loop. It never ends. Sometimes I feel I win a battle ... Sometimes I think I've done somebody some good ... But the war goes on forever ... and I'm only one soldier. Only one wounded soldier.[49]

Despite the fact that he embraces the military analogy, Batman's internal monologue shows that he realizes that violence, even when it is useful and even required in particular situations, is not a long-run solution to anything.

This brings up another moral conflict that many of us may have encountered ourselves: having good reason to do something now that may end up making things worse in the long run. Do you sacrifice some good now to promote more good later? And who has to suffer that loss now? In general, it may be a good thing for one side or the other in an armed conflict to lay down their weapons to stop the hostilities, but why should the people they represent have to pay for their sacrifice when the other side takes advantage of the surrender? Even if Batman could stop the cycle of violence in the future by refusing to engage in it himself from this point forward, surely violent criminals would take advantage of that in the short run, and how would Batman explain to the people hurt now that their sacrifice is helping those in the future? On the other hand, if he doesn't stop now, when will he stop? No matter when he stops, someone will get hurt. And as the end of the passage above indicates, by continuing, he not only perpetuates the cycle of violence, but he suffers from it as well.

The Leslie Thompkins Objection

We're familiar with Dr. Leslie Thompkins from our discussion of Batman's value in Chapter 4, in particular how he contributes to the cycle of violence in Gotham City (to which he alludes in the passage above). A colleague and friend of Thomas Wayne, Leslie was present in Crime Alley the night Thomas and Martha were shot, and comforted young Bruce when he needed it the most. Along with Alfred, with whom she would become romantically involved, she helped to raise Bruce, but was unaware he had begun crimefighting until well into his first year as Batman.[50]

From the beginning, we can see that Leslie Thompkins will serve as a fascinating contrast to Batman, both of them dedicated to helping and saving the residents of Gotham but in very different ways. In her first appearance, while Batman is paying his annual visit to Crime Alley on the night of his parents' deaths, he asked Leslie why she continued to live there, with all of its ... well, crime. She said the memory of seeing a child lose his parents to murder drove her to devote her life "to doing what I can to prevent such tragedy! Forgive me ... but I live for the time when you and your kind will be unnecessary!"[51] Later, we learn that the first night Bruce Wayne donned the mantle of the bat was to protect Leslie from thugs; after he threatened them, beat them, and drove them away, Leslie asked him, "Was all that necessary? All that violence?" Batman answered, "We live in a sick city. You cure your way, doctor, and I'll cure mine," again referencing their similar ends and opposite means.[52] Years later, when Barbara Gordon (in her role as Oracle) told Batman that Leslie wanted to talk to him, he said, "She doesn't exactly approve of my methods," to which Barbara replied, "Well, staunch pacifism and hyper-violent vigilantism don't exactly mix."[53]

There is ample evidence of Leslie Thompkins' pacifism aside from her debates with the little boy she helped raise. After she committed to helping Zsasz heal during No Man's Land, despite Batman and Huntress's warnings that he is an uncontrollable killer, he got loose and confronted her, but she told him, "You certainly have the power to do away with me, Zsasz—and I will not resist that by doing harm in return." She tried to appeal to whatever humanity remained in him by telling him that killing her will only endanger the lives of those she is treating, and placed her hand on his chest so he could feel her compassion toward him, which would also be lost if he killed her. It was a futile gesture, though; as he told her, "What a brave soul you are. How inspiring to see someone act out their true nature ... My true nature is to kill. So perhaps you should say your prayers now, old woman ..."

She muttered, "I won't—I won't resist you with violence—" and curled up in a ball on the ground.[54]

During the long seconds she waits for Zsasz to strike his killing blow, Leslie wondered which she was more ashamed of: the fear that paralyzed her, "or the fear that spurs me on towards action, fanning thoughts of rage and uproar—wishing my enemy harm, wishing someone would just finally kill this son of a—." Her thoughts were interrupted when Killer Croc pulled Zsasz away from her, seeking vengeance for a friend Zsasz killed. Even though Leslie did not violate her pacifism in action, she was still troubled that she even wished violence on Zsasz—a "sin in her heart," as some might say. As she reflected immediately afterwards, "I recognized the thought, and I acknowledged the thought. But I did not act on that thought. And I am trying to let that be enough." And if it weren't, Cassandra Cain, the trained assassin who continually struggles to combat that impulse herself, offered her "the bow of a warrior," a fist in an open hand: "the fist represents the ever-present ability to inflict harm, while the straight hand shields it, respectfully promising not to."[55] This recalls the incident recounted in the last chapter with Lady Shiva—later revealed to be Cassandra's mother—and the small boy in Calcutta who almost died protecting Batman, whom Shiva recognized as a true warrior but, as Batman pointed out, chose not to kill.[56]

Bruce Wayne learned about Leslie's attitude toward violence very early. When he was eleven, training in martial arts and boxing, she left Gotham to join a relief effort in a war-torn area in Africa. When he and Alfred visited her, Leslie told them of the horrors of the civil war: "So many lives have been lost and no ground gained … just violence begetting more violence. And I dress the wounds of their petty retributions."[57] When local guerrillas attacked the clinic, Bruce fought them off while Alfred grabbed a machine gun, fired some rounds in the air, and ordered the men to leave—after which Leslie sent the two home. Upset and afraid of the guerrillas' return, she moved her clinic, but the violence only escalated, and eventually she returned to Gotham. Later, after they delivered a baby together by caesarian section (as described earlier), Leslie revealed to Bruce that he was her inspiration to return to Gotham: "your incredibly foolish act of bravery made me see what a coward I was for leaving Gotham."[58]

Although Bruce's "foolish bravery," even if it was expressed in violence, may have inspired her to new levels of heroism and altruism, Leslie maintained her pacifism as young Bruce grew into the Dark Knight. When Bruce was arrested for the murder of Vesper Fairchild, Leslie was one of his few close associates who entertained the thought that he might have done it.

Talking with Alfred, who insisted that Master Bruce was innocent and recounted the hero's exemplary record of dedication of sacrifice, she argued, "It's not as simple as that, Alfred. Of course he means well. He's motivated almost solely by compassion, and his efforts to keep this city safe put mine to shame. But he is at the mercy of violence." Alfred countered that "It's self-defense! And not something from which he derives enjoyment—" to which Leslie asserted, "Alfred—violence is never the answer. Violence never creates peace. All of our great teachers have tried to impart this to us: Gandhi, Hanh, King, Tolstoy, Day … not to mention Buddha, Jesus …" Alfred said that "the employ of physical aggression does not inevitably transform a man of high standards and morals into a murderer," which Leslie agreed with, but went on to cite what she saw as Bruce's "emotional instability."[59]

To Leslie—and many of the thinkers she cites—violence corrupts the soul of the violent person as much as it harms the victims of his or her actions. As the Stoic philosopher Seneca wrote on anger, "It is easier to exclude the forces of ruin than to govern them … once they have established possession, they prove to be more powerful than their governor, refusing to be cut back or reduced."[60] As opposed to Batman's advice to Tim to "accept" his anger about his mother's death and use it for good, many such as Seneca (and Leslie) are less optimistic about the degree to which we can control anger and "use it," fearing that inevitably it uses us instead. Much earlier, during one of Batman's annual visits to Crime Alley, he saw some street punks attacking Leslie. Batman lost it, telling them that "the woman you attacked means more to me than anyone alive—and I'm going to break you for it! Do you hear—? Break you!" Leslie told him that violence would do no good, and asked him if he realized what happened there years ago—which, of course, he did—and he said, "Yes, yes … there's a curse here, Leslie! A curse of endless violence!" Leslie corrected him: "No, Batman! If there is a curse, it lives in human hearts—including yours! When we have the wisdom to use mercy and compassion instead of force—we human creatures will finally be on the path to perfection!"[61] Again, she emphasizes the way violence corrupts the heart and becomes the "easy way out" of problems, just as Batman regards killing to be the "easy way out" and one that is far too tempting.

This perspective explains Leslie's own feelings of guilt and responsibility for Bruce's chosen path in life, which she expresses several times (as we've seen). During the citywide gang war, she asked Catwoman, "How could I have failed that child so badly, that he would think violence ever accomplishes anything positive? I'm ashamed of myself, Selina …"[62] She also said as much to Bruce after she discovered his identity. While dressing his wounds, she saw all of his scars, and he explained that "it's my work, Leslie—the fortunes of war." She told him, "I'm so sorry I failed you," and after he asked what she meant, she elaborated: "It's all my fault! If I'd raised you properly, you wouldn't feel the need to—," at which point he told her that his mission was his choice, not the result of any bad parenting.[63] Nonetheless, Leslie works tirelessly to try to keep Batman's heart as pure as possible, while looking the other way when he launches into action.

Leslie's concerns with the violence in Batman's heart come full circle in the episode with Zsasz during No Man's Land. When Leslie and Batman argued about her treating Zsasz, she foreshadowed her own violent thoughts about Zsasz, telling Batman,

> I am grateful every day for what you do for this city, but I do not approve of the way you do it! You're childish and stubborn in your anger, and now more than ever I fear that I've taught you nothing, I fear that—that I may sink to your level, instead of raising you to mind!

After Croc saved her and Batman recaptured Zsasz, Leslie told Batman, "I would have preferred to lose my life than be the cause of you committing violence. But I was so glad to see you. I'm always so glad to see you." Surprisingly, he broke down, fell to his knees in front of her, and told her, "I'm sorry it's so violent, I'm sorry ..." She held him and reminded him that "I've said this many times, and No Man's Land does not change it. You keep working toward peace in this city, and I'll keep working toward peace in your heart ... deal?"[64]

Leslie reiterated this "arrangement" between them when she met Bruce in prison after he had been arraigned on charges of murdering Vesper Fairchild: "We had a deal, you know. I would accept that violence was sometimes a necessary part of your work—as long as you would allow me to keep offering non-violent solutions."[65] She continued to be the anti-Batman, working to save Gotham in a different way, opposing yet accommodating his methods out of the acknowledgment that his way is (unfortunately) necessary. In a scene echoing their early meeting in Crime Alley, when Batman was doubting his own value, she affirmed not only his value, but also her recognition that he is important to Gotham: "I don't deny that I pray for the day when no one will die from crime or injustice ... when you and your kind are unnecessary ... but until then, there is a need for you—and I'm glad you're here to fill it."[66]

"Only When Necessary" ... Really?

Even though Alfred refers to their discussions as "philosophical debates between extremists," Bruce Wayne and Leslie Thompkins acknowledge and appreciate the wisdom in each other's points of view.[67] As we've seen, Leslie knows that the Batman is necessary in the violent world of Gotham City, and Bruce says repeatedly that he wishes he didn't have to engage in such violence. And it's not only Alfred, Leslie, and his flock of Robins he says this to. After Batman saved scientist Harris Blaine from Ra's al Ghul's abduction attempt, Blaine joined Batman in pursuit of the Demon's Head, despite his repeated pleas that he's a scientist, not an adventurer or fighter. While Batman fought several of Ra's' thugs, Blaine commented, "You do enjoy using your fists, don't you?" Batman replied, "As a matter of fact, Blaine ... no!—But this isn't the place to discuss my methods!"[68] He has even said this to his enemies, especially those who want to fight him for its own sake. When the Demon (a Russian agent trained by the KGBeast, and nobody related to Etrigan or Ra's) became mad because Batman set him up rather than fighting him, and complained that this was "no battle between peers. This was a lie," Batman replied, "I'm not here to play games with you. I don't fight for the thrill of battle. And I don't fight unless there's no recourse."[69]

But ... is he sincere when he says he takes no pleasure in violence? After all, Alfred scoffed when Bruce said this to him, thinking to himself, "Takes no pleasure in it? Hmph!"[70] We have more than enough evidence to doubt his repeated denials, ranging from dismissive and sarcastic quips to outright expressions of joy.

Batman's repeated jokes about his own violence, even the most brutal or gratuitous instances, suggest his true attitudes about it. When an intruder alarm went off in the Batcave, Bruce told Alfred to "stand by to activate the anti-personnel protocols." When Alfred asked, "Lethal or nonlethal, sire?" Bruce answered, "Nonlethal just this once, old friend. You're getting on in life and shouldn't have to clean up bodies this late at night."[71] After Batman defeated Poison Ivy, with the help of Catwoman, Superman, and his dog Krypto—Ivy's tougher than you might think—Catwoman clocked her. (Ivy may be tough, but she's not as tough as Selina.) When Superman asked if that was necessary, Batman and Catwoman looked at each other and together said, "Yes."[72] Batman even jokes about his violence to himself: once, while beating some criminals, he thought, "I give them every break I can. Mostly cartilage, some bone."[73] These comments are easily laughed off, but that's the point: we wouldn't expect a person who reviles violence as much as Batman claims to treat it in such a manner (except, perhaps, as a coping mechanism).

Batman repeatedly excuses his penchant for excessive violence by citing his rule against killing, implying that his refusal to cross that line allows him to do anything on this side of it. He told Slade Wilson, the superhuman assassin known by the subtle name Deathstroke the Terminator, that "while my personal code prevents me from killing—I've got no problem with hurting you."[74] When Vox, the terrorist who threatened to blow up Wayne Tower, asked Batman if he'll kill him, Batman replied, "No. I'll stop you. And I will hurt you. Badly."[75] Similarly, while looking for Ra's al Ghul's daughter (and Talia's sister) Nyssa, Batman attacked his bodyguard Ubu, who taunted Batman, saying, "You are revealed to us, detective. Spineless, you lack the will to kill," to which Batman replied, "Maybe ... but I'll sure as hell hurt you a lot."[76]

These statements can be interpreted as instances of what philosophers and psychologists call *moral licensing*, the tendency of people to use a morally good act to excuse a morally bad one. For example, a driver who lets one car merge in front of him may feel justified in cutting off another one later. Moral licensing suggests that people implicitly have a "target" level of morality they regard as "good enough" that allows them, once they reach that target, to behave immorally otherwise, in the same way that sticking to your diet for a week may "earn" you a cheat day.[77] Whereas philosophers normally assess the ethics of individual acts, which would judge each decision a person makes as moral or immoral, the existence of moral licensing implies that people look at their own ethical behavior over a period, accepting that they won't behave ethically *all* the time—which is true—so they try to behave ethically *most* of the time. Although this is a reasonable approach that recognizes human imperfection, it is not particularly aspirational: we can acknowledge that we are not perfectly ethical without explicitly endorsing and excusing immoral behavior because we "did enough" already. This is especially strange to see on the part of Batman, who normally pushes himself very hard and does not easily admit failure—suggesting that, to him, using violence is not a failure or a fault, but a reward for sticking to his resolution not to kill.

This way of looking at Batman is supported by the sheer glee he often takes in violence, especially when considered against his steadfast refusal to kill. When Batman reluctantly stopped the Joker and Black Mask from killing each other by attacking them himself, he thought, "Still, doing it this way does have its compensations. My fists fit so nicely into their guts. And impact meat and bone with perfectly satisfying thumps."[78] Speaking of the Joker, during his first encounter with Batman, he was poised to fall into a tank of poisoned water, and Batman considered letting him fall. He didn't, of course, but he still beat the stuffing out of him, thinking to himself, "this'll have to do."[79] After mentally torturing Batman, the religious cult leader the Deacon wanted the Dark Knight to kill him and make him a martyr, but Batman refused, beating him instead while thinking:

> I go to work on him. I've never gone at a man like this before. I'm not trying for the knockout or the kill. I go for the pain. I concentrate on the nerve centers. My aim is to break the man, just the way he broke me. May God forgive me. I enjoy it.[80]

At least in this case, he acknowledged the problem with the joy he gets out of the violence he practices.

Even when it's not presented as an alternative to killing, Batman is shown to take a sadistic degree of pleasure in violence that directly contradicts his noble statements about the sanctity of life and his limited role of fighting and catching criminals rather than punishing them. After a group of vigilantes savagely beat Alfred, Batman—somewhat understandably—lost control on them. "I think of the streets awash with blood," he pondered. "I see Alfred lying there, his skull cracked open—I've been holding my fury in check, nursing it. Now, I let it explode. It feels good."[81] The last part suggests that it wasn't just revenge that motivated him, but rather that he took advantage of Alfred's situation to indulge his violent impulses. We see this again when Alfred was suffering from the deadly virus known as the Clench, and Batman divided his time between staying at Alfred's side, continuing his duties to Gotham, and beating criminals for the sheer joy of it. In a section of the story titled "Day 12: Tension Breaker," Batman found the Riddler, who asked while fleeing, "Don't you have anything better to do?!" Batman hit him, and Riddler said (through a busted mouth), "Oh-kay! I give up already! I thaid I give up … uncle. Take me back to Arkham and we'll cawl it a night, oh-kay?"[82] But Batman continued to beat him, long after he surrendered, simply because it felt good (and helped "break the tension").

Naturally, threats to those he cares about the most trigger his violent impulses. In addition to Mr. Pennyworth, we've seen this in how protective Batman is of Leslie Thompkins, and also Jim Gordon. While Batman and Nightwing were busting up a routine robbery, they heard news that Gordon had been shot. Batman went into a rage and started throttling one of the thieves, yelling, "Think it's all a damn joke! Nothing matters, does it? People die and it's nothing to you! Nothing!" Nightwing tried to pull his mentor off the thief, but Batman punched him hard enough to throw him across the room, shouting, "Get off me!"[83] The fact that even his closest partners are not immune to his outbursts shows, as Seneca wrote, how difficult anger can be to control once a person indulges it too much.

Just as Batman can lose control when someone he loves is in danger, it also happens when someone he cares about hurts him. After his beloved Silver St. Cloud left him because she couldn't live with the stress of his double life, Batman caught some burglars and brutalized them while saying,

> You picked a bad night to tangle with me, little man ... a real bad night! This morning, someone who was very precious to me walked out of my life forever—and tonight I'm hurting, deep down in my soul where there's no way to ease the pain! But it's pain you're going to share with me, punks! It's pain you deserve! Because it's scum like you that cost me the women I love![84]

Similarly, when the Joker used "neuroscience" to turn Catwoman "bad," Batman nearly thrashed him for it, yelling "Stop laughing! Do you hear me, Joker? For years, you've sneered and laughed at everything decent ... but no more, do you hear me? No more!" When Jason Todd—of all people—begged, "Stop! You'll kill him!" Batman replied, "He took her from me, Robin ... every woman I love, something always takes her from me ...," which anticipates his worries about her eventual death at the hands of the Joker after he seems to have killed Tommy Elliot.[85]

Other times, Batman simply takes his violence too far while excusing it as necessary. We often see this in the way he treats the Penguin, a criminal strategic mastermind but no physical threat to the Dark Knight. Nonetheless, as we saw earlier, Batman is often just as savage with him as he is with Zsasz or Killer Croc. When the Penguin attacked a party Bruce Wayne was attending—worst luck ever for Mr. Cobblepot—Batman confronted him and asked him to drop his gun, then beat on him while thinking, "The demand was unnecessary. The singular solution is striking quickly. Relentlessly. Some would say ... savagely. Innocent lives are at stake. Almost any means are justified by the ends."[86] Even if we grant that some violent response was justified in taking down an armed criminal—even the Penguin—it is difficult to argue that Batman is free to use "any means" at his disposal. This conflicts with the principle of *proportionality*, a key rule in the ethics of war (and other violent situations) that governs the appropriate response to a threat or attack, as well as an idea that grounds any sincere claim to use violence only when necessary—and only to the degree necessary.[87]

As we discussed in Chapter 2, Batman also indulges his violent tendencies in the spirit of vengeance and punishment, despite his many statements to the contrary. When Batman savagely beat up a drug dealer named Frank "Cutter" Thompson whom he suspected of killing a woman Batman had just met, Jim Gordon told him, "I think he's had enough," to which Batman replies, "Not as much as he deserves. But I suppose it will have to do for now."[88] After a new killer drug claimed the life of another woman, Batman found its dealer in his high-rise apartment and, in an attempt to get information, tossed him around a bit and then threw him out a window. Cassandra Cain—who had been following Batman out of concern—caught the dealer and brought him back, after which Batman told him, "Sounds like you want another flight. And this time—I don't think I have any more associates waiting in the wings." Later, Cassie said to Batman, "The way you hurt that man … How you hurt him. You were … punishing him."[89] Finally, after the citywide gang war, Batman found himself alienated from both his crimefighting partners and the Gotham City police, and he adopted a new-found dedication to protecting his city on his own. While chasing a petty thief, he thought, "you will pay for what you have done to [Gotham]. You will pay with your screams. You will pay with the crunching of bones that give way so easily in my hands. You will pay in … blood." After fighting the thief's gang, he grabbed one member to get information, telling him, "Wake up. Wake up or I break something other than your ribs." When the gangster pleaded, "Don't … it hurts …," Batman said, "You don't know what 'hurts' means. But you will," and threatened to break his fingers one by one until he talks (a clear instance of the torture we discussed earlier in this chapter).[90]

Losing Control

If only Batman were as careful to restrain his violent impulses as he is with his desire to kill his worst enemies. Like most of us, he finds self-control more difficult when he's upset, tired, or personally involved—and he's very aware of this. After the episode described above, in which Jim Gordon had to stop him from beating "Cutter" Thompson for murder, Batman thought to himself, "Nearly blew it. I let it get too personal. Lost my detachment … nearly lost control. Almost beat Cutter to death. Wouldn't have been any big loss. Still, it would have been tough to live with." To make matters worse, he learned soon afterwards that Cutter was in fact innocent, and the real killer went on to kill again. As Batman reflected, "I allowed my feelings to cloud my judgments, made stupid leaps in logic, and came up with the wrong answers."[91] More relevant to our current discussion, he was also far too eager to pummel a man he only *suspected* of murder, highlighting the fact that, although the thugs he beats on are not necessarily upstanding members of society, Batman doesn't know for certain that they have committed a crime (unless he catches them in the act), and even if they have, it's not his job to mete out punishment.

Batman's tendency to lose control makes him truly dangerous, especially in light of the perverse joy he gets out of beating on criminals (or, to be precise, suspected criminals). As psychotherapist Sabra Temple told him, "while you may not be immune to societal constraints and rules of law, you certainly seem above them ... making self-control paramount."[92] But once again, he knows this: as the narration to one story read, "Long experience has taught Batman that, in the heat of the moment, few men can control themselves."[93] This is why the fact that violence and anger are among Batman's core character traits is important, not just to how he justifies or excuses his violent behavior, but also why he is so quick to jump to that solution. Because violence is such a core aspect of his moral personality, even if he can normally keep it check (when he wants to), he is more likely to lose control and become violent when he is tired or upset. This is what made Leslie Thompkins doubt his innocence in the murder of Vesper Fairchild: as she told Alfred, he is a violent man, and when he is upset, that violence is harder to control, even for an otherwise good man. In fact, the first time we meet Leslie, Batman lost it on a punk named Gooch who pulled a gun on him, the narration reading: "Trembling with fury, the Batman crashes his fist into Gooch again and again ..." Leslie begged him, "Stop ... stop! You've hit him enough!" Batman said, "Sorry ... I lost my head!" with which Leslie agreed: "Yes! You should calm yourself! It's not healthy to lose your temper!"[94]

We see this very human imperfection in several especially tense episodes throughout Batman's career. One was his gradual exhaustion at the hands of Bane, who orchestrated a series of attacks on Batman from his various enemies to weaken him so Bane could defeat him more easily. Early in Bane's campaign, Batman was already exhausted, thinking that he was "racing for my grave, already dead," when he fought the vicious and skilled fighter Zsasz. Batman succumbed to his taunts too quickly, savagely beating him, forcing Gotham City police officer Renee Montoya to step in, saying, "That's enough! I've got him!" Batman asked wearily, "Enough?" but thought to himself, "no ... too much ... way too much."[95] Even in his depleted state, Batman was able to defeat Zsasz, but that same state also weakened his control over his violent impulses—which wouldn't be as much as a problem if he didn't indulge them so much when he was at full strength.

Another significant time Batman lost control was after Jason Todd was killed, after which Batman became noticeably dark and violent, lashing out at any thug who was unlucky enough to cross his path. He reached what was perhaps his lowest point in the several months before meeting Tim Drake, when Nightwing and Alfred commiserated about Batman's behavior and mood. Nightwing noted his violence, remembering how measured his use of force once was, "using only enough force to frighten" thugs, not hurt them. As Alfred told him, "I fear he's acting irrationally. Definitely without caution. I've mended these wounds more these past weeks than I have in years. Since Master Jason's death, I wonder if he cares for his own life?"[96] Later in the same story, we see Batman brutalizing men in one bar after another, looking for information, and at the end, breaking the wrist of a man who dared pull a gun on him.[97] Playing the role of father, Alfred reminded Bruce of what he told his first Robin: "We're not brutalizers. We've got to think with our heads, not with our fists." He continued, "Since Master Jason's death, you've changed. It seems, sir, that you now do all your thinking with those sadly bruised and battered knuckles."[98] Only after Batman hit rock bottom did he realize that, however much he didn't want to put another child in danger's way again, he needed a Robin in his life to temper the darkness and the violence that always threatened to get out (whatever doubts we may have about this justification, as we discussed in Chapter 3).

As we know, Batman does realize his shortcomings in this area, even if he doesn't act on this self-awareness often enough. Recall his comments to Alfred after the Joker resurfaced following Jason Todd's murder, in which he worried, "What happens next time? Will I control myself?" Even though Alfred assured him he always has, Batman knew better, telling him "that doesn't mean I always will" and, later, "I wonder why I don't simply get a gun and shove it in the Joker's mouth. I'm scared, Alfred. Scared one day I may."[99] Sometimes he realizes his own rashness too late, such as after the incident with Cutter, when he said, "Made a pledge to myself in the beginning ... 'Never go out angry. Never go out reckless. And never, never ... make it personal,'" but he has failed at this pledge time and again.[100] Even when Batman recognizes his impulse control problems, he minimizes them. In one moving adventure, he reflected on the violent nature of Gotham City itself, comparing it to an infection that he wants to cure, but

> I am infected myself. I can only fight back my own violence, the hate that drives me on. Choking it with control, loosing it only when necessary, and in just the necessary dose. Despite the violence that faces me. Even with those who revolt me.[101]

As we've seen, however, his ability to "loose it only when necessary and in just the necessary dose" is questionable, and not only in particularly emotional circumstances.

In an especially meaningful recent adventure, Talia gave Batman the mystical Suit of Sorrows which, according to her father's people, was "rumored to impart strength and speed to those who wear it. But it comes with a warning: The Suit of Sorrows will destroy anyone who is not pure." He discovered that it performed exactly as promised, but also found himself acting more violently than usual, and wondered if it's "my imagination? Psychosomatic smoke and mirrors? Or does the Suit of Sorrows really tap into something violent and impure within me?" He investigated the history of the Suit and learned of its long association with hyperviolent and murderous behavior through the centuries, and was tempted to destroy it, but decided not to.

> To destroy the suit would have shown a lack of faith in myself. And what am I, if not an act of faith? Instead, the suit takes its place in the trophy room. Where it might serve as a warning. Reminding me of the need for vigilance. For no man is beyond committing acts of violence. No man is so pure he can drop his guard.[102]

In this shining moment of self-awareness, Batman acknowledged and admitted his own violent tendencies, and like an alcoholic who keeps a bottle of hooch in the kitchen cabinet to make sure he can resist it, he decided to keep the Suit of Sorrows as a constant reminder of the line he must never cross—a blurrier line than simply "do not kill," but an important line nonetheless.

Batman is to be admired for maintaining *any* lines that he refuses to cross, to the extent he sticks to them. As we have seen, however, the acts that he engages in and those he refuses to engage in, as well as the reasons he will break these rules, are inconsistent with each other. Killing, torture, and violence are all among the most heinous wrongs one person could do to another, all of them denying victims respect for their basic dignity and humanity. Understood this way, these three acts are too similar to be treated so differently by the Dark Knight. Even his most frequently given reason for not killing, his belief in the sanctity of life, would seem to imply much more than merely not killing. It would also require him to maintain a minimal respect for life, which contrasts starkly with Batman's use of extreme violence and especially torture, which as we saw, breaks a person psychologically if not physically, and often irreparably at that.

Finally, in the spirit of virtue ethics, if Batman is as concerned with his moral character as we saw in the last chapter with respect to killing—however much that defeats the pursuit of his mission—that same concern should also give him pause before he brutalizes and tortures people, especially when they have done far less evil than those he refuses to kill. The fact that one man who does so much good, and adheres to one bedrock moral principle, can so flagrantly violate others, should serve as a cautionary tale to those of us who would maintain inconsistent aspects of our own moral codes. We must apply the same reflection and reasoning to all the rules and principles we follow to ensure that we're not going easy on some things we do because they serve other purposes—even if those purposes, like Batman's mission, are noble ones.

Notes

1   *Batman: Gotham Knights* #5 (July 2000), "Locked."
2   *Batman: Legends of the Dark Knight* #121 (September 1999).
3   *Detective Comics* #746 (July 2000), "Evolution IV: Aftertaste."
4   The TV show *24*, starring Kiefer Sutherland as Jack Bauer, featured torture often, which was both celebrated and criticized. For the latter, see Adam Green, "Normalizing Torture on '24,'" *New York Times*, May 22, 2005, at http://www.nytimes.com/2005/05/22/arts/television/normalizing-torture-on-24.html, and various chapters in Jennifer Hart Weed, Richard Davis, and Ronald Weed (eds.), *24 and Philosophy: The World According to Jack* (Malden, MA: Wiley Blackwell, 2008). For an example closer to home, see Colin Smith, "Why I Loathe and Detest Spider-Man, That Torturing Piece of Slime," *Too Busy Thinking About My Comics*, May 31, 2012, at http://toobusythinkingboutcomics.blogspot.com/2012/05/why-i-loathe-and-despise-spider-man.html, and my own "On Spider-Man, Torture, and Character in Comics," *The Comics Professor*, June 3, 2012, at http://www.comicsprofessor.com/2012/06/on-spider-man-torture-and-character-in-comics.html.

5   *Batman: Legends of the Dark Knight* #135 (November 2000).

6   *Batman: Gotham Knights* #32 (October 2002), "24/7."

7   See Part 1, Article 1, of the Convention of December 10, 1984, at https://www. un.org/documents/ga/res/39/a39r046.htm. On the problem with defining torture in general, see section 1 of Seumas Miller's 2017 entry at the *Stanford Encyclopedia of Philosophy*, at https://plato.stanford.edu/entries/torture/.

8   *Detective Comics* #750 (November 2000), "Dependence."

9   *Batman: Legends of the Dark Knights* #214 (March 2007). This is the same fine chap who is more afraid of the mercenary Deadshot, as we saw in the last chapter.

10 *Batman* #643 (Early October 2005); *Batman Confidential* #32 (October 2009).

11 *Batman: Shadow of the Bat* #59 (February 1997).

12 *Batman: Gotham Knights* #31 (September 2002), "Clean."

13 *Batman* #478 (Late May 1992), emphasis added.

14 *Detective Comics* #684 (April 1995).

15 *Batman: Dark Victory* #11 (October 2000).

16 *Batman Confidential* #33 (November 2009). I trust I don't need to note the history of water-based torture, including waterboarding.

17 *Batman: Legends of the Dark Knight* #175 (March 2004).

18 Ibid.

19 *Batman: Legends of the Dark Knight* #205 (Early July 2006).

20 *Batman* #603 (July 2002).

21 *Detective Comics* #809 (Early October 2005), "To the Victor Go the Spoils."

22 *Batgirl*, vol. 1, #57 (December 2004).

23 *Batman* #394 (April 1986).

24 For more, see Bob Brecher, *Torture and the Ticking Bomb* (Malden, MA: Blackwell, 2007), pp. 24–31.

25 *Batman: The Dark Knight* #2 (May 2011).

26 Charles Fried and Gregory Fried, *Because It Is Wrong: Torture, Privacy and Presidential Power in the Age of Terror* (New York: W.W. Norton and Company, 2010), p. 55.

27 Brecher, *Torture and the Ticking Bomb*, pp. 75 and 77.

28 Although it's not the purpose of this section, I would be remiss if I didn't mention that there are philosophical defenses of torture, at least in the most extreme circumstances in which the consequences of maintaining an absolute prohibition exceed the threshold of tolerance. See, for example, Stephen Kershnar, *For Torture: A Rights-Based Defense* (Lanham, MD: Rowman & Littlefield, 2011), and Uwe Steinhoff, *On the Ethics of Torture* (Albany, NY: SUNY Press, 2013).

29 Recall his statement to Jason Todd about what he'd like to do to the Joker: "taking him and spending an entire month putting him through the most horrendous, mind-boggling forms of torture. All of it building to an end with him broken, butchered and maimed ... pleading—screaming—in the worst kind of agony as he careens to a monstrous death" (*Batman* #650, April 2006).

30 *Batman: Legends of the Dark Knight* #164 (April 2003).
31 *Batman: Legends of the Dark Knight* #201 (Early May 2006).
32 *Detective Comics* #793 (June 2004), "The Surrogate Part Three: Deliverance."
33 *Batman* #0 (October 1994).
34 *Detective Comics* #608 (November 1989).
35 *Detective Comics* #596 (January 1989).
36 *Batman: Legends of the Dark Knight* #100 (November 1997), "The Choice."
37 *Batman* #437 (August 1989). (That "anymore" stands out, doesn't it?)
38 *Batman: Legends of the Dark Knight* #100 (November 1997), "A Great Day for Everyone."
39 *Batman* #410 (August 1987).
40 *Detective Comics* #554 (September 1985), "Port Passed."
41 *Batman* #645 (November 2005).
42 *Batman* #422 (August 1988).
43 *Detective Comics* #621 (September 1990).
44 *Batman* #455 (October 1990). Batman said something very similar to Jason Todd when the boy explained that he was angry because Two-Face killed his father, telling him, "I appreciate the anger you feel, Robin ... but you have to channel it—you can't let it get the best of you!" Jason snidely said, "Like it never gets the best of you, huh?" to which Batman replied, "We're not talking about me" (*Detective Comics* #580, November 1987).
45 *Detective Comics* #796 (September 2004), "... And Red All Over." Stephanie admitted her role in starting the "War Games" in *Catwoman*, vol. 3, #34 (October 2004).
46 *Batman: Legends of the Dark Knight* #120 (August 1999).
47 *Detective Comics* #597 (February 1989). Batman continued, "Better that you get half-a-dozen live ones to treat than one corpse to bury! ... I'd sooner send you every hood in Gotham to patch up than let them ruin one more innocent life!" This is an interesting reversal of the jurist Sir William Blackstone's famous phrase that "it is better that ten guilty persons escape than that one innocent suffer" (from his *Commentaries on the Laws of England*). Blackstone's phrase is usually invoked in support of civil rights, whereas Batman's is motivated by a significantly different concern!
48 In the most general terms, the philosopher John Rawls discussed this kind of comprise in terms of "nonideal" versus ideal moral/political theory in his classic *A Theory of Justice* (Cambridge, MA: Harvard University Press, 1971), ch. 4. More specifically, this concept of justified violent response is at the root of *just war theory*; see Michael Walzer, *Just and Unjust Wars: A Moral Argument with Historical Illustrations*, 5th edn. (New York: Basic Books, 2015).
49 *Detective Comics* #597 (February 1989).
50 As with Alfred, Leslie's history has taken a convoluted path since her introduction in 1976, when there was no sign that she had medical training or had even

known Thomas Wayne. This summary tries to combine all the relevant points of her story while retaining her important early appearances as well. Comics!

51 *Detective Comics* #457 (March 1976), "There Is No Hope in Crime Alley!" At this point, Batman knew who she was, but she did not know yet that he was that same child.

52 *Batman: Legends of the Dark Knight* #1 (November 1989).

53 *Detective Comics* #791 (April 2004), "The Surrogate Part One: Lost and Found." When they finally spoke, Leslie asked Batman to find a missing woman, "and please, for me, try not hitting anyone to do it." When Batman found someone with information about her, the man attacked him, but Batman managed to defeat him simply by ducking and weaving until the man knocked himself out. Batman thought to himself, "and I didn't even touch him. Leslie would be so proud."

54 *The Batman Chronicles* #18 (September 1999).

55 Ibid.

56 *Batman* #534 (September 1996).

57 *Detective Comics* #792 (May 2004), "The Surrogate Part Two: The Blinding."

58 *Detective Comics* #793 (June 2004), "The Surrogate Part Three: Deliverance."

59 *Batman: Gotham Knights* #26 (April 2002), "Innocent Until."

60 Seneca, "On Anger," Book I, 7(2), collected in John M. Cooper and J.F. Procopé (eds.), *Seneca: Moral and Political Essays* (Cambridge: Cambridge University Press, 1995). For a modern view on the downsides of anger, see Martha C. Nussbaum, *Anger and Forgiveness: Resentment, Generosity, Justice* (Oxford: Oxford University Press, 2016).

61 *Detective Comics* #483 (May 1979), "The Curse of Crime Alley."

62 *Catwoman*, vol. 3, #34 (October 2004).

63 *Batman: Legends of the Dark Knight* #23 (October 1991).

64 *The Batman Chronicles* #18 (September 1999).

65 *Batman: Gotham Knights* #26 (April 2002), "Innocent Until."

66 *Detective Comics* #574 (May 1987).

67 *Batman: Legends of the Dark Knight* #203 (Early June 2006).

68 *Batman* #243 (August 1972).

69 *Batman* #445 (March 1990).

70 *Detective Comics* #596 (January 1989).

71 *Robin*, vol. 4, #126 (July 2004). The intruder was none other than Stephanie Brown, asking to replace the recently retired Tim Drake as Robin.

72 *Batman* #612 (April 2003). When Krypto tried to lick Catwoman's face afterwards, she warned him, "Don't even think about it, dog."

73 *Batman: Legends of the Dark Knight* #58 (March 1994).

74 *Detective Comics* #710 (June 1997).

75 *Detective Comics* #830 (Late May 2007).

76 *Batman: Death and the Maidens* #9 (August 2004).

77   For an overview of the psychological evidence, see Irene Blanken, Niels van de Ven, and Marcel Zeelenberg, "A Meta-Analytic Review of Moral Licensing," *Personality and Social Psychology Bulletin* 41 (2015): 540–558.

78   *Batman* #644 (Late October 2005).

79   *Batman: The Man Who Laughs* (April 2005).

80   *Batman: The Cult* #4 (November 1988).

81   *Batman: Legends of the Dark Knight* #176 (April 2004).

82   *Batman: Gotham Knights* #42 (August 2003), "20 Days Less One."

83   *Robin*, vol. 4, #86 (March 2001).

84   *Detective Comics* #478 (August 1978).

85   *Detective Comics* #570 (January 1987); his later concerns, discussed above, were expressed in *Batman* #614 (June 2003). (I'm sure I don't have to point out the irony of a young Jason Todd telling Batman not to kill the Joker.)

86   *Batman: Ghosts—A Legend of the Dark Knight Special* (1995). The text actually reads "almost any means justifies the ends," a clear error that I took the liberty of correcting above.

87   See Walzer, *Just and Unjust Wars*, ch. 8.

88   *Batman* #410 (August 1987).

89   *Detective Comics* #790 (March 2004), "Scarification."

90   *Batman Allies Secret Files and Origins 2005* (August 2005), "A Friend in Need."

91   *Batman* #414 (December 1987).

92   *Batman: Legends of the Dark Knight* #147 (November 2001). This storyline contains long and fascinating conversations between Batman and Dr. Temple, which are beyond the scope of this book; for more on Batman and psychology, see Travis Langley, *Batman and Psychology: A Dark and Stormy Night* (Hoboken, NJ: John Wiley and Sons, 2012), and Robin S. Rosenberg, *What's the Matter with Batman? An Unauthorized Clinical Look Under the Mask of the Caped Crusader* (CreateSpace, 2012).

93   *Batman: Shadow of the Bat* #71 (February 1998).

94   *Detective Comics* #457 (March 1976), "There Is No Hope in Crime Alley!"

95   *Batman* #493 (May 1993).

96   *Batman* #437 (August 1989).

97   *Batman* #439 (September 1989).

98   *Batman* #440 (October 1989).

99   *Batman* #450 and 451 (Early and Late July 1990).

100 *Batman: Legends of the Dark Knight* #207 (August 2006).

101 *Batman: Legends of the Dark Knight* #44 (April 1993).

102 *Detective Comics* #842 (May 2008).

8

Law, Justice, and the Police

Aside from the obvious moral issues with Batman's other methods, such as violence and torture, they are also examples of a more general ethical problem: his disregard for the law. As we'll see, Batman considers his extralegal status as an advantage in his mission to fight crime, the same mission that he uses to justify the fact that he breaks the law with impunity and abandon. This topic is further complicated by his status and relationship with the Gotham City Police Department and its best-known commissioner (and one of Batman's closest friends), Jim Gordon, as well as how Batman sees his role compared to that of the police and how he acts (or doesn't) within the law.

Although this moral issue may not be as salacious as his refusal to kill or his embrace of violence and torture, all of these share one aspect: they all reflect Batman's insistence on carving out exceptions for himself to rules he imposes on others. Also, this is the one moral transgression that we average folks in the real world most likely share with the Dark Knight: most of us abstain from extreme violence, torture, and putting children in danger, but many of us have broken the law, even in relatively minor ways such as speeding or cheating on our taxes. The difficulty some of us may have in reconciling these actions with our overall moral codes may give us our most direct insight into the problems with Batman's moral inconsistency.

Breakin' the Law

As we've seen throughout this book in various contexts, Batman takes a rather cavalier attitude toward the law. It almost goes without saying that citizens have a duty to obey the law, absent strong considerations to the

Batman and Ethics, First Edition. Mark D. White.
© 2019 John Wiley & Sons Ltd. Published 2019 by John Wiley & Sons Ltd.

contrary, such as extreme necessity or the injustice of certain laws themselves.[1] For the most part, laws—especially criminal laws—provide a sense of order to everyday social interactions between imperfect human beings, ensuring that we don't act on our less social impulses to assault other people, steal their property, or take their lives. Most of us, most of the time, are not even tempted to do these things, and even when we are, our inherent sense of morality prevents us from doing them. But when those safeguards fail—or if people don't have them at all, like many of the criminals Batman fights—the law is the last barrier, hopefully triggering our instinct to avoid punishment out of sheer self-preservation and stopping us before we do something we'll regret. And when that doesn't work … well, we have Batman. (And the police, of course. But also Batman.)

Batman, however, holds himself above the law, despite the fact that he expects everyone else to obey it. He grants himself permission to violate the law, permission ordinarily given only to the police and military in emergency situations, even though he isn't subject to their level of oversight and accountability (however imperfect). Even when he is granted quasi-official status by the police department or government of Gotham City, he never seems to be brought before a review board to answer for any of his actions, although many of them are certainly questionable, as even Jim Gordon is forced to admit.

Batman's assertion of special privilege violates the universality that is a key aspect of Immanuel Kant's system of deontological ethics. One of the versions of Kant's much-beloved categorical imperative holds that, in order to consider the permissibility of a plan of action (or *maxim*), we have to ask ourselves what would happen if everyone could also follow the same maxim at the same time: "act only according to that maxim whereby you can at the same time will that it should become a universal law."[2] This is the *universalization* formula of the categorical imperative that forces us to think, as an elder probably asked you a million times as a child, "what if everyone else did that?" (To be accurate, though, this is meant in a more general sense rather than "don't you dare even think of doing something so stupid.")

Take lying, for instance (as we will in the context of Batman in the conclusion to this book). If you want to tell a lie for your own advantage, you have to be willing to allow everyone to lie for the same reason. But if you did allow this, the standard prediction is that people would lie so often that no one would believe anybody, which would defeat the purpose of your plan to lie. Because your plan to lie for your own benefit is inconsistent with everyone else having the same permission, it fails this categorical imperative "test," generating a duty not to lie. This process generates other Kantian duties such as those forbidding theft and killing, as well as positive duties (as we mentioned in Chapter 6) such as helping others and cultivating one's talents (both duties that a young Bruce Wayne took very seriously as he trained for his future as a crimefighter).

The same logic of universalization applies to lawbreaking as well. When the Riddler sets out to break a law for his own purposes, he is usually counting on most other people to obey the law. (After all, even thieves don't want their property stolen!) According to Kant, though, if the Riddler wants to break a law, he has to be willing to let everyone else break the law. Although this may be fine for an admitted nihilistic anarchist like the Joker, the Riddler is generally portrayed as a more run-of-the-mill criminal who has no interest in chaos—he wants a relatively peaceful, law-abiding Gotham City to take advantage of. Because his lawbreaking is self-defeating if we universalize it, it's immoral according to the categorical imperative.

Oh, I'm sorry ... did I say the Riddler? I meant Batman. (See what I did there?) Of course, Batman's purposes for breaking the law are much nobler than Edward Nigma's, but nonetheless, his lawbreaking works best if most everybody else obeys the law—even if only to make the few remaining lawbreakers stand out better! After the No Man's Land period ended and the federal authorities took control of law enforcement in Gotham, an agent told Batman, "We don't approve of your brand of vigilantism, unofficially sanctioned as it is by local law enforcement. Where would we be if every citizen decided to take the law into their own hands and prowl the streets in a cape and cowl?" Batman answered, "If every citizen felt that much responsibility for law and order there wouldn't be any need for either of us."[3] This is a great response, but the truth is, Batman wouldn't want *everyone* running around in a mask and cape, chasing thugs and beating them for information. This would compromise his ability to be imposing and scary (and there are already too many "capes" running around Gotham for his tastes). He gets tremendous mileage out of being the only Dark Knight out there, and nonetheless seeming to be everywhere at once. His mystique is valuable, and if everyone were as creepy and scary as he is, no one would be.

Being the one and only Batman has no ethical relevance, but granting oneself the exclusive permission to perform immoral acts such as breaking the law does. When it comes to the universalization formula of the categorical imperative, how it works is less important than the spirit behind it. The process of universalizing our maxims forces us to extend any permissions we grant ourselves to everyone else, out of recognition of the equal moral worth and dignity of all persons. This prevents us from carving out special exceptions for ourselves—no matter how important our mission is, or how good we might look in a cowl and cape. To do otherwise is to claim special status for ourselves, to imply that we are more deserving of privileges than other people, which violates Kant's essential belief in the equal dignity of persons—a belief Batman would seem to share, given his dedication to helping the downtrodden of Gotham City.

Given that Batman allows himself a degree of leeway to violate the law that he would not grant to many others (at least outside his little Bat-circle), how does he justify his lawbreaking? When he asked Alfred to tap into the Social Security Administration's computer system, the butler said, "I'm sure I don't need to tell you this is illegal, sir," to which Batman responded, "It's in a good cause, Alfred."[4] Trivial as this particular example may be—unless you happen to work for the Social Security Administration—it is as straightforward an admission as we can expect.

As we saw with respect to his other violations of moral norms and principles, Batman defends his lawbreaking in terms of the greater good he does, the lives he saves, and the mission he lives for. Even Jim Gordon approves: in their early days together, Batman told Jim how he planted a tape recorder in a criminal's house to get information. After Jim made a snide remark, Batman asked him, "You don't approve?" Jim said, "Of you breaking and entering—or of me being in the hotseat" because of a recently appointed "vigilante task force" aimed at the Dark Knight. He continued, "So we both want to clean up Gotham—but you're going about it the wrong way." When Batman asked, "You really believe that, Gordon?" the young captain conceded, "That you're breaking the law? Of course, but ... damn it, you work."[5] Acknowledging that Batman "works" represents a conflict for Gordon and the police in general, given their charge to uphold the law as well as to serve and protect, but this lackadaisical attitude certainly works in Batman's favor.

Nonetheless, Batman receives his fair share of pushback and questioning about his lawbreaking—and not just from frustrated police commissioners, mayors, and federal agents. We've already seen that Alfred pokes him occasionally about it, such as when the hyper-violent Anarky showed up in Gotham and Alfred compared him to Batman, who objected strenuously, saying "I know, I know—my own methods aren't always legal, either," but argued that Anarky's violence is excessive, and "the fact is, no man can be allowed to set himself up as judge, jury, and executioner."[6] As with his use of violence, Batman finds it difficult to draw a line regarding lawbreaking that he is unwilling to cross. He feels Anarky's use of violence is excessive, but it's difficult to see how exactly it's worse than some of what we've seen Batman do himself—and it isn't the difference in their goals, seeing that Batman expresses sympathy for what Anarky is trying to do. As we will see later, Batman reserves the right to break the law himself simply because he is the only person he trusts to do it *right*.

His other allies also call him on his selective disregard for the law, including ones that have no particular love for the institution themselves. For example, on one of their first adventures together, the Huntress asked Batman why Robin never drives the Batmobile; when Batman answered that Robin wasn't old enough to drive, Huntress laughed, saying, "That little legal technicality you won't violate? Sure, makes perfect sense. Not."[7] Another example comes from Oliver Queen, the anti-establishment crusader Green Arrow, whom Batman criticized for his participation, alongside his partner Black Canary, in an illegal scheme to bring down a dirty chemical company. When Ollie told him the story and complimented one of their underworld allies, Batman was incredulous, asking, "So ... you aided and abetted escape from an illegal act simply because you 'like his style'?" Ollie didn't miss the chance to point out Batman's hypocrisy on this count:

> Yeah, sure! You can break and enter without a warrant, conduct illegal surveillance, coerce confessions, and violate each and every point of the Miranda rule night in and night out—but it's "different" because you're sustaining the system whose rules you can't abide! ... But ... I'm wrong because I'm not a hypocrite about it—because I bellow from the rooftops about how warped and corrupt and twisted and sick the system really is—because right along with coming down on the creeps who violate the system's good rules, I come down on the system's bad rules themselves![8]

Batman works within the system while breaking its rules when it's convenient for him, but Green Arrow wants to tear down the entire system, which he sees as warped and corrupt (or "twisted and sick"). Batman values the legal system and relies on most people acting "within" it while he operates "outside" it, as we saw in our discussion of Kant's categorical imperative above. What irks Ollie the most is Batman's self-granted exclusive license to violate the law, while criticizing others who, like Green Arrow and Black Canary, do the same.

This criticism cuts even worse when it comes from someone who used to walk the other side of the fence for a living. On one of their many adventures together, Catwoman shared some choice thoughts with

Batman about the arbitrary lines that he will or will not cross. When she suggested they break into an accountant's office to steal records related to Wayne Enterprises that could be traced to Batman, he told her, "I have no problem with breaking and entering on a case-by-case basis—but you're talking about larceny ... and that means crossing a line." Catwoman pointed out that for all his talk of law and justice, the two of them are actually not that different:

> Oh, please ... You're a guy who's built a whole second career using the discomfort of your appearance creates in your prey as a calling card ... and, as someone who used to be a big part of that particular subset of society ... welcome to my world, sweetie.[9]

When Batman tried to clarify, saying, "As I said, I have no innate objection to breaking and entering in the name of justice—" Catwoman cut him off: "There you go again. You call it justice—the system still considers you a criminal, whether you like it or not ..." When he again objected that what they were doing was wrong, she said, "Get over it, Bruce—everything you do is wrong," elaborating that "even back in the day, when you and I were dancing on opposite sides of the fence ... I always knew there was a very thin line between your world and mine."[10] Much like our hypothetical case involving the Riddler, even when Batman and Catwoman pursued different goals, their methods were the same, and as much as Batman would justify his lawbreaking "in the name of justice" or his mission, he was breaking the law nonetheless—and this wasn't just a personal rule or standard he was violating, but a key institution for holding society together.

Batman's Relationship with the Police ... and the Vigilante Question

Although most of the discussion of Batman's lawbreaking to this point has been in terms of deontological principle, there are also significant negative consequences to his illegal activities that would be of relevance to utilitarians. One particularly important one is the activity he inspires from copycat heroes or vigilantes, who often take even Batman's violence to a higher level (if not a lethal one). We've seen this already with the "Bat-men," the vigilante gang Batman and Leslie Thompkins were dealing with when she learned

Batman's true identity. The leader of the Bat-men told Jim Gordon that they were "the same" as Batman, prompting Gordon to think,

> Damn it, I knew this would happen. Once we let one vigilante operate, we opened the floodgates. Every one of them will think they have some kind of divine right to do what they do. Every one of them will want the same treatment you get. I can't have that. Not in this city. And if the choice is an army of vigilantes or none ... it'll have to be none. I hope it won't come to that.[11]

Gordon is willing to grant one vigilante permission to operate in his city and "bend" the law, based on the trust they had developed (even at this early stage), as well as the fact that it is only one man, but he realizes the danger of giving *carte blanche* to anyone who wants to do the same, and in doing so, questions whether he should allow it at all.

Of course, it isn't only wannabe Bat-men and vigilantes that are a concern, but also Gotham's self-appointed protector and his costumed friends. Television journalist Arturo Rodriguez sounded a common refrain in a broadcast during the citywide gang war in Gotham, which he blamed on

> Batman and his secret cadre of unelected, unaccountable vigilantes. Answerable to no one, least of all the citizens they claim to protect, many authorities now openly question whether we wouldn't be better off without Batman and his gang. This reporter, for one, now joins that chorus of voices, asking when Batman will submit himself to the lawful oversight of our civil authorities.[12]

This leads to a question we have yet to ask: what is a vigilante, and does the term apply to Batman?

Vigilantism usually refers to any law-enforcement activities that take place outside of the official system, and therefore in the absence of any safeguards required by the system, such as humane treatment of suspects, guarantees of a fair and speedy trial under the presumption of innocence, and proportionate punishment conducted in a dispassionate way (as we saw in our discussion of retributivist justice as opposed to personal vengeance in Chapter 2). In practical terms, vigilantism usually boils down to the use of more violent tactics than police are permitted to use, often extending to killing; indeed, this is what distinguishes the hero actually known as the Vigilante (plus that guy from another comics universe known primarily for punishing) from most other heroes.[13]

This understanding of vigilantism—without the killing—certainly applies to Batman, and this is what we can assume most people mean when they accuse him of being one. As Lieutenant Sarah Essen told him during an argument, "You're a vigilante, Batman. By rights you should be locked up! If it wasn't for the way Jim Gordon feels—and the good he swears you've done this city—I'd arrest you myself!"[14] Batman certainly regards himself as helping the police to investigate crimes, apprehend criminals, and stop crimes in progress, as well as deter them simply by his presence (enhanced greatly by his impressive shadow). As he told Robin after they witnessed a gang stealing a cache of weapons, "We have to alert Gordon. He has to know what he's up against." When Robin asked, "It's out of our hands now?" Batman clarified: "It's never out of our hands, Robin. As long as those animals roam the streets it's our task to bring them down. Gordon must do what he can. We must do what he cannot."[15]

As the end of that quote suggests, Batman embraces his nature as a vigilante to avoid many of the restrictions that official law enforcement has to deal with, and feels that he's more effective as a result. Recall the thug Micky from our discussion of torture in the last chapter: As Batman repeatedly smashes his hands in the trunk of his car, Micky said, "You ain't the cops!" to which Batman replied, "That's right, I'm not the cops—that's why I can get away with treating you like the slimy little reptile you are."[16] He often references the advantages he enjoys over the police, such as when he was frustrated at the law's inability to prosecute drug suppliers in Gotham due to their crafty lawyers: "Maybe the law can't touch them ... but the Batman can!"[17] Later in the same tale he pushed a criminal attorney's face into a bowl of soup while he told his client, "Maybe the police can't get anything on you—but now you're dealing with the Batman."[18] Yet another time, Batman and Huntress ran afoul of members of a terrorist state hiding behind diplomatic immunity; as Batman told Alfred later, "they want to bring their brand of terror to Gotham under the guise of a foreign mission. The law can't touch them. But I can."[19]

An important element of Batman's justification for breaking the law, one that is often invoked by vigilantes in general, is the distinction between justice and the law. In college, Bruce Wayne took a class in law in which the professor presented a hypothetical case about a pair of car thieves, one of whom changes his mind and wants to get out of the car, but before he can, the driver accidentally strikes and kills a pedestrian. The professor explained that both thieves are guilty of manslaughter, but

Bruce argued that the passenger should be charged with theft but not manslaughter because "he had no part in the accidental death." When the professor asserted that the law would find both guilty of manslaughter, Bruce asked, "but is that justice, Professor Rexford?" The professor answered, "No, Mister Wayne … that's the law." After he graduated, Bruce visited his parents' grave and told them he couldn't be a policeman as he'd intended, because "they're too hamstrung by the very laws they're sworn to uphold!"[20]

Bruce's graveside dramatics aside, there is an important distinction between law and justice, and it's more than just a convenient rationalization for vigilantes eager to justify their lawbreaking. According to a legendary tale (albeit one yet to be immortalized in comic book form), a fellow judge told the famed jurist Oliver Wendell Holmes Jr. to "do justice!" at which Holmes snapped back, "that's not my job!"[21] Holmes' point was that his task as a judge was to execute the law as written and passed by legislators, not to further ideals of justice as defined by philosophers and other idealists. In the best-case scenario, laws are written by human beings as approximations of justice, rules to guide human behavior toward what is right, but sometimes missing this goal—as in what Bruce saw as an unjust accusation of the passenger-thief of manslaughter, or more generally, criminals released on legal technicalities despite "obvious" guilt.

In one of their earliest meetings, Batman told Jim Gordon that "the only difference between us is that my hands aren't bound by red tape!" When Gordon replied that his "red tape" is the law, Batman proclaimed that he was more concerned with justice, explaining that "I love the law as much as you do … but if I have to bend it to see that justice is done, I won't hesitate!"[22] After Gordon retired as commissioner, and Batman once again found himself on the outs with the GCPD, they revisited this topic, the Dark Knight reminding his friend that "justice and the law are, sadly, two different things," and Jim expressing doubt: "I won't tell you you're wrong. But I'm still not convinced you're right, either."[23]

Even considering these exchanges, Batman is surprisingly blunt with Jim about the advantages he enjoys due to his extralegal status. When the Joker made one of his patented dramatic returns and Gordon asserted his plans to put his best detectives on the case, Batman said, "Go ahead, Commissioner—if it'll make you feel better! But I have an idea official methods will be too slow to prevent further killings—so I'll be investigating on my own."[24] For the most part, though, Gordon isn't resentful, and even goes as far as to acknowledge the benefits of having a vigilante on his side. When the Dark

Knight's presence first became known in Gotham, Gordon thought to himself, "He's a criminal. I'm a cop. It's that simple," but he knew already that the distinction wasn't that cut and dried, given that many of his fellow cops, at least at the time, were corrupt killers themselves.[25] Perhaps the distinction is drawn most simply when Gordon told Batman, "I'm under orders," and Batman replied, "I'm not."[26]

As you may expect, Jim has to deal with plenty of pushback from his fellow police for his acceptance of Batman's help. He usually defends his friend; as he told Batman during one case, "There are factions in the department who've been complaining that I tend to rely on you a little too often— but there are certain cases that seem far more suited to you than to the average cop on the beat!"[27] But he also suffers blows to his own reputation from relying on Batman too often. As No Man's Land began, his wife Sarah Essen told another police officer,

> The commissioner spent a few weeks on the outside looking for another city to be a cop in. But they all laughed at him ... all because of the "B." They told him—we don't want a chief who needs a bogey-man to help fight crime. We want somebody who's good enough to do it himself.[28]

Gordon told Batman the same thing near the end of No Man's Land: "No one would give me work. They didn't want a cop who needed an 'urban legend' to do his policing for him. They laughed at me. Some of them behind my back. Some to my face."[29] In many ways, Gordon pays a heavy price for his relationship with Batman, but the fact that he almost always sticks by him nonetheless suggests that, on the whole, he finds the association worthwhile.

Of course, not all of Gotham's finest are as comfortable with their local vigilante as Gordon is. As one cop told Batman in an early case, "Stay off my beat, Batman! Us professionals keep the peace here!"[30] The police do their best to deal with the eccentric costumed villains Batman usually fights, and often resent the fact that they often have call on him for help, whether to apprehend them or get them to talk in the interrogation room (by whatever means he may use, as we'll discuss soon). Detective Marcus Driver, who has no love for the bat, exemplified the attitude of many of his colleagues when his partner was killed by Mr. Freeze. After the police tried and failed to bring Freeze in, even Driver admitted that they needed to call Batman. When asked if he was fine with it, Driver said, "No, but I'm a cop in Gotham. I can't afford to live in denial."[31]

To his credit, Batman understands how the police feel about him, telling Alfred:

> Bear in mind that some cops don't really like the Batman. Some cops don't care for the Batman's methods—for the way he cuts through red tape to steal their thunder. I even think it's safe to say … some cops hate the Batman—for being what they can only dream.[32]

In one episode, he even acknowledged as much to Gordon: when the commissioner was under political pressure from candidates in the mayoral race, at the same time as the criminal Cluemaster's puzzles were "embarrassing" him, Batman told his old friend, "We're the ones who embarrass you, Jim. Cut free from the restraints of bureaucracy, we show the police up with every case we solve. But Robin and I aren't a replacement for the police. We could never be."[33]

Batman's uneasy cooperation with the police was on display during one confrontation in which an officer started reading the Miranda warning to him. Batman brashly asserted his extralegal status when he argued that the Miranda requirements, which were instituted to protect the rights of criminal suspects, didn't apply to him:

> I may not have to use it, officer, but I'm well aware of the Miranda speech … and any cop worth his blues should be aware it's out of place here. I'm no criminal and you know it. So why not turn your backs on an innocent shadow?

The officer replied, "Maybe you are innocent, Batman—but we've already seen you're no shadow." Batman assured him they were on the same side, and the cop echoed Gordon when he replied, "Maybe—but we got orders, you don't." Batman said, "Surely you understand I refuse to be taken?" to which the officer volleyed, "Right—and surely you understand … we must take you."[34] Surprisingly, these incidents rarely come to blows or gunfire— unless Batman goes too far, as we'll see very soon.

Although most Gotham police tolerate Batman even if they don't celebrate him, he has a few particularly harsh critics on the force. One of them is Detective Harvey Bullock, who never met a donut he doesn't like—who can blame him?—and never met a caped crimefighter he does. As he told Batman, "I think you're a freak and a menace. But Gordon thinks you serve a purpose so I go along."[35] Bullock makes the excellent point that some of the resentment that police in Gotham feel toward Batman isn't because of what he gets away with, but that they can't do the same. Once, Harvey complained to Gordon, "I gotta wait to do things by the book, meanwhile the Batman's free to roam the night and do things the way they oughta be one—and he'll prob'ly make my collar. Gettin' so's I hate that costumed gink all over again!" Jim assured him, "I felt that way once, Sgt. Bullock … before I realized the Batman has to do what he does." When Harvey asked why, Jim simply answered, "Because he's good at it. The best. And because I'm … only a cop."[36]

This may sound a bit self-effacing on Jim's part, but I read it more as an acknowledgment that Batman enables the police to cut some corners in the pursuit of justice (if not the law itself).[37] Jim often finds himself in a tough spot, having to represent law and order in a city that rejects it and deal with a vigilante-slash-best friend who ignores it when it's inconvenient. Things were even worse in the early days when Harvey Dent was district attorney (before the incident that transformed him into Two-Face). While Dent, Gordon, and Batman were working together to bring a member of the Falcone crime family to justice, Dent said about the Dark Knight, "I've … come to appreciate our mutual friend. And how he crosses a line we … can't." He said Falcone considered himself above the law, and when Jim denied that, Harvey said fine—then arrest him. Jim acknowledged that they couldn't, but told the other two, "I want to be clear on this. In our … zeal … to bring Falcone to justice. I'll let you bend the rules, but we cannot break them. Otherwise, how are we different from him?"[38] (It seems Batman isn't the only one here who's concerned with his moral virtue.)

Batman's willingness to disregard the restrictions of the law goes overboard on occasion, though, and Jim is usually there to call him on it. In one case, Batman asked Jim if he could release Two-Face from Arkham Asylum to help clear a wrongly accused man named Freddie Richards. When Gordon said no, Batman broke him out himself … and Two-Face escaped. When Gordon confronted his friend and ally, he said:

> You broke a homicidal maniac out of the nuthouse and then lost him in the Caribbean somewhere. And for what? To save "an innocent man"? What makes you think Freddie didn't kill that John Doe they left in the house? What makes you think the city's any safer with him free? What the blazes makes you so right?!! How many people do you think Two-Face will kill before he gets nabbed again?[39]

Batman had no answer, to his credit. There is a parallel here with Batman's refusal to kill his most homicidal enemies, only to implicitly allow them to kill again—except that, in this case, Batman created this situation himself. In the pursuit of his mission, he openly defied his closest legal ally's orders, and compounded his moral responsibility for any harm that might come from Two-Face's subsequent actions. This highlights the aspect of uncertainty in utilitarian decisions that we first saw in Chapter 1, requiring the use of judgment to anticipate the various consequences—judgment that definitely failed Batman in this case, at least according to Jim Gordon.

Taking the Law into His Own Hands

Batman's relationship with the Gotham City Police Department reached its low point during the citywide gang war. The episode began when Stephanie Brown, otherwise known as Spoiler and for a very brief time as Robin, tried to win her way back into the good graces of the bat by initiating one of Batman's secret plans to unite and take control of all the gang and crime families in Gotham—and then fouled it up, resulting in chaos.

It also didn't help that Michael Akins, Jim Gordon's successor as police commissioner, had far less affection for Batman than his predecessor did. Jim tried to win over Akins from the beginning, telling him,

> Some cops think he's more of a hindrance than a help. Some think he should just mind his own business. They think he's some vigilante in this for kicks. They're wrong. He's the best man I've ever known. I know you're going to make changes, Mike. It's your department now, you'll do things your own way. But trust me on this, there are times when he'll be the only option. You're going to want a friend like him. Let him be your friend … he's the best one I've ever had.[40]

Akins did manage to avoid calling Batman for a while, and when he finally did, he told him:

> I should explain why I haven't … called you before now. It's not that I disapprove of you … but I feel that my department has to … we have to be more self-sufficient. We can't rely on you all the time. We have to trust ourselves, you understand? And we have to be worthy of the city's trust. We shouldn't look to you for all the answers …[41]

… and Batman agreed, which would be the last time that would happen for a long time.

Once Stephanie set the plan in motion and the gang hostilities increased, Batman called on Akins, who greeted him by saying, "This better be important. I'm not at your beck and call. I'm not Jim Gordon." Batman replied, "It's always important. And no, you're not Jim Gordon." (OK, *that* time they agreed too.) Batman asked him to stay out of the Gotham neighborhood known as the Hill while his own team worked to calm the area, at which Akin balked, asking, "Excuse me? What gives you the right—?"[42] The next time they met, Akins was even more hostile to Batman, who had information the commissioner wanted. "Cut the games," Akins said. "If you know something, tell me. Or so help me—I will make your life difficult." Batman handed him the information he wanted—and the antidote to dangerous bacteria that workers at a waste treatment plant had been exposed to. Akins stammered, "I—thanks," and Batman said, "You're welcome. And … and don't ever threaten me again."[43]

As the gang war reached full steam, Batman asked Akins for control of the entire GCPD for eight hours to confront the gangs, whom he erroneously thought were unified under the control of his double-agent, the hero known as Orpheus. Akins, predictably, was reticent, asking "Who the hell do you think you are?" Batman answered, "No disrespect, Commissioner. You're still relatively new to Gotham, while I have a great deal of experience with—" Akins cut him off, saying, "My god, this isn't about my ego or who has more experience. This is about what's right or wrong." Batman exerted his "mission at any cost" position: "It's wrong not to take every measure to insure [sic] no more lives are lost." Akins countered that "It's wrong to take the law into one's own hands."[44] This was unfair, because Batman wasn't taking anything—he was openly asking the commissioner of police to lend it to him. Nonetheless, it was an extraordinary request, and did nothing to quell the misgivings of Akins or the rest of the force that Batman saw them merely as junior partners in the fight against crime in Gotham, to be used as he pleased.

Batman tried to overcome this perception, but not in the most politic way. Co-opting Oracle's communications technology to commandeer the GCPD's network, Batman broadcast a message to all the city's police:

> Some of you have seen me, some of you have worked with me before. All of you know I'm good to my word. Now I'm asking you to take me at that word, and follow my orders. If we work together, if you listen to me, we can end this war tonight. We can save our city. There is no other option left.[45]

As he did with Gordon when he broke Two-Face out of Arkham, Batman went over Akins' head and truly "takes the law into his own hands," relying on his experience and camaraderie with the GCPD to secure their trust and cooperation against the united gangs. In a heartwarming show of support, most police acknowledged that, however they may feel about their local vigilante, he does know what he's doing and usually gets the job done, and they decided to join him.

Unfortunately, their trust was misplaced in this case. The plan was for Orpheus to bring the gangs together under his leadership so the police could move in and arrest them. But unknown to all, Black Mask had killed Orpheus, and it was he (dressed as Orpheus) who emerged to speak to the gangs—and incited them to turn on the police. Akins responded how you might expect, telling his people:

> All right, everyone! The Bat's really got us over the table on this one. He's jeopardized all of our lives and the lives of every good citizen of this city. So from here on out—forget the rubber bullets. You see anyone in a mask … you shoot to kill.[46]

He reiterated this later when he said, "I don't know what game Batman's been playing throughout the war—but I'm damned sure of one thing. He's not on our side."[47]

Finally, after Batman asked Akins to lay off Tarantula—the "hero" who killed Blockbuster while Nightwing watched—so she could work to settle down an area of Gotham, Akins reached his limit, and told him,

> You may think you give the orders around here, Batman, but this is my city, and my department that you're trying to rip to pieces … I've tolerated you until now, but the past few days you've stepped way over the line. My men have their orders. They're bringing in that gang, and if you interfere, they have orders to shoot on sight.[48]

It wouldn't be long before Akins would come to think of Batman as just one of Gotham's other "criminal masterminds": "Well, that's what he is. He breaks the law. He's obviously a genius. In other words, 'criminal mastermind.'"[49]

At the end of the gang war—after Oracle blew up her watchtower headquarters to prevent Batman and Black Mask from killing each other, as we saw earlier—Gotham lay devastated, as did Batman's relationship with the Gotham City Police Department. After Akins had the Batsignal dismantled, Batman waited for him in the police garage, and tried to convince the commissioner that they still share a goal of protecting Gotham. Akins didn't buy it, and when Batman asserted that he would keep doing what he needs

to do, Akins told him in no uncertain terms, "if what you need to do conflicts with my people or my department … if it threatens their lives or my
authority … then not only will I stop you … I'll destroy you."[50] When Alfred
asked Bruce "how you plan to conduct business … when the police force
has orders to shoot you on sight," he answered, "Just like we did in the
beginning, old friend—very carefully."[51] This was confirmed soon thereafter when Alfred noted, "After recent events, your relationship with the
Gotham constabulary is … precarious, at best," to which Batman added, "I'd
say it's nonexistent."[52]

Speaking of Gotham City police commissioners, after the gang war Jim
Gordon decided to leave Gotham with his daughter Barbara, but before he
did, he and Batman had a chat. They reflected on their close friendship, and
Batman told him he appreciated how "you put your faith in me when you
had every good reason not to." Jim cut to the chase, saying, "I'm in no position to protect you from the police now. After what you did … I don't know
if they can ever forgive you. And to be honest, son, I don't know if they
should." But he recognized who he was talking to, and saved Batman the
trouble of having to repeat what he said to Akins. "I don't suppose being on
the 'most wanted list' is going to stop you from … well, being you."[53]

Batman's renewed outlaw status following the gang war was evident
when he defeated Black Mask and the Joker and handed them over to the
police, after which a grateful but anxious officer said, "I'm sorry, Batman,
but there're warrants on you, too. You'll have to come with us." Batman
replied, "No, I don't think so—I'm not in the mood. Use your heads, officers. These are career-making busts I've just handed you. Why spoil it by
going to the hospital—which is where anyone will end up who tries to
arrest me. Think of your families." After they let him leave, he thought,
"Good men. They know how to make a tactical judgment call when conditions warrant."[54] Despite his condescending snark to the rank and file, he
did begin mending bridges with the GCPD when he handed over evidence
to Detective Renee Montoya—albeit evidence he earlier took from a crime
scene. When he approached her, she pulled her weapon and said, "You
know I have permission to shoot you." Batman said she wouldn't, "because
you know what I mean to this city, even if your bosses don't." He gave her
the bullet he took from the crime scene, to which she said, "Swell. The
coroner said the slug was missing. Convictions are easier when masked
vigilantes don't tamper with crime scenes, you know."[55] The more things
change, the more they stay the same.

It's Just Procedure ... or Is It?

Montoya's snide comment points to another way in which Batman has a negative impact on law enforcement: the ways his operations affect procedure when it comes to apprehending, prosecuting, and convicting criminals. After all, just because Batman exempts himself from the rules that bind police officers doesn't mean they don't need to follow them, and when his activities compromise the proper handling of a cases, the criminals he helps catch may not even make it to trial, much less prison or Arkham Asylum.

Ideally, Batman tries to work within procedure; as he taught Robin, "Do your job well, and you make that arrest stick. Do your job badly ... and you might not get a second chance."[56] When he told the officers in the episode described above that he doesn't have to issue Miranda warnings, this isn't a denial of their importance, but simply an admission that he doesn't have the power to arrest suspects at all. Alfred is always there to remind him of his limited role in the criminal justice system, especially when Batman laments the fact that criminals often escape prosecution or are released often as soon as they are imprisoned: "Yours is a singular task you've set for yourself, Master Bruce. It starts at this tunnel ... and it ends at the front of the police station."[57] Even though Batman takes liberties at crime scenes, as we saw with Detective Montoya, he does realize the importance of retaining evidence: when working alongside the vigilante Ballistic to break up a drug deal, Ballistic destroyed the drugs, which Batman tells him could have been evidence for a DEO case that now cannot be made.[58]

On occasion, Batman even lectures the police themselves on procedure. When Harvey Bullock asked Batman to help him with someone at work who's harassing him, Batman asked why he can't work with someone in the department, and Bullock answered that he doesn't want anyone looking into his record. When Batman asked if he's on the take—not uncommon in the GCPD—Bullock assured him, "I never took a dime from anybody. I just sometimes bend the rules a little. Stuff that's better buried. Stuff you'd understand." Batman clarified for him, "We're on the same side. But we're not the same. I'll help you find out who's threatening you. But you've got to collar him clean. I'm not setting anyone up so you can gun them down."[59] At the end of the day, Batman appreciates the value of a "clean collar," even if he doesn't always live up to it in practice.

District Attorney Harvey Dent, before he was transformed by a mobster's acid into Two-Face, made Bullock look like a stickler for procedure. Nonetheless, Dent provided Batman with a model for how they should work together to maximize convictions:

> Our problems are essentially the same. We both want to put Gotham's criminals behind bars. But to do that, I need evidence. I don't want to impede your work—I just want our indictments to stick. I can be at your disposal for consultation. Whenever you get close to a collar, call me and tell me what you've got. If it's enough, you get to do your thing. The police will clean up after you.[60]

We see how this works: Batman catches them and Dent puts them away. Before long, though, Dent became frustrated and asked Batman to plant evidence to secure a conviction. "You've asked me to do that kind of thing before, Harvey," Batman said. "My feelings haven't changed—that's not my way."[61] It's one thing to interfere with the legal system by corrupting evidence, which might end up letting a guilty person go free, but Batman draws the line at planting evidence, which could end up convicting an innocent person—and even Batman's not confident enough in himself or Harvey to do that. (And when Dent asks him to kill ... well, you know the rest.)

Most of the time, however, Batman is more of a hindrance to official procedure than a help. As Jim Gordon told him early in their partnership:

> Ever wonder what happens to the creeps you bring in? The system has treated them very kindly. At least a dozen felons apprehended by you are back on the streets—and the reason is always the same—insufficient evidence. It's hard enough explaining to the mayor why we're coddling Gotham's resident vigilante ... the fact that your conviction rate isn't any better than ours doesn't help one bit. You're living right on the line, friend. You're not restricted to the rules like we are—but you won't take it upon yourself to finish off these guys either. I'm not suggesting you do, mind you ...[62]

(Of course not, Jim.) As Harvey Dent's successor as district attorney, Janice Porter, told Gordon when she saw Batman at a crime scene, "This is an ongoing investigation. Just his presence here contaminates the crime scene." Jim tried to defend his friend, saying, "His presence here helps solve crimes. Let the man do his job," but Porter objected, "Let me do mine! I saw him take evid—he's gone."[63] Even if he returned the evidence after analyzing it and fingering the guilty party, Batman would have corrupted the crime scene all the same, endangering the case and increasing the odds that a guilty person will go free, as Gordon pointed out.

Another procedural issue that often arises with regard to the Dark Knight deals with the *exclusionary rule*. The Fourth Amendment to the United States Constitution protects citizens from police searches and seizure of property without a proper warrant, and the exclusionary rule allows a judge to exclude from trial any evidence acquired through an illegal search or seizure. This rule is a staple of legal dramas on TV and film in which the "smoking gun" that would ensure a ruthless killer's conviction is ruled inadmissible on Fourth Amendment grounds. The killer then cackles ruthlessly as he saunters out of the courtroom, after which the rogue cop, who has just had it with this "$%^& technicality," vows to see justice done even if he has to do it himself. All melodrama aside, in reality the exclusionary rule helps ensure that the police and prosecutors don't unduly harass citizens in the process of a criminal investigation (as Batman often does) or fabricate evidence (as Dent tried to get Batman to do), with the unfortunate side effect that sometimes valuable evidence that would help secure an honest conviction is excluded.[64]

How does this apply to Batman? Well … it's complicated. In an early story, a judge ruled that an alleged murder weapon "obtained" by Batman was obtained illegally: "It is with great reluctance that I must rule in favor of Mr. Brodsky's motion to exclude the alleged murder weapon from evidence."[65] Technically, though, the Fourth Amendment only applies to agents of the state, such as police and prosecutors. However, it also includes any people working for them, such as private investigators hired by the prosecution to help with a case. You can see where this is going: If Batman is considered to be working with the police, then the Fourth Amendment might extend to him as well. Of course, this depends on how cozy Batman is with the GCPD at any given time, which, as we've seen, varies with the seasons. At its best, as Jim Gordon once told the Gotham City mayor, "my 'relationship' with Batman is like the relationship we have with our psychics, independent experts, and anyone else who pitches in to make police work in this city easier."[66] He made a similar point during a TV interview years earlier when asked if Batman is "an authorized representative of the force": "No, he operates strictly on his own, but he's offered me his services … and I've accepted."[67] If this is the understanding, and Batman acquired the evidence as Batman usually does, a judge would most likely be right to rule it inadmissible.

Sometimes, however, Batman submits evidence in secret. Alfred applauded one such instance: "Apparently, the police were sent an envelope full of evidence to insure [sic] a conviction. Nice of you to tip your hat to the laws of governance."[68] Another time, after the citywide gang war, Alfred questioned that tactic, asking Batman, "But will the courts actually allow into evidence the intercepted phone tapes and TV footage you secretly provided?" Batman answered, confidently, "I don't see why not. The laws against unreasonable search and seizure only apply to agents of the government. Sure, the lawyers will cry and squabble, but eventually it'll be allowed in."[69] Not so fast, old chum: Even though there is no Fourth Amendment issue here, without a witness to corroborate the evidence, a halfway decent criminal defense attorney would get it excluded anyway. Ironically, given Batman's "nonexistent" relationship with the GCPD at that point, there probably wouldn't have been a constitutional issue if he submitted the evidence openly. (He just can't win.)

This also gets to the issue of Batman and procedural or civil rights in general. We've seen Batman boast to thugs like Micky that he's not police and therefore can get away with things they can't; in fact, he regards this as key to his success as a vigilante. Then again, this comes back to haunt him in just those cases in which he cooperates with the police. For instance, District Attorney Janice Porter reopened the case against a mobster Batman captured because she claimed Batman violated his civil rights while Gordon watched.[70] It may be that Gordon's presence was more relevant here than Batman's actions, at least as far as a civil rights complaint is concerned; the comic isn't clear, but the charge probably relies on police brutality, which would apply only if Batman is considered as an agent of the police, which Gordon's presence supports.

A final example of the grey area when it comes to Batman and legal procedure relates to the interrogation of suspects, another mainstay of police and legal dramas. As we've seen, Batman has his own methods for getting people to talk, which would definitely not be officially sanctioned by any legitimate law enforcement organization (or government). But this doesn't mean they won't rely on his "special talents" to intimidate suspects into talking. After the GCPD apprehended a suspect named McDonald who Gordon said wouldn't talk without his lawyer present—as is his constitutional right, mind you, as reflected in the *Miranda* rules—Batman asked if he could try. Jim said, "It's against regulations, but … No violence. Remember that." Batman went into the room, returned quickly, and said, simply, "He talked." Jim asked, "Just like that?" and Batman confirmed,

"Just like that."[71] Never mind what Batman said, did, or threatened to get McDonald to spill—presumably on the Hamburglar—Gordon crossed the line when he sent Batman in when legal representation was already requested.

Happily, there is another member of the GCPD who has deeper ethical qualms about using Batman to interrogate suspects. Like many of his fellow police, Detective Crispus Allen doesn't like to call the Dark Knight to get suspects to talk—especially the man suspected of shooting Jim Gordon. Even threatening the guy with Batman and telling him that Batman and Gordon were best friends is too much for Allen:

> It's not that I mind scaring a guy into confessing. That's what the box is for. It's what I do. But we're basically telling this perp he's going to get killed by a vigilante we refuse to stop. That's like putting a gun against his head to extract a confession.[72]

From this passage, we can surmise that Crispus Allen has a more refined conception of torture than we usually see on the part of Batman himself—he realizes that threatening a suspect with a pissed-off Dark Knight is one small step away from violence, and one more small step away from torture.[73]

This also highlights what is perhaps the key issue with Batman and the police, and one that implicates the police themselves rather than Batman. To the extent that he cooperates with the police, Batman's legitimacy is enhanced and he would likely be thought of as less of a vigilante—although it's unclear whether he would welcome this, given his demonstrated reliance on criminals' fear of him being a free agent and loose cannon. The police, however, sacrifice some of their legitimacy to whatever extent they appear to endorse the activity of a confirmed lawbreaking vigilante. We've seen how Batman's actions in coordination with the police can backfire, compromising evidence and sometimes even triggering civil rights charges. As the only officially sanctioned users of violence in civil society, the police are held to a very high standard regarding their use of that violence—and we've seen the disillusionment and pushback police in the real world receive when they are witnessed abusing that authority. Given their historical record for corruption, the Gotham City Police Department can ill afford to associate with a vigilante such as the Batman, at least not officially. A middle ground between Gordon and Akins is probably best: work with Batman behind the scenes, if at all, but disavow his methods in public, as dishonest as this may be.

Lawbreaking for Me, But Not for Thee

Although Batman obviously feels free to break the law when he thinks it's justified by the mission, he is very hesitant to grant others the same latitude. For example, after a woman named Judy Koslosky set a trap for a murderer and then killed him, she told Batman and the police, "It might not have been legal … but it was right." Later, Jason Todd told Batman he agreed with her, but Batman did not:

> That's just it, Robin. Judy was wrong! People can't set themselves above the law. That way leads to anarchy. Even though you and I skirt along the edges of it, we still operate within the legal system. That's the way it has to be. Even though more than a small part of me sometimes wishes it could be otherwise.[74]

On the surface, this seems flatly hypocritical of Batman, given his repeated declarations of the difference between justice and the law—and more than a bit easy on himself, claiming that they "skirt along the edges" of the law rather than flat out breaking it.

The hypocrisy ties back to the Kantian concept we saw at the beginning of our discussion of Batman's lawbreaking: he extends freedoms to himself that he is unwilling to extend to others. But it's not quite that simple. For instance, he is willing to extend these permissions to people he's trained, such as the Robins, Batgirls, and—when he's feeling generous— even a Huntress. He also extends this understanding to fellow heroes he hasn't trained but works alongside, such as fellow members of the Justice League, Outsiders, and the other brave and bold heroes he's been known to team up with (about once a month, on the average). It isn't that he doesn't trust *anyone* else to break the law—he doesn't trust anyone without the training, experience, and skill to break the law, as well as the judgment to know when.

In other words, Batman wants to make sure those he trusts to break the law are doing so the right way, to the right extent, and for the right reasons. This language is familiar from virtue ethics, especially as recommended by Aristotle, in which traits such as honesty and courage are to be practiced "at the right times, with reference to the right objects, towards the right people, with the right motive, and in the right way"—all of which demand judgment to determine.[75] In other words, it takes good character to know when to break the law, or any other deontological rules, for the greater good.

We see this play out every time Batman has to take down unendorsed vigilantes who go overboard with violence or murder, are indiscriminate with their chosen targets, or create too much collateral damage because they're sloppy or negligent. It really hits home, though, when someone he trained or sanctioned goes rogue—the main example being Jean-Paul Valley, who replaced Bruce Wayne after Bane broke his back. As we've seen, Valley became more and more violent the longer he served as Batman, gradually succumbing to his training as an assassin under the Order of Saint Dumas, and even modifying the Batman costume with blades and claws (like some kind of wolverine or something, who knows).[76]

When Jim Gordon confronted Valley about his reckless and negligent behavior that killed a man and threatened to kill many more, Jim said "we have a system of law," which Valley dismissed by saying, "which the Batman has always worked outside of. I still do. Your rules do not apply to me!"[77] Valley is taking advantage of the precedent that Wayne set as Batman, but he lacks the judgment or restraint to use it in the right way, at the right time, and for the right reason. As Bruce Wayne realized as Shiva helped him return to fighting strength, "the man I chose—is completely out of control ... maybe even mad."[78] Along with his failure to guide and protect Jason Todd, Batman came to consider the coronation of Jean-Paul Valley to be "perhaps the greatest mistake of his career ... creating a nightmarish new Batman only one shade removed from the demons he opposed."[79]

This sense of failure was surely augmented by the fact that an ideal replacement was readily available in the form of Dick Grayson, the original Robin, whom Valley mocked as "the heir to the throne and the slighted prince."[80] Grayson took the fact that he was passed over very hard; when Bruce told him and Tim about Valley's training under the Order, Dick asked him point-blank, "and you chose him over me to carry the mantle of the bat? A programmed murderer? If I'd known, my feelings would have been more hurt than they were!"[81] Bruce said he didn't know about Valley's past at the time, which seemed to satisfy Dick for a moment, but later Dick asked Tim why they didn't see that Valley wasn't all there. When Tim explained that Bruce wasn't prepared to choose a replacement, Dick balked, saying, "Not prepared? I've been doing this all my life. He trained me for this. Instead he picks some psycho with a religious fixation. What was Bruce thinking?" Tim told him that Bruce felt Dick had moved on, "that you were your own man now," but Dick was still disappointed that Bruce didn't realize he would have put on the cape and cowl in a moment—not just for the thrill of it, but out of devotion to the man who trained him.[82]

Dick would get his chance soon enough. After Bruce defeated Valley, he still needed more time before he felt he could return permanently, so he handed Dick the cape and cowl, after which the former Robin and current Nightwing came to realize the burden of the mantle of the bat.[83] Nonetheless, after Bruce was finally ready to return to Gotham as its sworn protector, Dick confronted him about his choice to promote Valley in the first place. Bruce's explanation was not based on Dick's skill or devotion, but rather echoed Tim's reasoning, based on a reticence to ask the former Boy Wonder who had only recently flown the nest and begun a new life. "I assumed you wanted to get out from under my shadow. Make a name for yourself. You've done that. Created a life. Fought your own fights. I didn't have the right to call you back." Bruce then admitted such discussions aren't easy for him, "but that's the way it always is, isn't it … between fathers and sons."[84]

All in all, Batman's embrace of lawlessness is yet another example of a moral rule that he violates for the sake of his mission. By itself, this is not inconsistent, and could be a reasonable part of a moral code that combines utilitarian and deontological factors. What makes this troubling from the viewpoint of moral consistency is that he is so willing to break the law at the same time that he has sworn vengeance on all criminals—or, in other words, people who break the law. If Batman is afraid of becoming like those he fights, then breaking the law, like the use of extreme violence, would seem to be a more pervasive concern than more specific but less common acts such as killing.

As I mentioned at the beginning of this chapter, Batman's penchant for breaking the law may also be the one morally questionable behavior he shares with many of us. Although few of us use extreme violence to get what we want, many of us commit misdemeanors such as traffic violations, which we justify or excuse for a number of reasons, some more valid than others. (Speeding through stoplights to get a pregnant woman to the hospital is fine, but doing the same thing to get to your comic book store on a Wednesday before it closes is … well, I'm no legal expert, but that one sounds OK to me too.) What matters the most here is the consistency of our reasons: Did we break the law for the greater good (to save a life) or an important principle (such as racial justice), or did we obey the law even in the face of such concerns while breaking it for more selfish ones (because we were tired or lazy)? If we are going to cross that line, not only must our reasons be good ones, but for our own sakes we should be consistent in our reasons as well.

Notes

1 On this point, see Leslie Green's entry on "Legal Obligation and Authority" in the *Stanford Encyclopedia of Philosophy*, at https://plato.stanford.edu/entries/legal-obligation/, and Christopher Heath Wellman and A. John Simmons, *Is There a Duty to Obey the Law* (Cambridge: Cambridge University Press, 2005). For a profound argument for civil disobedience in the case of unjust laws, see Dr. Martin Luther King Jr.'s 1963 "Letter from Birmingham Jail," available at http://www.africa.upenn.edu/Articles_Gen/Letter_Birmingham.html.

2 Immanuel Kant, *Grounding for the Metaphysics of Morals*, trans. James W. Ellington (Indianapolis, IN: Hackett Publishing Company, 1785/1993), p. 421.

3 *Batman* #575 (March 2000).

4 *Detective Comics* #594 (December 1988). He added, "Besides, if you're caught, I know a good lawyer."

5 *Batman: Legends of the Dark Knight* #12 (November 1990).

6 *Detective Comics* #608 (November 1989).

7 *Detective Comics* #653 (November 1992).

8 *Detective Comics* #559 (February 1986).

9 *Batman/Catwoman: Follow the Money* #1 (January 2011).

10 Ibid.

11 *Batman: Legends of the Dark Knight* #21 (August 1991).

12 *Batman* #632 (November 2004).

13 There have been a number of Vigilantes, but I'm referring primarily to the Adrian Chase version introduced in *New Teen Titans* (vol. 1) *Annual* #2 (August 1983).

14 *Batman* #460 (March 1991).

15 *Batman* #467 (Late August 1991).

16 *Batman: Legends of the Dark Knight* #175 (March 2004).

17 *Detective Comics* #583 (February 1988).

18 *Detective Comics* #584 (March 1988).

19 *Detective Comics* #653 (November 1992). This isn't the only time Batman was frustrated by diplomatic immunity: remember the Joker's appointment as the United Nations ambassador from Iran following his murder of Jason Todd (*Batman* #428–429, December 1988–January 1989), as well as a later case in which a diplomat was implicated in a crime in Gotham about which the FBI could do nothing, leading Batman to think, "Diplomatic immunity! What sort of world is it when diplomacy is a euphemism for turning a blind eye to murder? Every fiber of me calls out for justice—for retribution!" (*Detective Comics* #590, September 1988).

20 *The Untold Legend of the Batman* #1 (July 1980).

21 On the veracity of this story, see Michael Herz, "'Do Justice!' Variations on a Thrice-Told Tale," *Cardozo Law Review* 82 (1996): 111–161, available at http://www.uniset.ca/terr/art/82VaLRev111.pdf.

22 *The Untold Legend of the Batman* #3 (September 1980).

23 *Detective Comics* #800 (January 2005), "Alone at Night."

24 *Batman* #251 (September 1973).

25 *Batman* #406 (April 1987). Later, Gordon thought to himself, "It could have been me … I could have been the night monster. But I chose to hit them from the other side. I chose law, not justice" (*Batman* #458, January 1991).

26 *Batman: Legends of the Dark Knight* #58 (March 1994).

27 *Batman* #308 (February 1979).

28 *Batman: No Man's Land* #1 (March 1999).

29 *Batman: Legends of the Dark Knight* #125 (January 2000).

30 *DC Special Series* #15 (June 1978), "I Now Pronounce You Batman and Wife!" I must mention however, that Batman and the GCPD are not always at odds. In a famous Christmas Eve tale, Batman joined the police for carols while the citizens of Gotham, inspired by his example, took care of themselves (*Batman* #219, February 1970, "The Silent Night of the Batman").

31 *Gotham Central* #2 (February 2003). Later, after the police managed to bring the Firebug down by themselves, Driver gloated about it to Batman, telling him "we did it alone, without your help." Batman's response? "Good. Thank you" (*Gotham Central* #5, May 2003).

32 *Detective Comics* #546 (January 1985), "Hill's Descent."

33 *Detective Comics* #647 (Early August 1992).

34 *Detective Comics* #546 (January 1985), "Hill's Descent." In the same issue, we see police officers debating Batman's value, covering all the bases, from one whose life Batman saved, to another who blames him for all the costumed crooks in Gotham.

35 *Detective Comics* #651 (Early October 1992).

36 *Detective Comics* #539 (June 1984), "Boxing."

37 While Batman went missing in the beginning of No Man's Land, Gordon told Montoya that "he gave up on Gotham like everybody else. He always took the easy way out. Being a vigilante was easier than being a cop" (*Batman: No Man's Land* #1, March 1999), showing that being "only a cop" is actually harder because of the tighter restrictions.

38 *Batman: The Long Halloween* #1 (December 1996).

39 *Batman Annual* #13 (1989), "Faces."

40 *Batman: Gotham Knights* #13 (March 2001), "Officer Down, Part Seven: The End."

41 *Detective Comics* #758 (July 2001), "Unknowing, Part One." In another story in that issue ("History Lesson"), Akins revealed to Renee Montoya that he dealt with a well-intentioned but amateur vigilante at his previous job in Gateway City, who got himself and an innocent killed. Although he recognizes that Batman is better, the fact that Gotham needs Batman is what scares him.

42 *Detective Comics* #794 (July 2004), "Monsters of Rot, Part One: Cleansing Fires."

43 *Detective Comics* #795 (August 2004), "Monsters of Rot, Part Two: Knee Deep."

44 *Detective Comics* #798 (November 2004), "Undertow."

45 *Catwoman*, vol. 3, #35 (November 2004).

46 *Detective Comics* #799 (December 2004), "Good Intentions."

47 *Batman: Legends of the Dark Knight* #184 (December 2004).

48 *Catwoman*, vol. 3, #36 (December 2004).

49 *Batman Allies Secret Files and Origins 2005* (August 2005), "Street Crime."

50 *Gotham Central* #25 (January 2005). The rest of this issue (as well as much of the series) contains fantastic conversations and debates among the Gotham City police regarding the value and role of the bat, far too many to quote here.

51 *Batman* #634 (January 2005).

52 *Batman Allies Secret Files and Origins 2005* (August 2005), "A Friend in Need."

53 *Detective Comics* #800 (January 2005), "Alone at Night."

54 *Batman* #644 (Late October 2005).

55 *Batman Allies Secret Files and Origins 2005* (August 2005), "A Friend in Need." Montoya also defended him to her GCPD colleagues, arguing with her partner Crispus Allen that Batman isn't one of "the freaks," as Allen believes, but a hero who "saves lives. He protects people when we can't" (*Gotham Central* #25, January 2005). Unfortunately for the Dark Knight, she's in a distinct minority among her fellow police.

56 *Batman* #438 (Early September 1989).

57 *Batman Confidential* #25 (March 2009).

58 *Batman* #557 (August 1998).

59 *Detective Comics* #651 (Early October 1992).

60 *Batman Annual* #14 (March 1990).

61 Ibid.

62 *Batman Annual* #14 (March 1990).

63 *Batman: Dark Victory* #8 (July 2000).

64 For more, see Tracey Maclin, *The Supreme Court and the Fourth Amendment's Exclusionary Rule* (Oxford: Oxford University Press, 2012).

65 *Batman* #422 (August 1988).

66 *Batman* #672 (February 2008).

67 *Detective Comics* #575 (June 1987). Gordon's successor held a distinctly different view: even before the citywide gang war, when Detective Driver asked him to call Batman, Akins told him, "the GCPD can't officially touch the bat-signal, or in any way acknowledge the existence of Batman," at the same time that he told their office worker Stacy to pull the switch. As he admitted to Driver, "It's a fine line," but probably a good one to walk (*Gotham Central* #2, February 2003).

68 *Batman Confidential* #7 (September 2007).

69 *Batman* #644 (Late October 2005).

70 *Batman: Dark Victory* #0 (November 1999).

71 *Detective Comics* #625 (January 1991).
72 *Detective Comics* #754 (March 2001), "Monster in a Box." This scenario frequently played out in the pages of *Gotham Central* where resentment of the bat was a key theme; see, for instance, issue #36 (December 2005).
73 In one of comics' great ironies, Crispus Allen would go on—after he died—to be the latest human host for the Spectre, God's agent of divine vengeance on Earth, in *Infinite Crisis* #4 (March 2006).
74 *Batman* #422 (August 1988).
75 Aristotle, *Nicomachean Ethics* (350 BCE), translated by W.D. Ross, Book II Chapter 6, available at http://classics.mit.edu/Aristotle/nicomachaen.html.
76 *Batman* #500 (October 1993).
77 *Batman: Shadow of the Bat* #28 (June 1994).
78 *Batman* #509 (July 1994).
79 *Batman* #0 (October 1994).
80 *Detective Comics* #677 (August 1994).
81 *Batman: Shadow of the Bat* #29 (July 1994).
82 *Detective Comics* #676 (July 1994).
83 *Batman* #512 (November 1994). Dick took to the role of Batman much more smoothly after Batman's "death," beginning with *Batman: Battle for the Cowl* #1 (July 2009) and *Batman* #687 (August 2009), with Bruce's son Damian joining him as his Robin (*Batman and Robin* #1, August 2009). He even led a version of the Justice League alongside fellow second-generation heroes such as Donna Troy (formerly Wonder Girl), Jade (daughter of Alan Scott, the Golden Age Green Lantern), Jessie Quick (daughter of golden age heroes Johnny Quick and Liberty Belle), and Supergirl (you know who she is). See, for instance, *Justice League of America*, vol. 2, #49 (November 2010).
84 *Robin*, vol. 4, #13 (January 1995).

Conclusion

Batman became one of the world's most popular superheroes in large part because of the example he sets: a person who deals with personal tragedy by devoting his life, with almost superhuman dedication, resolve, and sacrifice, to preventing others from suffering as he did. Although he lacks superpowers, alien technology, or gifts from the gods, he made himself into a superhero by pushing himself to the limits of human perfection, not just physically but mentally.

But Batman is far from perfect—and perhaps this adds to his universal allure as well. He is hardly the "boy scout" his friend Superman is, nor the emissary for love and peace that Wonder Woman serves as. He is but a man, driving himself as hard as possible to do the best he can in a world that will never appreciate it, and sacrificing any semblance of happiness, joy, or love that he works so hard to make sure the residents of Gotham enjoy. And as "just" a human being, each of us can identify with his goal to help others and emulate it as much as we can, given our unique capabilities and resources—which most likely don't match up to his, but we can each do our part nonetheless.

Although Batman's general impulse to help others is admirable, the precise nature of his mission and the things he will or will not do to further it are more problematic. We can acknowledge his tremendous heroism, as shown by the incredible sacrifices he makes for the sake of others, at the same time that we criticize the moral choices he makes in the pursuit of his heroic mission.

Batman and Ethics, First Edition. Mark D. White.
© 2019 John Wiley & Sons Ltd. Published 2019 by John Wiley & Sons Ltd.

Looking Back

It might be a good idea to summarize what we've discussed in the previous pages. This was hardly an exhaustive look at Batman's ethics—that would take more books than there have been Batman films—but we did cover what I feel are the major aspects of what Batman tries to do and how he does it.

Mission: In dedicating his life to fighting crime and saving lives, Batman has set himself a generally utilitarian mission to improve the well-being of the largest number of people. This mission is limited in a number of ways— chiefly his focus on Gotham City and his negative contribution through preventing harm rather than promoting happiness—which are understandable and defensible but also arbitrary and sentimental. As we discussed, these self-imposed restrictions on his altruistic efforts are completely within his rights—he can certainly decide how he chooses to help others— but may nonetheless reflect an insincere devotion to the general thrust of utilitarianism, and point instead to personal reasons for his particular altruistic impulses, which can be interpreted as indulgent and contingent on his own pain.

Endangering children: Batman directly contradicts his mission to protect the innocent when he trains children to be his sidekicks. Even though they are often injured, beaten, or even killed, Batman continues to train new ones, after a mandatory period of remorse and repeated vows of "never again." This egregious betrayal of his devotion to life and the safety of innocents is compounded by the fact that these are children, easily excitable but with diminished capacity to give consent, who make an ambiguous contribution to the mission. They are, however, helpful to him personally, which makes the "Robin program" ultimately selfish in nature.

Refusal to kill: Batman claims his mission is to protect and save lives, yet his one ironclad rule—to not kill—stands in clear opposition to this goal insofar as he lets murderous sociopaths live to kill again (as they inevitably do). It is quite reasonable to have deontological constraints on one's pursuit of utilitarian goals, but this one stands out because of its direct contradiction of Batman's claimed ends, as well as the personal agony he has endured because of his worst foes, such as the Joker. His refusal to kill seems to be based less on a dedication to the sanctity of life and more on his own self-image and maintaining his moral virtue, which is a decidedly unvirtuous motivation, especially in light of its cost in human lives.

Willingness to use violence and torture: The hypocrisy of Batman's refusal to kill is further highlighted by his easy comfort with extreme violence and torture in pursuit of his mission. Belief in the sanctity of human life is normally based on an appreciation of the inherent value or dignity of persons, which is violated by the use of brutal methods to reduce them to bloody tools in his war against crime. Batman acts like the people he beats and interrogates are not fully human, but instead mere means to his ends—and his only excuse is that they are "scum," either known criminals or other residents of the shady underworld, whether or not they are actually wanted or suspected for a crime. He won't kill anybody, even to save countless innocent lives, but he will beat them within an inch of their lives, or hang them off a tall building until they talk, even to help solve a minor crime—a comparable wrong for a much smaller benefit.

Willingness to break the law: Batman usually claims to be working with the police and helping them to apprehend, prosecute, and punish criminals. But he does this in a way that promotes lawlessness and the violation of civil rights, such as bragging that he can do what the law cannot, which denies the value of legal protections for those suspected of crimes. Furthermore, his example inspires others to break the law, even though he opposes this and wants the exclusive right to "bend" the law when he sees fit and to authorize others to do so (such as his partners in crimefighting). In the worst case scenario, those he inspires but does not authorize often do not share his refusal to kill or his keen detective skills, making them a positive danger to the community at large. And this does not even account for the extent to which his extralegal activities compromise official investigations and prosecutions or make the everyday work of the police force more difficult.

In summary, his utilitarianism is limited in the scope of its reach and his activity within it; it is limited by only one principle, which happens to be the one which would contribute to the mission the most if it were relaxed; and he breaks a number of other important deontological constraints to pursue his mission, even those that are parallel to the one he won't break in their defiance of the sanctity of life and the protection of innocents.

The Importance of Moral Consistency

As we detailed throughout the book, Batman does have justifications for these anomalies in his moral code. None of them are done out of malice or capriciousness, and only his training of Robins can be held to be truly selfish—a rare indulgence that might be forgivable, were it not for the effect on the Robins themselves. But taken as a whole, they reflect, at best, a complex and imperfect rational code and, at worst, a person who lacks a certain level of integrity to his moral character.

A lack of integrity is what we could consider a "second-level" moral failing. It doesn't mean that a person without moral integrity does bad things—far from it. We see that, for the most part, Batman does good things for good reasons. He is a hero who has saved or helped countless people in Gotham City and beyond. But his lack of moral integrity reflects poorly on him, showing that the various elements of his moral character are not in harmony with each other. For example, he protects life, but refuses to take one life to protect hundreds of others; he will ignore the humanity of those he needs information from by torturing them; and he will endanger the well-being of a child with little justification based on his mission. Furthermore, he fights crime, yet breaks the law himself with impunity—although he does it for the "right reason" (and, to be fair, often with the tacit agreement of the authorities). Someone with a more consistent moral code would find it harder to sanction these inconsistencies.

Batman's lack of moral integrity is rare among superheroes, who are often shown to have much more straightforward and simplistic moral compasses. This does not exempt them from moral dilemmas, and they still have to use their judgment to find acceptable solutions, but the ethical "material" they're working with is much simpler.[1] But Batman, with his essential moral conflict, echoes people in the real world just as does his lack of superpowers. Few of us—moral philosophers included!—have perfect integrity within our ethical codes. Most of us are morally inconsistent, acting altruistically one moment and selfishly the next, behaving honestly or courageously in one instance and deceitfully or cowardly the next. If you traced out any of our lives in terms of our moral actions or statements, such as we've done for Batman in this book, do you think we'd fare any better? For most of us, it's highly doubtful—again, this doesn't make us bad people, but it does suggest we could do more to make sure our moral characters hold together better.

Why is moral consistency or integrity important? Our moral characters make up an important part of who we are, and character is both expressed and reinforced by our choices, so everything we do is a reflection of who we are as moral agents. Philosopher Christine Korsgaard calls this the process of *self-constitution*, in the sense that "to be a person is to be constantly engaged in making yourself into that person."[2] Korsgaard sometimes frames the problem of self-integration in terms of roles. For example, each of us plays a number of roles in our lives: parent, child, spouse or partner, mentor, teacher, student, worker, boss, coach, and so forth. Each of these roles comes with its own duties and responsibilities, and sometimes the responsibilities associated with one role conflict with those of another. If we don't reconcile this conflict, we may start to feel we are several different people, and this will be true insofar as our actions in one role appear much different than others. People may wonder, "he's such a great guy at home with his wife and kids, so why is he such a jerk with his employees?" or "how come my sister is so great with her coworkers but not her friends?" They may even say that "it's like they're two different people."

As Korsgaard writes:

> The task of self-constitution involves finding some roles and fulfilling them with integrity and dedication. It also involves integrating those roles into a single identity, into a coherent life. People are more or less successful at constituting their identities as unified agents, and a good action is one that does this well. It is one that both *achieves* and *springs* from the integrity of the person who performs it.[3]

We are complete and consistent persons to the extent that we can integrate the various roles we play—or the aspects of our moral character. Korsgaard points out that in our common language, you "pull yourself together" and "make up your mind," reflecting the common experience of having to reconcile conflicting and competing parts of our nature.[4] And "in the course of this process, of falling apart and pulling yourself back together, you create something new, you constitute something new: yourself."[5] This is done through the choices we make, which not only reflect our characters but also reinforce them, crafting them over time like a sculptor molds a hunk of clay.

Batman often claims he and Bruce Wayne are two different people, and struggles with the question of "which is the real me?" from time to time, but actually he normally integrates these two roles extremely well. His problems with inconsistency lie mainly within his role as Gotham's sworn protector and, as we've seen, these problems reflect a failure to integrate the various aspects of his moral character. It isn't that he can't find a stable way to balance his utilitarian and deontological commitments—this is the regularly occurring and never-ending ethical dilemma that each of us faces in our lives. It is never easy to decide when doing what's right has to take precedence over doing what's good, and we can hardly hold Batman to account for struggling with this as well.

The problem is that Batman reconciles these ethical conflicts in ways that cast doubt on his grasp of his basic utilitarian and deontological principles themselves, much less how to make judgments between them. It seems that he is unclear about just how much his utilitarian mission to protect and save innocent people demands. Even though he sacrifices all of his personal life and a great deal of wealth toward this cause, he makes other decisions, such as limiting his activities to Gotham City and to fighting crime, that reflect his sentimentality and the psychological legacy of his parents' deaths. In terms of his deontology, his refusal to kill is supposedly based on his belief in the sanctity of life, but this principle is betrayed by his embrace, often with glee, of extreme violence and torture—again, all in service of his mission, even though his single rule against killing represents the greatest barrier to success in that mission.

Nonetheless, there is no doubt that Batman is a hero and a good person. But he could be *better*, both as a hero and as a person, if he worked harder to make sure the various actions he takes in expression of his moral character and in pursuit of his mission were more consistent with each other and with his character as a whole. And this is the greatest lesson we can take from the Dark Knight: We don't need to achieve moral perfection, but we do need to strive for moral improvement, especially regarding the integration of our various moral principles and goals. We can try to do what's right and what's good, and many times we can do both at the same time—but even when we can't, we need to make sure we form judgments to settle this contrast in ways that make sense and are consistent over time.

Take lying, for instance. Most of us avoid lying most of the time, only doing it when the stakes seem too negligible to matter (as in little white lies) or too large to ignore ("I hated to do it but I had no choice"). This approach represents a reasonable compromise of a deontological rule against lying and consequentialist considerations that may overwhelm that rule in certain situations. If we look at our records of lying over our lives, ideally we would find some consistency: most of our lies were told in the circumstances mentioned above, and few of them otherwise. But if we find that there was no rhyme or reason to when we chose to lie, that it seemed random with no consideration of right and wrong or good and bad, then we are either psychopaths with no regard whatsoever for morality—let's hope this isn't the case!—or else we are thinking of the ethics of our actions but making wildly inconsistent choices that reflect a lack of integration of our moral characters.

Batman's biggest lie is, of course, his secret identity. The justifications for it are well known: when Ra's al Ghul, who knows Batman's true identity, sent all of Batman's enemies after his loved ones, Batman said to Jason Todd that he needs to protect his secret because "my greatest vulnerability" is "the people closest to me."[6] When Batman suspected that Silver St. Cloud, Bruce Wayne's love interest at the time, had figured out his double life, he reflected on why it's important to him, thinking about Silver's safety as well as the "safe retreat" that his civilian identity provides him.[7] But Batman knows that, in the end, his secret identity is only of value insofar as it helps protect his loved ones and promote the mission. After the Cataclysmic earthquake, when it seemed he would need to expose the cave and Wayne Manor to save people trapped in a collapsed subway tunnel, he told Tim, "The loss of Bruce Wayne's secret won't 'kill' anything, Robin. The Batman will go on."[8]

Although Batman has come to live with this lie, letting his fellow heroes in on his secret when it's useful but keeping others in the dark—even such close friends as Jim Gordon—he regrets having to lie even when circumstances justify it. When Batman faked Bruce Wayne's death before pursuing Ra's al Ghul—to prevent his identity from being exposed in the battle—and had to discuss the "news" directly with Gordon, Batman thought afterwards, "I hated to lie! It was necessary, though!"[9] When Jason Todd discovered that Two-Face likely killed his father and he lashed out at Batman for keeping it a secret, Batman admitted to him, "I was wrong. But I was trying to protect you," keeping an already rash young man from succumbing to blind vengeance.[10] After Jason was killed, Bruce attended his funeral while thinking to himself, "The world doesn't know that the new Robin is dead. That's the way it has to remain, if I want to maintain a secret identity. Yeah, I know that's cold but that's how it's going to be," which mirrors his willingness to let the world believe that the original Robin was dead to protect Dick Grayson after a nearly fatal incident.[11]

Batman will never be an unscrupulously honest person, but his general reluctance to lie without sufficient justification is reasonable. Even if you disagree with his reasoning, though, we can say that his behavior with respect to honesty has consistency regarding the circumstances in which he lies and his reasons for it. How a person expresses his or her moral character doesn't have to be black and white, completely honest or dishonest, but can lie somewhere in between. In fact, his history with dishonesty may be the most consistent of his morally questionable acts (but also the one with the least impact on other people's lives and well-being).

Neither does consistency or integrity mean that one's character and behavior can never change. For example, over the years, Batman has become more paranoid, especially regarding his fellow superheroes in the Justice League of America, most of whom are many times more powerful than he is—even if none are as smart, cunning, or determined. In one adventure, Ra's al Ghul attacked each member in very specific ways tailored to each one's weakness. In time, the rest of the team discovered that Batman had made detailed plans to take each one out should he have to (in case they were mind-controlled, they became possessed by demons … or he was just bored), plans that Talia stole for her father to use against them.[12] Batman's fellow Leaguers naturally felt betrayed, more for his secretiveness than for the fact that he had developed the plans—after all, Superman gave him a kryptonite ring to use on exactly such an occasion.[13]

In a later story, Batman was surprised to find his teammates lobotomizing the villain Doctor Light after he raped Sue Dibny, wife of the Elongated Man. Fearing his reaction, the rest of the team voted to have the magician Zatanna wipe Batman's memories of that event.[14] Batman's eventual realization of this, years later, drove him to develop the Brother Eye satellite to keep tabs on his fellow heroes without their knowledge. When Batman confronted the League about their actions, Aquaman brought up the secret plans stolen by Talia, to which Batman responded, "events have proven their necessity time and again," citing the power present in only a small grouping of the League.[15] This gradual increase in his paranoia and trust issues was the organic result of new events, just as we all change and (ideally) grow over the years—until, that is, Bruce took a year-long vacation to Nanda Parbat with Dick and Tim to get his head straight and "rebuild Batman."[16]

There is much to admire in Batman, but we must be cautious about putting him on a pedestal (or a gargoyle, as the case may be). His dedication to the people of Gotham City and his selfless pursuit of justice inspire awe and aspiration, but we should not emulate his fractured, inconsistent ethical behavior, which reflects a lack of integration of the different aspects of his moral code. We've seen how these various components conflict and work against each other, which causes unnecessary turmoil for him and usually compromises the pursuit of his mission. This may add to the romantic sense of Batman as a tragic hero, giving all he can to help people while torturing himself because he can't do it all. Although this may make for great stories, it's no example to live up to—rather, it should be a cautionary tale. By all means, enjoy the comics, movies, and TV shows, and marvel at his attempts to do *everything he can do* to save the innocent people of Gotham City from the scourge of crime, but at the same time learn from his mistakes. It can be thrilling to read (or watch) the dramatic push and pull of his various moral impulses, but again, we should also see the mistakes he makes, and the inner turmoil he experiences from them, and use them in our own lives to make ourselves better.

Few of us can be Batman. But all of us, in a way, can be *better* than Batman, specifically by trying to do what he does, but doing it in a more consistent way that will better promote our goals and make us more inte-grated people. This may not result in as dramatic and exciting adventures as Batman has, but it will lead to more satisfied and successful lives in which we do more good—and maybe even be happy.

Notes

1   I've written about this with respect to both Superman and Captain America: see "Moral Judgment: The Power That Makes Superman Human," in my edited vol-ume *Superman and Philosophy: What Would the Man of Steel Do?* (Hoboken, NJ: Wiley Blackwell, 2013), pp. 5–15, and *The Virtues of Captain America: Modern-Day Lessons on Character from a World War II Superhero* (Hoboken, NJ: Wiley Blackwell, 2014), ch. 5.

2   Christine Korsgaard, *Self-Constitution: Agency, Identity, and Integrity* (Oxford: Oxford University Press, 2009), p. 43.

3   Ibid., p. 25 (emphasis mine).

4   Ibid., p. 126.

5   Ibid., p. 214.

6   *Batman* #400 (October 1986). Elsewhere, Dick explained to Tim what would happen to the team if Batman ever revealed his true identity, focusing on the reaction of the police, not to mention the criminal element (*Batman: Gotham Knights* #8, October 2000, "Transference, Part 1").

7   *Detective Comics* #475 (February 1978).

8   *Batman* #555 (June 1998).

9   *Batman* #242 (June 1972), "Bruce Wayne—Rest in Peace!" Although it took a while, near the end of the No Man's Land period Batman did unmask in front of Jim, in an effort to regain his friend's trust after operating separately during the crisis, saying his secret was the only thing he could offer him other than his word. Jim refused to look, however, saying, "If I wanted to know who you were, I could have discovered it" years ago. "And for all you know, maybe I did. Maybe I do. But that's not the point. Put it back on." Even though Batman's secret

remained, the gesture turned out to be enough to enable them to work together again (*Batman: Legends of the Dark Knight* #125, January 2000).

10   *Batman* #411 (September 1987).

11   *Batman* #428 (December 1988); *Batman* #408 (June 1987).

12   *JLA Secret Files and Origins* #3 (December 2000), "Blame."

13   *JLA* #46 (October 2000).

14   *Identity Crisis* #6 (January 2005). Batman and Zatanna, who were childhood friends and occasional flirts, discussed this incident in *Detective Comics* #833–834 (August–September 2007).

15   *JLA* #120 (December 2005). Unfortunately, Batman's precautions massively backfired when Brother Eye became sentient and started eliminating superheroes; see, for instance, *The OMAC Project* #2 (July 2005). This ties in with Maxwell Lord, who as head of the covert intelligence agency Checkmate colluded with Brother Eye, and led to his execution at the hands of Wonder Woman, discussed in Chapter 6 (*Wonder Woman*, vol. 2, #219, September 2005).

16   *Infinite Crisis* #7 (June 2006) and *52* #30 (November 2006).

References

Some notes about the way I listed the comics cited in this book:

1. Because most all of the comics referenced in this book were published before the New 52 relaunch in fall 2011, there is no need to list volume numbers with most of the comics. (In other words, all the listings for *Batman* and *Detective Comics* would be volume 1, before the second volumes were launched with the New 52.) There are a few exceptions, such as *Catwoman, Nightwing,* and *Robin,* which had several volumes before the relaunch, and other occasional titles cited (such as *Wonder Woman, Manhunter,* and *New Teen Titans*).
2. Story titles are listed only when there is more than one story in the comic.
3. Artists include pencillers, inkers, and colorists.
4. Collected editions are listed when appropriate; some of the older collections may be out of print but still available in libraries, used bookstores, or comics fans' bookshelves (in case you know one of those goofballs). Most all of these titles are also available digitally, both in individual comics and collections.
5. All comics and collections are published by DC Comics.

52 #30 (November 2006). Geoff Johns, Grant Morrison, Greg Rucka, and Mark Waid (w), Keith Giffen, Joe Bennett, Ruy José, and David Baron (a). Collected in *52 Volume 2* (2017).

Azrael #16 (April 1996). Dennis O'Neil (w), Barry Kitson, James Pascoe, Demetrius Bassoukos, and Digital Hellfire (a). Collected in *Batman: Contagion* (1996) and *Batman: Contagion* (expanded edition, 2016).

Batgirl, vol. 1, #3 (June 2000). Kelley Puckett and Scott Peterson (w), Damion Scott, Robert Campanella, and Jason Wright (a). Collected in *Batgirl: Silent Running* (2001) and *Batgirl Vol. 1: Silent Knight* (2015).

Batman and Ethics, First Edition. Mark D. White.
© 2019 John Wiley & Sons Ltd. Published 2019 by John Wiley & Sons Ltd.

Batgirl, vol. 1, #23 (February 2002). Kelley Puckett (w), Damion Scott, Robert Campanella, Jason Wright, and Digital Chameleon (a). Collected in *Batgirl: Death Wish* (2003) and *Batgirl Vol. 2: To the Death* (2016).

Batgirl, vol. 1, #57 (December 2004). Dylan Horrocks (w), Mike Huddleston, Jesse Delperdang, and Jason Wight (a). Collected in *Batman: War Games Act 3* (2005) and *Batman War Games Book Two* (2016)

Batgirl, vol. 1, #73 (April 2006). Andersen Gabrych (w), Pop Mhan, Jesse Delperdang, Adam DeKraker, and Jason Wright (a). Collected in *Batgirl: Destruction's Daughter* (2006).

Batman #0 (October 1994). Doug Moench (w), Mike Manley, Josef Rubinstein, and Adrienne Roy (a). Collected in *Batman: Zero Hour* (2017).

Batman #219 (February 1970), "The Silent Night of the Batman." Mike Friedrich (w), Neal Adams, Dick Giordano, and Jerry Serpe (a). Collected in *Batman Illustrated by Neal Adams Volume 2* (2004).

Batman #237 (December 1971). Denny O'Neil (w), Neal Adams and Dick Giordano (a). Collected in *Batman in the Seventies* (1999) and *Batman Illustrated by Neal Adams Volume 3* (2005).

Batman #242 (June 1972), "Bruce Wayne – Rest in Peace!" Dennis O'Neil (w), Irv Novick and Dick Giordano (a). Collected in *Batman: Tales of the Demon* (1991).

Batman #243 (August 1972). Denny O'Neil (w), Neal Adams and Dick Giordano (a). Collected in *Batman: Tales of the Demon* (1991), *Batman Illustrated by Neal Adams Volume 3* (2005), and *Batman Arkham: Ra's al Ghul* (2019).

Batman #244 (September 1972), "The Demon Lives Again!" Denny O'Neil (w), Neal Adams and Dick Giordano (a). Collected in *Batman: Tales of the Demon* (1991), *Batman Illustrated by Neal Adams Volume 3* (2005), and *Batman Arkham: Ra's al Ghul* (2019).

Batman #251 (September 1973). Denny O'Neil (w) and Neal Adams (a). Collected in *Batman Illustrated by Neal Adams Volume 3* (2005) and *Batman: The Greatest Stories Ever Told, Volume 1* (2005).

Batman #306 (December 1978), "The Mystery Murderer of 'Mrs. Batman'!" Bob Rozakis (w), Don Newton, David Hunt, and Adrienne Roy (a). Collected in *Tales of the Batman: Don Newton* (2011).

Batman #307 (January 1979). Len Wein (w), John Calnan, Dick Giordano, and Glynis Wein (a). Collected in *Tales of the Batman: Len Wein* (2014).

Batman #308 (February 1979). Len Wein (w), John Calnan, Dick Giordano, and Glynis Wein (a). Collected in *Tales of the Batman: Len Wein* (2014) and *Batman Arkham: Mister Freeze* (2017).

Batman #313 (July 1979). Len Wein (w), Irv Novick, Frank McLaughlin, and Glynis Wein (a). Collected in *Tales of the Batman: Len Wein* (2014).

Batman #315 (September 1979). Len Wein (w), Irv Novick, Frank McLaughlin, and Glynis Wein (a). Collected in *Tales of the Batman: Len Wein* (2014).

Batman #320 (February 1980). Denny O'Neil (w), Irv Novick, Bob Smith, and Glynis Wein (a).

Batman #331 (January 1981). Marv Wolfman and Michael Fleisher (w), Irv Novick, Frank McLaughlin, and Adrienne Roy (a).

Batman #333 (March 1981), "The China Syndrome!" Marv Wolfman (w), Irv Novick, Frank McLaughlin, and Adrienne Roy (a).

Batman #344 (February 1982). Gerry Conway (w), Gene Colan, Klaus Janson, and Adrienne Roy (a). Collected in *Tales of the Batman: Gene Colan Volume 1* (2011) and *Tales of the Batman: Gerry Conway Volume 2* (2018).

Batman #345 (March 1982). Gerry Conway (w), Gene Colan, Klaus Janson, and Adrienne Roy (a). Collected in *Tales of the Batman: Gene Colan Volume 1* (2011) and *Tales of the Batman: Gerry Conway Volume 2* (2018).

Batman #347 (May 1982), "The Shadow of the Batman." Roger Slifer (w), Trevor von Eeden, Pablo Marcos, and Adrienne Roy (a).

Batman #373 (July 1984). Doug Moench (w), Gene Colan, Alfredo Alcala, and Adrienne Roy (a). Collected in *Batman Arkham: Scarecrow* (2016) and *Tales of the Batman: Gene Colan Volume 2* (2018).

Batman #375 (September 1984). Doug Moench (w), Don Newton, Alfredo Alcala, and Adrienne Roy (a). Collected in *Batman Arkham: Mister Freeze* (2017).

Batman #390 (December 1985). Doug Moench (w), Tom Mandrake and Adrienne Roy (a).

Batman #394 (April 1986). Doug Moench (w), Paul Gulacy and Adrienne Roy (a).

Batman #397 (July 1986). Doug Moench (w), Tom Mandrake and Adrienne Roy (a). Collected in *Batman Arkham: Two-Face* (2015).

Batman #400 (October 1986). Doug Moench (w), Steve Lightle, George Pérez, Paris Cullins, Bill Sienkiewicz, Art Adams, Tom Sutton, Steve Leialoha, Joe Kubert, Ken Steacy, Rick Leonardi, Brian Bolland, John Byrne, Bruce D. Patterson, Larry Mahlstedt, Terry Austin, Ricardo Villagran, Karl Kesel, and Adrienne Roy (a).

Batman #402 (December 1986). Max Collins (w), Jim Starlin and Daina Graziunas (a). Collected in *Batman: Second Chances* (2015).

Batman #403 (January 1987). Max Collins (w), Denys Cowan, Greg Brooks, and Adrienne Roy (a). Collected in *Batman: Second Chances* (2015).

Batman #404 (February 1987). Frank Miller (w), David Mazzucchelli and Richmond Lewis (a). Collected in *Batman: Year One* (2007).

Batman #405 (March 1987). Frank Miller (w), David Mazzucchelli and Richmond Lewis (a). Collected in *Batman: Year One* (2007).

Batman #406 (April 1987). Frank Miller (w), David Mazzucchelli and Richmond Lewis (a). Collected in *Batman: Year One* (2007).

Batman #407 (May 1987). Frank Miller (w), David Mazzucchelli and Richmond Lewis (a). Collected in *Batman: Year One* (2007).

Batman #408 (June 1987). Max Allan Collins (w), Chris Warner, Mike DeCarlo, and Adrienne Roy (a). Collected in *Batman: Second Chances* (2015) and *Robin the Boy Wonder: A Celebration of 75 Years* (2015).

Batman #410 (August 1987). Max Allan Collins (w), Dave Cockrum, Mike DeCarlo, and Adrienne Roy (a). Collected in *Batman: Second Chances* (2015), *Batman Arkham: Two-Face* (2015), and *Two-Face: A Celebration of 75 Years* (2017).

Batman #411 (September 1987). Max Allan Collins (w), Dave Cockrum, Don Heck, and Adrienne Roy (a). Collected in *Batman: Second Chances* (2015), *Batman Arkham: Two-Face* (2015), and *Two-Face: A Celebration of 75 Years* (2017).

Batman #414 (December 1987). Jim Starlin (w), Jim Aparo, Mike DeCarlo, and Adrienne Roy (a). Collected in *Batman: Second Chances* (2015).

Batman #416 (February 1988). Jim Starlin (w), Jim Aparo, Mike DeCarlo, and Adrienne Roy (a). Collected in *Batman: Second Chances* (2015).

Batman #420 (June 1988). Jim Starlin (w), Jim Aparo, Mike DeCarlo, and Adrienne Roy (a). Collected in *Batman: Ten Nights of the Beast* (1994) and *Batman: The Caped Crusader Volume 1* (2018).

Batman #422 (August 1988). Jim Starlin (w), Mark Bright, Joe Rubinstein, Steve Mitchell, and Anthony Tollin (a). Collected in *Batman: The Caped Crusader Volume 1* (2018).

Batman #424 (October 1988). Jim Starlin (w), Doc Bright, Steve Mitchell, and Adrienne Roy (a). Collected in *Robin the Boy Wonder: A Celebration of 75 Years* (2015) and *Batman: The Caped Crusader Volume 1* (2018).

Batman #426 (December 1988). Jim Starlin (w), Jim Aparo, Mike DeCarlo, and Adrienne Roy (a). Collected in *Batman: A Death in the Family* (1995).

Batman #427 (December 1988). Jim Starlin (w), Jim Aparo, Mike DeCarlo, and Adrienne Roy (a). Collected in *Batman: A Death in the Family* (1995), *The Joker: A Celebration of 75 Years* (2014), and *Robin, the Boy Wonder: A Celebration of 75 Years* (2015).

Batman #428 (December 1988). Jim Starlin (w), Jim Aparo, Mike DeCarlo, and Adrienne Roy (a). Collected in *Batman: A Death in the Family* (1995) and *Robin the Boy Wonder: A Celebration of 75 Years* (2015).

Batman #429 (January 1989). Jim Starlin (w), Jim Aparo, Mike DeCarlo, and Adrienne Roy (a). Collected in *Batman: A Death in the Family* (1995).

Batman #431 (March 1989). James Owsley (w), Jim Aparo, Mike DeCarlo, and Adrienne Roy (a). Collected in *Batman: The Caped Crusader Volume 1* (2018).

Batman #436 (August 1989). Marv Wolfman (w), Pat Broderick, John Beatty, and Adrienne Roy (a). Collected in *Batman: The Caped Crusader Volume 2* (2019).

Batman #437 (August 1989). Marv Wolfman (w), Pat Broderick, John Beatty, and Adrienne Roy (a). Collected in *Batman: The Caped Crusader Volume 2* (2019).

Batman #438 (September 1989). Marv Wolfman (w), Pat Broderick, John Beatty, and Adrienne Roy (a). Collected in *Batman: The Caped Crusader Volume 2* (2019).

Batman #439 (September 1989). Marv Wolfman (w), Pat Broderick, Michael Bair, and Adrienne Roy (a). Collected in *Batman: The Caped Crusader Volume 2* (2019).

Batman #440 (October 1989). Marv Wolfman and George Pérez (w), Jim Aparo, Mike DeCarlo, and Adrienne Roy (a). Collected in *Batman: A Lonely Place of Dying* (1990) and *Batman: The Caped Crusader Volume 2* (2019).

Batman #441 (November 1989). Marv Wolfman (w), Jim Aparo, Mike DeCarlo, and Adrienne Roy (a). Collected in *Batman: A Lonely Place of Dying* (1990) and *Batman: The Caped Crusader Volume 2* (2019).

Batman #442 (December 1989). Marv Wolfman and George Pérez (w), Jim Aparo, Mike DeCarlo, and Adrienne Roy (a). Collected in *Batman: A Lonely Place of Dying* (1990), *Robin the Boy Wonder: A Celebration of 75 Years* (2015), and *Batman: The Caped Crusader Volume 2* (2019).

Batman #443 (January 1990). Marv Wolfman (w), Jim Aparo, Mike DeCarlo, and Adrienne Roy (a). Collected in *Batman: The Caped Crusader Volume 2* (2019).

Batman #445 (March 1990). Marv Wolfman (w), Jim Aparo, Mike DeCarlo, and Adrienne Roy (a).

Batman #450 (Early July 1990). Marv Wolfman (w), Jim Aparo, Mike DeCarlo, and Adrienne Roy (a).

Batman #451 (Late July 1990). Marv Wolfman (w), Jim Aparo, Mike DeCarlo, and Adrienne Roy (a).

Batman #452 (Early August 1990). Peter Milligan (w), Kieron Dwyer, Dennis Janke, and Adrienne Roy (a).

Batman #455 (October 1990). Alan Grant (w), Norm Breyfogle, Steve Mitchell, and Adrienne Roy (a). Collected in *Robin: A Hero Reborn* (1991), *Robin Volume 1: Reborn* (2015), and *Legends of the Dark Knight: Norm Breyfogle, Volume 2* (2018).

Batman #458 (January 1991). Alan Grant (w), Norm Breyfogle, Steve Mitchell, and Adrienne Roy (a). Collected in *Legends of the Dark Knight: Norm Breyfogle, Volume 2* (2018).

Batman #460 (March 1991). Alan Grant (w), Norm Breyfogle, Tim Sale, and Adrienne Roy (a).

Batman #464 (Early July 1991). Alan Grant (w), Norm Breyfogle, Steve Mitchell, and Adrienne Roy (a).

Batman #465 (Late July 1991). Alan Grant (w), Norm Breyfogle, Steve Mitchell, and Adrienne Roy (a).

Batman #467 (Late August 1991). Chuck Dixon (w), Tom Lyle, Andy Mushynsky, and Adrienne Roy (a).

Batman #468 (Early September 1991). Chuck Dixon (w), Tom Lyle, Andy Mushynsky, and Adrienne Roy (a).

Batman #469 (Late September 1991). Chuck Dixon (w), Tom Lyle, Scott Hanna, and Adrienne Roy (a).

Batman #475 (March 1992). Alan Grant (w), Norm Breyfogle and Adrienne Roy (a).

Batman #477 (Early May 1992). John Wagner (w), Cam Kennedy and Adrienne Roy (a).

Batman #478 (Late May 1992). John Wagner (w), Cam Kennedy and Adrienne Roy (a).

Batman #479 (Early June 1992). Alan Grant (w), Tom Mandrake and Adrienne Roy (a).

Batman #487 (December 1992). Doug Moench (w), Jim Aparo and Adrienne Roy (a). Collected in *Batman: Prelude to Knightfall* (2018).

Batman #488 (January 1993). Doug Moench (w), Jim Aparo and Adrienne Roy (a). Collected in *Batman: Prelude to Knightfall* (2018).

Batman #490 (March 1993). Doug Moench (w), Jim Aparo and Adrienne Roy (a). Collected in *Batman: Prelude to Knightfall* (2018).

Batman #491 (April 1993). Doug Moench (w), Jim Aparo and Adrienne Roy (a). Collected in *Batman: Knightfall, Part One: Broken Bat* (1993), *Batman: Knightfall, Volume One* (2012), and *Batman: Prelude to Knightfall* (2018).

Batman #493 (May 1993). Doug Moench (w), Norm Breyfogle and Adrienne Roy (a). Collected in *Batman: Knightfall, Part One: Broken Bat* (1993), *Batman: Knightfall, Volume One* (2012), and *Batman: Knightfall 25th Anniversary Edition, Volume 1* (2018).

Batman #497 (July 1993). Doug Moench (w), Jim Aparo, Dick Giordano, and Adrienne Roy (a). Collected in *Batman: Knightfall, Part One: Broken Bat* (1993), *Batman: Knightfall, Volume One* (2012), *Batman: Knightfall 25th Anniversary Edition, Volume 1* (2018), and—don't ask me why—*Batman: A Celebration of 75 Years* (2014).

Batman #498 (August 1993). Doug Moench (w), Jim Aparo, Rick Burchett, and Adrienne Roy (a). Collected in *Batman: Knightfall, Part Two: Who Rules the Night* (1993), *Batman: Knightfall, Volume One* (2012), and *Batman: Knightfall 25th Anniversary Edition, Volume 2* (2018).

Batman #500 (October 1993). Doug Moench (w), Jim Aparo, Mike Manley, Terry Austin, and Adrienne Roy (a). Collected in *Batman: Knightfall, Part Two: Who Rules the Night* (1993), *Batman: Knightfall, Volume One* (2012), and *Batman: Knightfall 25th Anniversary Edition, Volume 2* (2018).

Batman #505 (March 1994). Doug Moench (w), Mike Manley, Bob Wiacek, and Adrienne Roy (a). Collected in *Batman: Knightfall, Vol. 2: Knightquest* (2012) and *Batman: Knightquest: The Crusade 25th Anniversary Edition, Volume 2* (2018).

Batman #509 (July 1994). Doug Moench (w), Dick Giordano, Joe Rubinstein, and Adrienne Roy (a). Collected in *Batman: KnightsEnd* (1995), *Batman: Knightfall, Volume 3: KnightsEnd* (2012), and *Batman: KnightsEnd 25th Anniversary Edition* (2018).

Batman #510 (August 1994). Doug Moench (w), Mike Manley, Joe Rubinstein, and Adrienne Roy (a). Collected in *Batman: KnightsEnd* (1995), *Batman: Knightfall,*

Volume 3: KnightsEnd (2012), and *Batman: KnightsEnd 25th Anniversary Edition* (2018).

Batman #512 (November 1994). Doug Moench (w), Mike Gustovich, Romeo Tanghal, and Adrienne Roy (a). Collected in *Batman: Knightfall Volume Three—KnightsEnd* (2012), *Batman Arkham: Killer Croc* (2016), and *Batman: Prodigal* (2019).

Batman #519 (June 1995). Doug Moench (w), Kelley Jones, John Beatty, and Greg Wright (a). Collected in *Batman by Doug Moench & Kelley Jones Volume 1* (2014).

Batman #520 (July 1995). Doug Moench (w), Eduardo Barreto and Greg Wright (a).

Batman #521 (August 1995). Doug Moench (w), Kelley Jones, John Beatty, and Greg Wright (a). Collected in *Batman by Doug Moench & Kelley Jones Volume 1* (2014) and *Batman Arkham: Killer Croc* (2016).

Batman #525 (December 1995). Doug Moench (w), Kelley Jones, John Beatty, and Greg Wright (a). Collected in *Batman by Doug Moench & Kelley Jones Volume 1* (2014) and *Batman Arkham: Mister Freeze* (2017).

Batman #526 (January 1996). Doug Moench (w), J.H. Williams III, Mick Gray, Pat Garrahy, and Android Images (a).

Batman #534 (September 1996). Doug Moench (w), Jim Aparo, Bill Sienkiewicz, Lee Loughridge, and Android Images (a). Collected in *Batman: Legacy Vol. 2* (2018).

Batman #541 (April 1997). Doug Moench (w), Kelley Jones, John Beatty, Greg Wright, and Android Images (a). Collected in *Batman by Doug Moench & Kelley Jones Volume 2* (2018).

Batman #544 (July 1997). Doug Moench (w), Kelley Jones, John Beatty, Gregory Wright, and Android Images (a). Collected in *Batman by Doug Moench & Kelley Jones Volume 2* (2018).

Batman #546 (September 1997). Doug Moench (w), Kelley Jones, John Beatty, Gregory Wright, and Android Images (a). Collected in *Batman by Doug Moench & Kelley Jones Volume 2* (2018).

Batman #548 (November 1997). Doug Moench (w), Kelley Jones, John Beatty, Gregory Wright, and Android Images (a). Collected in *Batman by Doug Moench & Kelley Jones Volume 2* (2018) and *Batman Arkham: Penguin* (2018).

Batman #555 (June 1998). Doug Moench (w), John Beatty, Sal Buscema, Gregory Wright, and Android Images (a).

Batman #556 (July 1998). Doug Moench (w), Norm Breyfogle, Joe Rubinstein, Gregory Wright, and Android Images (a).

Batman #557 (August 1998). Doug Moench (w), Vince Giarrano, Sal Buscema, Gregory Wright, and Android Images (a). Collected in *Batman: Road to No Man's Land Vol. 1* (2015).

Batman #558 (September 1998). Doug Moench (w), Jim Aparo, Sal Buscema, Gregory Wright, and Android Images (a). Collected in *Batman: Road to No Man's Land Vol. 1* (2015).

Batman #560 (December 1998). Chuck Dixon (w), Jim Aparo, David Roach, and Lee Loughridge (a). Collected in *Batman: Road to No Man's Land Vol. 2* (2016).

Batman #561 (January 1999). Chuck Dixon (w), Jim Aparo, David Roach, and Lee Loughridge (a). Collected in *Batman: Road to No Man's Land Vol. 2* (2016).

Batman #562 (February 1999). Chuck Dixon (w), Jim Aparo, David Roach, and Lee Loughridge (a). Collected in *Batman: Road to No Man's Land Vol. 2* (2016).

Batman #564 (April 1999). Devin Grayson (w), Dale Eaglesham, Jaime Mendoza, Noelle Giddings, and Digital Chameleon (a). Collected in *Batman: No Man's Land Vol. 1* (1999) and *Batman: No Man's Land Vol. 1* (2011).

Batman #575 (March 2000). Larry Hama (w), Scott McDaniel, Karl Story, Roberta Tewes, and Wildstorm FX (a).

Batman #579 (July 2000). Larry Hama (w), Scott McDaniel, Karl Story, Roberta Tewes, and Wildstorm FX (a).

Batman #581 (September 2000). Larry Hama and Scott McDaniel (w), Scott McDaniel, Karl Story, Hector Collazo, John Nyberg, Roberta Tewes, and Wildstorm FX (a).

Batman #585 (January 2001). Ed Brubaker (w), Scott McDaniel, Karl Story, Roberta Tewes, and Wildstorm FX (a). Collected in *Batman by Ed Brubaker Vol. 1* (2016).

Batman #595 (November 2001). Ed Brubaker (w), Scott McDaniel, Aaron Sowd, and Roberta Tewes (a). Collected in *Batman by Ed Brubaker Vol. 1* (2016).

Batman #603 (July 2002). Ed Brubaker (w), Sean Phillips, Gregory Wright, and Wildstorm FX (a). Collected in *Batman: Bruce Wayne—Fugitive* (2014) and *Batman by Ed Brubaker Vol. 2* (2016).

Batman #604 (August 2002). Ed Brubaker (w), Scott McDaniel, Andy Owens, Gregory Wright, and Wildstorm FX (a). Collected in *Batman: Bruce Wayne—Fugitive* (2014) and *Batman by Ed Brubaker Vol. 2* (2016).

Batman #607 (November 2002). Ed Brubaker (w), Scott McDaniel, Andy Owens, Gregory Wright, and Wildstorm FX (a). Collected in *Batman: Bruce Wayne: Fugitive Volume Three* (2002), *Batman: Bruce Wayne—Fugitive* (2014), and *Batman by Ed Brubaker Vol. 2* (2016).

Batman #608 (December 2002). Jeph Loeb (w), Jim Lee, Scott Williams, and Alex Sinclair (a). Collected in *Batman: Hush* (2008).

Batman #612 (April 2003). Jeph Loeb (w), Jim Lee, Scott Williams, and Alex Sinclair (a). Collected in *Batman: Hush* (2008).

Batman #613 (May 2003). Jeph Loeb (w), Jim Lee, Scott Williams, and Alex Sinclair (a). Collected in *Batman: Hush* (2008) and Harley Quinn: *A Celebration of 25 Years* (2017).

Batman #614 (June 2003). Jeph Loeb (w), Jim Lee, Scott Williams, and Alex Sinclair (a). Collected in *Batman: Hush* (2008).

Batman #615 (July 2003). Jeph Loeb (w), Jim Lee, Scott Williams, and Alex Sinclair (a). Collected in *Batman: Hush* (2008).

Batman #618 (October 2003). Jeph Loeb (w), Jim Lee, Scott Williams, and Alex Sinclair (a). Collected in *Batman: Hush* (2008).

Batman #632 (November 2004). Bill Willingham (w), Kinsun, Aaron Sowd, and Tony Avina (a). Collected in *Batman: War Games Act 2* (2005) and *Batman War Games Book Two* (2016).

Batman #633 (December 2004). Bill Willingham (w), Kinsun, Aaron Sowd, Rodney Ramos, Adam DeKraker, and Tony Avina (a). Collected in *Batman: War Games Act 3* (2005) and *Batman War Games Book Two* (2016).

Batman #634 (January 2005). Judd Winick (w), Paul Lee, Brian Horton, and Guy Major (a). Collected in *Batman: War Games Book Two* (2016).

Batman #641 (August 2005). Judd Winick (w), Doug Mahnke, Tom Nguyen, and Alex Sinclair (a). Collected in *Batman: Under the Red Hood* (2011).

Batman #643 (Early October 2005). Bill Willingham (w), Giuseppe Camuncoli, Sandra Hope, and Jason Wright (a). Collected in *Batman: War Crimes* (2005) and *Batman: War Games Book Two* (2016).

Batman #644 (Late October 2005). Bill Willingham (w), Giuseppe Camuncoli, Sandra Hope, and Jason Wright (a). Collected in *Batman: War Crimes* (2005) and *Batman: War Games Book Two* (2016).

Batman #645 (November 2005). Judd Winick (w), Doug Mahnke, Tom Nguyen, and Jason Wright (a). Collected in *Batman: Under the Red Hood* (2011).

Batman #650 (April 2006). Judd Winick (w), Eric Battle, Rodney Ramos, and Alex Sinclair (a). Collected in *Batman: Under the Red Hood* (2011).

Batman #652 (June 2006). James Robinson (w), Don Kramer, Michael Bair, Wayne Faucher, and John Kalisz (a). Collected in *Batman: Face the Face* (2006) and *Batman/Two-Face: Face the Face Deluxe Edition* (2017).

Batman #657 (November 2006). Grant Morrison (w), Andy Kubert, Jesse Delperdang, and Dave Stewart (a). Collected in *Batman and Son* (2014) and *Robin the Boy Wonder: A Celebration of 75 Years* (2015).

Batman #658 (December 2006). Grant Morrison (w), Andy Kubert, Jesse Delperdang, and Guy Major (a). Collected in *Batman and Son* (2014).

Batman #659 (January 2007). John Ostrander (w), Tom Mandrake and Nathan Eyring (a).

Batman #672 (February 2008). Grant Morrison (w), Tony S. Daniel, Sandu Florea, Jonathan Glapion, Mark Irwin, and Guy Major (a). Collected in *Batman and Son* (2014).

Batman #681 (December 2008). Grant Morrison (w), Tony S. Daniel, Sandu Florea, and Guy Major (a). Collected in *Batman R.I.P.* (2010).

Batman #687 (August 2009). Judd Winick (w), Ed Benes, Rob Hunter, Ian Hannin, and J.D. Smith (a). Collected in *Batman: Long Shadows* (2010).

Batman Allies Secret Files and Origins 2005 (August 2005), "A Friend in Need." Russell Lissau (w), Brad Walker, Jimmy Palmiotti, and Giulia Fletcher (a). Collected in *Batman: War Games Book Two* (2016).

Batman Allies Secret Files and Origins 2005 (August 2005), "Street Crime." Will Pfeifer (w), Ron Randall and Brad Anderson (a). Collected in *Batman: War Games Book Two* (2016).

Batman and the Outsiders, vol. 1, #1 (August 1983). Mike W. Barr (w), Jim Aparo and Adrienne Roy (a). Collected in *Batman and the Outsiders Volume 1* (2017).

Batman and the Outsiders, vol. 1, #32 (April 1986). Mike W. Barr (w), Alan Davis and Adrienne Roy (a). Collected in *Batman and the Outsiders Volume 3* (2019).

Batman and Robin #1 (August 2009). Grant Morrison (w), Frank Quitely and Alex Sinclair (a). Collected in *Batman & Robin: Batman Reborn* (2010).

Batman Annual #8 (1982). Mike W. Barr (w), Trevor von Eeden and Lynn Varley (a).

Batman Annual #10 (1986). Doug Moench (w), Denys Cowan, Alfredo Alcala, and Adrienne Roy (a). Collected in *Batman Arkham: Hugo Strange* (2018).

Batman Annual #13 (1989), "Faces." Christopher Priest (w), Michael Bair, Gray Morrow, and Adrienne Roy (a). Collected in *Batman: The Caped Crusader Volume 2* (2019).

Batman Annual #14 (March 1990). Andrew Helfer (w), Chris Sprouse, Steve Mitchell, and Adrienne Roy (a). Collected in *Batman: Featuring Two-Face and the Riddler* (1995) and *Two-Face: A Celebration of 75 Years* (2017).

Batman Annual #25 (May 2006). Judd Winick and Jim Starlin (w), Shane Davis, Jim Aparo, Mark Morales, Mike DeCarlo, and Alex Sinclair (a). Collected in *Batman: Under the Red Hood* (2011).

Batman: Battle for the Cowl #1 (July 2009). Tony S. Daniel (w,a), Sandu Florea, Ian Hannin, and J.D. Smith (a). Collected in *Batman: Battle for the Cowl* (2009).

Batman: Bride of the Demon (December 1990). Mike W. Barr (w), Tom Grindberg and Eva Grindberg (a). Collected in *Batman: Birth of the Demon* (2012).

Batman/Catwoman: Follow the Money #1 (January 2011). Howard Chaykin (w,a) and Jesus Aburto (a).

Batman/Catwoman: Trail of the Gun #1 (October 2004). Ann Nocenti (w), Ethan Van Sciver and Chris Chuckry (a).

Batman/Catwoman: Trail of the Gun #2 (November 2004). Ann Nocenti (w), Ethan Van Sciver and Chris Chuckry (a).

The Batman Chronicles #8 (Spring 1997), "Secrets of the Batcave: Dinosaur Island." Graham Nolan (w,a) and Patricia Mulvihill (a).

The Batman Chronicles #18 (September 1999). Devin Grayson (w), Dale Eaglesham, Jaime Mendoza, John Floyd, Pamela Rambo, and Digital Chameleon (a). Collected in *Batman: No Man's Land Volume 4* (2000) and *Batman: No Man's Land Volume 4* (expanded edition, 2012).

The Batman Chronicles #19 (Winter 2000), "Got a Date with an Angel." Steve Englehart (w), Javier Pulido and Dave Stewart (a).

Batman Confidential #1 (February 2007). Andy Diggle (w), Whilce Portacio, Richard Friend, and David Baron (a). Collected in *Batman: Rules of Engagement* (2007).

Batman Confidential #7 (September 2007). Michael Green (w), Denys Cowan, John Floyd, and I.L.L. (a). Collected in *Batman: Lovers and Madmen* (2008).

Batman Confidential #25 (March 2009). Andrew Kreisberg (w), Scott McDaniel, Andy Owens, and I.L.L. (a). Collected in *Batman: Dead to Rights* (2010).

Batman Confidential #32 (October 2009). Peter Milligan (w), Andy Clarke and David Baron (a). Collected in *Batman: The Bat and the Beast* (2010).

Batman Confidential #33 (November 2009). Peter Milligan (w), Andy Clarke and David Baron (a). Collected in *Batman: The Bat and the Beast* (2010).

Batman Confidential #49 (December 2010). James Patrick (w), Steve Scott, Bob Petrecca, and David Baron (a).

Batman: The Cult #1 (August 1988). Jim Starlin (w), Bernie Wrightson and Bill Wry (a). Collected in *Batman: The Cult* (2009).

Batman: The Cult #4 (November 1988). Jim Starlin (w), Bernie Wrightson and Bill Wry (a). Collected in *Batman: The Cult* (2009).

Batman: Dark Detective #2 (July 2005). Steve Englehart (w), Marshall Rogers, Terry Austin, and Chris Chuckry (a). Collected in *Batman: Dark Detective* (2006) and *Legends of the Dark Knight: Marshall Rogers* (2011).

Batman: The Dark Knight #2 (May 2011). David Finch (w,a), Scott Williams and Alex Sinclair (a). Collected in *Batman: The Dark Knight: Golden Dawn* (2012).

Batman: Dark Victory #0 (November 1999). Jeph Loeb (w), Tim Sale and Gregory Wright (a). Collected in *Batman: Dark Victory* (2012).

Batman: Dark Victory #2 (January 2000). Jeph Loeb (w), Tim Sale and Gregory Wright (a). Collected in *Batman: Dark Victory* (2012).

Batman: Dark Victory #8 (July 2000). Jeph Loeb (w), Tim Sale and Gregory Wright (a). Collected in *Batman: Dark Victory* (2012).

Batman: Dark Victory #11 (October 2000). Jeph Loeb (w), Tim Sale and Gregory Wright (a). Collected in *Batman: Dark Victory* (2012).

Batman: Death and the Maidens #1 (October 2003). Greg Rucka (w), Klaus Janson and Steve Buccellato (a). Collected in *Batman: Death and the Maidens* (2004) and *Batman: Death and the Maidens Deluxe Edition* (2017).

Batman: Death and the Maidens #2 (November 2003). Greg Rucka (w), Klaus Janson and Steve Buccellato (a). Collected in *Batman: Death and the Maidens* (2004) and *Batman: Death and the Maidens Deluxe Edition* (2017).

Batman: Death and the Maidens #6 (March 2004). Greg Rucka (w), Klaus Janson and Steve Buccellato (a). Collected in *Batman: Death and the Maidens* (2004) and *Batman: Death and the Maidens Deluxe Edition* (2017).

Batman: Death and the Maidens #7 (April 2004). Greg Rucka (w), Klaus Janson and Steve Buccellato (a). Collected in *Batman: Death and the Maidens* (2004) and *Batman: Death and the Maidens Deluxe Edition* (2017).

Batman: Death and the Maidens #9 (August 2004). Greg Rucka (w), Klaus Janson and Steve Buccellato (a). Collected in *Batman: Death and the Maidens* (2004) and *Batman: Death and the Maidens Deluxe Edition* (2017).

Batman: Family #8 (February 2003). John Francis Moore (w), Rick Hoberg, Stefano Gaudiano, Steve Lieber, Carla Feeny, and Jessica Kindzierski (a).

Batman: Full Circle (1991). Mike W. Barr (w), Alan Davis, Mark Farmer, and Tom Ziuko (a). Collected in *Legends of the Dark Knight: Alan Davis Volume 1* (2012), *Batman: Year Two 30th Anniversary Deluxe Edition* (2017), and *Batman: The Dark Knight Detective Vol. 1* (2018).

Batman: Gates of Gotham #1–5 (July–October 2011). Scott Snyder, Kyle Higgins, and Ryan Parrott (w), Trevor McCarthy, Graham Nolan, Dustin Nguyen, Derec Donovan, and Guy Major (a). Collected in *Batman: Gates of Gotham* (2012).

Batman: Ghosts—A Legend of the Dark Knight Special (1995). Jeph Loeb (w), Tim Sale and Gregory Wright (a). Collected in *Batman: Haunted Knight* (1996).

Batman: Gotham Knights #3 (May 2000), "Bad Karma." Devin Grayson (w), Paul Ryan, Pamela Rambo, and Wildstorm FX (a).

Batman: Gotham Knights #4 (June 2000), "Letting Go." Devin Grayson (w), Paul Ryan, Pamela Rambo, and Wildstorm FX (a).

Batman: Gotham Knights #5 (July 2000), "Locked." Devin Grayson (w), Paul Ryan, John Floyd, Jean Segarra, and Wildstorm FX (a).

Batman: Gotham Knights #7 (September 2000), "Oblation." Devin Grayson (w), Dale Eaglesham, John Floyd, Pamela Rambo, and Wildstorm FX (a).

Batman: Gotham Knights #8 (October 2000), "Transference, Part 1." Devin Grayson (w), Roger Robinson, John Floyd, Pamela Rambo, and Wildstorm FX (a). Collected in *Batman Arkham: Hugo Strange* (2018).

Batman: Gotham Knights #13 (March 2001), "Officer Down, Part Seven: The End." Greg Rucka (w), Rick Burchett, Rodney Ramos, and Digital Chameleon (a). Collected in *Batman: Officer Down* (2001).

Batman: Gotham Knights #16 (June 2001), "Matatoa Part 1 of 2." Devin Grayson (w), Roger Robinson, John Floyd, and Rob Schwager (a).

Batman: Gotham Knights #17 (July 2001), "Matatoa Part 2 of 2." Devin Grayson (w), Roger Robinson, John Floyd, and Rob Schwager (a).

Batman: Gotham Knights #26 (April 2002), "Innocent Until." Devin Grayson (w), Roger Robinson, John Floyd, Gloria Vasquez, and Wildstorm FX (a). Collected in *Batman: Bruce Wayne—Murderer?* (2002).

Batman: Gotham Knights #27 (May 2002), "Never Say Die." Dwayne McDuffie (w) and Denys Cowan (a). Collected in *Batman: Black & White Volume Three* (2007).

Batman: Gotham Knights #31 (September 2002), "Clean." Devin Grayson (w), Roger Robinson, John Floyd, Gloria Vasquez, and Wildstorm FX (a). Collected in *Batman: Bruce Wayne: Fugitive Volume Two* (2003) and *Batman: Bruce Wayne—Fugitive* (2014).

Batman: Gotham Knights #32 (October 2002), "24/7." Devin Grayson (w), Roger Robinson, John Floyd, Gloria Vasquez, and Wildstorm FX (a). Collected in

Batman: Bruce Wayne: Fugitive Volume Three (2003), *Batman: The Greatest Stories Ever Told, Volume 1* (2005), and *Batman: Bruce Wayne—Fugitive* (2014).

Batman: Gotham Knights #40 (2003), "Knight Moves Part Three: Checkmate." Scott Beatty (w), Roger Robinson, John Floyd, Gloria Vasquez, and Wildstorm FX (a).

Batman: Gotham Knights #42 (August 2003), "20 Days Less One." Scott Beatty (w), Roger Robinson, John Floyd, Noelle Giddings, and Wildstorm FX (a).

Batman: Gotham Knights #43 (September 2003), "Batgirl & Robin." Scott Beatty (w), Roger Robinson, John Floyd, Noelle Giddings, and Wildstorm FX (a).

Batman: Gotham Knights #44 (October 2003), "Body of Evidence." Scott Beatty (w), Roger Robinson, John Floyd, Noelle Giddings, and Wildstorm FX (a).

Batman: Gotham Knights #45 (November 2003), "Knights Passed." Scott Beatty (w), Roger Robinson, John Floyd, Noelle Giddings, and Wildstorm FX (a).

Batman: Gotham Knights #74 (April 2006). A.J. Lieberman (w), Diego Olmos, Bit, and Laurie Kronenberg (a).

Batman/Huntress: Cry for Blood #1 (June 2000). Greg Rucka (w), Rick Burchett and Tatjana Wood (a). Collected in *Batman/Huntress: Cry for Blood* (2002).

Batman in Barcelona: Dragon's Knight #1 (July 2009). Mark Waid (w), Diego Olmos and Marta Martinez (a).

Batman Incorporated #6 (June 2011). Grant Morrison (w), Chris Burnham and Nathan Fairbairn (a). Collected in *Batman Incorporated* (2012).

Batman: The Killing Joke (1988). Alan Moore (w), Brian Bolland and John Higgins (a).

Batman: Legends of the Dark Knight #1 (November 1989). Dennis O'Neil (w), Ed Hannigan, John Beatty, and Richmond Lewis (a). Collected in *Batman: Shaman* (1992).

Batman: Legends of the Dark Knight #12 (November 1990). Doug Moench (w), Paul Gulacy, Terry Austin, and Steve Oliff (a). Collected in *Batman: Prey* (1992 and 2012 expanded edition).

Batman: Legends of the Dark Knight #21 (August 1991). Mike W. Barr (w), Bart Sears, Randy Elliott, and Steve Oliff (a).

Batman: Legends of the Dark Knight #22 (September 1991). Mike W. Barr (w), Bart Sears, Randy Elliott, and Steve Oliff (a).

Batman: Legends of the Dark Knight #23 (October 1991). Mike W. Barr (w), Bart Sears, Randy Elliott, and Steve Oliff (a).

Batman: Legends of the Dark Knight #24 (November 1991). Howard Chaykin and Gil Kane (w), Gil Kane and Steve Oliff (a).

Batman: Legends of the Dark Knight #26 (January 1992). Howard Chaykin and Gil Kane (w), Gil Kane and Steve Oliff (a).

Batman: Legends of the Dark Knight #27 (February 1992). Denny O'Neil (w), Chris Sprouse, Bruce Patterson, and Steve Oliff (a).

Batman: Legends of the Dark Knight #44 (April 1993). Steven Grant (w), Shawn McManus and Matt Hollingsworth (a).

Batman: Legends of the Dark Knight #46 (June 1993). Doug Moench (w), Russ Heath and Digital Chameleon (a).

Batman: Legends of the Dark Knight #47 (July 1993). Doug Moench (w), Russ Heath and Digital Chameleon (a).

Batman: Legends of the Dark Knight #54 (November 1993). Mike Mignola (w,a), Dan Raspler (w), and Mark Chiarello (a). Collected in *Batman: Dark Legends* (1996).

Batman: Legends of the Dark Knight #58 (March 1994). Andrew Donkin and Graham Brand (w), John Higgins and Digital Chameleon (a).

Batman: Legends of the Dark Knight #65 (November 1994). J.M. DeMatteis (w), Joe Staton, Steve Mitchell, and Digital Chameleon (a). Collected in *Batman: Going Sane* (2008).

Batman: Legends of the Dark Knight #66 (December 1994). J.M. DeMatteis (w), Joe Staton, Steve Mitchell, and Digital Chameleon (a). Collected in *Batman: Going Sane* (2008) and *The Joker: A Celebration of 75 Years* (2014).

Batman: Legends of the Dark Knight #67 (January 1995). J.M. DeMatteis (w), Joe Staton, Steve Mitchell, and Digital Chameleon (a). Collected in *Batman: Going Sane* (2008).

Batman: Legends of the Dark Knight #68 (February 1995). J.M. DeMatteis (w), Joe Staton, Steve Mitchell, and Digital Chameleon (a). Collected in *Batman: Going Sane* (2008).

Batman: Legends of the Dark Knight #83 (June 1996). Warren Ellis (w), John McCrea and Digital Chameleon (a).

Batman: Legends of the Dark Knight #100 (November 1997), "The Choice." Dennis O'Neil (w), Dave Taylor and Digital Chameleon (a).

Batman: Legends of the Dark Knight #100 (November 1997), "A Great Day for Everyone." James Robinson (w), Lee Weeks and Digital Chameleon (a).

Batman: Legends of the Dark Knight #116 (April 1999). Devin K. Grayson (w), Dale Eaglesham, Batt, Aaron Sowd, and Pamela Rambo (a). Collected in *Batman: No Man's Land Volume 1* (1999) and *Batman: No Man's Land Volume 1* (2012).

Batman: Legends of the Dark Knight #120 (August 1999). Greg Rucka (w), Mike Deodato Jr., Sean Parsons, Pam Rambo, and Wildstorm FX (a). Collected in *Batman: No Man's Land Volume 3* (2000) and *Batman: No Man's Land Volume 2* (2012).

Batman: Legends of the Dark Knight #121 (September 1999). Larry Hama (w), Rick Burchett, James Hodgkins, and Felix Serrano (a). Collected in *Batman: No Man's Land Volume 3* (2000) and *Batman: No Man's Land Volume 2* (2012).

Batman: Legends of the Dark Knight #125 (January 2000). Greg Rucka (w), Rick Burchett, James Hodgkins, Klaus Janson, and Wildstorm FX (a). Collected in *Batman: No Man's Land Volume 4* (2000) and *Batman: No Man's Land Volume 4* (2012).

Batman: Legends of the Dark Knight #129 (May 2000). Dennis O'Neil (w), Sergio Cariello, Matt Ryan, and Rick Taylor (a). Collected in *Batman: The Ring, the Arrow and the Bat* (2003).

Batman: Legends of the Dark Knight #135 (November 2000). Archie Goodwin and James Robinson (w), Marshall Rogers, Bob Wiacek, John Cebollero, Danny Vozzo, and Digital Chameleon (a). Collected in *Legends of the Dark Knight: Marshall Rogers* (2011) and *Tales of the Batman: Archie Goodwin* (2013).

Batman: Legends of the Dark Knight #140 (April 2001). Doug Moench (w), Paul Gulacy, Jimmy Palmiotti, James Sinclair, and Digital Chameleon (a). Collected in *Batman: Terror* (2003) and *Batman: Prey* (2012 expanded edition).

Batman: Legends of the Dark Knight #141 (May 2001). Doug Moench (w), Paul Gulacy, Jimmy Palmiotti, James Sinclair, and Digital Chameleon (a). Collected in *Batman: Terror* (2003) and *Batman: Prey* (2012 expanded edition).

Batman: Legends of the Dark Knight #143 (July 2001). Chuck Dixon (w), Jim Aparo, John Cebollero, Noelle Giddings, and Digital Chameleon (a).

Batman: Legends of the Dark Knight #144 (August 2001). Chuck Dixon (w), Jim Aparo, John Cebollero, and Noelle Giddings (a).

Batman: Legends of the Dark Knight #145 (September 2001). Chuck Dixon (w), Jim Aparo, John Cebollero, and Noelle Giddings (a).

Batman: Legends of the Dark Knight #147 (November 2001). Doug Moench (w), Barry Kitson, James Sinclair, and Digital Chameleon (a).

Batman: Legends of the Dark Knight #159 (November 2002). John Ostrander (w), David Lopez, Dan Green, James Sinclair, and Digital Chameleon (a).

Batman: Legends of the Dark Knight #160 (December 2002). John Ostrander (w), David Lopez, Dan Green, James Sinclair, and Digital Chameleon (a).

Batman: Legends of the Dark Knight #164 (April 2003). Dwayne McDuffie (w), Val Semeiks, Dan Green, James Sinclair, and Digital Chameleon (a). Collected in *Batman: Blink* (2015).

Batman: Legends of the Dark Knight #172 (December 2003). John Wagner (w), Chris Brunner and James Sinclair (a).

Batman: Legends of the Dark Knight #173 (January 2004). John Wagner (w), Chris Brunner and James Sinclair (a).

Batman: Legends of the Dark Knight #175 (March 2004). John Wagner (w), Chris Brunner and James Sinclair (a).

Batman: Legends of the Dark Knight #176 (April 2004). John Wagner (w), Chris Brunner and James Sinclair (a).

Batman: Legends of the Dark Knight #182 (October 2004). A.J. Lieberman (w), Brad Walker, Troy Nixey, and Javier Rodriguez (a). Collected in *Batman: War Games, Act One—Outbreak* (2005) and *Batman: War Games Book One* (2015).

Batman: Legends of the Dark Knight #184 (December 2004). Dylan Horrocks (w), Brad Walker, Troy Nixey, and Javier Rodriguez (a). Collected in *Batman: War Games, Act 3* (2005) and *Batman: War Games Book Two* (2016).

Batman: Legends of the Dark Knight #201 (Early May 2006). Christos N. Gage (w), Ron Wagner, Bill Reinhold, and James Sinclair (a).

Batman: Legends of the Dark Knight #202 (Late May 2006). Christos N. Gage (w), Ron Wagner, Bill Reinhold, and James Sinclair (a).

Batman: Legends of the Dark Knight #203 (Early June 2006). Christos N. Gage (w), Ron Wagner, Bill Reinhold, and James Sinclair (a).

Batman: Legends of the Dark Knight #204 (Late June 2006). Justin Gray (w), Steven Cummings and James Sinclair (a).

Batman: Legends of the Dark Knight #205 (Early July 2006). Justin Gray (w), Steven Cummings and James Sinclair (a).

Batman: Legends of the Dark Knight #207 (August 2006). Bruce Jones (w) and Ariel Olivetti (a).

Batman: Legends of the Dark Knight #209 (October 2006). Bruce Jones (w) and Ariel Olivetti (a).

Batman: Legends of the Dark Knight #214 (March 2007). Christos N. Gage (w), Phil Winslade and Mike Atiyeh (a).

Batman: Legends of the Dark Knight Annual #1 (1991). Denny O'Neil (w), Jim Aparo, Keith Giffen, Malcolm Jones III, Joe Quesada, Joe Rubinstein, Tom Lyle, Ty Templeton, Dan Spiegle, James Blackburn, Michael Golden, and Steve Oliff (a).

Batman: Legend of the Dark Knight Halloween Special #1 (December 1993). Jeph Loeb (w), Tim Sale and Gregory Wright (a). Collected in *Batman: Haunted Knight* (1996).

Batman: The Long Halloween #1 (December 1996). Jeph Loeb (w), Tim Sale and Gregory Wright (a). Collected in *Batman: The Long Halloween* (2011).

Batman: The Long Halloween #3 (February 1997). Jeph Loeb (w), Tim Sale and Gregory Wright (a). Collected in *Batman: The Long Halloween* (2011).

Batman: The Long Halloween #12 (November 1997). Jeph Loeb (w), Tim Sale and Gregory Wright (a). Collected in *Batman: The Long Halloween* (2011).

Batman: The Long Halloween #13 (December 1997). Jeph Loeb (w), Tim Sale and Gregory Wright (a). Collected in *Batman: The Long Halloween* (2011).

Batman: The Man Who Laughs (April 2005). Ed Brubaker (w), Doug Mahnke and David Baron (a).

Batman: No Man's Land #0 (December 1999). Jordan B. Gorfinkel and Greg Rucka (w), Greg Land, Drew Geraci, and Rob Schwager (a). Collected in *Batman: No Man's Land Volume 5* (2001) and *Batman: No Man's Land Volume 4* (2012).

Batman: No Man's Land #1 (March 1999). Bob Gale (w), Alex Maleev, Wayne Faucher, and Matt Hollingsworth (a). Collected in *Batman: No Man's Land Volume 1* (1999) and *Batman: No Man's Land Volume 1* (2012).

Batman: The Return #1 (January 2011). Grant Morrison (w), David Finch, Batt, Ryan Winn, and Peter Steigerwald (a). Collected in *Batman: The Dark Knight: Golden Dawn* (2012).

Batman: Scottish Connection (1998). Alan Grant (w), Frank Quitely, Matt Hollingsworth, and Brad Matthew (a).

Batman Secret Files and Origins (October 1997), "The Men Behind Gotham." Scott Beatty (w).

Batman: Shadow of the Bat #0 (October 1994). Alan Grant (w), Bret Blevins and Adrienne Roy (a). Collected in *Batman: Zero Hour* (2017) and *Batman: Shadow of the Bat Volume 3* (2018).

Batman: Shadow of the Bat #16 (Early September 1993). Alan Grant (w), Bret Blevins, Mike Manley, and Adrienne Roy (a). Collected in *Batman: Knightfall, Part Two: Who Rules the Night* (1993), *Batman: Knightfall, Vol. 1* (2012), *Batman: Shadow of the Bat Vol. 2* (2017), and *Batman: Knightfall 25th Anniversary Edition, Volume 2* (2018).

Batman: Shadow of the Bat #28 (June 1994). Alan Grant (w), Bret Blevins, Bob Smith, and Adrienne Roy (a). Collected in *Batman: Knightfall, Vol. 2: Knightquest* (2012), *Batman: Shadow of the Bat Volume 3* (2018), and *Batman: Knightquest: The Crusade 25th Anniversary Edition, Volume 2* (2018).

Batman: Shadow of the Bat #29 (July 1994). Alan Grant (w), Bret Blevins, Bob Smith, and Adrienne Roy (a). Collected in *Batman: KnightsEnd* (1995), *Batman: Knightfall, Volume 3: KnightsEnd* (2012), *Batman: Shadow of the Bat Volume 3* (2018), and *Batman: KnightsEnd 25th Anniversary Edition* (2018).

Batman: Shadow of the Bat #30 (August 1994). Alan Grant (w), Bret Blevins and Adrienne Roy (a). Collected in *Batman: KnightsEnd* (1995), *Batman: Knightfall, Volume 3: KnightsEnd* (2012), *Batman: Shadow of the Bat Volume 3* (2018), and *Batman: KnightsEnd 25th Anniversary Edition* (2018).

Batman: Shadow of the Bat #45 (December 1995). Alan Grant (w), Michal Dutkiewicz, Gerry Fernandez, Pamela Rambo, and Android Images (a).

Batman: Shadow of the Bat #54 (September 1996). Alan Grant (w), Dave Taylor, Stan Woch, and Pamela Rambo (a).

Batman: Shadow of the Bat #59 (February 1997). Alan Grant (w), Dave Taylor, Stan Woch, Pam Rambo, and Android Images (a).

Batman: Shadow of the Bat #62 (May 1997). Alan Grant (w), Dave Taylor, Stan Woch, Pam Rambo, and Android Images (a).

Batman: Shadow of the Bat #71 (February 1998). Alan Grant (w). Mark Buckingham, Wayne Faucher, Gloria Vasquez, and Android Images (a).

Batman: Shadow of the Bat #72 (March 1998). Alan Grant (w), Eduardo Barreto, Wayne Faucher, Pam Rambo, and Android Images (a).

Batman: Shadow of the Bat #74 (May 1998). Alan Grant (w), Mark Buckingham, Wayne Faucher, Pam Rambo, and Android Images (a). Collected in *Batman: Cataclysm* (1999) and *Batman: Cataclysm* (expanded 2015 edition).

Batman: Shadow of the Bat #76 (July 1998). Alan Grant (w), Mark Buckingham, Wayne Faucher, Pam Rambo, and Android Images (a). Collected in *Batman: Road to No Man's Land Vol. 1* (2015).

Batman: Shadow of the Bat #78 (September 1998). Alan Grant (w), Mark Buckingham, Wayne Faucher, Pam Rambo, and Android Images (a). Collected in *Batman: Road to No Man's Land Vol. 1* (2015).

Batman: Shadow of the Bat Annual #3 (1995). Alan Grant (w), Brian Apthorp, Stan Woch, and Linda Medley (a). Collected in *Batman: Four of a Kind* (1998) and *Batman Arkham: Poison Ivy* (2016).

Batman: Son of the Demon (September 1987). Mike W. Barr (w) and Jerry Bingham (a). Collected in *Batman: Birth of the Demon* (2012).

Batman: 10-Cent Adventure (March 2002). Greg Rucka (w), Rick Burchett, Klaus Janson, and Lee Loughridge (a). Collected in *Batman: Bruce Wayne— Murderer?* (2002).

Batman: Turning Points #2 (January 2001). Ed Brubaker (w), Joe Giella and Shannon Blanchard (a). Collected in *Batman: Turning Points* (2007).

Batman: Turning Points #3 (January 2001). Ed Brubaker (w), Dick Giordano, Bob Smith, and Glenn Whitmore (a). Collected in *Batman: Turning Points* (2007).

Batman: Two-Face—Crime and Punishment (1995). J.M. DeMatteis (w), Scott McDaniel and Pat Garrahy (a). Collected in *Batman Arkham: Two-Face* (2015).

Batman: Vengeance of Bane #1 (January 1993). Chuck Dixon (w), Graham Nolan, Eduardo Barreto, and Adrienne Roy (a). Collected in *Batman Versus Bane* (2012), *Batman: Knightfall, Volume One* (2012), and *Batman: Prelude to Knightfall* (2018).

Catwoman, vol. 3, #34 (October 2004). Ed Brubaker (w), Paul Gulacy, Jimmy Palmiotti, and Laurie Kronenberg (a). Collected in *Batman: War Games, Act 1* (2005) and *Batman: War Games Book One* (2015).

Catwoman, vol. 3, #35 (November 2004). Ed Brubaker (w), Paul Gulacy, Jimmy Palmiotti, and Laurie Kronenberg (a). Collected in *Batman: War Games, Act 2* (2005) and *Batman: War Games Book Two* (2016).

Catwoman, vol. 3, #36 (December 2004). Ed Brubaker (w), Paul Gulacy, Jimmy Palmiotti, and Laurie Kronenberg (a). Collected in *Batman: War Games, Act 3* (2005) and *Batman: War Games Book Two* (2016).

DC Special Series #15 (June 1978), "I Now Pronounce You Batman and Wife!" Denny O'Neil (w), Michael Golden, Dick Giordano, and Rick Taylor (a). Collected in *Batman: Tales of the Demon* (1991) and *Batman Arkham: Ra's al Ghul* (2019), and *Legends of the Dark Knight: Michael Golden* (2019).

Detective Comics #411 (May 1971), "Into the Den of the Death-Dealers!" Dennis O'Neil (w), Bob Brown and Dick Giordano (a). Collected in *Batman: Tales of the Demon* (1991).

Detective Comics #447 (May 1975), "Enter: The Creeper." Len Wein (w), Ernie Chua and Dick Giordano (a). Collected in *Tales of the Batman: Len Wein* (2014).

Detective Comics #457 (March 1976), "There Is No Hope in Crime Alley!" Dennis O'Neil (w), Dick Giordano and Terry Austin (a). Collected in *The Greatest Batman Stories Ever Told* (1988) and *Batman in the Seventies* (1999).

Detective Comics #475 (February 1978). Steve Englehart (w), Marshall Rogers, Terry Austin, and Jerry Serpe (a). Collected in *Batman: Strange Apparitions* (1999), *Legends of the Dark Knight: Marshall Rogers* (2011), and *The Joker: A Celebration of 75 Years* (2014).

Detective Comics #478 (August 1978). Len Wein (w), Marshall Rogers and Dick Giordano (a). Collected in *Batman: Strange Apparitions* (1999), *Legends of the Dark Knight: Marshall Rogers* (2011), *Tales of the Batman: Len Wein* (2014), and *Batman Arkham: Clayface* (2017).

Detective Comics #481 (January 1979), "Ticket to Tragedy." Denny O'Neil (w), Marshall Rogers and Adrienne Roy (a). Collected in *Batman in the Seventies* (1999) and *Legends of the Dark Knight: Marshall Rogers* (2011).

Detective Comics #483 (May 1979), "The Curse of Crime Alley." Denny O'Neil (w), Don Newton, Dan Adkins, and Adrienne Roy (a). Collected in *Tales of the Batman: Don Newton* (2011).

Detective Comics #485 (September 1979), "The Vengeance Vow!" Denny O'Neil (w), Don Newton, Dan Adkins, and Adrienne Roy (a). Collected in *Batman: Tales of the Demon* (1991) and *Tales of the Batman: Don Newton* (2011).

Detective Comics #486 (November 1979), "Murder by Thunderbolt." Denny O'Neil (w), Don Newton, Dan Adkins, and Adrienne Roy (a). Collected in *Tales of the Batman: Don Newton* (2011) and *Batman Arkham: Scarecrow* (2016).

Detective Comics #489 (April 1980), "Where Strike the Assassins." Denny O'Neil (w), Don Newton, Dan Adkins, and Adrienne Roy (a). Collected in *Batman: Tales of the Demon* (1991) and *Tales of the Batman: Don Newton* (2011).

Detective Comics #496 (November 1980), "Murder on the Mystery Ship." Michael L. Fleisher (w), Don Newton, Dan Adkins, and Adrienne Roy (a). Collected in *Tales of the Batman: Don Newton* (2011).

Detective Comics #500 (March 1981), "To Kill a Legend." Alan Brennert (w), Dick Giordano and Adrienne Roy (a). Collected in *The Greatest Batman Stories Ever Told* (1988) and *Batman in the Eighties* (2004).

Detective Comics #514 (May 1982), "Haven!" Len Wein (w), Don Newton, Frank Chiaramonte, and Adrienne Roy (a). Collected in *Tales of the Batman: Len Wein* (2014).

Detective Comics #529 (August 1983), "The Thief of Night!" Doug Moench (w), Gene Colan, Dick Giordano, and Adrienne Roy (a). Collected in *Tales of the Batman: Gene Colan Volume 1* (2011).

Detective Comics #539 (June 1984), "Boxing." Doug Moench (w), Don Newton, Bob Smith, and Adrienne Roy (a).

Detective Comics #542 (September 1984), "Between Two Nights." Doug Moench (w), Gene Colan, Bob Smith, and Adrienne Roy (a). Collected in *Tales of the Batman: Gene Colan Volume 2* (2018).

Detective Comics #546 (January 1985), "Hill's Descent." Doug Moench (w), Gene Colan, Bob Smith, and Adrienne Roy (a).

Detective Comics #554 (September 1985), "Port Passed." Doug Moench (w) and Klaus Janson (a).

Detective Comics #557 (December 1985), "Still Beating." Doug Moench (w), Gene Colan, Bob Smith, and Adrienne Roy (a).

Detective Comics #559 (February 1986). Doug Moench (w), Gene Colan, Bob Smith, and Adrienne Roy (a).

Detective Comics #567 (October 1986), "The Night of Thanks, But No Thanks!" Harlan Ellison (w), Gene Colan, Bob Smith, and Adrienne Roy (a).

Detective Comics #568 (November 1986). Joey Cavalieri (w) and Klaus Janson (a). Collected in *Batman: The Dark Knight Detective Volume 1* (2018).

Detective Comics #570 (January 1987). Mike W. Barr (w), Alan Davis, Paul Neary, and Adrienne Roy (a). Collected in *Legends of the Dark Knight: Alan Davis Volume 1* (2012) and *Batman: The Dark Knight Detective Volume 1* (2018).

Detective Comics #574 (May 1987). Mike W. Barr (w), Alan Davis, Paul Neary, and Adrienne Roy (a). Collected in *Legends of the Dark Knight: Alan Davis Volume 1* (2012), *Batman: A Celebration of 75 Years* (2014), and *Batman: The Dark Knight Detective Volume 1* (2018).

Detective Comics #575 (June 1987). Mike W. Barr (w), Alan Davis, Paul Neary, and Adrienne Roy (a). Collected in *Legends of the Dark Knight: Alan Davis Volume 1* (2012) and *Batman: Year Two—Fear the Reaper* (2002).

Detective Comics #577 (August 1987). Mike W. Barr (w), Todd McFarlane, Alfredo Alcala, and Adrienne Roy (a). Collected in *Batman: Year Two 30th Anniversary Deluxe Edition* (2017).

Detective Comics #578 (September 1987). Mike W. Barr (w), Todd McFarlane and Adrienne Roy (a). Collected in *Batman: Year Two 30th Anniversary Deluxe Edition* (2017).

Detective Comics #580 (November 1987). Mike W. Barr (w), Jim Baikie and Adrienne Roy (a). Collected in *Batman: The Dark Knight Detective Volume 1* (2018).

Detective Comics #583 (February 1988). John Wagner and Alan Grant (w), Norm Breyfogle, Kim DeMulder, and Adrienne Roy (a). Collected in *Legends of the Dark Knight: Norm Breyfogle Volume 1* (2015) and *Batman: The Dark Knight Detective Volume 2* (2018).

Detective Comics #584 (March 1988). John Wagner and Alan Grant (w), Norm Breyfogle, Steve Mitchell, and Adrienne Roy (a). Collected in *Legends of the Dark Knight: Norm Breyfogle Volume 1* (2015) and *Batman: The Dark Knight Detective Volume 2* (2018).

Detective Comics #589 (August 1988), "The Burning Pit." Alan Grant and John Wagner (w), Norm Breyfogle and Adrienne Roy (a). Collected in *Legends of the Dark Knight: Norm Breyfogle Volume 1* (2015) and *Batman: The Dark Knight Detective Volume 2* (2018).

Detective Comics #590 (September 1988). Alan Grant and John Wagner (w), Norm Breyfogle and Adrienne Roy (a). Collected in *Legends of the Dark Knight: Norm Breyfogle Volume 1* (2015) and *Batman: The Dark Knight Detective Volume 2* (2018).

Detective Comics #594 (December 1988). Alan Grant and John Wagner (w), Norm Breyfogle and Adrienne Roy (a). Collected in *Legends of the Dark Knight: Norm Breyfogle Volume 1* (2015).

Detective Comics #596 (January 1989). Alan Grant and John Wagner (w), Eduardo Barreto, Steve Mitchell, and Adrienne Roy (a).

Detective Comics #597 (February 1989). Alan Grant and John Wagner (w), Eduardo Barreto, Steve Mitchell, and Adrienne Roy (a).

Detective Comics #598 (March 1989). Sam Hamm (w), Denys Cowan, Dick Giordano, Frank McLaughlin, and Adrienne Roy (a). Collected in *Batman: Blind Justice* (2005).

Detective Comics #600 (May 1989). Sam Hamm (w), Denys Cowan, Dick Giordano, Frank McLaughlin, and Adrienne Roy (a). Collected in *Batman: Blind Justice* (2005).

Detective Comics #603 (August 1989). Alan Grant (w), Norm Breyfogle, Steve Mitchell, and Adrienne Roy (a). Collected in *Legends of the Dark Knight: Norm Breyfogle, Volume 1* (2015).

Detective Comics #606 (October 1989). Alan Grant (w), Norm Breyfogle, Steve Mitchell, and Adrienne Roy (a). Collected in *Legends of the Dark Knight: Norm Breyfogle, Volume 1* (2015).

Detective Comics #608 (November 1989). Alan Grant (w), Norm Breyfogle, Steve Mitchell, and Adrienne Roy (a). Collected in *Legends of the Dark Knight: Norm Breyfogle, Volume 2* (2018).

Detective Comics #609 (December 1989). Alan Grant (w), Norm Breyfogle, Steve Mitchell, and Adrienne Roy (a). Collected in *Legends of the Dark Knight: Norm Breyfogle, Volume 2* (2018).

Detective Comics #610 (January 1990). Alan Grant (w), Norm Breyfogle, Steve Mitchell, and Adrienne Roy (a). Collected in *Legends of the Dark Knight: Norm Breyfogle, Volume 2* (2018) and *Batman Arkham: Penguin* (2018).

Detective Comics #621 (September 1990). Alan Grant (w), Norm Breyfogle, Steve Mitchell, and Adrienne Roy (a). Collected in *Robin Volume 1: Reborn* (2015) and *Legends of the Dark Knight: Norm Breyfogle, Volume 2* (2018).

Detective Comics #625 (January 1991). Marv Wolfman (w), Jim Aparo, Mike DeCarlo, and Adrienne Roy (a).

Detective Comics #627 (March 1991), "The Case of the Chemical Syndicate." Marv Wolfman (w), Jim Aparo, Mike DeCarlo, and Adrienne Roy (a).

Detective Comics #646 (July 1992). Chuck Dixon (w), Tom Lyle, Scott Hanna, and Adrienne Roy (a).

Detective Comics #647 (Early August 1992). Chuck Dixon (w), Tom Lyle, Scott Hanna, and Adrienne Roy (a).

Detective Comics #649 (Early September 1992). Chuck Dixon (w), Tom Lyle, Scott Hanna, and Adrienne Roy (a).

Detective Comics #651 (Early October 1992). Chuck Dixon (w), Graham Nolan, Scott Hanna, and Glenn Whitmore (a).

Detective Comics #653 (November 1992). Chuck Dixon (w), Graham Nolan, Scott Hanna, and Adrienne Roy (a).

Detective Comics #662 (June 1993). Chuck Dixon (w), Graham Nolan, Scott Hanna, and Adrienne Roy (a). Collected in *Batman: Knightfall, Part One: Broken Bat* (1993), *Batman: Knightfall, Volume One* (2012), and *Batman: Knightfall 25th Anniversary Edition, Volume 1* (2018).

Detective Comics #665 (August 1993). Chuck Dixon (w), Graham Nolan, Dick Giordano, and Adrienne Roy (a). Collected in *Batman: Knightfall, Part Two: Who Rules the Night* (1993), *Batman: Knightfall, Volume One* (2012), and *Batman: Knightfall 25th Anniversary Edition, Volume 2* (2018).

Detective Comics #676 (July 1994). Chuck Dixon (w), Graham Nolan, Scott Hanna, and Adrienne Roy (a). Collected in *Batman: KnightsEnd* (1995), *Batman: Knightfall Volume Three—KnightsEnd* (2012), and *Batman: KnightsEnd 25th Anniversary Edition* (2018).

Detective Comics #677 (August 1994). Chuck Dixon (w), Graham Nolan, Scott Hanna, and Adrienne Roy (a). Collected in *Batman: KnightsEnd* (1995), *Batman: Knightfall Volume Three—KnightsEnd* (2012), and *Batman: KnightsEnd 25th Anniversary Edition* (2018).

Detective Comics #684 (April 1995). Chuck Dixon (w), Graham Nolan, Scott Hanna, and Adrienne Roy (a).

Detective Comics #696 (April 1996). Chuck Dixon (w), Graham Nolan, Scott Hanna, Gloria Vasquez, and Android Images (a). Collected in *Batman: Contagion* (1996) and *Batman: Contagion* (expanded edition, 2016).

Detective Comics #702 (October 1996). Chuck Dixon (w), Graham Nolan, Scott Hanna, Gloria Vasquez, and Android Images (a). Collected in *Batman: Legacy Vol. 2* (2018).

Detective Comics #710 (June 1997). Chuck Dixon (w), Graham Nolan, Bill Sienkiewicz, Gloria Vasquez, and Android Images (a).

Detective Comics #721 (May 1998). Chuck Dixon (w), Graham Nolan, Klaus Janson, Gloria Vasquez, and Android Images (a). Collected in *Batman: Cataclysm* (1999) and *Batman: Cataclysm* (expanded 2015 edition).

Detective Comics #722 (June 1998). Chuck Dixon (w), Jim Aparo, James Hodgkins, Gloria Vasquez, and Android Images (a). Collected in *Batman: Road to No Man's Land Vol. 1* (2015).

Detective Comics #724 (August 1998). Chuck Dixon (w), Jim Aparo, James Hodgkins, Gloria Vasquez, and Android Images (a). Collected in *Batman: Road to No Man's Land Vol. 1* (2015).

Detective Comics #725 (September 1998). Chuck Dixon (w), William Rosado, Tom Palmer, Gloria Vasquez, and Android Images (a). Collected in *Batman: Road to No Man's Land Vol. 1* (2015).

Detective Comics #730 (March 1999). Bob Gale (w), Alex Maleev, Wayne Faucher, and Dave Stewart (a). Collected in *Batman: No Man's Land, Volume One* (1999) and *Batman: No Man's Land, Volume One* (2011).

Detective Comics #736 (September 1999). Larry Hama (w), Mike Deodato Jr., Sean Persons, and Pamela Rambo (a). Collected in *Batman: No Man's Land, Volume Four* (2000) and *Batman: No Man's Land, Volume Three* (2012).

Detective Comics #741 (February 2000). Devin Grayson and Greg Rucka (w), Dale Eaglesham, Damion Scott, Sal Buscema, Sean Parsons, Rob Hunter, Pamela Rambo, and Wildstorm FX (a). Collected in *Batman: No Man's Land Volume 5* (2001), *Batman: No Man's Land Volume 4* (2012), and—get this—*The Joker: A Celebration of 75 Years* (2014).

Detective Comics #746 (July 2000), "Evolution IV: Aftertaste." Greg Rucka (w), Shawn Martinbrough, John Watkiss, Steve Mitchell, and Wildstorm FX (a). Collected in *Batman: Evolution* (2001) and *Batman: New Gotham Vol. 1* (2017).

Detective Comics #750 (November 2000), "Dependence." Greg Rucka (w), Shawn Martinbrough, Steve Mitchell, and Wildstorm FX (a). Collected in *Batman: Evolution* (2001), *Batman: New Gotham Vol. 1* (2017), and *Batman Arkham: Ra's al Ghul* (2019).

Detective Comics #754 (March 2001), "Monster in a Box." Nunzio DeFilippis (w), Mike Collins, Steve Bird, Jesse Delperdang, and Wildstorm FX (a). Collected in *Batman: Officer Down* (2001).

Detective Comics #757 (June 2001), "Air Time." Greg Rucka (w), Rick Burchett, Rodney Ramos, and Wildstorm FX (a). Collected in *Batman: A Celebration of 75 Years* (2014) and *Batman: New Gotham Vol. 2* (2018).

Detective Comics #758 (July 2001), "History Lesson." Ed Brubaker (w), Steve Lieber and Gloria Vasquez (a).

Detective Comics #758 (July 2001), "Unknowing, Part One." Greg Rucka (w), Shawn Martinbrough, Steve Mitchell, and Wildstorm FX (a). Collected in *Batman: New Gotham Vol. 2* (2018).

Detective Comics #765 (February 2002). Greg Rucka (w), Rick Burchett, Jesse Delperdang, Rodney Ramos, and Wildstorm FX (a). Collected in *Batman: New Gotham Vol. 2* (2018).

Detective Comics #768 (May 2002), "Purity: Part 1 of 3." Greg Rucka (w), Steve Lieber, Mick Gray, Jason Wright, and Wildstorm FX (a). Collected in *Batman: Bruce Wayne: Fugitive Volume Two* (2002) and *Batman: Bruce Wayne—Fugitive* (2014).

Detective Comics #780 (May 2003), "Dead Reckoning Part Four." Ed Brubaker (w), Tommy Castillo, Wade von Grawbadger, Jason Wright, and Wildstorm FX (a).

Detective Comics #783 (August 2003), "More Perfect Than Perfect." Paul Bolles (w), Shawn Martinbrough, Jason Wright, and Wildstorm FX (a).

Detective Comics #784 (September 2003), "Made of Wood: Part One of Three." Ed Brubaker (w), Patrick Zircher, Aaron Sowd, Jason Wright, and Wildstorm FX (a).

Detective Comics #785 (October 2003), "Made of Wood: Part Two of Three." Ed Brubaker (w), Patrick Zircher, Aaron Sowd, Jason Wright, and Wildstorm FX (a).

Detective Comics #790 (March 2004), "Scarification." Andersen Gabrych (w), Pete Woods, Cam Smith, and Jason Wright (a). Collected in *Batman: War Drums* (2004).

Detective Comics #791 (April 2004), "The Surrogate Part One: Lost and Found." Andersen Gabrych (w), Pete Woods, Cam Smith, and Jason Wright (a). Collected in *Batman: War Drums* (2004).

Detective Comics #792 (May 2004), "The Surrogate Part Two: The Blinding." Andersen Gabrych (w), Pete Woods, Cam Smith, and Jason Wright (a). Collected in *Batman: War Drums* (2004).

Detective Comics #793 (June 2004), "The Surrogate Part Three: Deliverance." Andersen Gabrych (w), Pete Woods, Cam Smith, and Jason Wright (a). Collected in *Batman: War Drums* (2004).

Detective Comics #794 (July 2004), "Monsters of Rot, Part One: Cleansing Fires." Andersen Gabrych (w), Pete Woods, Cam Smith, and Jason Wright (a). Collected in *Batman: War Drums* (2004).

Detective Comics #795 (August 2004), "Monsters of Rot, Part Two: Knee Deep." Andersen Gabrych (w), Pete Woods, Nathan Massengill, and Jason Wright (a). Collected in *Batman: War Drums* (2004).

Detective Comics #796 (September 2004), "… And Red All Over." Andersen Gabrych (w), Pete Woods, Nathan Massengill, and Jason Wright (a). Collected in *Batman: War Drums* (2004).

Detective Comics #798 (November 2004), "Undertow." Andersen Gabrych (w), Pete Woods, Cam Smith, and Jason Wright (a). Collected in *Batman: War Games Act 2* (2005) and *Batman War Games Book Two* (2016).

Detective Comics #799 (December 2004), "Good Intentions." Andersen Gabrych (w), Pete Woods, Cam Smith, and Jason Wright (a). Collected in *Batman: War Games Act 3* (2005) and *Batman War Games Book Two* (2016).

Detective Comics #800 (January 2005), "Alone at Night." Andersen Gabrych (w), Pete Woods, Cam Smith, Drew Geraci, and Jason Wright (a). Collected in *Batman War Games Book Two* (2016).

Detective Comics #809 (Early October 2005), "To the Victor Go the Spoils." Andersen Gabrych (w), Pete Woods, Bit, and Jason Wright (a). Collected in *Batman: War Crimes* (2005), *Batman: War Games Book Two* (2016), and *Batman Arkham: Killer Croc* (2016).

Detective Comics #821 (September 2006). Paul Dini (w), J.H. Williams III and John Kalisz (a). Collected in *Batman: Detective* (2007) and *Batman: A Celebration of 75 Years* (2014).

Detective Comics #830 (Late May 2007). Stuart Moore (w), Andy Clarke and Nathan Eyring (a). Collected in *Batman: Death and the City* (2007).

Detective Comics #832 (July 2007). Royal McGraw (w), Andy Clarke and Nathan Eyring (a). Collected in *Batman: Death and the City* (2007).

Detective Comics #833 (August 2007). Paul Dini (w), Don Kramer, Wayne Faucher, and John Kalisz (a). Collected in *Batman: Death and the City* (2007).

Detective Comics #834 (September 2007). Paul Dini (w), Don Kramer, Wayne Faucher, and John Kalisz (a). Collected in *Batman: Death and the City* (2007).

Detective Comics #842 (May 2008). Peter Milligan (w), Dustin Nguyen, Derek Fridolfs, and John Kalisz (a). Collected in *Batman: Private Casebook* (2009).

Detective Comics #848 (November 2008). Paul Dini (w), Dustin Nguyen, Derek Fridolfs, and John Kalisz (a). Collected in *Batman: Heart of Hush* (2009).

Detective Comics #849 (December 2008). Paul Dini (w), Dustin Nguyen, Derek Fridolfs, and John Kalisz (a). Collected in *Batman: Heart of Hush* (2009).

Detective Comics #850 (January 2009). Paul Dini (w), Dustin Nguyen, Derek Fridolfs, and John Kalisz (a). Collected in *Batman: Heart of Hush* (2009).

Final Crisis #6 (January 2009). Grant Morrison (w), J.G. Jones, Carlos Pacheco, Doug Mahnke, Marco Rudy, Christian Alamy, Jesús Merino, Alex Sinclair, and Pete Pantazis (a). Collected in *Final Crisis* (2014).

Gotham Central #2 (February 2003). Ed Brubaker and Greg Rucka (w), Michael Lark, Noelle Giddings, and Digital Chameleon (a). Collected in *Gotham Central, Book One: In the Line of Duty* (2011).

Gotham Central #5 (May 2003). Ed Brubaker (w), Michael Lark, Noelle Giddings, and Lee Loughridge (a). Collected in *Gotham Central, Book One: In the Line of Duty* (2011).

Gotham Central #25 (January 2005). Greg Rucka (w), Michael Lark, Stefano Gaudiano, and Lee Loughridge (a). Collected in *Gotham Central, Book Three: On the Freak Beat* (2011).

Gotham Central #26 (February 2005). Ed Brubaker (w), Jason Alexander and Lee Loughridge (a). Collected in *Gotham Central, Book Three: On the Freak Beat* (2011).

Gotham Central #36 (December 2005). Ed Brubaker and Greg Rucka (w), Kano, Stefano Gaudiano, and Lee Loughridge (a). Collected in *Gotham Central, Book Four: Corrigan* (2012).

Hawkgirl #63 (June 2007). Walter Simonson (w), Renato Arlem and Alex Bleyaert (a). Collected in *Hawkgirl: Hath-Set* (2008).

The Huntress #1 (April 1989). Joey Cavalieri (w), Joe Staton, Bruce Patterson, Dick Giordano, and Albert DeGuzman (a).

Huntress: Year One #1 (July 2008). Ivory Madison (w), Cliff Richards, Art Thibert, and Jason Wright (a). Collected in *Huntress: Year One* (2009).

Identity Crisis #4 (November 2004). Brad Meltzer (w), Rags Morales, Mike Bair, and Alex Sinclair (a). Collected in *Identity Crisis* (2005).

Identity Crisis #6 (January 2005). Brad Meltzer (w), Rags Morales, Mike Bair, and Alex Sinclair (a). Collected in *Identity Crisis* (2005).

Infinite Crisis #1 (December 2005). Geoff Johns (w), Phil Jimenez, Andy Lanning, Jeromy Cox, and Guy Major (a). Collected in *Infinite Crisis* (2008).

Infinite Crisis #4 (March 2006). Geoff Johns (w), Phil Jimenez, George Pérez, Ivan Reis, Oclair Albert, Marc Campos, Drew Geraci, Andy Lanning, Jimmy Palmiotti, and Lary Stucker (a). Collected in *Infinite Crisis* (2008).

Infinite Crisis #7 (June 2006). Geoff Johns (w), Phil Jimenez, George Pérez, Ivan Reis, Joe Bennett, Andy Lanning, Jerry Ordway, Sean Parsons, Art Thibert, Jeremy Cox, Guy Major, Tanya Horie, and Richard Horie (a). Collected in *Infinite Crisis* (2008).

JLA #5 (May 1997). Grant Morrison (w), Howard Porter, John Dell, and Pat Garrahy (a). Collected in *JLA Volume One* (2011).

JLA #39 (March 2000). Grant Morrison (w), Howard Porter, John Dell, and Pat Garrahy (a). Collected in *JLA Volume Four* (2014).

JLA #46 (October 2000). Mark Waid (w), Steve Scott, Mark Propst, John Kalisz, and Heroic Age (a). Collected in *JLA: Tower of Babel* (2001) and *JLA Volume 4* (2014).

JLA #120 (December 2005). Bob Harras (w), Tom Derenick, Dan Green, and David Baron (a). Collected in *JLA: World without a Justice League* (2006) and *JLA Volume 9* (2016).

JLA Secret Files and Origins #1 (September 1997), "Star-Seed." Grant Morrison and Mark Millar (w), Howard Porter, John Dell, and John Kalisz (a). Collected in *Secret Origins Featuring JLA* (1999), *Justice League of America: The Greatest Stories Ever Told* (2006), and *JLA Volume One* (2011).

JLA Secret Files and Origins #3 (December 2000), "Blame." D. Curtis Johnson (w), Pablo Raimondi, Claude St. Aubin, Dave Meikis, Tom McCraw, and Digital Chameleon (a). Collected in *JLA: Tower of Babel* (2001).

Joker: Last Laugh #6 (January 2002). Chuck Dixon and Scott Beatty (w), Rick Burchett, Mark Lipka, Dan Davis, Gina Going, and Digital Chameleon (a). Collected in *Batman: Joker's Last Laugh* (2008).

Justice League of America, vol. 2, #49 (November 2010). James Robinson (w), Pow Rodrix, Robson Rocha, Christian Alamy, John Dell, Julio Ferreira, Sandra Hope, Keith Champagne, Rodney Ramos, Don Ho, Tom Nguyen, Derek Fridolfs, and Rod Reis (a). Collected in *Justice League of America: Omega* (2011).

Manhunter, vol. 3, #26 (February 2007). Marc Andreyko (w), Javier Piña, Robin Riggs, and Jason Wright (a). Collected in *Manhunter Vol. 4: Unleashed* (2008).

New Teen Titans, vol. 1, #39 (February 1984). Marv Wolfman (w), George Pérez, Romeo Tanghal, and Adrienne Roy (a). Collected in *The New Teen Titans: The Judas Contract* (1988) and *The New Teen Titans Volume 6* (2017).

New Teen Titans Annual, vol. 1, #2 (August 1983). Marv Wolfman (w), George Pérez (w,a), Pablo Marcos and Adrienne Roy (a). Collected in *The New Teen Titans: Terra Incognito* (2006), *The New Teen Titans Volume 5* (2016), and *Vigilante by Marv Wolfman Volume 1* (2017).

New Titans #60 (November 1989). Marv Wolfman (w), George Pérez (w,a), Bob McLeod and Adrienne Roy (a). Collected in *Batman: A Lonely Place of Dying* (1990).

New Titans #61 (December 1989). Marv Wolfman (w), George Pérez, Tom Grummett, Bob McLeod, and Adrienne Roy (a). Collected in *Batman: A Lonely Place of Dying* (1990).

Nightwing, vol. 2, #93 (July 2004). Devin Grayson (w), Patrick Zircher, Andy Owens, and Gregory Wright (a).

Nightwing, vol. 2, #98 (December 2004). Devin Grayson (w), Sean Phillips and Gregory Wright (a). Collected in *Batman: War Games Act 3* (2005) and *Batman War Games Book Two* (2016).

Nightwing, vol. 2, #101 (March 2005). Scott Beatty and Chuck Dixon (w), Scott McDaniel, Andy Owens, and Gregory Wright (a). Collected in *Nightwing: Year One* (2005) and *Robin the Boy Wonder: A Celebration of 75 Years* (2015).

The OMAC Project #2 (July 2005). Greg Rucka (w), Jesús Saíz, Cliff Richards, Bob Wiacek, and Hi-Fi Design (a). Collected in *The OMAC Project* (2005).

Robin, vol. 1, #4 (April 1991). Chuck Dixon (w), Tom Lyle, Bob Smith, and Adrienne Roy (a). Collected in *Robin: A Hero Reborn* (1991) and *Robin Vol. 1: Reborn* (2015).

Robin, vol. 4, #9 (August 1994). Chuck Dixon (w), Tom Grummett, Ray Kryssing, and Adrienne Roy (a). Collected in *Batman: KnightsEnd* (1995), *Batman: Knightfall Volume Three—KnightsEnd* (2012), *Robin Vol. 4: Turning Point* (2017), and *Batman: KnightsEnd 25th Anniversary Edition* (2018).

Robin, vol. 4, #13 (January 1995). Chuck Dixon (w), John Cleary, Phil Jimenez, Ray Kryssing, and Adrienne Roy (a). Collected in *Batman: Knightfall Volume Three—KnightsEnd* (2012), *Robin Vol. 4: Turning Point* (2017), and *Batman: Prodigal* (2019).

Robin, vol. 4, #14 (February 1995). Chuck Dixon (w), Tom Grummett, Ray Kryssing, and Adrienne Roy (a). Collected in *Batman: Troika* (2019).

Robin, vol. 4, #86 (March 2001). Ed Brubaker (w), Jacob Pander, Arnold Pander, Tom McCraw, and Jamison (a). Collected in *Batman: Officer Down* (2001).

Robin, vol. 4, #126 (July 2004). Bill Willingham (w), Damion Scott and Guy Major (a). Collected in *Batman: War Drums* (2004) and *Robin the Boy Wonder: A Celebration of 75 Years* (2015).

Robin, vol. 4, #128, September 2004). Bill Willingham (w), Damion Scott and Guy Major (a). Collected in *Batman: War Drums* (2004).

Robin, vol. 4, #131 (December 2004). Bill Willingham (w), Tom Derenick, Robert Campanella, and Guy Major (a). Collected in *Batman: War Games Act 3* (2005) and *Batman War Games Book Two* (2016).

Robin: Year One #1 (October 2000). Chuck Dixon and Scott Beatty (w), Javier Pulido, Robert Campanella, and Lee Loughridge (a). Collected in *Robin: Year One* (2001) and *Batgirl/Robin: Year One* (2013).

Robin: Year One #2 (November 2000). Chuck Dixon and Scott Beatty (w), Javier Pulido, Robert Campanella, and Lee Loughridge (a). Collected in *Robin: Year One* (2001) and *Batgirl/Robin: Year One* (2013).

Robin: Year One #3 (December 2000). Chuck Dixon and Scott Beatty (w), Javier Pulido, Robert Campanella, and Lee Loughridge (a). Collected in *Robin: Year One* (2001) and *Batgirl/Robin: Year One* (2013).

Robin: Year One #4 (January 2001). Chuck Dixon and Scott Beatty (w), Javier Pulido, Marcos Martin, Robert Campanella, and Lee Loughridge (a). Collected in *Robin: Year One* (2001) and *Batgirl/Robin: Year One* (2013).

Secret Origins #6 (September 1986), "The Golden Age Batman." Roy Thomas (w), Marshall Rogers and Terry Austin (a). Collected in *Batman: The Greatest Stories Ever Told, Volume 2* (2007) and *Legends of the Dark Knight: Marshall Rogers* (2011).

Secret Six, vol. 3, #2 (December 2008). Gail Simone (w), Nicola Scott, Doug Hazlewood, and Jason Wright (a). Collected in *Secret Six: Unhinged* (2009).

The Spectre #51 (March 1997). John Ostrander (w), Tom Mandrake and Carla Feeny (a).

Suicide Squad #23 (January 1989). John Ostrander and Kim Yale (w), Luke McDonnell, Karl Kesel, and Carl Gafford (a). Collected in *Suicide Squad Vol. 3: Rogues* (2016).

Superman #710 (June 2011). J. Michael Straczynski and Chris Roberson (w), Eddy Barrows, J.P. Mayer, Rod Reis, Travel Foreman, John Dell, and Dave McCaig (a). Collected in *Superman: Grounded Volume 2* (2012).

Tales of the New Teen Titans #44 (July 1984). Marv Wolfman (w), George Pérez (w,a), Mike DeCarlo, Dick Giordano, and Adrienne Roy (a). Collected in *The New Teen Titans: The Judas Contract* (1988) and *The New Teen Titans Volume 7* (2017).

Underworld Unleashed: Batman—Devil's Asylum #1 (1995). Alan Grant (w), Brian Stelfreeze, Rick Burchett, and Linda Medley (a).

The Untold Legend of the Batman #1 (July 1980). Len Wein (w), John Byrne, Jim Aparo, and Glynis Wein (a). Collected in *Tales of the Batman: Len Wein* (2014) and *Legends of the Dark Knight: Jim Aparo Volume 3* (2017).

The Untold Legend of the Batman #2 (August 1980). Len Wein (w), Jim Aparo and Glynis Wein (a). Collected in *Tales of the Batman: Len Wein* (2014) and *Legends of the Dark Knight: Jim Aparo Volume 3* (2017).

The Untold Legend of the Batman #3 (September 1980). Len Wein (w), Jim Aparo and Glynis Wein (a). Collected in *Tales of the Batman: Len Wein* (2014) and *Legends of the Dark Knight: Jim Aparo Volume 3* (2017).

Wizard the Comics Magazine #0 (September 2003), "Interlude: The Cave." Jeph Loeb (w), Jim Lee, Scott Williams, and Alex Sinclair (a). Collected in *Batman: Hush* (2008).

Wonder Woman, vol. 2, #219 (September 2005). Greg Rucka (w), Tom Derenick, Georges Jeanty, Karl Kerschl, David Lopez, Rags Morales, Nelson DeCastro, Bit, Bob Petrecca, Mark Propst, Dexter Vines, Tanya Horie, and Richard Horie (a). Collected in *The OMAC Project* (2005), *Superman: Sacrifice* (2006), and *Wonder Woman: Mission's End* (2006).

Wonder Woman, vol. 2, #220 (October 2005). Greg Rucka (w), David Lopez, Bit, and Wildstorm FX (a). Collected in *Superman: Sacrifice* (2006) and *Wonder Woman: Mission's End* (2006).

Index

List of Comics Writers and Artists

Batman and Ethics, First Edition. Mark D. White.
© 2019 John Wiley & Sons Ltd. Published 2019 by John Wiley & Sons Ltd.